New Age Thinking

RELIGIONS AND BELIEFS SERIES

The series includes books bearing on the religions of the Americas, the Bible in its relationship to cultures, and on ethics in relation to religion. The series welcomes manuscripts written in either English or French.

Editorial Committee

Robert Choquette, Director
Margaret Dufour-McDonald
David Jeffrey
Pierre Savard

In the Same Series

RELIGIONS AND BELIEFS SERIES, NO. 5

New Age Thinking
A Psychoanalytic Critique

M. D. FABER

University of Ottawa Press

This book has been published with the help of a grant from the Canadian Federation for the Humanities, using funds provided by the Social Sciences and Humanities Research Council of Canada.

University of Ottawa Press gratefully acknowledges the support extended to its publishing programme by the Canada Council, the Department of Canadian Heritage, and the University of Ottawa.

CANADIAN CATALOGUING IN PUBLICATION DATA

Faber, M. D. (Mel D.)

New Age Thinking: A Psychoanalytic Critique

(Religions and Beliefs Series; no. 5)

ISBN 0-7766-0421-X (bound)
ISBN 0-7766-0417-1 (pbk.)

1. New Age movement—Controversial literature.   2. New Age movement—Psychological aspects.   I. Title.   II. Series.

BP605.N48F32 1996   239'.9   C95-920899-2

Cover: Robert Dolbec
Typesetting: Infographie G.L.

Distributed by Cardiff Academic Press Ltd., St. Fagans Road, Fairwater, Cardiff CF5 3AE.

© University of Ottawa Press, 1996

ISBN 0-7766-0421-X (cloth)
ISBN 0-7766-0417-1 (paper)

Printed in Canada

For Jared Faber

CONTENTS

PREFACE

As I went about preparing to write this book, I found myself involved in the related problems of breadth and depth. I wanted to include enough material to make the inquiry representative of New Age thinking as a whole, and at the same time I wanted to afford the reader the experience of sampling particular authors in depth: New Age thinking comes through most vividly when one has the opportunity to become very familiar with specific writings, to examine closely, in a leisurely fashion, the thought, indeed the *mind*, of the author who has committed himself to the perspectives of the New Age. Needless to say, the reader will have judged for himself by the book's conclusion whether I managed to accomplish my purpose.

The book's Introduction has three aims: first, to let the reader know what I mean by New Age thinking, to indicate the focus and the scope of the inquiry; second, to present in very general terms the theoretical, psychoanalytic direction from which the analysis will be coming ("object relations"—a neo-Freudian outlook); and third, to state the book's thesis concisely and unequivocally. As I perceive it, the New Age is loaded with regressive, undesirable elements, with infantilism and magical, wishful thinking. I want the reader to be aware of my perception from the outset. I do not wish to pussyfoot around when it comes to cultural developments that I consider to be inimical to the culture's intellectual and psychological well-being.

Chapter 2 attempts to set forth meticulously the theoretical context of the book, the psychoanalytic presuppositions and arguments that will be used again and again to disclose the unconscious meaning of New Age beliefs and practices. I rely very heavily in this chapter on the work of Margaret Mahler, Daniel Stern, and Christopher Bollas, as that work presents what in my view are the chief developmental struggles of our lives, namely the attempt to get separate and autonomous while retaining an internalized tie to the caregiver; the endless, lifelong search for parental substitutes with the miraculous capacity to transform one's existence; and the reluctance to relinquish the omnipotence and narcissism of the early period. The New Age is overwhelmingly absorbed in these issues.

Chapter 3 comprises the heart of the book and devotes itself to a thorough examination of four major areas of New Age thought: crystals, shamanism, channelling, and Witchcraft (capitalized because it claims to be a religion). Here, the reader is able to ponder at length the psychoanalytic nature and quality of New Age thinking as it emerges from a number of major texts. The "data" I offer are both theoretical and practical; they tell us what New Agers are *thinking*, or how they view philosophically their spiritual enterprise, and they tell us what New Agers are *doing*—their rituals and activities, their behavioural *routes* to the emotional, psychological goals of the movement: omnipotence, symbiotic fusion, and narcissistic inflation, or grandiosity.

Chapter 4 shifts the focus to spiritual or psychic healing, a popular, far-reaching aspect of New Age thought. Here, the reader can concentrate on the methods and beliefs of an influential New Age healer as he presents his life and work to his audience, and of course to his potential customers. New Age texts on healing invariably display what we can call an invitational dimension. They aim to explicate the nature of health and illness, and also to encourage the reader to take his problems, whatever they are, to the healer, to the guru, of his choice.

Chapter 5 consists of interviews and experiences as the author goes to the New Agers themselves to learn what they have to say about their activities, and to learn, also, what they *do* as they put their commitments and beliefs into practice. My aim is to offer the reader a cross-section of New Age practitioners, those typical, working, functional, "everyday" New Agers who may be said to comprise the reality of the movement as it develops and takes shape around us. However, I caution the reader at the inception of chapter 5 to read it in the full context of the discussion. The material makes rich, psychoanalytic sense *only* as it is examined in the psychoanalytic light which I hope emerges from chapters 1 through 4. In the end, of course, I must simply cross my fingers.

The final chapter concentrates on the New Age's version of the universe around us, and above all on what that version *means* to the emotional goals of the movement. We hear a great deal these days about the new physics, the new cosmos, quantum theory, relativity. Well, the New Age is very interested in these matters because, as I endeavour to demonstrate, the New Age can *use* them, or *apply* them, in the service of its all-pervasive unconscious agenda: collapsing the gap of separation that yawns when infantile symbiosis fades; restoring the perceptual and emotional omnipotence that characterizes the phenomenology of the neonate; and re-establishing psychically the narcissistic glow of the baby who is, like most babies, the *centre* of the parents' world. It seemed fitting to bring the book to a close with the "big picture" or the "whole show" in the reader's analytical eye.

As the next millennium nears, New Age thinking sweeps vigorously through Western culture. Realistically, there is not very much we can do to stop it. The human appetite for wishful thinking, for magical solutions to the ancient and inescapable problems of separation, smallness, and death, has always been robust, and is presently quite as robust as ever. Still, the discussion to follow may persuade a few New Agers to think twice about their involvement, and it may well enable the curious and/or the concerned to understand more fully, more completely, just what New Age thinking is—where it comes from and what it means. I have no illusions. If this book manages to fulfil the promise of its title, if it does offer the reader an incisive, effective critique of New Age thinking, I will feel gratified in the part of me that longed to share my views with other people.

MDF
Vancouver, Canada

CHAPTER I

INTRODUCTION:
TARGETS, METHODS, THESES

Sᴏᴍᴇᴡʜᴇʀᴇ in Manhattan a young male stockbroker has decided to spend a Friday night at home practising his shamanism. Donning a feathered headdress, a crystal necklace, and beaded moccasins, he walks about his apartment chanting aloud and beating a small, painted drum. "Ayaa! ayaa! ayaa!" he cries as he induces the shamamic trance and begins his spiritual journey to the realm of the power animals. Somewhere in Vancouver, British Columbia, a female university student has traced a circle of about two metres circumference on the floor. Standing in the brilliant sunshine which streams through her bedroom window, she makes ordered, ritualistic gestures to the north, south, east, and west. She then steps into the circle's centre and utters invocations to the Great Wiccan Goddess, invocations that will (she hopes) draw down the supernatural power she requires to fulfil her present wish: an outstanding performance on her upcoming biology examination. Somewhere in London, England, the middle-aged female leader of a small group of channellers (ten persons) has gone into a profound trance. She is endeavouring to contact a spirit-guide for the purpose of determining whether one of her loyal followers (in attendance) should embark upon an approaching business opportunity. As she passes over to the other, spiritual side of the universe, the guide, whose name is Koba, speaks in low, sibilant tones through her throat. Her eyes stare wide as the words come through: "Go forward," says Koba, "the franchise will be a success." Somewhere in San Francisco, California, an elderly male healer chats with a forty-year-old woman who has come to him with painful bursitis in her arms and shoulders. Nothing, apparently, will make the inflammation go away; drugs, rest, soaking in a variety of remedies—all are to no avail. Telling his client that he loves her unconditionally and that he is about to transfer healing energies to her offending joints and tissues, the healer moves his chair very close to the chair of his patient, extends his open hands toward the patient's afflicted parts, and concentrates. Three minutes later the energetic transference is completed. Somewhere in Toronto, Ontario, a young mother and housewife has placed a lovely piece of quartz crystal underneath her pillow. She is about to retire for the night in the belief that by morning the magical stone will have enhanced not only her tranquillity of mind but also her perceptual capacities. The quartz, she has read, holds within its shimmering atoms the very powers of the cosmos as they are manifested through the mineral kingdom of the Earth. Switching off the light, she lays her head confidently down. Somewhere in Dallas, Texas, an enthusiastic male New Ager in his early twenties is listening to a sceptical female friend question the validity of his experience. The New Ager has just come from a channelling session in which he has contacted, at long last, his very own guardian angel. "But how do you know it really happened?" asks his friend. "How do you know it's true?" "True?" replies the young man. "I *experienced* it. It happened to me. Why should I question what I just went through? And besides, I've already gotten a great deal out of it. I've already begun to feel empowered. I'm not going to start *analyzing* what *worked for me*." The friend persists: "But what if I told you I had just flown up to heaven and had a glass of sherry with St. Peter? Would you not wonder about that? Would you not at least entertain the possibility that my *experience,* as you put it, was delusional?" Hisses the New Ager, "Oh, shut up!"

Defining the New Age

The foregoing vignettes may help the reader understand what I mean by New Age thinking. During the past three or four decades something rather unusual, and very conspicuous, has been occurring in the culture that surrounds us. We might describe it as a rise of alternative religions, or a rise of occult and spiritual practices, or a resuscitation of ancient, metaphysical systems of belief. From the perspective of *critique,* psychoanalytic or otherwise, we might describe it as a retreat into magic in an age of science. If we are *part* of the movement, we might allude to an awakening of higher consciousness on a global scale, or perhaps the *evolution* of higher consciousness on a global scale.

Marilyn Ferguson (1980) calls the whole business "the Aquarian conspiracy" in a volume with that title—a volume dubbed by *USA Today* "the handbook of the New Age."[1] Here is a publisher's note that immediately precedes Catherine Bowman's (1992) *Crystal Awareness*. The note is headed "About Llewellyn's New Age Series":

> The "New Age"—it's a phrase we use, but what does it mean? Does it mean that we are entering the Aquarian Age? Does it mean that a new Messiah is coming to correct all that is wrong and make Earth into a Garden? Probably not—but the idea of a *major change* is there, combined with awareness that Earth *can* be a Garden; that war, crime, poverty, disease, etc., are not necessary "evils."
>
> Optimists, dreamers, scientists ... nearly all of us believe in a "better tomorrow," and that somehow we can do things now that will make for a better future life for ourselves and for coming generations.
>
> In one sense, we all know there's nothing new under the Heavens, and in another sense that every day makes a new world. The difference is in our consciousness. And this is what the New Age is all about: it's a major change in consciousness found within each of us as we learn to bring forth and manifest powers that Humanity has always potentially had.
>
> Evolution moves in "leaps." Individuals struggle to develop talents and powers, and their efforts build a "power bank" in the Collective Unconscious, the "soul" of Humanity that suddenly makes these same talents and powers easier access for the majority.
>
> You still have to learn the "rules" for developing and applying these powers, but it is more like a "relearning" than a *new* learning, because with the New Age it is as if the basis for these had become genetic.

I present this material not because I consider it to be penetrating and accurate; indeed, it strikes me as barely intelligible. I present it, rather, as a memorable example of the way in which the New Age thinks and writes about itself. "Evolution" moves in "leaps," one of which is the "struggle" to build a "power bank" in the "Collective Unconscious," the "soul" of "Humanity." The "rules" for applying this "power bank," although not yet known, have become somehow "genetic" and will therefore be "relearned." Such material brings to mind Wendy Kaminer's (1992, 101) biting suggestion that a good motto for the New Age would be "Stop Making Sense." Let's try to pin the matter down, now, in the standard historical fashion.

In the "wake of the sixties counterculture," write Lewis and Melton (1992, ix) in the Introduction to their edited volume, *Perspectives on the New Age*, there emerged in North America and Europe "a large-scale decentralized religious subculture," which "drew its principal inspiration from sources outside the Judeo-Christian tradition." Although this subculture was "in many respects" the continuation of a "preexisting occult-metaphysical tradition," the "addition to its ranks of a sizeable number of former counterculturists in the postsixties period meant that metaphysical religion was no longer a marginal phenomenon." By 1980, it had become "an integral part of a new, truly pluralistic mainstream." In North America, Lewis and Melton maintain (ix), "the single most important event prompting general awareness of this subculture was the airing of the televised version of Shirley MacLaine's *Out on a Limb* in January of 1987." The popularity of this miniseries prompted the media to begin investigating and eventually to begin generating programs and articles about what came to be called the New Age movement. Among the articles was a *Time* feature titled "New Age Harmonies" in December of 1987. "This piece was the most significant general article on the movement to appear in a major news magazine," and it caused some of the more dedicated individuals within the subculture to "back away" from what was suddenly becoming a kind of spiritual fad (Lewis and Melton, x).

Striving to avoid "some of the confusion" which has come to be associated with the label "New Age," Lewis and Melton (1992, x) distinguish two meanings: the first "is what we might think of as New Age in the *narrow* sense," which we can take to refer "to the phenomena, personalities, and events given prominence by the media," such as channelling, Shirley MacLaine, large public gatherings on behalf of global harmony, psychic fairs, and so on; the second we can take to refer to the "broad, spiritual subculture" which devotes itself to a variety of practices and beliefs (crystal healing, Wicca or Witchcraft, meditation, shamanism, the forging of a compassionate, loving world) in a manner that befits a genuine metaphysical and religious movement, at least in the historical sense. If the reader has not already surmised it, let me point out immediately that the psychoanalytic discussion to follow is devoted overwhelmingly to the *second* of these meanings of "New Age."

Lewis and Melton (1992, xi) conclude by reminding us that "a significant portion of New Agers are baby boomers," people who two decades earlier "were probably participating at some level in the phenomenon known as the counterculture." As the counterculture began to fade away in the early 1970s, many former "hippies" found themselves "embarking on a spiritual quest—one that in many cases departed from the Judeo-Christian mainstream." Thus one way "to date the beginnings of the New Age Movement" is from "the period of the rather sudden appearance of large members of unconventional spiritual seekers in the decade following the sixties." By the early 1970s the focus of the movement "was somewhat different from what it had become by the mid-eighties when the media began to pay attention." The early years were marked by "the prominence of newly imported Asian groups, although many of the older occult-metaphysical organizations (New Thought, Christian Science, Theosophical Society) were also experiencing a growth spurt." These "various groups, in combination with a significant number of less formally affiliated individuals, constituted a fairly substantial spiritual subculture (the New Age) that became the successor movement to the counterculture." Finally, observe Lewis and Melton (xii), "one of the traits of the New Age is that major subjects of interest vary from time to time, so that, particularly to the outside observer, this subculture appears to go through transformation after transformation." Eastern spiritual teachings have given way to an emphasis on channelling, which appears, in turn, to be giving way to an emphasis on shamanism, Witchcraft, and crystals. It is impossible to know, as I write, what will be in, or back in, and what will be out, or back out, in a year or two. Still, the topics on which this book focuses most of its psychoanalytic attention appear to be hearty survivors of the New Age's shifting interests.

Lewis (1992, 4) states in a subsequent discussion, "My impressionistic sense of the New Age is that it is merely the most visible part of a more significant cultural shift. While the popularity of phenomena like channelling and crystals may well be on the decline, the larger spiritual subculture which gave birth to these more particular phenomena is growing steadily." In support of this view, Lewis cites Gallup Poll statistics which indicate that one out of every four Americans believes in astrology, and one out of five in reincarnation. Similar surveys in Britain put the belief in reincarnation at more than thirty percent. "Statistics of this magnitude," observes Lewis (1992, 4), "indicate that we are no longer talking about a marginal phenomenon. Rather, we appear to be witnessing the birth of a new, truly pluralistic mainstream." This especially seems to be the case in the San Francisco Bay area, where "a recent newspaper survey found that roughly 25 percent of ... residents agree with certain key New Age ideas, such as the notion that nature, or Mother Earth, has its own kind of wisdom, a planetary consciousness of its own." While it might be inaccurate to conclude from such a survey that one quarter of all Bay area residents are New Agers, it would not be inaccurate to assert that one quarter "adhere to certain holistic, ecological, and metaphysical points of view that depart significantly from traditional perspectives" (Lewis 1992, 5). Needless to say, observations and conclusions such as these give the following psychoanalytic critique not only a manifest relevancy but a certain urgency as well.

Building upon the work of Lewis and Melton, and recognizing fully the New Age's amorphous, changing nature, I would suggest in the way of a comprehensive summary that the New Age has its roots in the many alternative religions which have emerged in North America and Europe during the last two centuries (Swedenborgianism, New Thought, Christian Science, Transcendentalism, Theosophy); that it is given a major, almost birthing impetus by the counterculture of the 1960s and the spiritual seekers who emerge from that counterculture in the 1970s and 1980s; that it evinces a compelling interest in many ancient spiritual and occult beliefs and practices which may be regarded as alternative religions (channelling, shamanism, Witchcraft, crystal healing, Tantrism, Zen, yoga, meditation); that it is centrally preoccupied with the theme of individual and societal transformation, as it is derived, in part, from the writings of Teilhard de Chardin and Jung, and as it emerges, by implication, from the world of modern physics where the notions of *relativity* and *indeterminacy* are taken by New Agers to indicate the interconnectedness of all things in the universe; that it is devoted to the hoary art of *psychic healing* in its endless and often bizarre manifestations; and finally, that it increasingly aligns itself with, indeed merges into, the self-help movement with its emphasis upon self-empowerment, self-esteem, positive thinking, and personality change.

In keeping with the old adage that a concrete example is worth a thousand abstract explanations, I will present a brief summary of what I take to be a quintessential New Age book, namely Wayne W. Dyer's (1992) *Real Magic: Creating Miracles in Everyday Life*. This will give us a good "feel" for the nature and the quality of New Age discourse, and it will afford us the added bonus of glimpsing the direction from which our psychoanalytic critique will arise. Dyer begins by telling his readers how much he loves them, one and all. He then declares, "We can soar to new and higher levels of awareness, allowing ourselves to transcend our environment and literally create a world of our own—a world of real magic ... You are capable of achieving perfect equilibrium of the mind [Dyer has a penchant for using the second person]. The path requires a commitment on your part to your own inner transformation. Your inner transformation cannot be completed from an intellectual or scientific perspective. Instruments of limitation will not reveal the limitless. This is a job for your mind and your soul, the invisible segment of you that is always there but often ignored" (xv). "You" will learn in this book, Dyer claims, how to "realign yourself in the invisible world" (xv). Well, we may ask, how do "you" do this, exactly? Simply by coming to realize that "you can create your own reality," says Dyer helpfully. You can "actualize the divine forces at work within you." You can know that ultimately everything is "blessed and for the greater good." You can realize there is "order in chaos in a universe that is in perfect order" (xvi). You can "take these ideas and make them work" in yourself, in your family, and in your world (xvii). "God bless you," breathes Dyer as he brings his prefatory pep talk to a close. With his reader (or "you") primed for the meat of the discussion, Dyer proceeds to create a veritable smorgasbord of spiritual goodies. He grabs at everything and anything he can get his hands on; it is a kind of New Age self-help free-for-all, a riot of clichés and generalizations, of emotional appeals and sacrosanct advice—in short, a nonsensical hodgepodge. Dyer proceeds *stochastically:* if he lets fly enough arrows, one will probably find the mark. "Reexamine your life" (5), he commands authorially; learn from recalling your past experiences; bear in mind that everything has a purpose (7). Study the *Bhagavad Gita;* it will guide you to "real magic" (17); remember, "no man is an island" (18); find the teacher and wise man in yourself (18); look closely at the life of Christ (19); do not forget that powerful, invisible forces dwell within you, that you have no limits (20); everything is possible (23); be spiritual, not sceptical (27); get rid of "negativity" (27); your "soul" is timeless and "non-local," tied to the "divine," indeed to the whole "universe" with which you can unite on a higher level (29); your soul is immortal, and therefore death is an illusion (31); follow your intuition as it guides you to any of the world's great religions (45); feel connected to everyone and love everyone (47); forgive (47); meditate (47); visualize yourself blending into everything that surrounds you, including the non-material universe (53–55); become peaceful (55); relax (55); keep your spirits up (58); bolster your self-esteem (58); practise inner affirmations (66); "a world of form surrounds you" (72); surrender to "Satori" (enlightenment in Zen Buddhism, usually achieved after years of ardent practice); cut out bad habits (80); don't be greedy (90); "as you think so shall you be" (111); you can change (176); it's up to you (176); create your own "magical personality" (183); you will "radiate magic" in the world around you (245); "we are in an age of spiritual revolution" (247).

From the psychoanalytic angle, three items stand out clearly: first, we have an overarching presence of *infantile omnipotence,* the egocentric, unconscious belief in one's unlimited powers as those powers are derived (and internalized) from the omnipotent caregiver of life's first years (the phenomenology here is the *baby's, not* the caregiver's); second, we have the urge to *fuse regressively* with the environment, to attach oneself to the surrounding world (universe) in a way that denies, erases, cancels out the ever-present sense of *separation* which the chronologically mature individual must cope with during the course of his days on the planet; third, we have the longing for *narcissistic inflation*, the longing to go about in the belief that one is somehow magical, wonderful, unique, *radiating* special qualities and energies, as opposed to being simply another regular person in the world.

New Age bookstores everywhere are loaded with works like Dyer's (1992), works that say everything and nothing at all, works that have no time or inclination to stop and examine their assumptions, works that promise, admonish, and flatter all to the end of inducing in the reader an instantaneous transformation, which never, of course, occurs. It is all in Dyer's title, *Real Magic*: reality gives way to magic; magic becomes reality, real, factual. Make the real world go away; make all my dreams come true in a land where omnipotence, fusion, and narcissism once again rule, just as they ruled during the early period of my existence. Other fine examples of such "spiritual" New Age volumes would be Shakti Gawain's (1986) *Living in the Light: A Guide to Personal and Planetary Transformation*, Deepak Chopra's (1992) *Unconditional Life: Discovering the Power to Fulfill Your Dreams*, and Thomas Crum's (1987) *The Magic of Conflict*. But let us look more closely, more intensely, at the psychoanalytic methodology we will be employing in subsequent sections.

Internalization of Psychological Objects

I do not take New Age thinking at face value. To put a crystal on one's body in the belief that it will foster one's emotional integration, to "journey" in a meditative trance to "another reality" where one converses with one's "animal companions," to contact "spirit guides" on a "higher plane" and then open one's mouth and throat so they may deliver supernatural messages aloud, to cast a circle on the ground and then step inside of it to receive "energy" from an invisible "Goddess," to offer oneself to the world as a "healer" whose "unconditional love" can cure cancer, to pick up books in a drugstore and take them home in the expectation that one's life will be "transformed" by reading them—all of this requires interpretation; all of this requires us to ask: What is going on? What is this person doing? What is the meaning, and in particular the psychoanalytic meaning, of such behaviour?

Obviously in my view psychoanalysis is a marvellous instrument with which to grasp both individual and group conduct. It gives us a particular, crucial kind of insight into what people are *doing* and what their actions mean. Because psychoanalysis is not an exact science, many regard it as unreliable and of little value as an investigative instrument. I will not venture into this hot and apparently endless debate here but only say to the reader that my analyses are supported by the clinical and theoretical edifice which psychoanalysis has built up over the years. While it is true that studying human beings, as opposed to, say, table salt, will always be a "soft" or inexact science, it is also true that the psychoanalytic net can catch a great deal in the way of underlying motivational significances. What all this boils downs to, I suppose, is that the reader who is sceptical about or hostile to psychoanalysis may not discover as much in what follows as the reader who is open to it. As for the objection that the analytic approach places considerable emphasis on the early period of life, what can I say except that *is* psychoanalysis, that is how it views our existence. We are profoundly, ineluctably influenced in a thousand ways by the early stages of our development and by the internalizations which arise therefrom. With this, of course, I agree. My point is simply that to object that psychoanalysis has the tendency to spy aspects of the early period in life's later stages is like going to the opera and objecting that the characters on the stage are *singing*. It's the nature of the beast.

During the first two decades of this century psychoanalysis concentrated its efforts primarily upon repression, and upon the relation of repression to the dynamic unconscious. As Freud viewed the matter, the requirements of civilized existence obliged the individual's sexual and aggressive tendencies, or, more correctly, the individual's sexual and aggressive "drives," to "go under," to manifest themselves but partially, in an "inhibited" way. The tension between one's urgent instinctual demands and their truncated expression in culture led in a good many instances to "neurotic" disorders with repression at their centre, and in *all* instances, for *all* people, to a life of "discontent" and conflict. It was through slips of the tongue, free associations, organic and behavioural symptoms, and above all through dreams, that such conflicts and discontentments revealed themselves to the "analyst of the psyche." As he continued to work with people, however, Freud came increasingly to recognize the extent to which the problem of neurosis involved not merely the repression of instinct, the struggle between nature and culture, unconscious and conscious experience, but the extent to which one's *conscious* life, lived primarily at the level of ego processes, was itself a vehicle for the expression of unconscious aims.

From the inception of his career, Freud was scornful of psychology's readiness to deal *only* with the phenomena of consciousness. He regarded the "psychoanalytic assumption of unconscious mental activity" as an "extension of the corrections begun by Kant in regard to our views on external perception." Just as Kant "warned us not to overlook the fact that our perception is subjectively conditioned and must not be regarded as identical with the phenomena perceived," so psychoanalysis "bids us not to set conscious perception in the place of the unconscious mental process which is its object." The "mental," like the "physical," is "not necessarily in reality just what it appears to us to be." Still, Freud concluded, it is gratifying to discover that the "correction of inner perception" does not "present difficulties so great as that of outer perception," that the "inner object" is "less hard to discern truly than is the outside world" (Freud [1915] 1971, 104). Freud gives us here, for the first time in Western intellectual history, not merely two kinds of philosophical objects, those of the inner and those of the outer world, but an *inner object with an unconscious, dynamic, perceptual dimension.*

Psychoanalysis, as an originator of knowledge and understanding, culminates in our full appreciation of the significance of *internalization* in human life. It has long been stressed, perhaps to the point of becoming a cliché, that man is distinguished from the other animals by his proclivity to create and to dwell within a world of symbols, that his existence must not be regarded dualistically as of the mind over here and of the body over there but must be grasped in terms of his psychobiological propensity to unite mind and feeling in a symbolic mode of expression. Indeed, the entire shape of modern philosophy, anthropology, and sociology is determined in an important way by its concentration on the symbolic style of social and individual organization. Yet to stress this aspect of our behaviour is to stress what is merely a visible, "higher" manifestation of a considerably more basic human tendency. As we concentrate on the nature of internalization we find ourselves in possession of a more powerful analytic instrument than that which inheres in the symbolistic approach—which deals, truth be told, with materials that take shape *after* the elemental events of our lives have transpired. I do not believe we can genuinely grasp the symbolic—including above all the symbols of New Age thinking—without first having grasped the psychoanalytic, and by psychoanalytic I do not mean the libido theory, the Oedipus complex, the classical "Freudian" scheme. I mean, rather, those close, "neo-Freudian" investigations of the infant-mother symbiosis which have occurred within the past four decades and which are offered to the reader *in detail* during the course of chapter 2, where we ready ourselves in earnest for a psychoanalysis of the New Age.

The human infant, perhaps from the inception of his extrauterine life, evinces a powerful urge to internalize the universe around him, to take in and to retain a sizeable portion of the materials with which he comes into contact during the long course of his development toward childhood. It is customary in psychoanalytic circles to approach the problem of internalization by referring to introjection, incorporation, and identification. We do not have to worry too much about these terms here, but it is probably a good idea to mention that introjection and incorporation are generally regarded as the kinds of "primitive" or pre-cognitive internalizing processes that are employed by the infant and the pre-Oedipal child of three to four years, and identification as the kind of internalizing activity that is characteristic of the Oedipal child, the adolescent, and the adult. I say "generally regarded" because the child, the adolescent, and the adult retain (and often express) the capacity to incorporate and introject other persons and things in a deep, tenacious, "primitive" way when circumstances provoke intense psychological pressure and recall the aims and disappointments of life's early stages. Indeed, as I will soon work to establish, New Age thinking as a whole may be considered a striking exemplification of *just this point.* "All those processes" by which we "transform real or imagined interactions" with the environment, and "real or imagined characteristics of the environment" into *inner* relationships and *inner* characteristics, might be thought of as that to which the term *internalization* refers (Schafer 1968, 8–9).

We must note in this connection that the tendency to internalize the environment is prompted by *both* the developing cortex and the growing organism's *defensive needs.* It is the infant's helpless condition, his long period of dependency, his anxiety over separation and loss, along with his accompanying urge to master, to control, a world that is frequently at odds with his wishes and threatening in itself, that goads the internalizing process into life. What we have here is in large measure a kind of "magical" activity based on the feeling-belief that one is safe only when vital external objects and relationships (including paradoxically "bad" objects and relationships) are *taken and held inside.* Of particular importance in all of this, of course, is the caretaker.

That the child's interaction with the parent is the foundation of human psychology everyone appreciates in a "soft," general way. What I wish to emphasize here is that the child's interaction with the parent is the foundation of human psychology in a "hard," structural, perceptual sense that has yet to be recognized by large numbers of people. Internalization transpires at the sensorial, *bodily* level. The materials that are taken in—and these are largely aspects of the caretaker—are taken into the child's *perceiving organism.* It is there that they root themselves, and it is there that they remain, for the duration of the individual's life. In the remarks of Freud, cited earlier, Kant was called explicitly to mind. We must call him to mind again here by declaring that the very *a priori* ground of our perceptual participation in the world is connected inextricably to the internalization of the early period in which the parental object functions as the dynamic, emotive centre of the neonate's existence. It is in this perceptual-structural context that I may begin to suggest what the psychoanalytic term "object" refers to.

It is used to indicate the child's "caregiver," the individual who accompanies the child through all the successive stages of development. This person is, first of all, a partner in a variety of reflexive, biological urges and responses; she/he then becomes a "somebody" who can be recognized and represented, as well as respected, feared, hated, needed, and loved. With regard to the perceptual complexity embedded in this general picture, "object" may refer to the *breast* that provides appetitive pleasure or frustration, to the *person* who provides the breast, to the *perception* of that person, and to the psychical *representation* of that perception. In subsequent chapters I range among these distinctions, relying upon the reader to apprehend the nuance of the moment. The extent to which such "objects," through the process of internalization, come to be integrally bound up with the individual's existence is captured dramatically by the current trend in psychoanalysis to refer to a person's "selfobjects" when probing into issues of identity formation and conflict-inducing situations. It is precisely here that we find the deepest meaning of the psychoanalytic commonplace that virtually all relationships between human beings contain an element of the transference—that is, an unconscious element tied developmentally to significant figures of the past. Behind the transference stand the primary internalizations of the early period. More specifically in regard to New Age thinking, behind the crystal, behind the power animal, behind the guardian angel, the Wiccan Goddess, the numinous healer, the holographic universe—indeed, behind the symbols and ideas of New Age thinking as a whole—stand these basic internalizations, these basic projections, these creators of the obiquitous *transference* in human behaviour and perception.

Those "inner objects" of Freud's essay, then, are not entirely "inner" or "mental" in the customary sense, the sense he had in mind. They have a kind of physical or "objective" existence in the body. As for the "objects" of the "outside world" also mentioned by Freud, they themselves are not entirely external or "physical"—again in the sense he had in mind; for they are "coloured" or *projectively* "touched" by the perceiving organism with which they come into contact. Notably, the methodological angle I am developing here does not simply leave Freud's dualism (inner vs. outer) behind, it reflects the most recent models of the physical universe in which the interactions of the forces under investigation (the relational field) contribute overwhelmingly to the reality, and in which the observer's participation in the event comprises an integral part of the picture. Psychological objects must be regarded accordingly. They are no more and no less real than anything else in this new, fluid universe of ours.

New Age thinking also uses the relational field to make many of its central points and observations. However, the New Ager usually employs the field to *justify* his particular view of reality, whatever that happens to be (relativism), while I employ the field exclusively to establish the inescapable presence of *the object* in human affairs, the inescapable presence of *projection* and *transference* in virtually everything we say and do. This lands me, I confess, in the midst of an epistemological dilemma: what about the argument I am presenting here? Is it not also coloured by the object, the transference, the tendency to project? My reply is twofold: first, I do not claim for one moment to have a God's-eye view of New Age thinking, or of anything else. I claim only to have a handle on the truth *as I see it,* or *as I have come to understand it in the light of my psychoanalytic perspective.* Second, I work diligently in every sentence, paragraph, and chapter to offer the reader a candid, carefully examined and pondered view of the matter under consideration—in short, to be as objective as I can possibly be. That writers will ever succeed, either individually or as a group, in liquidating their unconscious minds I very much doubt. To the reader who longs to turn the pages of a perfectly objective text, I can only say, in as patient and friendly a spirit as I am able to muster, give me a break.

Postmodernism

The vast subject of New Age thinking is sometimes linked in the literature to the vast subject of postmodernism, a kind of mating of monsters. Pauline Rosenau's (1992, 15) definitive *Post-Modernism and the Social Sciences,* for example, cites "New Age religion" as one of several "hopeful" responses to the failure of "modernity" and to the scepticism of the postmodern era, while Wendy Kaminer's (1992, 158) *I'm Dysfunctional, You're Dysfunctional* finds it perfectly understandable that people feel, in the midst of a "crisis of postmodernity," an urge to "seek refuge" in the "dawn of a New Age." Charlene Spretnak's (1991, 217) *States of Grace,* a treatise composed largely from a Wiccan angle and fast becoming a New Age classic, devotes itself explicitly to "the recovery of meaning in the postmodern age," indeed to the refutation of "deconstructive postmodernists" and their "triumphal denial of nearly everything." For Spretnak, this becomes a "spiritual quest." Now, as it turns out, I explore the connection of postmodernism to the New Age rather fully in this book's conclusion where contextual materials cast strong light on my observations and arguments. However, I want to outline my position very briefly here, in this Introduction, because doing so will help the reader to understand the *kind* of discussion he is about to examine.

While social conditions (or trends) bear powerfully upon the advent of alternative religions, while we cannot hope fully to appreciate the quality of religious ideas without tracing them to the cultural soil in which they take root, and while psychoanalysis itself would be foolish to ignore the social dimension of the items on which it chooses to focus its attention, it would be mistaken, just plain wrong, to regard the New Age as an outgrowth or spinoff of the postmodern world. The matters to which New Age thinking devotes its "spiritual" attention are primarily matters that preoccupy *and have preoccupied* all human beings, of all social classes and educational backgrounds, in all parts of the world, always, simply because they are *existential matters* which are tied inextricably to the nature of human development and growth. I am referring to separation, limitation, self-esteem (or narcissism), disease, and death—what might be called the "inescapables" of human experience. Accordingly, New Age thinking comprises a reaction to, or a way of dealing with, *timeless anxieties, wishes, and fears,* timeless human preoccupations which will disappear from the scene as soon as people (1) lose entirely their sense of differentiation from their parents and from the environment; (2) achieve omnipotence; (3) manage to avoid completely all frustration, rejection, and abuse of whatever kind during the course of their lives; (4) gain total immunity from all sickness and disease; and (5) become immortal. Although the postmodern world may well lend to New Age beliefs and practices a certain accent, a certain emphasis, a certain "feeling" and ideational dimension, it no more *causes* the New Age, or *produces* the New Age, or *gives rise* to the New Age than *I* as *ego* cause or produce or give rise to the bodily functions in which I find myself involved each and every day of my life on the planet. The book to follow applies psychoanalysis to what its author takes to be one particular, idiosyncratic response, namely New Age thinking, to several *generic* human concerns.

This Book's Thesis

I suspect the reader by this time has a fairly good idea of my overall thesis. Still, I want to spell it out here as clearly, as explicitly, as I can. I want the reader to know exactly what it is that I will strive to establish, to demonstrate, to *prove* in subsequent sections. I do not wish there to be any equivocation at all on the principal issue. I regard New Age thinking as essentially *regressive* or *infantile* in nature. It is absorbed, I contend, in matters of symbiotic merger, omnipotence, narcissistic inflation, and in magical thinking and wishing generally. New Age thinking makes war on reality; it denigrates reason; it denies and distorts what I consider to be the existential facts of our human experience; it seeks to restore the past, specifically, the before-separation-world, in an idealized, wish-fulfilling form that has little or no connection to the adult estate. Latching on to the notion of "transformation" in Jung (the outcome of arduous psychoanalytic work between analyst and patient [Jung 1966, 219]), New Age thinking hijacks and debases it toward magical, occult, and simplistic practices—from channelling the "transformational" messages of angels to reading "transformational" texts in the bookshop; latching on to the idea of "evolution" in Teilhard de Chardin (the uncertain outcome of *biological* tendencies in nature, including man), New Age thinking hijacks and debases it toward a religio-political agenda (the "Aquarian conspiracy"), which has nothing to do with evolution in the strict (or even loose) scientific sense. Teilhard was a professional paleontologist; New Age evolutionists are utopian dreamers. As for the *adaptive* value of New Age thinking (individuals "feel better" or "function better" when under the spell of this or that ritual or guru) (1) it bears *no relevance whatsoever* to any and all questions of veracity, authenticity, actuality, or validity, as it is a purely *practical* or *pragmatical* criterion; (2) it exacts too high a price, namely loss of reason, autonomy, and maturity, for whatever adaptive reward it offers the practitioner. In its mildest and least virulent expression New Age thinking is merely frivolous and vaguely neurotic; in its most severe and most virulent expression, it is destructive of intelligence and clear perception, and seriously or even pathologically delusional to boot.

Is there nothing good at all about New Age thinking, then? Is it entirely "bad news"? What of its emphases on brotherhood, harmony, peace, the environment, the deepening of one's spiritual and emotional nature? Are not *these* good? No question they are, but we do *not* need New Age thinking in any or all of its expressions to lay a social, cultural, national, or international emphasis upon brotherhood, harmony, peace, the environment, and the deepening of one's spiritual and emotional nature. We do *not* require crystals, shamans, channellers, Witches, psychic healers, or New Age star-gazers and "physicists" to devote our energies to the actualization of these ancient and venerable goals.

Let me hasten to add, however, that by negating the New Age through psychoanalytic critique I do not mean simply to tear down; I mean also to assist the reader (and myself) in understanding that *human relations are truly foundational,* that human relations stand behind *all* the spiritual and religious conduct we discover in the world around us, that human relations comprise the bedrock from which are sculpted the myriad "higher" manifestations of human creativity. The aim of this book is as much to underscore the human, *feeling* origin of all spiritual and religious behaviour and belief as it is to disclose the self-deception and regressive magic which reside at the heart of New Age thought. It is when our omnipotence, narcissism, and symbiotic longing attempt to transform our human projections into external reality that we as a species betray our better selves, sacrificing our reason and our existential courage to the deceptive and always temporary comforts of superstition and self-flattering fantasy. This book asks the reader, finally, to stay *here,* among his limited, fallible, mortal fellow creatures. This book asks the reader, finally, to realize there is no place else to go.

Note

1. The comment from *USA Today* appears on the cover of Ferguson's book.

References

BOWMAN, C. 1992. *Crystal Awareness.* St. Paul, Minn.: Llewellyn.

CHOPRA, D. 1992. *Unconditional Life: Discovering the Power to Fulfill Your Dreams.* New York: Bantam.

CRUM, T. 1987. *The Magic of Conflict.* New York: Simon and Schuster.

DYER, W. 1992. *Real Magic: Creating Miracles in Everyday Life.* New York: HarperCollins.

FERGUSON, M. 1980. *The Aquarian Conspiracy: Personal and Social Transformation in Our Time.* Los Angeles: Tarcher.

FREUD, S. [1915] 1971. "The Unconscious." In *Collected Papers,* ed. J. Riviere, Vol. 4, 98–136. London: Hogarth.

GAWAIN, S. 1986. *Living in the Light: A Guide to Personal and Planetary Transformation.* San Raphael, Ca.: New World Library.

JUNG, C. 1966. *Two Essays on Analytical Psychology.* Bollingen Series, Vol. 7. Princeton, N.J.: Princeton University Press.

KAMINER, W. 1992. *I'm Dysfunctional, You're Dysfunctional.* New York: Vintage.

LEWIS, J. 1992. "Approaches to the Study of the New Age Movement." In *Perspectives on the New Age,* ed. J. Lewis and J. Melton. Albany: State University of New York Press.

LEWIS, J., and J. MELTON, 1992. "Introduction." In *Perspectives on the New Age*, ed. J. Lewis and J. Melton. Albany: State University of New York Press.

ROSENAU, P. 1992. *Post-Modernism and the Social Sciences.* Princeton, N.J.: Princeton University Press.

SCHAFER, R. 1968. *Aspects of Internalization.* New York: International Universities.

SPRETNAK, C. 1991. *States of Grace: The Recovery of Meaning in the Postmodern Age.* San Francisco: HarperCollins.

CHAPTER II

THE PSYCHOLOGICAL MATRIX OF NEW AGE THINKING

Part 1

Separation and Merger

The conflict between separation and merger not only dominates the life of the infant but also extends itself far beyond infancy and childhood into the life of the adolescent and adult. It revolves around the struggle to become an autonomous, separate person, differentiated and distinct, and, *at the same time*, to retain one's connection to significant others—either the actual parents or their later substitutes in a protean variety of shapes and forms. For the human creature, two of life's most powerful needs are, paradoxically, to be attached and to be separate, to be related and to be independent, to be autonomous and to be connected; and it is precisely this paradoxical and in some sense contradictory thrust in human growth and development, this antithetical, two-sided inclination of people, that makes human behaviour so problematical, so maddeningly difficult to see and to fathom, and that brings so much confusion to the lives of individuals and societies. Ethel Person, in her wonderful book *Dreams of Love and Fateful Encounters* (1989, 132), renders the matter this way: "The self is delineated only through separation, but the sense of being separated proves impossible to bear. The solitary self feels cut off, alone, without resources. The solitary self feels impelled to merge with a new object." What Dr. Person has captured, if I may be permitted to indicate the issue still again, is that the two needs, to be separate and joined, independent and connected, are, from a deep psychological angle, *one* need, neither side of which finds expression without engaging the other, like a crab going backwards and forwards at the same time. When the desire for merger is felt, it typically engages the need to be separate; and the need to be separate engages the wish to be connected, joined. While it is easy to write about the matter, to employ such terms as alogical, paradoxical, and antithetical, it can be most unpleasant to experience the actual conflict when it occurs, along with the inner confusion that it often engenders. I would suggest, in fact, that we have here a major source of human stress.

From the many psychoanalytic accounts of infancy and childhood, of the growth and development of the human creature, I choose what is generally regarded as the most methodologically sophisticated, accurate, and helpful, namely Margaret Mahler's *Psychological Birth of the Human Infant* (1975). A child psychiatrist and pediatrician working with normal children in a specially constructed facility in New York City during the 1950s and 1960s, Mahler (and her associates) places the accent immediately on the struggle between separation and union.

We take for granted, she reminds us (Mahler 1975, 3), our experience of ourselves as both fully "in" and fully separate from the "world out there." Our consciousness of ourselves as distinct, differentiated entities, and our concomitant absorption into the external environment, without an awareness of self, are the polarities between which we move with varying ease, and with varying degrees of alternation or simultaneity. Yet the establishment of such consciousness, such ordinary, taken-for-granted awareness, is a slowly unfolding process that is not coincident in time with our biological emergence from the womb. It is tied closely and developmentally to our dawning experience of our bodies as separate in space and belonging only to us, and to our dawning experience of the primary love object as also separate in space, as having an existence of her/his own.[1] Moreover, the struggle to achieve this "individuation" reverberates throughout the course of our lives: "It is never finished; it remains always active; new phases of the life cycle find new derivatives of the earliest processes still at work" (3). As we shall see, the writings and rituals of the New Age are designed in large measure to address the endless transformations of these "early processes."

What must be stressed in particular here is the strength of *both sides* of the polarity. Children, with every move toward maturation, are confronted with the threat of "object loss," with traumatic situations involving separation from the caregiver. Thus they are constantly tempted to draw back, to regress, to move *toward* the object and the old relation as opposed to *away* from the object and the anticipated future, the new reality. At the same time, the normally endowed child strives mightily to emerge from his early fusion (we could say confusion) with the mother, to *escape* and to *grow*. His individuation consists precisely of those developmental achievements, those increasing motor and mental accomplishments, that begin to mark his separate existence, his separate identity as a separate being. The ambivalent impulses toward and away from the object, the great urge to differentiate and at the same time stay connected, are, in Mahler's words, forever intertwined (1975, 4), although they may proceed divergently, one or the other lagging behind or leaping ahead during a given period.

Mahler makes plain that this process is not merely one of many equally important processes which transpire during the early time. On the contrary, the achievement of separation constitutes the very core of the self (Mahler 1975, 4), the foundation of one's identity and being as a person. Yet this foundation can be gained (and here is the echo of a paradox again) only if the parent gives to the child a persistent, uninterrupted feeling of connection, of union—a tie that encourages the very breaking of it. This delicate balancing act is never perfect, and Mahler emphasizes throughout the course of her study that old conflicts over separation, old, unresolved issues of identity and bodily boundaries, can be reawakened or even remain active throughout the course of one's existence, at any or all stages of the life cycle. What appears to be a struggle for connection or distinctness in the now of one's experience can be the flare-up of the ancient struggle in which one's self began to emerge from the orbit of the *magna mater*. We will shortly be exploring the degree to which this last observation sheds light upon New Age thinking.

By separation, then, Mahler does not mean primarily the physical separation of the baby in space or the distance from the caregiver, the kind of separation we associate, for example, with the work of John Bowlby. What Mahler has in mind is an *inward* or *intrapsychic separation* from both the mother and her extension, the world. The gradual development of this subjective awareness, this inward perception of the self and the other, leads eventually to clear, distinct inner representations of a "self" that is distinguished from "external objects." It is precisely this sense of being a separate individual that psychotic children are unable to achieve.

Similarly, when Mahler uses the term *symbiosis* the accent is not upon a behavioural state but an inward condition, a feature of primitive emotional life wherein the differentiation between the self and the mother has not occurred, or where a regression to an undifferentiated state has occurred. This does not necessarily require the presence of the mother; it can be based *on primitive images of oneness, or on a denial of perceptions that postulate separation.* Thus, for Mahler, identity during the early period does not refer to the child having a sense of *who* he is; it refers to the child having a sense *that* he is (1975, 8). Indeed, the sense that he is can be regarded as the first step in the process of an unfolding individuality. The achievement of separation-individuation is a kind of "second birth," a "hatching" (9) from the symbiotic mother-infant "membrane" in which the child is originally contained.

The Stages of Development

Mahler calls the earliest stage of development "autistic."[2] The infant "spends most of his day in a half-sleeping, half-waking state" (1975, 41). He awakens mainly to feed and falls asleep again when he is satisfied, or relieved of tensions. "Physiological rather than psychological processes are dominant," and the period as a whole is "best seen" in physiological terms. There is nothing abnormal about this "autism," as Mahler employs the term. The baby simply lacks awareness of the mother as a ministering agent and of himself as the object of her ministrations.

From the second month on, however, the baby increasingly feels the presence of the mother, and it is just this sense of the caretaker (or the "need-satisfying object") *being there* that marks the inception of the normal symbiotic phase, which reaches a peak of intensity at about six to nine months. The most remarkable feature of this phase (and one that will be of great significance for us as we study New Age thought) is contained in Mahler's point that the infant "behaves and functions as though he and his mother were an omnipotent system—a dual unity with one common boundary" (1975, 44). The symbiotic infant participates emotionally and perceptually in a kind of delusional or hallucinatory fusion with the omnipotent mothering figure. Later in infancy and childhood, and indeed later in life at all stages when we experience severe stress, "this is the mechanism to which the ego regresses." Mahler hypothesizes that the symbiotic stage is "perhaps what Freud and Romain Rolland discussed in their dialogue as the sense of boundlessness of the oceanic feeling" (44). Psychoanalytic discussions of religion, and in particular of mystical states, generally begin with a reference to the Freud-Rolland exchange. In a subsequent section, I'll offer my own view of what constitutes the essence of religious feeling.

Thus, when the autistic phase subsides, or, to use the metaphors characteristic of Mahler's treatise, when the "autistic shell" has "cracked" and the child can no longer "keep out external stimuli," a "second protective, yet selective and receptive shield" begins to develop in the form of the "symbiotic orbit," the mother and the child's dual-unity. While the normal autistic phase serves postnatal physiological growth and homeostasis, the normal symbiotic phase marks the all-important human capacity to bring the mother into a psychic fusion that comprises "the primal soil from which *all subsequent relationships form*" (Mahler 1975, 48, my emphasis). We commence our existence as people in the illusion that the other (who appears to be omnipotent) is part of the self. Although the mother is actually *out there*, ministering to the child, she is perceived by the latter to be a facet of his own organism, his own primitive ego. What the mother "magically" accomplishes in the way of care—the production of milk, the provision of warmth, the sensation of security—the baby omnipotently attributes to the mother and *to himself*. At the emotional, pre-verbal level he declares, in effect, "I am not separate from my symbiotic partner; my partner and I are one. Whatever my partner appears to possess and to do, I possess and do as well. Whatever power my partner has, I also have. We are *one*, one omnipotent indestructible unit, twin stars revolving around each other in a single orbit of emotion and will." As D. W. Winnicott (1974, 13) unforgettably expresses it, the feeling of omnipotence is so strong in the infant (and so persistently clung to in the growing child when the dual-unity of the symbiotic stage begins to break down) that it is "nearly a fact."

What this means, of course, is that the decline of symbiosis, or the increasing awareness of separation on the part of the child, will be experienced as a loss of *self*. If union with mother means wholeness, then dis-union will mean less than wholeness. As Mahler phrases it elsewhere (1968, 9), the cessation of the symbiotic phase marks the "loss of a part of [one's] ego." Let us examine Mahler's account of this original human trauma (the expulsion from paradise), and let us bear in mind as we proceed, first, that the transition from symbiosis to individuation is a multi-faceted, complex process that consumes the first three years of life, and second, that for many, many people the loss of omnipotent merger and the narcissistic gratification that goes with it is never entirely accepted at the deep, unconscious level. I am not suggesting that the infant's growing abilities and independence fail to provide him with satisfaction; to be sure, they do, and Mahler is careful to emphasize *both* sides of the equation, the drive to remain with and to relinquish the mother. I am suggesting only that the movement away is attended by powerful anxiety and by the irrational wish to have it *both* ways: separateness and symbiotic union. Also, as one would suspect, the babies in Mahler's study often differ dramatically in their developmental inclinations and capacities, but more of that later.

Separation Underway

What Mahler calls the "first subphase" of "differentiation" occurs "at the peak of symbiosis" when the infant is about six months old. During his more frequent periods of wakefulness the field of his attention gradually expands "through the coming into being of outwardly directed perceptual activity" (1975, 53). No longer is the "symbiotic orbit" the exclusive focus of his limited yet evolving "sensorium." In addition, the baby's attention gradually combines with "a growing store of memories of mother's comings and goings, of good and bad experiences" which comprise the mnemic core of what psychoanalysis calls the "good" and the "bad" object. The infant is more alert, more goal-directed, and his attendants begin to talk of his "hatching," of his emergence from the "autistic shell."

As the seventh month approaches, "there are definite signs that the baby is beginning to differentiate his own body" from that of his mother (Mahler 1975, 54). "Tentative experimentation at individuation" can be observed in such behaviour as "pulling at the mother's hair, ears, or nose, putting food into the mother's mouth, and straining his body away from mother in order to have a better look at her, to scan her and the environment. This is in contrast to simply moulding into mother when held." The infant's growing visual and motor powers help him to "draw his body together" (55) and to commence constructing his own, separate ego on the basis of this bodily awareness and sensation. At times, the baby even begins to move away from the mother's enveloping arms, to resist the passive "lap babyhood" which marks the earliest months of life. As he does this, however, he constantly "checks back" to mother with his eyes. He is becoming interested in mother as "mother" and compares her with "other" people and things. He discovers what belongs and what does not belong to the mother's body—a brooch, eyeglasses, a comb. He is starting to discriminate, in short, between the mother and all that which is different from or similar to her.

This incipient individuation on the baby's part is accompanied by considerable anxiety, the most striking manifestation of which occurs in the presence of strangers. Like so much else in the area of separation-union, "stranger anxiety" evinces two distinct yet interrelated aspects. On the one hand, strangers fascinate the infant who, in Mahler's words, shows great "eagerness to find out about them" (1975, 56). On the other hand, strangers terrify the infant by reminding him of the other-than-mother world, the world of separation, the world that appears as symbiosis and dual-unity fade. (When we come to New Age thinking we can refer conveniently to the before-separation-world and the after-separation-world in our efforts to pinpoint the underlying significance of various New Age practices and beliefs.) After stating that babies vary in their susceptibility to stranger anxiety (and other anxiety as well), Mahler offers us the example of Peter who at eight months reacts initially with wonder and curiosity to a stranger's mild overtures for his attention; two minutes later, although he is close to his mother, even leaning against her leg, Peter bursts into tears as the stranger touches his hair (57). Such is the emotional turbulence that accompanies the onset of individuation during the first subphase.

Increasing Autonomy, Persistent Ambivalence

Mahler divides the second subphase into the early practising period and the practising subphase proper. During the former, the ten- to eleven-month infant becomes more and more deeply absorbed in his expanding mental and physical universe. He begins rapidly to distinguish his own body from his mother's, to actively establish a specific (as opposed to symbiotic) bond with her, and to indulge his autonomous, independent interests while in close proximity to her. In a word, he begins to *transfer* his absorption in mother to the world around him. He explores the objects in his vicinity—toys, bottles, blankets—with his eyes, hands, and mouth; his growing locomotor capacity widens his environment; not only does he have a "more active role in determining closeness and distance to mother," but the "modalities that up to now were used to explore the relatively familiar" suddenly transport him to a new reality. There is more to see, to hear, to touch (Mahler 1975, 66).

Yet in all of this, Mahler is careful to point out, the mother is "still the center of the child's universe" (1975, 66). His experience of his "new world" is "subtly related" to *her*, and his excursions into the other-than-mother realm are often followed by periods of intense clinging and a refusal to separate. For an interval the baby is absorbed in some external object and seems oblivious to mother's presence; a moment later he jumps up and rushes to her side expressing his need for physical proximity. Again and again he displays a desire for "emotional refuelling" (69), that is to say, for a dose of maternal supplies—hugging, stroking, chatting—after a period of independent activity. What Mahler's children (and all children) want—and we come here to a crucial utterance—is to "move away independently" from the mother and, *at the same time*, to "remain connected" to her (70).

The practising subphase proper (eleven to fifteen months) marks the high point of the child's move toward a separate existence. Not only does he experience a dramatic spurt in cognitive development, he also achieves what Mahler calls "the greatest step in human individuation," his upright locomotion (1975, 71). These "precious months" of increasing powers and skills comprise "the child's love affair with the world": the "plane of his vision changes ... he finds unexpected and changing perspectives ... The world is the junior toddler's oyster ... Narcissism is at its peak ... The chief characteristic of this period is the child's great narcissistic investment in his own functions, his own body, and the objectives of his expanding reality" (71). Adding to the exhilaration, notes Mahler, is the child's "elated escape from fusion with, from engulfment by, mother." Here is the movement *away* in its most striking biological and psychological expression.

Yet even here, in the midst of this great expansion, this "love affair with the world," the paradoxical, ambivalent aspect of human development rears its head as mightily as ever in the form of deep-seated, pervasive anxiety. "The course of true love never did run smooth," observes Shakespeare, and the words would seem to apply to our earliest developmental experiences. The child's rapidly expanding ego functions bring with them both the threat of "object loss" and the fear of being "re-engulfed" by the mother. One minute he expresses a need for "checking back," for "emotional refuelling," for knowing exactly the mother's whereabouts; the next minute he forcibly removes himself from mother's caressing arms in an effort to assert his capacity for active, independent functioning. Sometimes the baby runs away to make sure mother *wants* to catch him up; yet when she does, he shows resentment at being held and stroked.

Even the enormous step of upright locomotion, and the increase in perception that it brings to the child, holds both sides of the dual-unity equation. It is the need for mother's emotional support at the instant he learns to walk that Mahler captures unforgettably: "The child walks alone with his eyes fixed on his mother's face, not on the difficulties in his way ... In the very same moment that he is emphasizing his need for her, he is proving that he can do without her." In this way, the toddler "feels the pull of separation from his mother at the same time he asserts his individuation. It is a *mixed* experience, the child demonstrating that he can and cannot do without his mother" (Mahler 1975, 73, my emphasis). As for the mother's *physical* absence during this period (she may be working, ill, etc.), it typically sparks sadness, or even depression, in the infant. The "symbiotic mothering half" of the "self" is "missed" during the very subphase that is most obviously filled with the joys of separation (74).

Undeniably Alone

The entire separation-individuation process culminates at approximately thirty months in what Mahler terms "the rapprochement subphase," the period during which the infant perceives with growing clarity and certainty that he and mother are separate beings, that the old symbiosis and the narcissistic gratifications (including omnipotence) that go with it are illusory, that he is physically and psychically *alone*. Here is Mahler's (1975, 78) powerful description of this watershed in a person's life: "With the acquisition of primitive skills and perceptual cognitive faculties there has been an increasingly clear differentiation, a separation, between the intrapsychic representation of the object and the self-representation. At the very height of mastery, toward the end of the practising period, it had already begun to dawn on the junior toddler that the world is *not* his oyster, that he must cope with it more or less on his own, very often as a relatively helpless, small, and separate individual, unable to command relief or assistance merely by feeling the need for it or by giving voice to that need" (omnipotence). We may note parenthetically at this juncture that much magical and religious activity is designed to *deny* precisely this momentous event, and not only deny it but bring about its *reversal* through just those mechanisms that Mahler mentions here, namely "mere feeling" (wishing) and "giving voice" (prayers and invocations). During the course of the next chapter we will explore these denials and reversals in depth.

With the erosion of symbiosis the "fear of losing the *love* of the object" (Mahler 1975, 78), as opposed to losing the object, makes itself felt increasingly in the child. Up to this point (the rapprochement subphase) the object and the self have been more or less psychically indistinguishable. Now, as differentiation occurs in earnest, the object's love becomes the focus of the child's attention. This does not mean that the original anxiety over loss of the object as part of the self disappears. It means only that an additional, more conscious or even cognitive anxiety has been superimposed upon the original, primal dread. Accordingly, the toddler begins to demand the mother's constant attention. He is deeply preoccupied with her whereabouts. He expresses enormous anger and anxiety at her leave-taking, and anguish at being left behind. He clings to mother, seeks her lap, and may begin to show a dependent interest in maternal substitutes. In a thousand ways he attempts to coerce the mother into fulfilling his wishes. He tries at times to be magnificently separate, omnipotent, rejecting: he will gain the mother's love and attention by showing her the proverbial "cold shoulder." At other times he plays the helpless baby. For weeks on end his wooing of mother alternates sharply with his expressions of resentment and outrage (97).

How do the mothers react to all this? "Some cannot accept the child's demandingness; others are unable to face the child's gradual separation, the fact that the child can no longer be regarded as a part of her" (Mahler 1975, 78). Yet whatever the relational dynamics happen to be, they cannot stop the process: "No matter how insistently the toddler tries to coerce the mother, she and he can no longer function effectively as a dual unit—that is to say, the child can no longer maintain his delusion of parental omnipotence, which he still at times expects will restore the symbiotic status quo." The child must "gradually and painfully give up the delusion of his own grandeur, often by way of dramatic fights with mother—less so, it seemed to us, with father. This is the crossroads of what we term the rapprochement crisis" (79). Mahler observes in a sentence at which we prick up our ears as we near the study of New Age thinking that "many uniquely human problems and dilemmas" which are "sometimes never completely resolved during the entire life cycle" have their origin here, during the end of symbiosis and the onset of separation (100).

Resolving the Dilemma

The resolution of the rapprochement crisis comes about in a variety of ways, the description of which concludes the first half of Mahler's study. As the child experiences a growing capacity to be alone, his clamouring for omnipotent control starts to diminish. He shows less separation anxiety, fewer alternating demands for closeness and autonomy. Not only does he begin to understand empathetically what his mother is going through, which allows him to "unify the good and bad objects into one whole representation" (Mahler 1975, 110), but he begins to identify with the problems and struggles of the youngsters around him. In this way, he begins to turn to other people, and in many instances to his own father, in his effort to satisfy his needs. And with the wholesale emergence of gender differences, he starts to participate in those activities that are peculiar to his/her sex.

Equally important, the child's capacity for verbalization and symbolization begins to lead him toward the cultural realm, toward an endless variety of substitutive or, in Winnicott's (1974, 118) famous expression, "transitional" objects, which characteristically take the form of "blankies," story-books, toys, pets, and so on, and which exist somewhere "between the child's fantasies and reality," in what Winnicott calls "transitional space." We might say that the child's growing ability to incorporate the world into his burgeoning ego leads him to a series of new internalizations, new inward presences, which are appropriate to his age and to the problems he confronts. He is beginning to live with his own thoughts and with the companions of his inner world. This is what we usually mean by "being alone."

In the majority of cases, and generally for all normal children, such developments culminate in the establishment of what Mahler calls "object constancy" (1975, 110), and, with it, the inception of an individuated life. By "object constancy" Mahler has in mind "the presence of a reliable internal image that remains relatively stable irrespective of the state of instinctual need or inner discomfort. On the basis of this achievement, temporary separation can be lengthened and better tolerated" (110). This is the necessary step, the vital inward accomplishment, that permits further growth, further individuation, further ego strength in the pre-schooler and eventually in the schoolchild.

Mahler devotes the second half of her treatise to several lengthy case histories in which we see children struggling, from normal autism and symbiosis to separation and individuation. She strives in these sections to illustrate her theoretical position at the clinical level, the level from which the theoretical materials originally arose, of course. As she does this, Mahler makes clear something that she stresses in many places in part 1, namely that it is the *combination* of a particular caretaker interacting with a particular child that ultimately shapes the child's emerging character in terms of both conscious and unconscious processes. Projections pass not only from the baby to the mother, but from the mother to the baby as well. "It seemed that the ability to cope with separateness, as well as with actual physical separation," declares Mahler (1975, 103), "was dependent in each case on the history of the mother-child relationship, as well as on its present state. We found it hard to pinpoint just what it was in the individual cases that produced more anxiety in some and an ability to cope in others. Each child had established by this time his own characteristic ways of coping." Thus, when we look at the whole picture, we spy an element of mystery, a unique, intangible quality that pertains to each mother-infant bond and that can never be fully explained by observers, or indeed by the mother and infant who are involved in the relationship. What occurs early on is not strictly an enigma but it has its enigmatic aspect, and we must always bear this in mind. Human behaviour finally escapes whatever logical space we try to fit it into. Reality *happens*, from the *inside*, and can never be perfectly reconstructed.

As I have been suggesting all along, the struggle for and against separation extends itself powerfully not only into New Age thinking but into the nature and development of our perceptual lives generally, including the whole of culture. Although it may appear a bit strange to express the matter thus, our ordinary consciousness in the widest, most all-inclusive sense is inextricably bound up with the early struggle over separation *and cannot be grasped apart from it*. We must remember as we move through the next few pages that what Mahler

(1975) describes in the final paragraphs of her theoretical section is the passing of the rapprochement crisis, not the passing of the separation-union conflict. Indeed, it is the thesis of this book, and has been from the outset, that this conflict never ceases, that it so forcefully shapes and directs our conduct as to gain a place among the central conflicts of our experience as a form of life.

As Mahler herself makes clear (1975, 115), a "sound image" of the maternal figure does not mean that the old longing for merger stops, that the fear of re-engulfment goes away, that anxiety, ambivalence, and splitting suddenly vanish, along with feelings of omnipotence and narcissistic grandiosity; it does not mean that the primal terrors of rejection and loss miraculously disappear forever. The establishment of a sound maternal image simply means that the little person can stumble ahead *still loaded* with the great, absorbing issues of the early time, still loaded with the stress that attends the erosion of symbiosis, still wishing contradictorily for both merger and differentiation, still smarting from the collapse of dual-unity. What occurs as the infant undergoes separation has been described by Ana-Maria Rizzuto (1979, 49) as a "life-long mourning process that triggers an endless search for replacement." To express the matter from a different yet crucially related angle, the passing of the rapprochement crisis simply means that one is now in a position to act-out among others this basic human dilemma, this rooted, unconscious issue as it manifests itself projectively at the levels of both individual and group conduct. It means that one can now seek omnipotence, fusion, and narcissistic gratification in the wider world. In a manner of speaking, one is loose. The old cliché that we are all more or less neurotic emerges with fresh clarity, it is to be hoped, at this juncture.

Let us deepen and enrich Mahler's findings, then, and conclude our psychoanalytic investigation of origins by concentrating once more on the first years of life, this time with evoked companions, attunement, and transformation as the focus.

Part 2

Evoked Companions, Attunement, Transformation

The genesis and the formation of the self derive from the baby's initial mirroring experience with the mother. For the past few decades this remarkable aspect of our origins has been studied intensively and has come to be regarded as a central feature of our development. The investigations of René Spitz (1965, 81) and his associates during the 1950s and 1960s established at the clinical level the baby's inclination to concentrate on the mother's face—and in particular on her eyes—during periods of feeding. For three or perhaps four months the nursing infant does not look at the mother's breast (or at the bottle held close to her breast) but at her face. "From the moment the mother comes into the room to the end of nursing he stares at her face." What is especially interesting in this regard is the connection between such primal gazing and the mouth, or "oral cavity."

While the child takes into his mouth and body his physical nourishment, he takes into his dawning awareness or his "visceral brain" the emotional, psychological materials that he discovers in the face, eyes, and bodily attitude of the mother. It is often remarked that the first ego is a body ego and that our later life is influenced at the perceptual level by the foundational experiences our bodies undergo as consciousness awakens. We have here a compelling instance of how this works. When Spitz calls the "oral cavity" in its conjunction with the mother's body "the cradle of human perception," he reminds us that sucking in and spitting out are the first, the most basic, and the most persistent *perceptual* behaviours among humans. They underlie at the bodily level our subsequent rejections and acceptances, our subsequent negations and celebrations, of experience.

Although Spitz established the baby's inclination to stare at the mother's face, notes H. M. Southwood (1973, 235–39), he did not state that mother and infant spend considerable time looking at each other, nor did he contend that such looking, along with the mother initiating the infant's facial expressions and sounds, provided the means for the baby to regard the mother's face and sounds as his own. An inborn tendency on the part of the infant prompts him to seek out his mother's gaze and to do so regularly and for extended periods. The mother, because of tendencies developed during the course of her relationship with her own mother, sets about exploiting this mutual face-gazing activity. As the eye-to-eye contact becomes frequent, and easily observed by the investigator, the mother's inclination to continually change her facial expression, as well as the quality of her vocalizing, emerges with striking clarity. Usually she smiles and nods and coos; sometimes, in response to an infant frown, she frowns. In virtually every instance the mother's facial and vocal behaviour comprises an imitation of the baby's.

Thus, as the mother descends to the infant's level she provides him with a particular kind of human reflection. She does not simply give the baby back his own self; she reinforces a portion of the baby's behaviour in comparison with another portion. She gives the baby back not merely a part of what he is doing but in addition something of her own. In individual development, "the precursor of the mirror is the mother's face" (Winnicott 1974, 130). The upshot may be stated as follows: the kind of behaviour we connect with the ego or the perceptual apparatus derives in large measure from the behaviour of the mother. Not only does she trigger the ego's formation, she determines the kind of stimuli to which the child will attend, including the stimuli that will eventually come through language.

Early Excitement, Early Affect

These social interactions must not be viewed as purely cognitive events. In the words of Daniel Stern (1985, 74, 75), to whose *Interpersonal World of the Infant* I now turn: "They mainly involve affect and excitement" and become part of the infant's effort "to order the world by seeking invariants." When the pre-verbal, inward Representation of such Interaction becomes Generalized into what Stern calls a RIG, the infant's "sense of a core self" (90), or what we called the "ego" in the previous section, is well upon its developmental way. "Affects," writes Stern (89), "are excellent self-invariants because of their relative fixity," which means, of course, that affects are a central part of mirroring. By creating a "continuity of experience" (90), and in particular a "continuity of *affective* experience" (93), the RIG provides the baby with the psychic, emotional foundation of his subsequent perceptual interactions with the world. As the Duke of Gloucester observes in Shakespeare's *King Lear*, we see the world "feelingly."

Thus mirroring in its early stages (we'll come to the later stages very soon) comprises for Stern a "mediation" in which the caregiver "greatly influences the infant's sense of wonder and avidity for exploration" (1985, 103). It is "only the feeling state" that belongs to the nascent self—that is, a "self-invariant"—and "merger experiences" become simply "a way of being with someone" (109). The infant lays down over and over again the memory of specific affective episodes; he/she develops RIGs; and he/she becomes susceptible to subsequent experiences which recall the foundational ones. Later affective exchanges *reactivate* the original exchanges; they "pack the wallop of the original lived experience in the form of an active memory" (110). This is the *essence* of the infant's affective world.

Evoked Companions

Employing terminology that will help us enormously in understanding a host of New Age beliefs and practices, Stern calls these active memories "evoked companions" (1985, 113) and suggests that they constitute what psychoanalysis usually refers to as internalized relationships. "For instance," Stern (113) writes in an effort to let us know exactly what he has in mind, "if a six-month-old, when alone, encounters a rattle [I will refer the reader to this very passage when we come to examine the role of the rattle in New Age shamanism] and manages to grasp it and shake it so that it makes a sound, the initial pleasure may quickly become extreme delight and exuberance, expressed in smiling, vocalizing, and general body wriggling. The extreme delight and exuberance is not only the result of successful mastery, but also the historical result of similar past moments in the presence of a delight-and-exuberance-enhancing (regulating) other." It is partly a "social response," but in this instance it takes place in a "nonsocial situation." At such times, the original pleasure born of mastery acts as a "retrieval cue" and activates the RIG, resulting in an "imagined interaction with an evoked companion," which includes of course the "shared and mutually induced delight" about the mastery.

Equally crucial for our grasp of New Age thinking is Stern's observation that evoked companions "never disappear" (1985, 116). They "lie dormant throughout life," and while they are always retrievable "their degree of activation is variable" (116). He writes: "Various evoked companions will be almost constant companions in everyday life. Is it not so for adults when they are not occupied with tasks? How much time each day do we spend in imagined interactions that are either memories, or the fantasied practice of upcoming events, or daydreams?" (118) Robert Rogers (1991, 41) comments on these materials: "The seemingly unaccountable experience by an adult of strong emotion, such as love or anger, as a response to a relatively trivial situation involving a comparative stranger might be accounted for by assuming that an 'evoked companion' has suddenly been mobilized, however unconsciously. Where else could all that affect come from?" Thus "attachment is the internalized representation of repetitive interactions with caregivers" (Rogers, 41). What is internalized in the earliest representations "is not simply the infant's own action, nor the environment's response, but the dynamic interplay between the two" (Rogers, 41). Can anyone fail to spy here the manner in which these citations touch upon, indeed mesh with, our earlier discussion of separation anxiety as presented in Mahler?

Many individual and group behaviours and beliefs, particularly those which occur in the religious or spiritual realm, are designed unconsciously to address the problem of separation (and/or other psychological problems) by offering practitioners experiences that *evoke companions*. Such experiences grant the *solace of companionship* to those who are struggling in the after-separation-world, those whose aloneness, self-alienation, or persistent separation anxiety prime them to respond to an unseen universe of powerful forces and beings to which they are ostensibly *connected*. Indeed, many of the figures at the heart of religious ritual (God the Father, the Son, Mary, guardian angels) and New Age beliefs and behaviours (visitors from past lives or outer space; shamanic guides; channelled entities, including Jesus) may be regarded in significant measure as projective, psychological expressions, or complex, multi-layered symbolifications, of those longed-for, inward *companions* associated originally with the *dynamic affects* included in the dual-unity situation, the baby's delicious, regulating, invariant and *internalized* encounters with the caregiving figures of the early period.

In preparation for the next section, I want to stress once more the dynamic, energetic, affective, powerful quality of these social interactions. "During this period the mother very often enters into the infant's play by lending some things animate properties. She manipulates toys so that they swoop in and out and speak and tickle. They take on the organic rhythms and feelings of force—that is, the vitality affects of persons" (Stern 1985, 122). New Age thinking is obsessed with "energy," and we must keep our eye on everything that contributes to our ultimate grasp of what "energy" means from the standpoint of psychoanalysis.

Affect Attunement

What Stern (1985, 124) calls "the next quantum leap in the sense of self" occurs when the infant discovers that he/she "has a mind and that other people have minds as well." At about nine months, infants come gradually upon "the momentous realization" that subjective experiences are "potentially shareable with someone else." The infant "must arrive at a theory not only of separate minds but of interfaceable separate minds" (124). This is not, of course, a "theory" in the usual sense, but a "working notion that says something like, what is going on in my mind may be similar enough to what is going on in your mind that we can somehow communicate this without words and thereby experience intersubjectivity" (125). Now, intersubjective relatedness or the "new organizing subjective perspective about the self" is built upon a foundation of "core relatedness," the sharing of affective states. Stern dubs this empathetic responsiveness between caregiver and child "affect attunement," observing that it comprises what is meant when clinicians speak of parental mirroring (138).

After presenting a wealth of clinical evidence for the existence of affect attunement, Stern (1985, 139) writes in a crucial passage: "Strict imitation alone won't do ... The parent must be able to read the infant's feeling state from the infant's overt behaviour, must perform some behaviour that corresponds in some way to the infant's, and the infant must be able to read this parental response as having to do with his own original feeling." When these "conditions" are met, the "transaction" occurs. Moreover, just as evoked companions never disappear, just as they lie dormant throughout life waiting to be activated, so affect attunements become *deeply internalized*, providing the emergent self with a foundational legacy of feeling that is sought over and over again in subsequent years. Indeed, it is "attuning" with "vitality" that permits us as humans to *be* with one another in the sense of "sharing likely inner experiences" on a continuous basis (Stern, 157).

To cast all this in terms which anticipate New Age beliefs and behaviours, what is created as mother and baby interact in affect attunement is a kind of vibrational tie or frequency arrangement. The infant and the caretaker are on the same subjective "wavelength," the same "band"; they are "tuned in" to one another, sharing their aliveness, their mutual participation in feeling states, their individual "humming," their energy. No matter what the affective state may involve—joy, tenderness, anger—if attunement is there then vibrational or energetic *connection* is there, which means that just as evoked companions may address the issue of separation as depicted in Mahler, so may affect attunement. In fact, evoked companions and affect attunement are part of the same psychological picture. They give us our longing for life as *vital attachment*, as *intimate relation*. This is what we never outgrow, and crave forever after. We look for it in our exchanges with other people, as well as in our participation in the worlds of art, religion, and nature. We *want* the sweet, ancient hit of energetic attachment, of attuned interaction, of *power* that speaks for life and union, "the vibes." May I suggest that this is in large measure the "fix" of life itself, life that is tied inextricably to the vital, dual-unity exchanges of the early period? "My heart leaps up when I behold the rainbow in the sky," writes Wordsworth rendering the essence of the matter. And when we experience *the absence* of companions and attunement, when there *is* no attachment and connection in our lives, we feel downcast, lonely, separated, dead—some individuals more than others, of course. Here is

a memorable consequence: when we discover (or re-discover) an attunement, an evoked companion, an energetic, affective fix, we often feel
transformed.

The Transformational Object

Guiding us toward the psychoanalytic heart of New Age thinking,
toward the essence of its interrelations with the early period, Christopher Bollas (1987, 13–14) observes in *The Shadow of the Object* that
the infant's experience of his first object, "the mother," is fundamentally transformative in character: "It is undeniable that as the infant's
other self, the mother transforms the baby's internal and external environment ... [She] is less significant and identifiable as an object than as
a process that is identified with cumulative internal and external transformations." Just as evoked companionship and affect attunement
never disappear, so this feature of early existence "lives on in certain
forms of object-seeking in adult life." The object is sought for its "function as a signifier of transformation." The quest is not to possess the
object but to "surrender to it as a medium that alters the self," that
promises to "transform the self" (14). It is an old refrain: having met
you, or found Jesus, or joined the Party, or started channelling, *I'm
changed*. In significant measure, and in psychoanalytic terms, the
refrain translates into something like this: I've rediscovered (through a
degree of emotional regression) the transformational essence of the
early period, of dual-unity, of mirroring. My new connection reunites
me with a transforming internalized caretaker and thus diminishes my
sense of separation. I am restored to the before-separation-world.

This conception of the maternal figure as transformational is supported by the overriding fact that she regularly alters the baby's environment to meet his need; she "actually transforms his world" (Bollas
1987, 15). The infant identifies his own emerging capacities of motility,
perception, and integration with the presence of the mother, and the
failure of the mother to provide a facilitating environment can result in
the ego's collapse. With the infant's creation of the transitional object
(upon which I'll expand in a moment), the transformational process is
"displaced from the mother-environment, where it originated, into
countless subjective objects." The transitional phase is "heir to the
transformational period." Not only can the infant play with the illusion
of his omnipotence, he can experience the "freedom of metaphor" (15).

In a section titled "The Search for the Transformational Object in
Adult Life," Bollas (1987, 15) declares that psychoanalysis has failed to

take notice of the "wide-ranging collective search for an object that is identified with the metamorphosis of the self." For example, in religions faith, when a person believes in the deity's potential to transform the environment, he "sustains the terms of the earliest object tie within a mythic structure." Such knowledge is "symbiotic" (16), writes Bollas, touching implicitly on the theme of separation in Mahler. It (the symbiotic knowledge) "coexists alongside other forms of knowing." Aesthetic objects, too, frequently elicit transformational response from the individual, who may feel a "deep subjective rapport" with a painting, poem, song, symphony, or landscape and experience "an uncanny fusion" with the item, an event which "re-evokes an ego state that prevailed during early [pre-verbal] psychic life" (16). Such occasions are "less noteworthy as transformational accomplishments" than they are for their "uncanny quality," the sense of being reminded of something "never cognitively apprehended but existentially known." They draw forth a sense of "fusion," which is the individual's recollection of the transformational object. Thus, as *psychological categories,* transformation and separation are integrally related once again.

As I just suggested, and wish to re-emphasize here, the search for symbolic equivalents to the transformational object, and the experience with which it is identified, continues throughout the life cycle. We develop faith in a God whose absence is held ironically to be "as important a test of man's being as his presence" (Bollas 1987, 17). We visit the theatre, the museum, the landscape of our choice, to "search for aesthetic experience." We may imagine the self "as the transformational facilitator," and we may invest ourselves with abilities to change the environment that are not only "impossible" but, upon reflection, "embarrassing" (17). In such daydreams the self as transformational object is somewhere in the future, and even meditative planning about the future is often a "kind of psychic prayer for the arrival of the transformational object," a "secular second coming" of a relation experienced in the earliest period of life (17).

How does such transformation *look* during the early time? What are its phenomenological features? If the infant is "distressed," the "resolution of discomfort is achieved by the apparition-like presence of mother" (Bollas 1987, 33). The "pain of hunger" is "transformed by mother's milk" into an experience of "fullness." This is a "primary transformation": emptiness, agony, and anger become fullness and contentment. The "aesthetic" of this experience is the "particular way the mother meets the infant's need" and "transforms his reality" (33). This, says Bollas, is the "first human aesthetic" (32). The baby internalizes both the content and the *form* of the mother's ministrations and communications.

In his discussion of transformational variants, Bollas (1987, 22) reminds us of the tie between transformation and *healing*, a key concern for many New Agers. The healer is frequently experienced as a "transformational maternal presence" by the patient, who is "searching" for miraculous *change*. The patient's certainty that the healer will "deliver transformation" is based upon the healer's "nominated capacity" to reactivate the memory of "early ego transformation" (27). What happened *then* will happen *now*. I will make considerable use of these points in chapter 4 when I turn to the healing arts of Dr. Richard Moss, one of the New Age's chief "medical" gurus.

We come now to a culminating point, the psychoanalytic heart of New Age thinking, and perhaps the psychoanalytic heart of spiritual or sacred sentiments in general. Because, as Bollas (1987, 33) puts it, the "experience of rapport with the other" is the "essence of life before words exist," and because our earliest experience with the mother is *prior* to our knowing her as "an object in her own right," *the sacred precedes the maternal*. It (the sacred) is not the result of having internalized *the mother* and having regressed to *that* internalization, that unconscious, projective *image*. It is the result of having internalized and regressed to the *process of the mother's transformational ministrations*, the unconscious *foundation* of one's subsequent bonding to her. This explains why individuals sometimes feel irritated when their spiritual experiences are reduced by others to regressive love for *the mother specifically*, for mama *as mama*. Such reduction, again in Bollas's (39) words, is "an insult to the integrity of the uncanny experience." The upshot is obvious: the sacred and the spiritual are loaded with pre-verbal feelings of fusion and transformation, connection and change, union and the wondrous sense of the self's *alteration*. One is tied uncannily to an "other" who is numinous, *magical*, because specific pre-verbal memories rooted in the dynamic unconscious awaken affects that "say so." The attainment of "grace" in its myriad, endless shapes and forms, and in its ultimate *mystery*, is the sharp reinfusion of the infantile transformational process into the life of the "changed" or "saved" individual.

In partial summary, then, we will examine New Age thinking with an eye to disclosing its absorption in matters of (1) separation/union, (2) companionship, (3) attunement, and (4) transformation. We will psychoanalyze its images, symbols, and rituals in an effort to reveal its preoccupation with, even its obsession with, these four themes.

The Tie to the Culture

As we saw in Mahler, the child's frantic efforts to resolve the rapprochement crisis culminate in his ability to create an entire symbolical universe and to have it inside himself in a space that Winnicott (1974) calls transitional—the word *transition* indicating the movement away from the caregiver and toward the wider world. In favourable circumstances, or when mothering is "good enough" to prompt ordinary development, the child's potential space becomes filled with the products of his own creative imagination. If he is given the chance, the baby will begin to live creatively and to use actual objects to be creative into. If he is not given the chance, then there is no area in which the baby may have play, or may have cultural experience; then there is no link with the cultural inheritance, and no contribution to the cultural pool.

Here is the process in some detail. The "good-enough mother" begins by adapting almost completely to the infant's needs. As time goes on, "she adapts less and less completely according to the infant's growing ability to deal with her failure through his own experience." If all goes well, the infant can actually gain from his frustration by developing his own idiosyncratic style of relative independence. What is essential is that the mother give the baby, through her good-enough care, "the illusion that there is an external reality that corresponds to the infant's own capacity to create." It is precisely within this area of creativity that the infant will begin to make his transition away from the maternal figure by choosing "transitional objects"—blankets, teddy bears, story-books—which afford him the magical or illusory belief that he is moving toward, or staying with, the caretaker at the same time that he is moving away from her or giving her up. Such magic, such illusion, such creativity provides the child with his primary link to the "cultural realm," to the religious, artistic, and scientific symbols that comprise the shared, illusory reality of grown-ups. In this way, there is a direct development from transitional concerns to playing, and from playing to shared playing, and from this to cultural experience (Winnicott 1974, 12).

On the one hand, then, our ability to make symbols, to imagine, to create, to use our powerful brains, is an innate ability that is nourished into production by maternal care. On the other hand, however, that ability is prodded into action by the very real problem of maternal separation. In the development of symbolic thought, and in the perceptual style that arises from it, there is an element of that rooted anxiety which we have been describing all along. Thus Geza Roheim's famous contention that culture itself, at the deepest psychological level, is a way back to the parent, a symbolic connection to the early time, rings true. Thinking, says Roheim (1971, 131), is deeply rooted in the emotions, and between thinking and the emotions the mental image magically resides. It means *both* away from the object (separation accomplished) and back to the object (separation overcome). Civilization originates "in delayed infancy, and its function is security." It is a "huge network of more or less successful attempts to protect mankind against the danger of object-loss, the colossal efforts made by a baby who is afraid of being left alone in the dark." I would suggest that the life of ordinary consciousness in culture is not merely a dream but a projective dream, one that invariably projects the objects of the inner world upon the objects of the environment.

The Oedipus

Internalization of stress does not cease with the close of the primary years. On the contrary, the newcomer emerges from this turbulent period to confront the strain of the Oedipal phase during which the emotional and sensual desire for the parent of the opposite sex creates a fear of castration in the male child (we will come to the female in a moment), as well as powerful feelings of ambivalence and jealousy toward the male parent.

This is a time of great anxiety for the boy, whose dilemma will be imperfectly and paradoxically resolved through identification with the father. That is to say, perceiving the hopelessness of removing his rival, the child begins to identify with him (identification is a form of internalization) and to strive and compete in the male world of which the father is the chief representative. As his wounded narcissism benefits from his boyish accomplishments and interactions, he gradually adopts the male point of view. Typically, his wishes and aims are now bound up with heroic achievements, glory, domination; yet the wish for the mother persists at the deepest levels, and a conflicted dependency on the father develops as a refuge from separation and loss.

The entire syndrome—to use the presently popular term—finds its expression in romantic and/or authoritarian fantasies and behaviours. As males, we go through life longing for the perfect woman (which means for mother), fearing emasculation at the hands of both women and men, identifying with symbols of power and control (the nation, the leader, the company, the winning team, wealth), and making the best of what we perceive to be our failures and shortcomings. It is a pathetic picture, and would even be ridiculous were it not so replete with deep and genuine discontentment. When the Buddha thousands of years ago bluntly maintained that life is suffering he probably had some ancient version of this syndrome in mind.

For the female child the dynamics of the Oedipal phase are rather different; the stress that results, however, can be just as intense. If a single utterance had to be made to get at the essentials of the matter it would point out that the girl's partial absorption (as opposed to the boy's almost total absorption) into the father's socially oriented universe during the resolution of the Oedipal crisis leaves her more directly and uninterruptedly in the midst of the pre-Oedipal, maternally centred issues which characterize the first years of life. Hence the girl is more prone than the boy to evince open, on-going concern with "boundary issues," or issues of separation and merger, and to regard the male parent (and his later substitutes) not so much as an avenue away from the mother's world as a means of resolving problems inextricably tied to the imperfections of the mother's care.

In even briefer compass, girls (and women) remain absorbed in the issue of closeness, and when girls (and women) discover themselves involved with normal males who fear such closeness, whose pursuits have been directed away from precisely such closeness, the old, familiar tension between the sexes results. Women tend to experience confusion when the needs of the self, particularly the assertive, aggressive self, clash with the need to preserve and enhance relationships, to express care and concern. Men, placing the emphasis on separation and achievement, typically experience less confusion as the needs of the self arise during periods of interpersonal and professional crisis; but they may also harbour an underlying sense of isolation, a loneliness and disconnectedness, which often plagues them throughout the course of their lives.

Qualifications and Reaffirmations:
A Final Preparatory Word

The question arises: does the generalized model that I have presented thus far apply to all children, in all families, in all cultures, in our rapidly changing world? My reply is as follows: no one will deny that children, mothers, fathers, and families vary considerably in regard to developmental tendencies and interrelational styles. Mahler herself is careful to point out again and again that quality of response and rate of maturation differ dramatically among her youthful subjects and that such difference is compounded by the uniqueness of each parent and each familial situation. Recently, Mary Ainsworth (1983) and her associates have confirmed that babies do not react uniformly to specifically the problem of physical separation. For some, the departure or the absence of the caretaker is far more traumatic than it is for others. As for reunion, some children are reluctant to "make up" for a lengthy period; others are happily in their parent's arms right away. Yet the

separation-union conflict is there to one degree or another in all children, in all parents, in all families. We know babyhood and symbiosis
at the beginning; later, we know individuation and relative autonomy.
Mahler's "phases," and the issues that pertain to them, appear to be
universal. As for Stern and Bollas, who can doubt that infants everywhere thrive on feelings of attunement and companionship, and on the
transformations that accompany maternal care? Stern and Bollas are
writing about "life" as we know it as humans.

Similar reflections may be brought to bear when Peter Neubauer
(1985) informs us that the mother is not always the central presence
during the early period, that our rapidly changing culture increasingly
witnesses the father (and others) assuming a pivotal role. Undoubtedly
this is so. But even here, where fathers or uncles or nannies or aunts are
conspicuous, the issue of separation-union will still be crucial for the
developing child. Motivational dynamics may shift direction, yet the
scheme that Mahler gives us will continue to disclose essential conflicts and provide a useful foundation. I am not denying that future decades may require wholesale reformulation; I am only suggesting that
we should continue to make theories, based on our best evidence,
while the world around us continues to change. What choice *have* we,
after all? Were we to wait for change to stop so that we could begin to
make theories we would never make any theories.

With regard to cross-cultural issues, which we can only apprehend as formidable, we must remember, first, that New Age thinking
is overwhelmingly a Western phenomenon and thus very hospitable to
Mahler's scheme, along with the expansion of it (Stern, Bollas) that we
have undertaken in this chapter. Secondly, psychoanalytic studies of
maturational problems among non-Western peoples reveal, on the one
hand, the enormous differences at work in the world, and on the other,
the ubiquity of the separation-union conflict.

East Indians, for example, struggle mightily to achieve a coherent,
separate self amidst a consuming and often maddening network of familial ties and responsibilities (Roland 1988). The Japanese struggle
similarly with the powerful demands of the work group, a conformist,
authoritarian extension of the original family structure (Roland). And
the struggles of *both* these peoples are complicated and deepened by
the arrival of Western, often American, ideas and attitudes. Yet for all
the differences, which I do not for one minute propose to minimize, we
still see the basic, core conflict over union and separation as it emerges
from Mahler and as it may be cautiously extrapolated to the adoles-
cents and adults of other societies. Indeed, this primal struggle exists
worldwide and is perhaps best illustrated in Eli Sagan's (1985) study of

various cultures, each of which appears to be negotiating a stage of Mahler's scheme.

Maintaining that "the psyche is the paradigm for the development of culture and society," and following closely Mahler's depiction of psychic development, Sagan (1985) views the human community as a whole passing from (a) early kinship organizations rooted in the familial bond, to (b) complex organizations based on chieftainship and comprising the first, wrenching move *away* from kinship, to (c) monarchic and archaic civilizations (Egypt, China) based on the elaborate, hierarchical arrangements which ensure individual security through stable social order. Sagan writes,

> Society may choose to resist ... the drive toward development, but once advance is resolved upon, society is not free to take any direction ... it wants. No primitive society develops into an archaic or classical civilization. Every primitive society that embarks on a developmental journey becomes a complex society. The logic within this advance is not primarily economic, or scientific, or even rational ... it is primarily a psychological logic. The stages in development from primitive to chieftainship to early monarchies to complex monarchies to archaic civilizations are projections and magnifications onto society as a whole of stages in the development of psyche. The journey of the psyche through the various phases in the process of separation and individuation is recapitulated in social development. (Sagan 1985, 363)

As for the advanced, democratic society in which we exist today, it is "the least dependent upon fundamental kinship ties of any political system ever invented" (Sagan 1985, 375). For Sagan, then, the developmental conflict described by Mahler is ubiquitous not only for the individual but for the group as well; the *world* struggles with problems of merger and separation, with the clashing needs for cohesion and personal, independent expression. With all of this in mind, let us turn to New Age thinking.

Notes

1. The term "object" is used customarily in psychoanalysis because the infant has yet to perceive the caretaker, usually the mother, as a separate, full-fledged *person* in the way we normally intend that term. "Object" is a psychoanalytic attempt to render the phenomenology of the infant's perception.

2. Mahler's postulation of a normal autistic phase in which the infant experiences and internalizes symbiotic merger with the mothering figure, and in particular Mahler's suggestion that we as adults can regress to this autism, and *know* it regressively, has stirred controversy of late. G. E. Zuriff (1992) has synthesized and summarized the

literature, and I refer the reader to his paper cited in the reference section. Incidentally, Zuriff finds nothing objectionable in Mahler's postulation of primary autism, remarking (30) that it is not, strictly speaking, "empirical," yet retains its "scientific status" as a "theoretical postulate."

References

AINSWORTH, M. 1983. "Patterns of Infant-Mother Attachment." In *Human Development*, ed. D. Magnusson and V. Allen. New York: Academic.

BOLLAS, C. 1987. *The Shadow of the Object: Psychoanalysis of the Unthought Known*. London: Free Association Books.

MAHLER, M., and M. FURER. 1968. *On Human Symbiosis and the Vicissitudes of Individuation*. New York: International Universities Press.

MAHLER, M., F. PINE, and A. BERGMAN. 1975. *The Psychological Birth of the Human Infant*. New York: Basic.

NEUBAUER, P. 1985. "Preoedipal Objects and Object Primacy." *The Psychoanalytic Study of the Child*, 40: 163–82.

PERSON, E. 1989. *Dreams of Love and Fateful Encounters*. London: Penguin.

RIZZUTO, A. 1979. *The Birth of the Living God*. Chicago: University of Chicago Press.

ROGERS, R. 1991. *Self and Other: Object Relations in Psychoanalysis and Literature*. New York: New York University Press.

ROHEIM, G. 1971. *The Origin and Function of Culture*. New York: Doubleday.

ROLAND, A. 1988. *In Search of Self in India and Japan*. Princeton, N.J.: Princeton University Press.

SAGAN, E. 1985. *At the Dawn of Tyranny*. New York: Knopf.

SOUTHWOOD, H. 1973. "The Origin of Self Awareness and Ego Behaviour." *International Journal of Psychoanalysis*, 54: 235–39.

SPITZ, R. 1965. *The First Year of Life*. New York: International Universities Press.

STERN, D. 1985. *The Interpersonal World of the Infant*. New York: Basic.

WINNICOTT, D. W. 1974. *Playing and Reality*. London: Penguin.

ZURIFF, G. 1992. "Theoretical Inference and the New Psychoanalytic Theories of Infancy." *Psychoanalytic Quarterly*, 61: 18–35.

CHAPTER III

A PSYCHOANALYSIS OF NEW AGE THINKING

Part 1

The New Ager's Goal

What are New Agers trying to do? What is the central aim of their practice, be it shamanism, or channelling, or Witchcraft, or arranging
crystals in arcane arrays? From a psychoanalytic perspective, and in
particular from the perspective of the second chapter in which we
viewed the child's struggle to deal with the devastating loss of fusion
and omnipotence by turning to substitute objects, I would suggest that
New Age thinking has been designed at the deep unconscious level to
undo the realities that attend the passing of the symbiotic stage and the
dawning of separation and smallness. To turn the same coin onto its
other side, I would suggest that New Age thinking has been designed
to *restore* the past in a fantastic, wish-fulfilling, idealized form that
reunites the practitioner with the symbiotic object and with the
omnipotence and narcissism which accompany the before-separation
interplay. Such restoration is characterized by powerful feelings of
attunement (often described as vibrational energy), by powerful feelings of companionship (often described in terms of guides and best
friends), and by powerful feelings of transformation. More specifically,
in reference to this last item, the New Age's obsession with transformation, its endless questing for and discussion of transformation (there
are literally hundreds of references to it in Marilyn Ferguson's New Age
Bible, *The Aquarian Conspiracy* [1980], subtitled *Personal and Social
Transformation in Our Time*), may be regarded psychoanalytically as a
search for the transformational object of the early period and the

before-separation-world (Eden) with which that object is associated. New Age thinking aims to stand reality on its head, and, by doing so, to erase the early traumas we are all obliged to experience.

The Persian poet Omar Khayyám wrote,

Ah, Love, could you and I with Him conspire
To grasp this sorry scheme of things entire,
Would we not shatter it to bits—and then
Remold it nearer to the Heart's Desire?

(Rubáiyát, Stanza 99)

This is precisely what New Agers want to do. The "scheme of things" is "sorry" because it entails separation, smallness, and, of course, death. The New Ager purports through his/her rituals to "conspire" with the Divine, or with the Cosmic Powers That Be, and thereby to turn "things" around. He "shatters" reality "to bits," which means that he *undoes* separation and smallness (the "sorry scheme"), and he then "remoulds" it in accordance with his "heart's desire," namely his wish for union and the attunement, companionship, and feelings of transformation (including omnipotence) that go with union. In the most general psychoanalytic sense, this is the system, the *motive*, of New Age thinking.

The New Ager's Method

The next question must be, of course, how do New Agers bring all this about? How do they undo those developmental realities that we discovered in Mahler and that comprise the very scaffolding on which our characters are built? What is their method for achieving such a colossal purpose? The answer emerges immediately, and there is only one answer: magic. Let us look briefly at what psychoanalytic investigators have had to say about its nature and function.

Malinowski (1925) pointed out more than half a century ago that magical acts, one and all, are "expressions of emotion," and, more particularly, emotion bound up with the possession or the lack of power. Engaged in a series of practical actions, an individual often comes to what Malinowski calls "a gap" (242). The hunter loses his quarry, the sailor his breeze, the warrior his spear, or his strength. What does an individual do in such a case, "setting aside all magic and ritual"? Whether he is savage or civilized, in possession of magic or without it, his "nervous system and his whole organism drive him to some substitute activity. He is possessed by his idea of the desired end; he sees it and feels it. Hence, his "organism reproduces the acts suggested by the anticipations of hope." The individual who is swayed by "impotent fury" clenches his fists or imagines an attack upon his enemy. The lover who aches for the unattainable object sees her in visions or mentally addresses her. The disappointed hunter imagines the prey in his trap. Such behaviours are natural responses to frustrating situations and are based on "a universal psycho-physiological mechanism" (242). They engender "extended expressions of emotion in act or word," which allow the individual to "forecast the images of the wished-for results," and, by doing that, to regain equilibrium and harmony with life. Thus a "strong emotional experience which spends itself in a ... subjective flow of images, words, or gestures" leaves a "very deep conviction of its reality." To the "primitive man," or to the "credulous and untutored" of all ages, the spontaneous spell or rite or belief, with its power "born of mental obsession," "must appear as a "direct revelation" from an external, impersonal force.

Now, when one compares this "spontaneous ritual and verbiage of overflowing passion or desire" with "traditionally fixed magical ritual," one cannot but note a "striking resemblance." The two "products are "not independent of each other" (Malinowski 1925, 243). Magical rituals "have been revealed to man" in those "passionate experiences which assail him in the impasses of his instinctive life and of his practical pursuits, in those gaps and breaches left in the ever-imperfect wall of culture which he erects between himself and the ... temptations and dangers of his destiny" (244). We must recognize "in this," writes Malinowski, "the very fountainhead of magical belief." Magic does not come "from the air" but from "experiences actually lived through." As for magic's *persistence*, its ability to survive failure and disappointment, it comes from the fact that positive cases always overshadow negative ones ("one gain easily outweighs several losses"). Also, those who espouse and practise magic, at least in "savage societies," are individuals of "great energy" and "outstanding personality," that is to say, individuals who are capable of swaying others to their view. In every "savage society," stories of a "big magician's wonderful cures or kills" form the "backbone of belief" and contribute to the pool of living "myth" which gives the authority of tradition to current formulas and rites.

To these insightful remarks I would immediately add the following: the magical rites and practices of the New Age, with their consuming interest in fusion and transformation, also derive from "experience actually lived through," also address "a gap," or "impasse of instinctive life." I am referring, of course, to the primal, traumatic experience of disruption that attends the passing of the symbiotic stage, which brings with it feelings of separation and smallness, and which reverberates powerfully and painfully in the psyche of many individuals forever after, as Mahler suggested. Certainly New Agers often address the kind of "gap" Malinowski has in mind here—the practical problem in search of a practical solution; but their deepest unconscious aim (and the foundational goal of their methods) is to close what we can think of as *the* gap—the big, lifelong one that opens as the child loses the symbiotic mother, leaves the symbiotic orbit, and confronts for the first time his existence as a small, separate creature in the world.

Roheim (1955) was among the first psychoanalysts to spy the connection between magic and the traumas of the early period, and, like Malinowski, he drew upon his anthropological work in making his observations. "Magic must be rooted in the child-mother situation," he writes, "because in the beginning the environment simply means the mother. Therefore, wishing or manifesting the wish is the proper way to deal with the environment" (11). Roheim then goes on to say—and let us keep our eyes open for the "gap" we found in Malinowski—"the mother is not only known by the fact that she gratifies the wishes of the child. In truth, she would never be discovered were it not for the fact that there is a gap between desire and fulfilment." More specifically, "magic originates from the child's crying when he is abandoned and angry; it is not merely the expression of what actually takes place in the dual-unity situation, but is also a *withdrawal of attachment from the object to the means by which the object is wooed*, that is, from the mother to the word and back again to the mother" (12, my emphasis). Thus it is "obvious," asserts Roheim (44), "that we grow up via magic." We "pass through the pregenital to the genital phases of organization, and concurrently our mastery of our own body and of the environment increases. This is our own 'magic,' and it is analogous in some ways to the invocation of his own 'luonto' (or nature) by the Finnish wizard" (44). In a series of key, summarizing sentences Roheim states that "magic" is our "great reservoir of strength against frustration and defeat. Our first response to the frustrations of reality is magic, and without this belief in our own specific ability or magic, we cannot hold our own against the environment." The baby "does not know the limits of its power. It learns in time to recognize the parents as those who determine its fate, but in magic it denies this dependency. The ultimate denial of dependency comes from the all-powerful sorcerer who acts out the role which he once attributed to the projected images." While the "magical omnipotence fantasy of the child is a part of growing up, magic in the hands of an adult means a regression to an infantile fantasy" (45–46, my emphasis). Magic says, in the end, I refuse to give up my desires.

There is a sharp qualitative difference, then, between the kind of "magic" we use naturally during the course of our everyday lives and the kind that marks a regression to infancy. The first is rooted in what Mahler (1975, 71) calls "sound secondary narcissism," or the realistic pride we take in our accomplishments at all ages; and it is rooted also in the supportive feelings that are directed toward us by other people, including of course the parents. This is the "magic" we associate with a "positive attitude," with a healthy confidence, and above all, with an ability to "bounce back" and "carry on" when things go badly. The second kind of magic is rooted in the "primary narcissism" of the symbiotic stage, in what might be thought of as a primitive identification with parental omnipotence. We associate it not with everyday confidence and resilience but, as Roheim (1955) suggests, with grandiosity, with claims of supernatural power or divine gifts. One thinks here not only of the "sorcerer" Roheim mentions but of the dictator, the guru, and certain film stars as well. This basic distinction will help us to place the varieties of New Age practice and belief on a continuum of magical thinking.

Magic Stones

Those are not my words. They are the way Korra Deaver, president of the Parapsychology Education Center of Little Rock, and Doctor of Parapsychology from St. John's University in Louisiana, describes rock crystals, which she characterizes further as "things of unparalleled beauty" and "hidden power" (Deaver 1987, 1). Magic, beauty, power: terms that remind us in our present, specialized context of Malinowski's and Roheim's discussion of magical actions which we just examined, of Christopher Bollas's point (chapter 2) that the form of the mother's ministrations to the baby constitutes our first aesthetic experience, and of Daniel Stern's observation (chapter 2) that affects and only affects comprise the foundation of the core self.

I will dispense with the customary description of the crystal's chemical composition, geological history, and long usage in occult and religious practice. The reader can go to the encyclopedia and get this information for himself if he chooses. I want to confront the heart of the issue immediately by asking, what exactly *is* the magic that this "magic stone" accomplishes for people now, during the so-called New Age? What can it *do*? What is its "hidden power"?

According to Melody's (1992, 1) international best-seller *Love Is in the Earth: Laying-on of Stones*, crystals "possess a vibratory energy," or a "vital energy force," that is linked on the one hand to the "mineral kingdom" and on the other to the "entire universe." Thus, when an individual works with crystals (gazing at them in a trance, or holding them in his hands as he "heals" someone), he is in a position to "meld his personal energy" with the "mineral kingdom" and with the "universe" of which the mineral kingdom is an integral part. "Each of us," writes Melody (1), calling to mind the wish for omnipotence that we explored in chapter 2, "has the infinite power of the universe within the self." Infinite power: this could be Mephistopheles addressing Faust. As we will see increasingly, New Age thinking has little patience with human limitations.

Ra Bonewitz (1987, 9–10) in his book *The Cosmic Crystal Spiral* expresses the matter this way; note the familial, parental spin that he puts on the discussion: "In the beginning the Universe was in a pure state of energy ... was a seething mass of energy." Then came "the big bang" (10). Just as "your life was set in motion by a single, explosive event, so was the life of the universe" (14). Indeed, continues Bonewitz, "we can liken the processes shaping the newly born Universe to the ovum. As the ovum begins to divide and multiply, what develops is almost entirely dependent on the genetics of the ovum; likewise the early Universe was governed by the laws of physics." Because stars create through their "birthing" process and subsequent "life processes" what we think of today as "heavy matter," and because human beings are composed of that very stuff, stars are made of "what you and I are made of" (18). But what is the *first* thing the universe does with its "newly minted heavy stuff," asks Bonewitz (37)? The answer: "Make crystals out of it." Crystals "are fundamental structures of Creation" and the "first stage of making heavy matter into you" (37). There is, then, a "basic connection between you and the Mineral Kingdom" (37). The "energy" of its "crystal structure" is potentially *your* energy. You can interact with the stone in a way that brings its power to *you*. Bonewitz is drawn once again toward the familial emphasis: "We now know with absolute certainty that the Universe and all in it are made from *energy* ... The root of your being is the same as all that lives in the Universe, and the Universe itself [the ovum] ... Energetically, your roots are the same as the stars and the planets ... Scientists and mystics are in agreement at last ... In the beginning it was all energy," all "vibration" (6–7). Incidentally, if the reader is wondering how Bonewitz has come to *know* all this, he need wonder no more: "I have been gifted with certain insights," he tells us toward the beginning of his book (4).

Catherine Bowman's *Crystal Awareness* (1992, xiii) boils everything down nicely for us: "Because crystals absorb energy patterns, they are capable of servicing our need as conductors of energy information ... You are like a crystal-pure energy that vibrates with your

Universe." Hence, you can "resonate with all the knowledge of eternity." Your personal crystal stone will "amplify this knowledge for you until the day comes when *you are as one with this energy*" (xiv, my emphasis). With their "unlimited power," crystals are the "basic energy source" for the accomplishment of our wishes (2). When we add their "energy" to ours we create a new and irresistible "vibrational force" (19). What exactly do we have in all this—I mean, from the psychoanalytic angle?

Crystals are psychoanalytically compelling because of their aesthetic features and because of their putative *vibrational or energetic essence.* When we are informed that crystals contain the vibrations of the mineral kingdom, the earth, and the universe, we must recognize that all three have become projectively mixed up with the caregiver and with the before-separation-world at the centre of which the caregiver resides. Bonewitz's (1987) references to the universe as ovum and womb ("stars are the womb of creation," 37) reveal this, of course, but so does the very title of Melody's (1992) book: *Love Is in the Earth.* The universe, the earth, and the mineral kingdom of which the crystal forms an integral part have become *psychological objects* at the unconscious, projective level. In this way, the crystal appeals powerfully to the emotions because it represents a means of recontacting the vibrational essence, the resonance, the energetic, affective *attunement* of the first symbiotic relationship—the dual-unity that lives on urgently at the self's mnemic, wishful core. The fascination with the crystal as a vibrating energy source thinly masks the unconscious longing for the original vibrational fusion. As Bowman (1992, xiii) says, you can become one with this energy, this irresistible vibrational force. You can "resonate" with all the "knowledge of eternity"—that is, with the omnipotence of the original merger.

Let us also recall here Christopher Bollas's (1987, 32) point that the particular way in which the mother meets the infant's need and transforms his reality comprises the first human aesthetic. The baby internalizes both the content and the *form* of the mother's ministrations. To gaze at the beautiful vibrating crystal, the "magic stone" that is linked to the universe, the originator of all life and being, is to reactivate unconsciously the original *mirror relationship* with the caregiver, the original mutual face-gazing activity in which the mother and the baby stare at one another on the same affective "band," the same affective "wavelength," tuned in to the aesthetic of their interaction. Needless to say, when all of this occurs, when aesthetic delight goes forward in hand with a sense of vibrational attunement and increase of power, separation is undone—one is *attached*, fused psychically with the magical object that restores the past in a wish-fulfilling, idealized form. One is *not* alone, and small; one has one's pretty vibe-stone, one's link to the seething, universal energy, the source. And to have that is, of course, *transformational*. One is changed, altered, made whole again in the fantasied dual-unity. As the back cover of Bonewitz's (1987) book puts it, employing a defensive intellectuality that masks the raw wish for the transformational object: "As the universe moves increasingly into a mineral state of being and the level of consciousness in all matter continues to rise, crystals—the fundamental structures of all creation—are revealed as being at the center of the *change* taking place in the universe and *within ourselves*" (my emphasis). *That* is the "magic" one accomplishes when one plays (in the deepest psychoanalytic sense) with his crystal.

Crystal Attunements, Crystal Transformations: Vibrational Stones

I shall present and then discuss a few selected passages that corroborate strikingly, even unforgettably, the psychoanalytic theses of the previous two paragraphs. "Crystal can be skilfully fashioned into powerful psychic tools such as meditation stones and crystal balls," writes Korra Deaver (1987, 7). "The crystal can be used by amateurs and professionals alike ... yet to each person *there is a personalized sense of attunement with his own stone* ... Some stones will absorb energy quickly, others more slowly, according to the ability of the user *to harmonize his/her vibratory rate with that of the stone*" (7, my emphasis). The crystal, claims Deaver (17), "will actually generate a vitalizing current that the body's own electrical field will be able to pick up." One does not, then, choose just *any* stone; one chooses the stone that brings forth a "personalized sense of attunement," a harmonious "vibratory rate," and doing this engages, of course, all the significant stages of the early period, from the pre-verbal transformational stage (Stern 1985, Bollas 1987) to the later verbal, symbolic, transitional stage (Winnicott 1974). One gets the early attunement and transformation, and one gets the later transitional object, the symbolic link to the caretaker. The crystal permits differentiation from the actual mother at the same time that it allows regression to the primal, Edenic experience of omnipotence and fusion, the "strong time" of "magical" happenings, the time during which one felt and got hooked on the *vibrations* of the maternal figure. As Deaver tells us, the stone "actually" generates a "vitalizing current" that the practitioner can "pick up." One can "actually" *be* in the old, vibrational relationship. Needless to say, to *believe* this and to *go for it* is itself addicting, whether or not there is any "actual" meeting of "current" or mixing of "vibes." The *fix* is in the hope and the belief, the inward persuasion, that something transformational is happening. This is the deepest emotional bribe of New Age thinking as a whole.

"Vibrations surround all matter," writes Catherine Bowman (1992, 19). "Sound, color, light, minerals, humans, all vibrate at varying frequencies but still have the ability to interact with one another." This interaction, Bowman (19) goes on, "can best be compared to the rippling action of simultaneously throwing two stones into a still pond ... Crystals are like one stone, we are like the other. When placed together, our vibrations will merge in perfect harmony to help us raise our energies into higher levels of awareness." Could there be a more perfect metaphorical description of vibrational dual-unity? We "merge" our "vibrations" with those of the crystal and become *one*. Such "merger," Bowman (19) declares in a line at which we have already glanced, "creates a new vibrational force." However, such a "force" is "new" *only* in the after-separation-world. This force is, in fact, the old vibrational attunement of mother and baby, the centre and the essence of the before-separation-world. It seems "new" because it is a force that is now regressively *restored* to the problematical (or dreaded) after-separation-world. As for Bowman's point that such "merging" of crystal and human vibrations will lead us to "higher levels of awareness," it gives us a chance to point out in a preliminary way that "higher" in New Age thinking invariably indicates an interest in and a gravitation toward some version of the dual-unity situation, the *original* state of merger with the object. One can't go wrong psychoanalytically always to translate "higher" into "merger" when exploring New Age texts.

Bowman (1992, 20) asserts in an equally striking passage the psychoanalytic significance of which should be clear at the juncture: "Crystals can become an extension of our own vibrations. Their energy will intermingle with our own, and when properly programmed, can *liberate the mind* into discovering potentially *unlimited awareness* ... These interactions will excite electrons into *transforming* energy" (my italics). Here the emphasis is squarely on the crystal as a transformational object and an avenue to that omnipotence and limitlessness which are so dear to New Age thinking generally. To rediscover the object of the early period through a compelling symbolic equivalent such as the vibrating, magical stone is to rediscover also those *facets* of the object which are internalized so deeply into the budding self as to become, in Winnicott's (1974, 13) terms, "nearly facts." As we "couple" our "vibrations" with those of the "quartz" (Bowman, 25), we are on the road to unlimited perceptual capacity and power, omniscience itself. *There* is a change; *there* is a transformation.

We may recall Stern's (1985, 103) crucial observation that only the *affects* of the early period become part of the individual, nascent, core self, or the pre-verbal aspect of the developing personality. Bonewitz (1987, 78) engages this notion memorably when he writes in *The Cosmic Crystal Spiral*, "If there is one thing I fervently wish to teach you about crystals, it's this: don't *think* about crystals, *feel* about them. Just like everything else you encounter in your life." In other words, go to the affective, pre-verbal level and get your hit *there*. Stay away from analysis, for analysis interferes with the gravitation toward vibrational fusion, the "merging" of one's "energy" (including one's *aesthetic* energy) with the magical stone. Bonewitz (80) states a few paragraphs later that it is "resonance" which allows us to "attune" our individual "energy" with that of a particular crystal. "Resonance" is, of course, an ideal word to describe the primary, pre-verbal, vibratory relation between mother and baby. "Like attracts like," claims Bonewitz (80) in a rather unoriginal moment; "your soul pattern recognizes a like pattern in a particular crystal." Such words translate directly into a wish for vibrational reunion with the object. We'll deal with "soul patterns" more thoroughly in a subsequent section.

Here is Melody (1992, 4–5) writing about crystals as they are used in dyadic healing—that is, as one person places stones on or near another to address a medical or emotional problem: "Cleanse the area and the crystals which will be used ... *Attune* between self and the stones and between self and the subject ... It is necessary for the practitioner to *attune* with the stones ... The practitioner *attunes* to the stones ... Be well *attuned* to the stones ... *Attune* your self with the subject via *attunement stones* to be placed on the body of the subject ... Allow the healing power of the universal source to run through you" (my emphasis). What we have here, clearly, is a magical method of *rebuilding the old, affective attunement with the original object*. The "practitioner" draws the original caretaker into the present moment, brings the "patient" into the before-separation-world of dual-unity, and derives a "healing" from the wholesale regression. When Melody (5) instructs, "Place your hands over the hands of the subject and direct the subject to relax and to allow the healing power of the universal source to run through you, from your hands into his/her hands, in order to facilitate energization and *well-ness*" (my emphasis), she is calling for the return of vibrational fusion, the early, energetic *two-ness* that comprises the foundation of the core self. Whatever the "patient's" problem, he will "feel better" as he is restored to the security of the primal merger, as he escapes the feeling of separateness which frequently accompanies ill health, and which is in fact for many the root cause of ill health itself.

As for Melody's "healer," the human instrument of the *change* that occurs during the interaction, he/she is a version of the transformational object, the numinous figure who long ago turned discomfort into pleasure on a regular basis. With the aid of the magical stones, the all-powerful crystals that are linked to the "universal source," Melody's "healer" succeeds to *that role.* "Both crystals and touch promote the healing of the subject," declares Melody (1992, 6–7); whatever ails him will thus be "transformed" into a "purified" condition. The "black hole" of illness will be "filled with white light." For "black hole" we may read existential *angst,* the dreaded state of primal aloneness, the stench of separation and death in one's psychic nostrils. For "white light" we may read the vibrational, transformational object as she originally appeared, "apparition-like" in Bollas's (1987, 33) words, over and over again to the anxious, soon-to-be gratified baby.

Melody (1992, 6) also claims that vibrational crystals can be used to remove the "blockages" which often prevent a successful healing, a successful exchange between transformer and languishing subject. "The use of the hands in conjunction with stones has produced intensified contact of the unique energies of the stones and the universal healing energy. They assist the practitioner in connecting with the electrical flow within the subject and in directing the vital flow to remove and melt energy blockages." Moreover, such use is further facilitated when the stones are placed "at the areas of the chakras." A "wand-type crystal, rotated in a counter-clockwise direction" is particularly effective in the "opening of the chakras" and the "removal of blockages" (7). The term *blockage* refers merely to any *resistance* the "patient" might experience during the regression to dual-unity, the return to the before-separation-world—in short, the "transformation" that New Age thinking describes as "healing." Just as "higher" invariably indicates some kind of regressive merger in New Age texts and workshops, so "blockage" invariably indicates a reluctance to relinquish one's rational, grown-up, analytic perspective, routinely and degradingly referred to by New Agers as "the ego."

As for the *chakras,* an East Indian term that appears everywhere in New Age literature, they are designated areas of the body that are supposed to be particularly sensitive to the input of energy (through touch, pressure, or cosmic rays) and that are supposed to be instrumental in a person's attempt to achieve relaxation, centredness, and enlightenment. Jeff Chitouras (1993, 38) writes in the magazine *Gnosis,* "Chakras are vortices of energy situated along the center of the body. There are seven major chakras situated over the seven major plexuses of the body where the main network of ganglia are located. They are also located around each of the seven endocrine glands. The chakras play a major role in connecting us directly to higher levels of consciousness. Cosmic rays vibrating at an extremely rapid rate are received and distributed by the second chakra to the others which act like transformers stepping down the vibrations to a rate our bodies can integrate." Bow-man (1992, 64) puts it this way: "Chakras are force centers or symbolic spots that originate in the etheric body. Some esoteric schools refer to these areas as wheels or petals. It is believed that through these open-ings energy is passed from the etheric to the physical body." The chakras are dear to New Age thinking and continually brought into New Age discussions of enlightenment and healing because they are tightly associated with matters of *energy* and *vibrational frequency*. They provide a certain pseudo *tangibility* to the intangible and uncon-scious longing for refusion with the vibrational object of the early period. In a manner of speaking, New Agers are prone to fall into the chakras or "force centres" as magic, vibrational *holes* which transport them emotionally to Wonderland, to the psychic place in which vibra-tional attunement with the caretaker can be regressively savoured, the place in which separation and smallness are denied. Once again in Bow-man's (60) words, when we "open" the chakras by passing crystals over them or concentrating on them meditatively (imaging), we "open up" ourselves to "new vibrational frequencies"—that is, to the old vibra-tional, *transformational experience of merger, the Edenic mirror of mother and baby enjoying affective attunement together.* Melody's (1992) crystal wand is an apt instrument indeed for bringing this expe-rience about.

Crystals as Companions

I will return to the subjects of attunement, transformation, power, and healing as they are bound up with the "magical stones." I want now to concentrate explicitly on the connection between crystals and Daniel Stern's (1985) concept of evoked companionship, the pre-verbal, inward relationship with the self that is derived from the internalization of the object and that comprises, early on, a kind of primitive symbiosis, and, later, a transitional bonding in the sense we have come to associate with Winnicott's (1974) work. I wish to stress that crystals function at *both* levels in New Age thinking; they are pre-verbal, evoked compan-ions and they are transitional objects linked symbolically and aesthet-ically to the divine, the traditional source and the traditional security of human beings. As Korra Deaver (1987, 4–5) informs us, "One com-mon ancient belief held that rock crystal was originally holy water that God poured out of Heaven. As the holy water drifted earthward, it became frozen into ice in outer space. This holy ice was then miracu-lously petrified by guardian angels so that it would remain in solid form for the protection and blessing of mankind ... The Japanese believed that rock crystals were the congealed breath of the White

Dragon, emblematic of the highest powers of creation ... American Indians have treasured crystal as a sacred stone to be used in healing and in communicating with the Spirits ... As a magic talisman crystal cannot be equalled. Ancient priests believed it to be a God-given force which defies all evil and destroys all black magic." Obviously these are transitional, fully symbolic significances, the kind that fit neatly into religious and quasi-religious (such as Jungian) frameworks. But we must also be sensitive to the early, pre-verbal significances that are embedded *in* these "higher" meanings at a more fundamental and foundational level. Indeed, *all* the psychic levels of development are at work when magic is at work, including the most primitive ones which address the most basic of wishes: to undo separation, to be returned (through miraculous transformation) to the before-separation-world.

"In order for the crystal to acquire your vibrations," writes Deaver (1987, 56), "let it be a *companion*. When you meditate, hold it in your hand; place it near or on top of your body so that it is within your auric field and will pick up your vibrations. Wherever you go, take it with you. Keep it on your person. The longer it is in your presence and within your vibrations, the sooner it will become *an extension of your-self* and can be used as such" (my emphasis). Just as mother and baby function as extensions of each other during the early period, just as dual-unity *is* this mutuality of being or mutuality of existence, so does the New Ager's magical, vibrational stone become an extension of himself, an object of mutuality, of magically integrated existence (the externalization of the internalized caretaker). And just as it is the mutual *vibrations* of the mother and the baby, the *attunement* of the mother and the baby, that comprise the energetic, affective root of this bonding, so it is the New Ager's vibrations, along with the postulated vibrations of the crystal, that forge this magical dual-unity in the now of his "mature," separate life, thus undoing or at least palliating the traumatic, never-to-be accepted reality of dual-unity's demise. Once it has become saturated with the New Ager's vibrations, once it represents at the deep, emotive level the vibrational attunement and symbiosis of the early period (evoked companionship), the stone can "rise" to the next developmental level and become the New Ager's transitional object, the object that represents the differentiating move away from the caretaker and the regressive move toward the caretaker, all in the same psychological moment. The evoked companion linked to the maternal figure as she is internalized during the pre-verbal stage melds with the full-fledged transitional companion of the symbolic stage, the energized, aesthetic "talisman" that can be toted around as the toddler totes around his blankie or favourite stuffed animal. Just as one level of development merges into another in our actual lives as described by

Mahler, so one level of development merges into another here, as reality is magically remade to suit the regressive wishes of the separated subject.

Melody (1992, 60) tells us that specific crystal arrays, in this case a "seven-ray circle," along with the "visualization" of one's "favourite crystal," will result in the "subject's" feeling himself "filled with an effusion of energy" and confronting on the intuitive, emotional level the appearance of his "spiritual guide," a psychic being to whom Melody (60) refers as the "best friend." This material comprises a kind of projective "slip," one that captures the ardent wish for and regressive move toward evoked companionship (an affective expression of symbiotic merger). As we saw in chapter 2, certain *energies* of mother and baby, certain "vibrations," are converted by the infant into what Stern (1985, 90) calls a RIG, a pre-verbal "representation of interaction that has been generalized." Such RIGs provide the basis of what psychoanalysis usually calls internalized relationships and are a major source of the feelings one experiences in relation to oneself. An evoked companion, then, is a way of *being with someone on the inside* that is based upon previous, powerful interactions on the outside. Here, the "seven-ray circle" or crystal rite is designed to produce an *energy rush*, or, as Melody puts it, an "effusion," that is *followed immediately* by the appearance of the "best friend" or "guide." The rite, in short, is a projective version of what actually happens early on, during the delicious period of internalized interaction with the object. And the result, of course, is also a version of the emotional state that arises during the original exchange: *separation is over*. The "best friend," or "guide," originally the mother, is now *there*. As for the visualization of the crystal, the concentrative trance in which the "best friend" appears, it is pure, unalloyed regression, an approximation of the very state the infant is in as he bonds with the mother, as he "mirrors" her behaviour and as she mirrors his. Melody has captured for us phenomenologically the manner in which the "friend" *appears out of the stone* or *comes from the stone* (take "stone" in two senses here: (1) the crystal and (2) the trance, the "stoned" condition of the practitioner). Psychically, then, there is very little difference between the crystal and the friend, or guide. From the standpoint of the unconscious, *they are interchangeable*.

Continuing with the theme of companionship, we may note how Bowman (1992, 189–90), in a series of remarkable passages, urges the reader to take his crystal to bed with him, or into the bath: "Crystals may be used in bed. Many configurations can be made to increase spiritual and physical aspects while you are asleep ... To sleep with your personal crystal, direct the point away from your head, under the pillow. Its vibrations help in the dream state to guide and direct you on new paths of awareness." We have here in part the crystal as the New Ager's vibrating, magical teddy bear, the transitional object in the sense Winnicott (1974) intends. We also have, however, another instance of the New Ager's persistent attraction to omnipotence of thought, achieved in this instance through a complete and marvellous *passivity*. One discovers "new paths of awareness," new spiritual and physical directions, not through study or work or research but simply by lying in bed with a pretty stone under the pillow. Here is magical thinking in all its primitive glory. "Crystals may be put in the bath water with points directed away from the tub. If a revitalizing of energies is needed, turn the points inward while you bathe." This is the crystal as magical rubber duck, filling the subject with "good vibrations" as he bathes—a perfect reconstruction of "bath time" in babyhood and childhood. Yet one does not *ever* have to be without the crystal companion: "A new crystal should be carried on or near the body as it needs time to absorb, blend with, and become an extension of your personal vibrations. Keep it close when performing such daily routines as working, reading, and relaxing. It should even be slept with by tucking the quartz between the bottom pillow case and the bed" (Bowman, 29). One can have the magical stone about one always, which means, of course, that one can have a continuous, vibrational *fix*, a continuous energetic tie to the mineral kingdom: mother earth. As Bowman (28) pronounces: "After holding the stone for a few minutes some people experience energy vibrations in the form of body temperature changes, colors flashing through the mind, or a feeling of peaceful compatibility." This is, needless to say, the way "people" often describe the effects of hallucinogenic or intoxicating substances.

Bowman (1992, 148–49) is particularly revealing when she discusses "rose quartz" as companion: "Its energies are linked to the heart chakra, having soft, feminine vibrations. In today's impersonal society, we can never be exposed too much to its comforting, loving vibrations ... Through use of this crystal, we can begin to open up to the inner beauty of ourselves. When we have self-love, others will be attracted to our radiating, pure energies." Here we have the crystal as "good object," the "soft," comforting maternal figure infusing her vulnerable offspring with "loving vibrations" and instilling into him/her the emotive foundations of primary narcissism ("self-love"). Bowman's "impersonal society" is in some measure a screen for the after-separation-world, the world in which the child must deal with the *loss* of the good object and find ways to recoup the loss, the chief way being, of course, the creation of transitional substitutes, such as the *rose quartz* that we have before us now, and the "other people" who will be, in Bowman's words, "attracted to our energies" if we "use this crystal."

Does one have a stomach ache? Is one feeling "tense" and "fearful" in "the stomach" (Bowman 1992, 149)? What does one do about it? One places a "yellow crystal" directly "over the navel." This will not only "absorb" the tension and fear, it will "restore lost confidence" and "stimulate" one's "creativity." Here we have the crystal as substitute umbilicus, retying the subject to the maternal object and to the before-separation-world, the loss of which is commonly felt in the *stomach*, the seat of *angst* and dreaded aloneness and powerlessness. The picture of a crystal held over a navel is in a very real sense a picture of the New Age as a whole, with its refusal to accept the realities of separation and loss, and its absorption in magical methods of regaining the before-separation-world (see the opening paragraphs of this chapter).

Has one hurt oneself? Does one have an injury, a pain—a "boo-boo," as we say? What does one do about it? Korra Deaver (1987, 41) tells us: "Hold a crystal in your left hand. Place your right hand over the pain area. Energy flows in the left hand and out the right hand. Energy opens the blocked channels and promotes healing." Just as mama "kisses and makes better," so does our magical, maternal stone. The "boo-boo" will go away. This is a tiny but vivid example of what Bollas (1987) has in mind when he talks of the caretaker as "transformational object" routinely changing discomfort into pleasure for the infant and creating in the infant a life-long appetite for transformation, as well as for the symbiotic fusion that is experienced concomitantly during the transformational period. Crystals do not merely comfort and soothe the subject, however; they actually *protect him from harm*—another patently maternal (and paternal) function: "The wave and form configuration is established by placing the crystals in the pattern of two zig-zag lines, one placed on each side of the subject's body and each line having seven apexes ... This acts to transmit a white healing light around the subject that provides for his safety and security" (Melody 1992, 104). Who can forget the wonderful feeling of protection he enjoyed when in the care of his magical, omnipotent parents? Yet one must be careful *not to upset* this transformational, transitional, and companionable stone, this magical quartz bearing the vibrations of mother earth. One must, in fact, take precautions: "Do not expose your crystals to artificial light ... do not reuse a salt solution after cleansing ... do not touch other people's crystals [hands off the other person's mama] ... do not allow anyone to handle your crystal [stay clear of my maternal object]" (Bowman, 47). And finally, "Do not go near your crystals when depressed or angry. They will pick up your negativity, amplify it, and release it back to you" (Bowman 1992, 47). In other words, be careful not to *transform the good object into the bad object through your negative projections*. Be careful not to shatter the idealized, magical version of the before-separation-world that you have been working to create. Especially interesting here is the extent to which the stone has become a kind of *living thing* capable of absorbing and responding to the emotions of the practitioner. This perfectly expresses, of course, the psychic reality of internalization, the way our inner objects achieve quasi-independent authenticity when we project them into the objects of the world, in this case the quartz. Also, Bowman's *splitting* of the stone reflects the way the baby splits the caregiver during the early period, on the one hand fearing the caregiver's changeability and ambivalence, and on the other craving the caregiver's succouring and support. The perdurable unconscious aim that arises from this emotive situation is to keep the split aspects apart, repressing the bad and cleaving to the good.

The theme of companionship is perfectly summed up in this unforgettable passage from Bonewitz (1987, 103): "The more you focus on something, the more you think about it, the more energy you give it ... Just sit with your crystal and love it for what it is. A little clear spot here, a little cloudiness there, a beautiful angle, a reflection of sunlight ... It is perfect, just like you ... Or sit with your crystal and attune to it, and if you feel like crying, then cry." A number of items stand out here: sitting quietly with the maternal stone and loving it, just as the mother sits quietly and lovingly with baby; attuning with the crystal, sending into it one's "energy," one's "vibrations"; enjoying the feeling of fusion that accompanies the aesthetic trance and that reflects the *form* of the mother's ministrations to the infant; and, finally, we have Bonewitz's suggestion that all of this may make us feel like *crying*. Why, we may ask? Why should the New Ager, cuddled up with and loving his pretty little stone, feel like crying? The answer sheds considerable light on New Age thinking as a whole, which means of course that Bonewitz's suggestion is loaded with underlying significance: This is crying as *release*—release from the painful after-separation-world, from differentiation and separation, from object loss and being on one's own, vulnerable, limited, mortal, no longer in the magical care of the omnipotent and transformational maternal figure, one's first and unforgettable *home.* Now, at long last, resting in regressive fusion with one's vibrational quartz, enjoying the return of affective attunement, the agonizing, apparently endless thirst for merger is over, the before-separation-world is back again, dual-unity is back again; one is "perfect"; life is "perfect"; and as the stress of autonomy begins to fade away, one cries and releases into magic: boo-hoo, what a bad, nasty dream all that separation was; now I'm back in the Wonderland of dual-unity and I can cry at that awful interval of isolation. If we add this picture of the New Ager sitting and crying with his dear, dear stone to the one we looked at earlier, namely the New Ager holding his crystal over his navel to soothe and heal his anxious stomach, we get very close indeed to the psychodynamics of New Age thinking.

Travelling with and Entering into the Stone:
A New Psychoanalytic View of Religious Feeling

One does not merely sit with one's crystal, or sleep with it, or bathe with it—one travels with it psychically, or enters into it for extended periods of time through a kind of "spiritual" (read regressive) trance. "Holding a crystal in your left hand with the point toward your head," instructs Korra Deaver (1987, 48), "lie on the floor or bed with your head to the north so that you are in line with the polar energies of the earth." As your "body and brain slow down, feel the pulsing of the life force in your body. Submerge yourself into it. Flow into this pulsating, living part of the universe." Feel as if "you are being swept off head-first, still in a prone position, and floating into a sea of energy." Deaver (48) continues: "Mentally float off into the stratosphere, with the earth becoming smaller and smaller as it recedes from your inner view. Go with the tide; gently move along in outer space in a spiral motion, and be completely immersed in the cosmic rhythms ... Visualize a brilliant white light all around you, and know that the light is God." In chapter 2, I noted Mahler's (1975, 44) hypothesis that the "symbiotic stage" is "perhaps what Freud and Romain Rolland discussed in their dialogue as the sense of boundlessness of the oceanic feeling" to which "the ego regresses" in mystical and profoundly religious moments. I also promised to offer my own view of what constitutes the essence of religious feeling.

The study of crystals as a whole, and the examination of the just-cited passage by Deaver, prompt me to suggest that the boundless ocean of regression is a *dynamic* place loaded with mnemic *vibrations*; it is, as Deaver says, a "sea of energy" in which one feels the *pulse*, the *force*, the *photons*, as it were, of the universe with which one suppos-edly has merged. Spiritual or mystical or religious individuals are not seeking a passive regression, a passive symbiosis, mere merger with the caregiver (or the breast) in a kind of autistic night of the soul. They are unconsciously looking for the *hit*, the *charge*, the *vibrational excita-tion* that transpires during the time of affective attunement, the time during which both mother and baby *resonate* mutually within their mirror relationship. Such individuals want to be infused with feeling, with "energy," want to be back on the delicious wavelength (the "buzz") that exists during the early period and that is now projected onto the universe as object (becoming one with the universe) or onto God as object (union with the Divine). The "oceanic feeling" is more active, more energetic, more affectively *charged* than Mahler's notion of regressive merger with the mother may imply. This is crucial; in fact, it leads to everything else. When one feels the affective attunement of the early time, the *vibrational transference* of the early time, one feels also the companionship, or the sense of evoked companionship, that is associated inextricably with attunement insofar as the important affective exchanges between caregiver and neonate are *internalized* by the latter. Indeed, internalization of affect is the pre-verbal foundation of the core self, the very feeling base of the individual for the remainder of his days. Moreover—and we come now to the heart of the matter—when one feels the regressive vibrational hit, along with the sensations of companionship and attunement that go with it, one feels changed, altered, renewed, *transformed*; one feels as one does during the early period when the transformational object turns discomfort (here, the after-separation-world) into pleasure or relief (the before-separation-world, fusion).

Profound religious experience (mystical oneness, the discovery of grace or salvation) *charges the individual with affect,* energizes him, switches him on, and this is a direct echo of the *vibrational* charge one feels during the early time when the caregiver in her role as attuner-transformer touches the infant powerfully at the affective level. All of this—vibrational charge, attunement, companionship, and transformation—is at work when the parishioner shouts at the foot of the pulpit, "I'm changed! I belong to Jesus now! The Holy Spirit is moving in me!" or when the mystical New Ager, crystal in hand, floats off into the "sea of energy" that is, in his mind, the great body of the universe itself. We perceive from this angle once again why the crystal is a central New Age obsession: it holds the "vibes" that are connected directly to the great mother earth and to the great mother's mother, the mother of all mothers, the cosmos. That the crystal is *aesthetically* pleasing, that it reflects the *form* of the mother's ministrations to the baby and induces thereby the kind of *trance* we associate with mystical moments, only makes the line of reasoning we are taking here more psychoanalytically compelling, of course.

What we may term oceanic passages of immersion crop up everywhere in the New Age literature. Returning to Melody's (1992, 60) "seven-ray circle," an array of stones that surrounds the prone practitioner, we find the following instructions: "After centering the self, one enters the Seven-Ray Circle. Deep circular breathing is initiated and focus is directed to the crown chakra. At this time one can feel the inflow of pure energy from the universal source. One now visualizes a *grand version of one's favorite crystal* located on the spiritual plane at the end of the center ray of energy. *One follows the ray to inside the crystal* envisioning a beautiful lush garden, the top of a mountain, the serenity of the autumn, the vitality of the ocean, and establishes a comfortable location in which to await the arrival of one's guide. When the guide appears, an effusion of energy fills the subject" (my emphasis). Here one does not travel outward into the universe with the aid of one's stone; one enters into the "grand" body of the vibrational object itself. *One goes in.* And one finds there "lush gardens," mountain peaks, the serene autumnal landscape, and "the vitality of the ocean"—objects of beauty, power, and abundance which express the longing for omnipotence and for symbiotic fusion with the caregiver. Particularly revealing, and helpful, is the combination of serenity and vitality that is captured in this passage. It illustrates perfectly the dynamic, vibrational, *energetic* aspect of the "ocean" to which one regresses during the course of one's mystical experience.

What the New Age practitioner is *doing* here, within his circle of magical stones, should be "crystal" clear to the reader by this time: he is returning to the before-separation-world; or, alternatively, he is *dropping out of the after-separation-world,* the world of isolation, smallness, and mortality to which his own developmental differentiation has consigned him. And why not, we may ask? Why not go back to the before-separation-world where one is radiant and powerful and safe, and connected to one's "guide"? Why remain in the after-separation-world at all? No one compels the New Age practitioner, or anyone else, to do that; and besides, all one has to do to escape, to fulfil one's unconscious purpose, is make a circle of pretty, sparkling objects, a kind of fairy ring, and lie down in it. Is it surprising that such regressions, such "trips," such magical entrances into the before-separation Wonderland, become a kind of psychic *fix,* something the anxious subject wishes to do again and again? There is a magic in the magic.

Let us note another choice passage of immersion from Melody (1992, 236). Called "The Gate," it anticipates the section on shamanism, which is coming up soon. The practitioner is told to make four small lines of stones and to place "a photograph of the self" between the first two lines and a "written description" of one's "final desire" between the second two lines. Facing these, the practitioner lies down between two long lines of stones ("the gate"), which stretch from head to foot and proceeds to "focus" his thoughts on his "desire" and his "photograph." Melody (237) goes on: "Continue deep circular breathing, visualizing the intake of the vitality of the universe. Allow the essence of this vitality to completely fill the body and mind; it is usually perceived as a continuing flow of pulsing golden light, filling one's totality with purity and freshness. Envision the flow of energy coursing through the body as a fountain of perfection, and refreshing the self with *inner re-birth* ... One now visualizes a grand version of one's favorite crystal and progresses to the interior to actualize his final desire in the light of love." Thus does one achieve, concludes Melody (238), the "control of [his] reality" (my emphasis). Here, the universal energies, the universal vibrations, lead the practitioner to a central focus of New Age literature, which has at its core a transformational significance, namely *rebirth*. What are the psychoanalytic implications of this idea?

Having been *born again* between the lines of magical stones (the "gate" that serves as a symbol for the birth canal), the practitioner is no longer in the land of his *actual* birth—that is, he is no longer in the after-separation-world to which his *actual* birth and *actual* development delivered him. "Birth" is Mahler's (1975) *developmental process*—separation, differentiation, anxiety, the transitional phase, the entry into culture and the realm of substitute objects which can never entirely replace the precious original ones. To experience a magical "rebirth" on the inside is to experience a "second coming," one that *undoes* the first coming, that allows the individual to enjoy things as they "should be," that *gets it right*. It is to undergo a *transformation* in which dual-unity returns to one's existence, along with power and all-encompassing narcissism, Melody's (1992, 237) "fountain of perfection" that bathes the practitioner with rich, self-congratulatory feelings. Note too that Melody asks the practitioner to keep a photograph of himself in view: one regresses to the *mirror* stage but now the "object in the mirror" is not the mother but the *self*, the anxious individual who in the after-separation-world must seek the original object by looking at a picture of the self *into which the original object was internalized.* At the level of unconscious process, it is the internalized version of the caregiver that is to shine out of the photograph and into the eyes of the practitioner. As for the idea that magical acts are one and all "expressions of emotion" that allow the individual to "forecast the images of wished-for results" and to regain thereby a "harmony with life"—an idea we discovered in Malinowski (1925, 242) toward the begining of this chapter—could we have a better example than the one we have before us in "the gate"? The practitioner lies down among his crystals and thinks of his "final desire," which he has just written down and placed before him, believing it will now "come true." Thus, in Malinowski's (242) words, do the "credulous and untutored of all ages" seek to actualize their "wishes" and manifest their "powers" in this world.

Melody's (1992, 138) introduction of "the rebirthing process" gives me a chance to say a word or two on what Melody (138) calls "the reality of reincarnation," a psychoanalytically related idea and one to which New Agers subscribe in large numbers.

Reincarnation appeals powerfully to people not only because it is a denial of death and of the separation that death comprises in the unconscious, but also because it implies *transformation*. Indeed, reincarnation at its conceptual, definitional core is a primitive, pristine expression of a transformational occurrence. The transformations themselves are, of course, projective outgrowths of one's early interactions with the transformational object (Bollas 1987). One is changed from one form into another form as one continues to exist forever, immortally. Thus reincarnation offers us an idealized version of the early period—there is no separation (and consequently no death); there is no truncation of the tie to the vibrational caregiver (now projected onto the universe); and there is constant change, constant transformation, not merely "world without end" but transformation without end. To express the whole business from another angle, reincarnation appeals powerfully to people because it promises a universe that is modeled on the before-separation-world, a universe in which separation is denied and *transformation is the big, ongoing feature of one's reality*. To believe in reincarnation is to walk around with the feeling that transformation is on its way, that transformation is one's ultimate fate; accordingly, it is to feel without interruption *the presence of the transformational object in the psyche*. Thus reincarnation, at its emotional centre, is a kind of regressive addiction shielding the individual from the harsh realities of his existence: separation, and the permanence, or *changelessness*, of death. Because "life" as we experience it is inextricably connected in the unconscious to the transformational object who constantly changes unpleasure into pleasure, death becomes "the most terrible of all things" (Aristotle) because it means the total lack of change, inertness, which signifies to the psyche the *absence* of the transformational caregiver: see how still the dead lie. That is death's terror. The powerful appeal of reincarnation must be understood in this context.

Returning briefly to passages of immersion, we find the following in Bowman's (1992, 38) *Crystal Awareness*: "Crystals to be either worn, used in meditation or for personal development may be programmed with self-images. This is accomplished by mentally picturing yourself in perfect health and happiness. In other words, see yourself as you wish to be." Once again we are reminded of Malinowski's (1925) notion that magical actions are mere emotional wishing for "harmony with life." Bowman's use of the modern cybernetic term *programmed* does not diminish the primitiveness of the instruction one bit. Bowman (38–39) continues: "When projecting this image into the crystal, it is advisable to surround your body with a protective shield to repel any type of negativity from entering into your auric [that is, vibrational] field. This is done by creating an imaginary bubble around your entire physical structure. Its size may be six inches to three feet, whatever is most comfortable. Create this protective coating so that you may see out and experience the world, but no negative emotions or situations may enter into your vibrations ... This will attract the higher vibrations from the universal frequencies to hasten your development. You are placing your physical and spiritual bodies in the hands of the higher forces." As usual in New Age thinking, Bowman's "higher" means simply *regressive,* a return to the early period during which the child placed himself entirely in the parents' (forces') hands for his security and protection. Most compelling here, however, is the practitioner's psychic immersion into a magical construction that recalls the before-separation-world in its idealized form. Entering a "bubble," a "protective coating" which surrounds one's "entire physical structure," the practitioner gets "comfortable" and then resonates with positive vibrations as he peeps out at the world—a baby kangaroo in the mother's pouch. Yet the practitioner does not merely resonate; the rite is more active than that: he "attracts the higher vibrations from the universal frequencies"; he creates the two-way street, the two-way "wavelength" that exists between mother and baby during the early time; he strives for the affective attunement and evoked companionship that he experienced long ago in the dual-unity situation. Bowman's "universal frequencies" are a projective version of the *original* "frequency," which aroused a perdurable longing, indeed a *fixation,* in the subject. As we will see eventually, these "universal frequencies" are the central symbiotic projection of New Age physics, which has fastened upon quantum theory and holography to create a universal, cosmic version of the before-separation-world, a kind of vibrational, quantum caregiver, or big Holographic Mama, who surrounds us all and to whom we are all connected—the New Age substitute for the traditional God. As for one's "aura," a popular New Age idea lifted from Kirlian photography and arbitrarily put to spiritual purposes, it constitutes another transparent expression of the longing for affective attunement, companionship, dual-unity: *one is surrounded continuously by vibrations,* one's "aura"—a primitive, pre-verbal version of the first vibrational object whose ministrations and affect surrounded the baby during the very early time.

Here is a passage from Bowman (1992, 62) designed for individuals who meditate with crystals in *advanced classes,* individuals who "are capable of tolerating more powerful energy vibrations"—in short, individuals who are given to regressions that are deeper and more serious than those indulged in by ordinary practitioners. "Create the pyramid structure using the blue color for understanding, acceptance and peacefulness. Mentally begin to push this blue energy up from the base of the pyramid. Feel it raising slowly until the energy flows from your head to the apex of the structure. The inside space will become a *cocoon of warm, soothing blue light*. With the crystal pointed up, you will have the vibrational energy of the earth flowing from your feet into the crystal. It, in turn, directs the energy back down to your feet—a completion and a continuation" (my emphasis). Thus the practitioner, having inserted himself psychically into his warm cocoon of light, hooks himself up with the vibrations of the mother (here called "earth") and basks in the resulting "energetic" experience. Bowman calls this a "completion" and a "continuation," and it is indeed just that: a completion of the longing for dual-unity which drives the practitioner to the regressive trance, and a continuation of the original fusion which separation and differentiation (Mahler) have disrupted. The circular, mirror relationship of the early period, or the *circuit of attunement* between mother and baby, has been re-established.

Bowman (1992, 63) goes on: "Begin to focus your awareness on the crystal. Feel its texture, temperature, and shape. Allow it to grow larger and larger *until it is big enough to hold your body*. Seek an entrance through its base, sides or point. Metally project the body through this doorway. Experience a gently pulling sensation as the transaction is completed ... Imagine your physical self floating inside the crystal's clear, white interior. *Become the crystal* by seeing, tasting, feeling, and becoming aware of all the sensations. When fifteen minutes are up create an exit opposite your initial entry point. Envision your body passing slowly through this opening ... Experience a gentle pushing as awareness enters back" (my emphasis). Well, here we are finally doing what we've been wanting to do all along, and arriving at the "place" that's been "in the air" from the beginning. We have *merged totally* with the magical, vibrational, maternal surrogate and have, consequently, discovered ourselves again in the womb of dual-unity, or psychic fusion. We go in, and we come out, whenever we wish to do so. We feel the "gentle pulling" of the regression to the object of the early period, and the "gentle pushing" of our rebirth into the ordinary or after-separation-world, now made palatable by our magical capacity to undo it and deny it—cancel it out—according to our wish and our will. And because the after-separation-world is now *defeated*, because it is now in the sphere of *our control* and unable to prevent us from regaining the before-separation-world, the world of energetic attunement and companionship, because we are now able to *transform* one world into the other, the after-separation-world becomes itself a version of the before-separation-world. Thus reality is made to stand upon its head. We will have fusion, and dual-unity, and rebirth, and transformation, and power, and control—in a word, we will have things *our way* even though the before-separation-world is *gone*. This is the ultimate aim and purpose of New Age thinking as a whole.

Finally from Bowman (1992, 72): "Place a crystal point up in the center of your forehead over the third eye area ... Relax your mind and body by deep breathing ... Imagine the shape of an egg. Visualize being inside and being able to look out through its shell ... With your shell securely in place, begin to open the chakras ... Focus your awareness on the crystal over your third eye. Relax and float." What Mahler (1975, 48) termed the "cracking of the autistic shell," or the "hatching" of the baby into the pre-verbal realm of mother-infant relations, is here reversed, undone, denied. The practitioner goes back to the egg-womb and puts the "shell" of it securely in place. Ensconced psychically therein, he proceeds to focus his attention on his pretty, coloured stone, to open his "chakras" (his emotional "holes") to the reactivation of the old, vibrational union, and to float off in his rediscovered state of autistic fusion. As in a speeded-up film running *backwards*, the shattered pieces of "shell" resume their condition of wholeness, intactness. Humpty Dumpty *is* put together again. What all the king's horses and all the king's men *couldn't* do, the regressive magic of New Age thinking accomplishes happily in a trice: presto-changeo! Surely there can be no question at this juncture as to what constitutes the *enemy* of New Age thinking, namely *hatching*, leaving the egg-womb, undergoing separation and differentiation, saying goodbye to the Garden of dual-unity and merger. In her instructions for terminating this egg-womb "meditation" (read regression), Bowman (71) writes: "Close the petals of each chakra, leaving a simple red petal open at the base chakra. It is thought never to be completely closed, because this is where one of the main streams of energy flows into the body." In other words, always go about with an open vibrational hole; always go about with the conviction that one is *still tied* energetically to the maternal figure, still *attuned* to the wavelength of the mirror relationship, still resonating with the deliciousness of merger. *Chakra* here and elsewhere in New Age literature is just a name for holding oneself in a particular emotional state that comprises a vibrating psychic umbilicus linking the practitioner to the object of the early period. To be without this connection is the dreaded condition that New Age thinking is designed to avoid. It is also, of course, the condition that most of us have accepted as the plain reality of our post-paradisal existence.

Telepathy, Healing, Gazing, and the Question of Scientific Evidence

The way in which crystals are used to accomplish telepathic aims perfectly illustrates the practitioner's urge for the old, vibrational union, the affective attunement of the early period and the *power* one knows therein. Melody (1992, 51–56) provides us with all the fascinating details in her section titled "Telepathic Spiral Arrays." She writes: "The left spiral configuration is established by placing the crystals in a helical pattern starting at the side and ending at the navel. The right spiral starts at the navel and ends on the left side of the subject ... These arrays facilitate the teleportation and reception of thoughts via thousands of invisible threads which provide a connection between self and object ... These threads of ethereal material are perfect conductors of vital electrical force through which thought-forms can be transmitted from dispatcher to receiver ... One enters the array, breathes deeply, and transmits the information via the electrically charged invisible threads that connect the two individuals ... During transmittal of the message it is helpful to visualize a white beam of crystalline light tied to one's senses and radiating from the area just beneath the solar plexus ... At the conclusion of the broadcast, one exits the array." What an elaborate, pseudo-scientific rigmarole do we have before us here for restoring dual-unity, for restoring the energetic tie between the mother and the baby. The wish to bridge the gap of separation, to collapse the after-separation-world and the *limitations on the self* that one experiences therein, simply knows no bounds. The anxious, power-hungry human animal will have its way. By means of "invisible threads" of "energy" emanating from one's "navel" towards which a number of magical stones have been pointed—in other words, by means of a psychically re-established *umbilicus* of vibrating power (here called "electrical force")—one recoups the *omnipotence of thought* he experienced during life's early stages, as well as the "vibrational connection" to the "other person" that made up the emotive core of affective attunement. New Age magic is single-minded. In every case it wants some aspect, if not the entire psychological shape, of the before-separation-world. The fascination of telepathic exchange, indeed the motive for its *invention*, lies in its capacity to become a version, or screened expression, of the mysterious, empathetic, power-laden communication that occurs between infant and caregiver during the first years of life when "messages" are exchanged pre-verbally along affective or vibrational lines. Those who believe in telepathy, who feel certain that, somehow, "there must be something in it," are merely recalling unconsciously their own early experience.

The question arises, what evidence is there for the power New Agers attribute to the crystal, not only in regard to telepathic events but generally? Is there any empirical support—the kind we associate with mainstream science—for the many claims put forward in the context of this chapter? Yes, says Melody (1992, 1), who asserts: "Crystals have been scientifically proven to possess vibratory energy, to generate and to emit electrical charge, and to possess the vital energy force which sustains all that exists. The energies of the mineral kingdom are universal energies and are available to those who are willing to both receive and meld this energy with their own. The arrays in this guide-book assist one in the exercise of personal creativity, merging with the Higher Will, contacting the energies from which the entire universe is comprised, and in healing the self and facilitating the healing of others while continuing on the path to enlightenment." Apparently it never occurs to Melody that all sorts of earthly objects vibrate and emit energy without possessing the capacity to effect human transformation. Yet Melody's support for the efficacy of crystals is contained entirely in these few lines, which are, we must assume, sufficient for her followers. One wonders why Melody and her adherents do not attempt their transformational magic while clutching on to vibrating electrical wires, or chunks of low-level uranium—or snakes, for that matter. Might not these things assist one on the "path to enlightenment"? Do not they also contain "universal energies"?

Bowman (1992, 5) takes a somewhat different line: "To date, there is no hard scientific, medical or psychological evidence to corroborate the fact [the *fact*?] that crystals help to raise conscious awareness. Our scientific measuring tools are still too primitive. Instead, it is a private personal confirmation, a knowingness of being in balance with all aspects of the self that reveals how crystals assist us." The fault, dear Brutus, lies not in the crystals but in ourselves. We are still too backward, too "primitive" in our scientific endeavours to "corroborate" the claims of New Age crystal-gazers. One day, perhaps, we'll catch up to the Melodys and Bowmans of this world. In the meantime, however, we can validate the claims of transformation "personally," through mere subjective "knowingness" and "being in balance" with ourselves. As the reader recalls Bowman's instructions for psychically entering into "blue cocoons" and enormous "bubbles of light" where practitioners can indulge themselves in a variety of ethereal trances, he can make up his own mind as to what is "primitive" and what is not in Bowman's presentation. As for relying on one's personal "knowingness" and "balance" for the determination of truth, it would well serve pretty much *everyone* who has strolled through the corridors of history, from paleolithic hunters of the woolly mammoth, to Roman vestal virgins, to the masters of the Inquisition, and to ardent Hitlerian Nazis. I just don't understand the value of such a position; it means, quite simply, anything goes.

Perhaps the most reasonable (and refreshing) statement on the matter comes from Leslie Shepard (1987, 15), writing in *Occultism Update.* After informing us that "quartz crystals are a natural product formed by movements in the earth's crust," a product that can "receive, amplify, convert, and focus energy" in a variety of "modern devices such as watches and microcomputers," Shepard observes, "it is widely claimed that if a crystal is placed in a room it will bring harmony and peace, that it will keep food fresh, and that it accelerates healing and relieves tension." He goes on: "It should be said, however, that Dr. William Jarvis of the National Council Against Health Fraud in Loma Linda, California, has stated: 'There is no convincing published data to indicate that crystals have any efficacy in healing. The effects that are claimed are more in the realm of the metaphysical than the physical. They cannot really be measured and can be readily understood as placebo effects [the placebo is the restoration of dual-unity]. Until there is scientific documentation, these treatments should be presented only as experiments.' The chiropractic Board of Examiners in Massachusetts has banned the use of crystals in Chiropractic work." Shepard (16) concludes by pointing out that "a new word, crystaphile, has been coined to indicate lovers of crystal who believe it may have occult applications," and that "occult powers have been claimed for many precious stones since ancient times."

Now, the question of scientific "documentation" or evidence is crucial and must be kept in view during any discussion of New Age practices and beliefs. At the same time, the question of scientific evidence must be posed *in conjunction* with the question of psychoanalytic evidence, or the degree to which New Age practices and beliefs call to mind the clinical and theoretical picture of human behaviour that psychoanalytic investigation has built up over the past century. It is *this* evidence, from the work of Mahler and Stern and Bollas and Malinowski and others, that allows us to grasp what is going on as New Agers interact with their pieces of quartz. It is this evidence that allows us to appreciate that we are journeying analytically into the realm of the *wish*, the realm of magical thinking, the realm in which fusion and omnipotence and vibrational attunement are restored to the practitioner, to the individual who, hungry for transformation, eager to be rid of ordinary reality, has bought into the claims of the occult.

"Always remember," writes Melody (1992, 227), "that the information which is transmitted to the inner self consists of definite and insistent desires, aspirations, ambitions, and dreams," which may be "actualized" as follows: "Transcribe the first chosen desire to a piece of paper upon which the crystal array for 'reprogramming' has been placed. Enter the larger crystal array for 'reprogramming' and after centering the self and deep breathing create a clear mental picture of the desire or goal you wish. Recognize that the most ardent mental visualization transfers the desire to the self. Maintain for thirty minutes."

There is no denying, of course, that one *has* a desire: to be healthy or famous or rich or beloved or whatever. Yet what Melody misses—and this applies to New Agers generally—is the big, unmentioned wish, the big, unconscious wish, that underlies not only this magical procedure but all the magical procedures of New Age thinking, namely the wish that is "actualized" by the very *doing* of the magic, the wish that is "actualized" by indulging in a game the underlying assumptions of which say to the practitioner, "You are omnipotent; you are connected to the all-powerful object of the early period; you are special and wonderful and in control of everything; you have not relinquished the advantages of the before-separation-world; let the magical vibrations of the universe help you to achieve your dreams, to *transform* your existence." The fix of New Age thinking, its seductiveness, lies not so much in what actually results from one's esoteric activities as in the *emotional position one adopts* as he takes part in those activities. To be *doing* magic is a wish-fulfilment *in and of itself.*

Deaver (1987, 36–37) writes on the matter of healing with crystals: "In most cases of healing diseased organs or tissues, the crystal is held in the area of disturbed energy on the body ... The patient himself must try various distances and orientations of the crystal until he feels an appropriate response, a feeling of well-being ... The best guidance is what feels right ... Using a crystal in each hand helps to amplify the healing forces that are flowing through the healer to the patient ... Healings done through spiritual love vibration are the most effective. Failing the necessary love donor, one can supply his own love vibration. The desire to be a healing channel is in itself a love vibration." The most obvious psychoanalytic significance here is, of course, the re-establishment of dual-unity, the placebo effect to which we referred a moment ago. The "vibrations" of the crystal-bearing "healer" flow to the "patient" as they become *one* in an updated version of the old, affective attunement that existed betweeen mother and baby during the early period. (If the "patient" is alone with the crystal, he can, as Deaver suggests, try to split himself up into a version of the internalized object and his own needy self and proceed from there.) That the "patient" in this duo may be expressing some sort of illness or discomfort I am not denying for a moment. I am merely suggesting that whatever "healing" occurs here is the result of the "patient" finding himself once again in the dual-unity situation, *linked* to the significant other, feeling the affective attunement and companionship that he felt and *thrived on* long ago in his infancy and childhood. New Age "healing" creates a powerfully seductive "bedside manner" in the "healer," who is saying to the patient, in effect: "You're not alone; you're connected once again to the maternal vibrations on which you originally flourished;

you've returned to the before-separation-world, the Garden of magical merger; in the midst of this fusion, this vibrational exchange, you will be altered, transformed, made whole." Once again, it is the *doing of the magic* that breeds the result, the improvement (if it "works" and there is improvement). The "patient" *gets better* because at the unconscious level where he is responding, the "patient" likes the before-separation-world *better* than the world in which he got "sick." *That* is the significance, ultimately, of Deaver's (37) emphasis on the "spiritual love vibration" that is passed between the "healer" and the "patient": it is a *transference version* of the *first* vibration that ties the infant to the caregiver during the time of affective attunement. As always in New Age literature, "spiritual" here means parental, and in particular the parental paradise of symbiotic merger, the magical *resonance* of the two-way interaction that occurs in life's first stages as mother and baby enjoy their mutual mirroring.

The "sickness" to which New Age healing addresses itself should now be clear: it is the anxiety and stress that comes automatically and inescapably with the advent of the after-separation-world; it is the anxiety and stress that attends the realization of one's separateness and smallness and mortality—in a word, *the facts*, now made more brutal than they usually are by the collapse of the family and the community, the decline of traditional religion, and the emergence of a violent, impersonal, polluted, and over-crowded world.

The underlying psychoanalytic significance of *gazing* into crystals for the purpose of divining the future or disclosing the unknown should also be clear now. Deaver (1987, 18–22) instructs the practitioner as follows: "Easy naturalness is the key. One is merging one's consciousness with the elemental consciousness and purpose of the stone, which is a natural harmonizer and balancer ... Practice is best carried out alone ... You may prefer to hold the crystal in your hands ... An inner peace is required ... Begin your practice with an active visualization. Take a simple object such as a spoon or pen and try to see it in the crystal ball ... Don't just look at the crystal—look into its depths ... Concentrate ... With practice the pictures will become clear and brilliant ... You will feel inside that you know the answer to the question or problem ... Some day you will find yourself in complete control of the mental faculties that function through the crystal ball." Deaver (24) concludes by asserting: "Think only positive thoughts if you want the crystal to amplify and enhance the energies within you." Just as the deepest purpose of wishing or healing with crystals is not the result but the return to the before-separation-world of dual-unity and omnipotence which is accomplished by the doing of the magic, so the deepest purpose of *gazing* is not the information or the prediction that ostensibly comes from it, but *being in the state of gazing*, being in connection with the crystal, being tied to the magical stone by means of a regressive trance. One may come away from the crystal with *nothing* in the way of information or prediction, but it feels good to be doing this sort of thing; it feels good to be indulging one's omnipotence, one's narcissism, one's *connection* to the lovely quartz. It is the *state of staring* at the numinous, translucent object that is ultimately craved because it is the *state of staring* that restores the original *mirror relation* between mother (crystal ball) and infant (New Age practitioner). To put the matter as bluntly as possible, in the crystal ball we have a version of the mother's face.

Part 2

Shamanism, New Age Style

I will rely on a number of sources including Michael Harner's *The Way of the Shaman* (1990), universally regarded by New Agers as the Bible on the subject. Here are a few blurbs from the jacket of the paper edition: "Harner has impeccable credentials, both as an academic and as a practicing shaman. Without doubt (since the death of Mircea Eliade) the world's leading authority on shamanism"—this from "Neville Drury, author of *The Elements of Shamanism.*" Again, "an intimate and practical guide to the art of shamanic healing and the technology of the sacred. Harner is not just an anthropologist who has studied shamanism; he is an authentic white shaman"—this from "Stanislav Grof, author of *The Adventure of Self-Discovery.*" Finally, from the legendary guru Carlos Castaneda, "wonderful, fascinating ... Harner really knows what he's talking about." The jacket concludes by informing us that Harner has practised shamanism and shamanic healing "for more than a quarter of a century" (more impressive, I take it, than a mere twenty-five years) and that he is the founder and director of the Foundation for Shamanic Studies in Norwalk, Connecticut. After completing the analysis of shamanism that I intend to set out here, the reader may wish to glance at these glowing quotations, and this information, once again. An irony or two may just be visible. I consider my other sources to be significant and valuable, of course, but the Harner book is the one New Agers are usually discussing.

Because Carlos Castaneda (whose portrait appeared on the cover of *Time* twenty years ago) may be regarded as the inceptor of the current, popular fascination with shamanism, and because Castaneda's writings have enjoyed such a large audience, the question quite naturally arises, why not take up Castaneda here? To those who have read him and who have followed the sizeable literature that has spring up around him, the answer to this question is obvious. From all indications, Castaneda turns out to be one of the twentieth century's great hoaxers; his writings are in large measure bogus, put forward as authentic and factual investigative reporting and exposed (by Richard de Mille [1985], for example) as faked. Some of what Castaneda reports may have actually occurred; some of it may not have actually occurred; that is, some of it may have been *made up*. Some of what Castaneda presents as his own writing and theorizing may be his own; some of it may be plagiarized and presented as his own. There is no way I wish to carry this burden. A writer who is under such a cloud and who may pass into history as an intellectual charlatan is best left out, particularly when other texts can take us to the heart of the matter.

Shamanism, New Age style, is currently on the rise, even replacing (perhaps) some of the other practices of the day. "One of the traits of the New Age," write Lewis and Melton (1992, xii) in a passage cited earlier, in chapter 1, "is that major subjects of interest vary from time to time, so that, particularly to the outside observer, this subculture appears to go through transformation after transformation. The movement away from the prominence of Eastern spiritual teachers (particularly characteristic of the seventies) to an emphasis on channelled entities (in the eighties) is an example of one such transformation. In a similar manner, the interest in channelling seems to be waning as we move into the nineties, and the new emphasis appears to be shamanism and Native American spirituality." Lewis and Melton are wise to write "appears to be" in the foregoing passage. My own impression in researching this book and interviewing many New Agers is that all the pistons of the New Age engine are pounding rather vigorously, including crystals, channelling, psychic healing, meditation, and Wicca. Harner (1990, xi) informs us that "during the last decade" shamanism "has returned to human life with startling strength." Today, his sweeping prose declares, "from Zurich to Auckland, from Chicago to Sao Paulo, humans are again taking up the ancient way of the Shaman, often in drumming circles or groups which meet regularly for practice, healing work, and shamanic journeying" (xiii). Nor are present-day adherents to the shaman's way mainly deviants, extremists, or cultists. In Harner's (32) words again, it is "middle-class Americans from a variety of backgrounds" who are getting involved. The question becomes, what exactly has psychoanalysis to say about all this?

The Shamanic Myth of Connection and Disruption

Just as New Agers involved with crystals stress the tie between human beings and the surrounding universe, so do the practitioners of New Age shamanism underscore the connection between people and nature as a whole. However, the shamanic myth, in contrast to the mythic backdrop of the magical stones, holds that this connection was *severed* long ago, as culture, and the ordinary, socialized consciousness that arises with culture, seduced people away from direct and unalloyed participation in the natural world. These two symbolically (and psychoanalytically) related ideas—the ultimate connection of everything to everything else and the experience of a *fall* or disjunction of perception in the human creature—comprise the mythic framework in which all shamanic beliefs and practices transpire. Let us look closely at both sides of the framework, beginning with the notion of union.

"The shaman knows," writes Harner (1990, 54), "that humans are related to all forms of life, that they are all our relations, that all life is one." Shamans "are not lonely even if alone, for they have come to understand that we are never really isolated" (xiv). As they go about their shamanic work, journeying psychically to other realms and levels of existence, "shamans discover the incredible safety and love of the normally-hidden universe. The cosmic love they repeatedly encounter in their journeys is increasingly expressed in their daily lives ... They realize that everything is alive. Everywhere they are surrounded by life, by family. They have returned to the eternal community of the shaman, unlimited by boundaries of space and time" (xiv–xv). Surely one cannot miss the psychological scent of the before-separation-world in such images and metaphors.

Inextricably woven into shamanic notions of connection is the notion of the earth as *magna mater*, as great mother, as the *root* connection which underlies and establishes the connective network in its intricate and infinite totality. The shaman, writes Harner (1990, xiii), "has reverence for, and spiritual communication with, the other beings of the earth and with the Planet itself." He is "able to talk with all of nature, including the plants, the streams, the air, the rocks, and the animals," and he "considers such communication essential for his survival" (xiii). Nature, the very earth itself, is "prepared to reveal to him in his altered state of consciousness things that are not ascertainable to others who exist in the ordinary state" (54). Shall we sample briefly the expression of such ideas in one or two additional shamanic texts?

"Everything is interdependent and mutually supportive," writes Kenneth Meadows in *Shamanic Experience* (1991, 3). "We are of the Earth and dependent on the Earth for our survival. The Earth itself is a living being—an organism within the greater organism of the universe" (3). Again from Meadows—and we prick up our ears at the entrance of vibrational explanations—"shamanism recognizes that everything is an energy-system in itself within a greater energy-system, and therefore linked to the energy-systems of everything else ... Everything is alive. Everything vibrates: animals, trees, plants, even rocks ... Everything interconnects in a universal web of energy ... This concept of the Web is used by shamans as an explanation of the connected wholeness of all that is in existence" (6, 41). According to Loren Cruden (1993, 12), writing in the journal *Shaman's Drum*, "The spirit of shamanism remains one of awareness of the sacred, of services to the web of life and of bridging the realms." Solveig Turpin (1993, 32) observes, also in *Shaman's Drum*, "Shamanism holds that all natural objects and natural phenomena are part of a common consciousness ... All things, living or inanimate, and all creatures, human and animal, share in a cosmic soul." Finally, to sum up the matter with a line from Meadows (171), shamanism is rooted "in a respect for the Earth as a Mother who provides the opportunity to incarnate, and who nurtures, sustains, and protects one in physical existence." The intricate, shamanic web of the world has, ultimately, a maternal meaning.

However, as I mentioned a moment ago, the shamanic oneness of the universe, the magical *union*, was broken in the distant past as people and animals, or indeed people and the whole of nature, underwent *separation* through the rise of culture and ordinary consciousness. Shamanism's deepest aim is to end this separation, to reunite the disjunctive worlds, and in doing so to regain not only primal unity but all the advantages or *powers* that came with access to the other realm. Here is the way it goes in Harner (1990, 57): "While the mystical *paradise* [my emphasis] of animal-human unity is lost in ordinary reality, it still remains accessible in nonordinary reality to the shaman. The Australian aborigines' concept of 'The Dream Time' embodies this awareness, for it refers to a mythological past that still exists parallel in time to present-day ordinary reality, and which is penetrated by dreams and visions. The shaman, alone of humans, is regularly able to effect the animal-human unity by entering the shamanic state of consciousness. For the shaman in the altered state of consciousness, the mythical past is immediately accessible." Turpin (1993, 32) puts it this way in *Shaman's Drum:* "In the beginning, all human beings could move easily between the world of the flesh and of the spirit. All were male and female, all were animal and human. In the shamanic version of the *fall from grace* [my emphasis] this ability was lost, the two domains became separated, and a no-man's land fraught with difficulties sprang up between. Only the shaman in the trance state can return to the oneness that was the original state of the universe." We are getting to the first decisive point—I mean, from the psychoanalytic angle.

Everything is connected, everything is one, everything is tied to earth as object; there *is no separation*, ultimately. But most of us cannot see, or feel, or participate in the magical, interconnecting web. We are "fallen," cut off, shut out, alone. Only the shaman may bridge the gap; only the shaman may, in his trance, embark on the journey toward the original wholeness and all the fantastic rewards that accompany such wholeness. This in a nutshell is the ancient system. Now, in New Age thinking, *we, all of us,* can bridge the gap that separates the ordinary from the non-ordinary world. *We* can be the special one. *We* can end the alienation and aloneness that belongs to the "fallen" state, the state of egotic differentiation that was both achieved and thrust upon us during the early years (Mahler) and that elicits a constant anxiety and ambivalence within us in our so-called adult or grown-up condition. *We* can have the union, the paradise, the garden-like existence that we associate with the prelapsarian realm, the shamanic, mythic version of the before-separation-world into which every mother's son or daughter is born in a thousand locations on earth thousands of times each and every day. What the ancient shamans supposedly did in Siberia and Guatemala, and what present-day shamans supposedly do in those and other locations, *we* can do in our apartments and town houses with our rattles and beads and feathers, and our handy instructions as available in Harner's "practical guide," which prepares the practitioner for shamanism in about an hour (Harner [1990] writes on page 30, "Now you are ready for your first exercise in shamanism") and which costs about $15 at your local New Age bookstore. Harner's "first exercise in shamanism" is, of course, the "journey of exploration," the "trip" that takes one to the "other reality" in which one's prelapsarian affinities and powers are regained. I want to have a look now at this journey. I want to examine the behaviours and metaphors which surround it, to probe its underlying nature and meaning. From the standpoint of psychoanalysis I want to ask, what's going on?

The Shamanic Journey

The shaman, Harner (1990, 20) informs us, is distinguished from "other kinds of magicians by his use of a state of consciousness which Mircea Eliade calls 'ecstasy.'" However, Harner continues, "the practice of ecstasy alone does not define the shaman, for the shaman has specific techniques of ecstasy ... He specializes in a trance during which his soul is believed to leave his body and ascend to the sky or descend to the underworld." Also, he commonly strives in his trance "to heal a patient by restoring beneficial or vital power, or by extracting harmful power." Thus the shamanic state of consciousness involves "not only a trance or a transcendent state of awareness, but also a learned awareness of shamanic methods and assumptions while in such an altered state" (21). Harner (47) writes in another place that "a perception of two realities is typical of shamanism, even though some Western armchair philosophers have long denied the legitimacy of claiming such a dual division between the ordinary world and a hidden world among primitive peoples, apparently assuming that primitives cannot distinguish between the two." Yet, Harner goes on, "if primitive peoples do not consciously make such a dichotomy they do in fact unconsciously order their cognitions according to this model." One "proof" of this is the "shamanic trance," the "world of ecstasy and supernatural powers" into which the shaman "dives." He exists "in two worlds: outside the trance he lives the daily life of his tribesmen; inside the trance he is part of the supernatural world." Being a shaman and being in this peculiar, magical, trance-like state are indistinguishable at the level of operational definition.

Meadows (1991, 84) expresses the business this way: "In making a spirit or soul journey we switch our brain circuits to a different frequency from the one we use in ordinary reality. This produces a change of awareness and a state of shamanic consciousness which is not hypnotic, for the traveller is in complete control of his will and actions at all times." Meadows (84) continues: "Some describe this condition of shamanic consciousness as a trance, but in my understanding it is not even that, for there is no suspension of sensation or awareness. Indeed, sensation is actually enhanced and consciousness is expanded ... It is a transcendent state of awareness which might be likened to a waking dream." As we will see in a moment, Meadows's emphasis on "brain waves" and "frequencies," in other words on *vibrations*, turns out to be significant and accurate, but in ways far different from those he intends in his book.

As for the *methods* employed to induce both trance and journey, Harner (1990, xii) declares, "Shamanic methods require a relaxed discipline, with concentration and purpose. Contemporary shamanism, like that in most tribal cultures, typically utilizes *monotonous percussion sound* to enter an altered state. This classic, drug-free method is remarkably safe. If practitioners do not maintain focus and discipline, they simply return to the ordinary state of consciousness" (my emphasis). And then, in a passage apparently designed for those "middle-class Americans" (32) bent upon sharing shamanic enlightenment, Harner (xii) writes: "The classic shamanic methods work surprisingly quickly, with the result that most persons can achieve in a few hours experiences that might otherwise take them years of silent meditation, prayer, or chanting. For this reason alone, shamanism is ideally suited to the contemporary life of busy people." Grab a sandwich, grab a coffee, grab a bit of shamanic reality, and still have plenty of time left over for the evening news.

Here are a few of Harner's actual instructions to the reader: "Undertake this exercise in a quiet, half-darkened room free of furniture . . . It will help if you have two good rattles . . . There are two phases in the exercise: the starting dance and dancing your animal [we will come to "animals" shortly]. In both dances steadily and loudly shake a rattle in each hand, and dance in time with the rattles . . . Keep your eyes half-closed to cut down on light . . . Standing still and erect, face east and shake one rattle rapidly . . . shake the rattle above your head . . . shift into a faster rate of rattle-shaking and dancing . . . Stop dancing and welcome your animal and the shamanic state of consciousness" (1990, 65–67). Again: "Eat only a light lunch and no dinner . . . Use a room free of light and external noises. Clear the area of furniture . . . beat the drum in time to your rattle . . . shake your rattle until there is an alteration in your consciousness." Harner includes here (77) a drawing of a bald, bearded male wearing glasses, seated on the grass, and beating a drum that rests on his lap. Finally: "The beginning of the steady, monotonous sound of the rattle and the drum, which has been associated with the shamanic state of consciousness on previous occasions, becomes a signal to return to it . . . In this state part of the shaman's consciousness is usually still lightly connected to the ordinary reality of the physical or material environment where he is located. The lightness of his trance is a reason that a drumbeat often must be maintained by an assistant to sustain him in the shamanic state . . . If the drumming stops he might come back rapidly to ordinary consciousness" (50). Do other shamanic texts place a similar emphasis on rattling, drumming, and the production of monotonous percussion sound?

Drumming, states Meadows (1991, 57), is "used to induce an altered state of mind so that perceptions are extended to deeper levels in which shamanic work can be done. The drum also represents the spiralling power that is associated with the Life Force. The beat of the drum *synchronizes the heartbeat*—the rhythm of your own Life Force—*with the rhythm of the Cosmos, the heartbeat of the Universe.* The monotonous beat and the low amplitude of the drum sound relaxes the brain and neurons which then come into tune with the *vibratory rates* of the invisible worlds" (my emphasis). As for the rattle: it is, says Meadows (63), "an ancient sonic device which is used to create an atmosphere of expectancy in a process of change from one level of reality to another. It is primarily a tool of transformation. A rattle is usually made from gourds or leather and contains seeds or beans ... The shaking of it has great significance. It symbolizes the *vibratory* movement of the Cosmic forces that expand in all directions and give rise to Law ... Repeated shaking of the rattle is a signal to consciousness to switch to an altered frequency" (my emphasis). Thus does Meadows *combine* for us the emphases on *monotony and vibration*.

The question of where the practitioner *goes* on his shamanic journey is multi-faceted, and I will soon devote several pages to it. But a good clue comes, as a preliminary indication, in a passage of Harner (1990, 51) which states: "Siberian and other shamans sometimes refer to their drums as horses or canoes that transport them into the Lower-world or Upperworld. The steady, monotonous beat of the drum *acts like a carrier-wave*, first to help the shaman enter the altered state, and then to sustain him on his journey" (my emphasis). A Siberian poem called *Shaman Drums* cries out in one place, "Sonorous drum, fulfill my wishes!"

The "sonorous drum" of "shamanic exercise" rhythmically induces a regressive trance in the practitioner, a regressive trance, or "stone," that is loaded with *vibratory* excitation. Meadows (1991, 57) intuits the psychoanalytic essence of the matter when he writes that the beat of the drum "synchronizes" one's "heartbeat"—one's own life-rhythm—with the rhythm of the "cosmos," the "heartbeat" of the "universe." What is "synchronized" here as the regressive trance proceeds is the heartbeat of the practitioner and the *internalized heartbeat of the original object*, the *dual* heartbeat of *dual-unity* when mother and baby are *joined* in affective attunement, the blissful merger, the blissful oneness that comprises the central emotional feature of the before-separation-world. So dependent upon the rhythmic vibration of the drum is the journey to shamanic consciousness that its interruption endangers the trip. As Harner (1990, 50) says, if the drumming ceases, the practitioner may return "rapidly" to ordinary awareness. This dependency constitutes an affective throwback (atavism) to the dependency of the early period during which the infant's security, the infant's *fusion*, is inextricably tied to the maternal "vibes," the "heartbeat," of the infant-caregiver interaction. Thus the rhythmic "carrier-wave" (Harner, 51), which takes the practitioner to shamanic reality and which is created by the drum, is the current, physical version of the *vibrational wave* which carries the baby along affectively during the early time and which is here recalled associatively and unconsciously as the practitioner gives in to his longing for the prelapsarian domain. When the Siberian poet cries out to the drum, "fulfill my wish," the *wish* is for *vibrational* union, the *attunement* of the early period, the months and years during which the infant basks narcissistically in the glow of the caretaker's love and shares in her magical omnipotence: one is the "star," special, precious, all-powerful, the *centre* of the world.

This poetical cry, "drum, fulfill my wish," reminds us, too, that the realm of the shaman is the realm of the *wish*, the realm of magical thinking in which the ordinary realities of separation, smallness, and death are set aside through one's absorption in the trance, the rhythm, the *heartbeat* that Meadows, in typical New Age fashion, projects onto the "universe" or the "cosmos" as a macrocosmic, symbolic version of the *individual* whose heartbeat is sought in all these magical behaviours, namely the individual *who comprises the universe, the cosmos of the baby:* the actual, living, breathing, breast-bearing mama. With crystals, as we saw, it is the putative vibration of the quartz that is projectively tied to the universe and that the practitioner ostensibly engages through his magical interactions with the stone. With shamanism, *the actual vibrations of the drum* (and rattle), the *actual sounds* of the magical instrument, elicit the practitioner's projections and become the means of regaining the attunement, the fusion of the past. The regression and projection are equally primitive in the two instances. With crystals, one believes in the vibrations, in a very special sense *hallucinates* them, and then taps into their magical properties through ritualistic interactions with the quartz. With shamanism, the vibrations actually enter the organism; one has a distinct vibrational sensation which is then put to an hallucinatory purpose in the belief that such "waves," or "carrier-waves" to quote Harner (1990, 51) again, take one to another place, namely the before-separation-world of affective attunement which is *also* the destination of the crystal-gazer.

As for the *rattle's* significance, it is in many ways similar to that of the drum: its monotonous, vibrational sounds carry the practitioner toward the realm of the wish, the realm of affective attunement conjured up symbolically and persuasively by the general mythic context and the practitioner's unconscious longing. Additionally, the control of the rattle (this also applies to the drum) as in Harner's (1990, 66) instructions—"start shaking your rattle loudly; shift to a faster rate; increase your speed," and so forth—recreates the sense of simple mastery that Stern (1985, 113) describes as among the first "evoked companions" of the early period: "If a six-month-old, when alone, encounters a rattle and manages to grasp it and shake it so that it makes a sound, the initial pleasure may quickly become extreme delight and exuberance, expressed in smiling, vocalizing, and general body wriggling. The extreme delight and exuberance is not only the result of successful mastery, but also the historical result of similar past

moments in the presence of a delight-and-exuberance-enhancing other."
It is partly a "social response," but in this instance it takes place in a
"nonsocial situation." At such times, the original pleasure born of
mastery acts as a "retrieval cue" and activates the internalized memory, resulting in an "imagined interaction with an evoked companion,"
which includes, of course, the "shared delight about the mastery"
(Stern, 113). Here, in our shamanic instructions, the actual rattling
recalls the actual rattling or similar simple action that was performed
and shared with the caregiver during the time of mutual mirroring.
Internalized and later called up as "companions," these artless, natural
masteries become the earliest, most primitive experiences of being
with the other when alone. In this way, they recall the *primal merger*,
and the *primary narcissism*, of the early period exactly as does the
"carrier-wave" of the drum, another prong in this many-pronged program of regression to the prelapsarian realm. That one's *whole body* is
involved in the rattling as one sways and dances only deepens the
somatic aspect of the regression (Stern's "wriggling") and recalls further and more fully the early period in which one's body is integrally
involved in all egotic or proto-egotic behaviours. As Freud (1960, 37)
noted, the "first ego" is a "bodily ego," and it is the first ego that is
engaged here as the practitioner, hungry for omnipotence and narcissistic gratification, eager to undo separation, eager to set aside ordinary
awareness, eager to stand reality on its head, takes up the tools of the
shamanic trade and heads for the shamanic never-never land.

Harner (1990, 21) captures the essence of the matter when he
writes, "In the shamanic state of consciousness, the shaman typically
experiences an ineffable joy in what he sees, an awe of the beautiful and
mysterious worlds that open before him. His experiences are like
dreams, but waking ones that feel real and in which he can control his
actions and direct his adventures. While in the shamanic state, he is
often amazed by the reality of that which is presented. He gains access
to a whole new, and yet *familiarly ancient universe* that provides him
with profound information about the meaning of his own life and death
and his place within the totality of all existence. During his great adventures in the shamanic state, he maintains conscious control over
the direction of his travels, but does not know what he will discover.
He is a self-reliant explorer of the endless mansions of a magnificent
hidden universe" (my emphasis). Exactly! The trance and the journey
do indeed involve transportation to a world one *did* know—*during the
early period. That* is why the "hidden," "ancient universe" to which
one travels is, in Harner's own words, "familiar." This "universe" comprises precisely the before-separation-world of life's initial stages, the
"ancient" world of dual-unity, suddenly become "new" in the "now"

of one's regression or psychic revisiting, yet *familiar* by virtue of the deep internalization that transpired as the *mirror* of the mother-infant interaction worked its developmental spell. And yes, this "universe" *is and was* tied integrally to the issue of one's "life" and "death"—that is, to the issue of *union* and *separation, merger* and *loss*, apprehended existentially and unconsciously by the baby in the real terms of his or her actual survival. When we involve ourselves emotionally and speculatively with the conceptualizations of "life" and "death" we are indulging in the projection of the good object (union, the breast) and the bad object (separation, naughtment) onto the world.

As for the "joy" (Harner 1990, 21) the shaman experiences when he gets to the other side, it is, of course, the joy of *getting back* what he had to *give up* as he *grew up*, namely union with the object and the omnipotence and narcissism that accompany such union, or, to use the shamanic terminology, the world as it was before the fall into ordinary consciousness, before the disjunction with the natural realm: Paradise, the Garden. No wonder the shaman who has regressively crossed over feels "ineffable joy" (Harner, 21). He has defeated reality. He has undone the past through magic. He has successfully denied the developmental events of his existence. What a triumph for the ego! The "mystery" and "awe" that he also experiences constitute, in turn, an expression of what is commonly referred to in psychoanalysis as "the uncanny"—an anxiety-laden, fear-laden sensation of *strangeness* which often accompanies hallucinatory regression and the general collapse of one's normative perception. This is the unconscious leaking through from the area of the bad object and the superego, and reminding our shaman, if he has indeed made some headway, that he is on *strange ground* or even *forbidden territory*, that he has entered the maternal past of blurred boundaries and potential engulfment—a realm that most of us have had the strength and the inclination to relinquish in our struggle to gain a separate, autonomous, differentiated self.

It is in *this* sense, this psychoanalytic sense, that the shaman's experience is, in Harner's words, "like a dream" (1990, 21), for the dream is the realm of the *wish* and, in a famous phrase, "the royal road to the unconscious," the psychic mechanism through which the dreamer's wilful and forbidden desires, often of a regressive nature, are disguisedly made manifest and, as manifest, made accessible to interpretation, accessible to the analytical effort that can disclose the nature of the unconscious longing, the passion and the pull behind the images and symbols of the dream itself. Harner (21) declares that the shaman perfectly "controls" his actions in his "dreams": here is the illusion of mastery, the foolish belief that the symbolized goals of the will are to be taken at face value, accepted at the conscious, surface level. As it turns out, the shaman is entirely controlled, guided, led by his time-less, regressive longing for the before-separation-world of fusion, om-nipotence, and narcissistic gratification. This is the "mansion" he craves as he journeys to his "hidden universe."

New Age Shamanism Underway:
A Few Representative Trips

Keeping a sharp eye out for metaphors and symbols that may further reveal the underlying nature of New Age shamanism, let us look now at the actual *commencement* of the journey as Harner and his fellow experts present it in their writings. "The basic form of the journey, and the one usually easiest to learn," states Harner (1990, 24), "is the jour-ney to the Lowerworld." To undertake this, "a shaman typically has a special *hole* or entrance into the Lowerworld" (my emphasis). Among "California Indian shamans" the "hole" is often a "hot spring"; among the shamans of the Kalahari in Africa, "waterholes" are the place of "entrance"; Australian shamans of the "Chapara tribe" simply "dive into the ground" where they please; similarly, "those of Fraser island are said to 'go into the earth'"; another "entrance" employed "by California Indians" is a "hollow tree stump"; the Conibo Indians taught Harner himself to "follow the roots of the giant catahua tree down into the ground." Where, exactly, do these *holes*, these *entrances*, lead?

"Entrances into the Lowerworld," observes Harner (1990, 25), "commonly lead down into a *tunnel* or *tube* that conveys the shaman to an *exit*, which opens out upon bright and marvellous landscapes" (my emphasis). From there, Harner continues, "the shaman travels wherever he desires for minutes or even hours, finally returning back up through the tube." Harner then cites "a fine description given by Rasmussen" for the Eskimo of Hudson Bay (25): "A way opens right from the house whence they invoke their helping spirits; a road down through the earth, or down through the sea; by this route the shaman is led down. He almost glides, as if *falling through a tube so fitted to his body that he can check his progress by pressing against the sides.* This *tube* is kept open for him until he returns" (26, my emphasis). Of this material, Harner writes: "Most of us who are engaged in shamanic work do not find the Tunnel constricting. Usually it is spacious and provides ample room for movement. Sometimes obstacles may obstruct passage, but one normally can find a *crack* to go through" (26, my em-phasis). Harner (27) then includes a photograph of the "entrance to the Hopi Lowerworld." It consists of a large, round hill, shaped exactly like the distended belly of a pregnant woman, with a hole precisely in the centre of it. The size of the hole in relation to the hill is about the size of a navel in relation to a stomach.

Meadows's (1991, 86–96) version of all this is essentially like Harner's, with a bit more emphasis on the energetic, vibrational aspect: the New Age shaman must have "a hole" going "down into the ground" (87); this "hole" leads to a "tunnel," which is the "access to the Lower World," and "an opening in a vortex of energy within one's own energy system" (90); one "journeys" to a "higher vibrational level" (94); and one "returns to the starting place outside the tunnel entrance" (96). So much for the trip's *commencement*, so much for the *hole* and the *tube*, or *tunnel*. What of the trip itself?

There is much to be presented and said on this score, but let's get going with a few instructional suggestions from Harner. "Now you are ready for your first experiential exercise in shamanism," he writes (1990, 30–31). "This will be a simple journey of exploration down through the tunnel into the Lowerworld. Your only mission will be to traverse the tunnel, perhaps see what lies beyond, and return ... You will need a drum, or a cassette player, or a tablespoon and hardcover book ... Eat only lightly ... Take off your shoes ... Relax ... Now visualize an opening into the earth, a hole or a spring ... The right opening is the one that feels comfortable ... Spend a couple of minutes *visualizing the hole* without going into it ... start the drum beat ... *enter the opening* ... Go down through the opening and *enter the Tunnel* ... it may be dark and dim ... The Tunnel sometimes appears ribbed and often it bends ... *At the end of the Tunnel you will emerge out of doors.* Examine the landscape ... Come back, sit up, and open your eyes" (my emphasis). Surely what is going on here must be fairly clear by now, at least from a psychoanalytic standpoint.

Concentrating upon the monotonous rhythms of drum and rattle, swaying and dancing to the steady beat of the percussive sounds, our budding New Age shaman induces a regressive trance that opens the way psychically to a re-participation in affective attunement (mother and baby on the same vibrational frequency) and evoked companionship (the accomplishment of simple mastery shared with another and then internalized). Such re-participation, triggered ultimately by a persistent and unconscious wish for the before-separation-world, allays the anxiety engendered by separation, differentiation, smallness, and mortality—in other words, by ordinary consciousness. It comprises a generalized (and of course regressive) disavowal of the facts, reality, the actual world one perceptually and emotionally inherits when fusion and symbiosis fade. The shamanic subject, discontent with the realm of transitional objects (Winnicott 1974), the realm of illusory substitutes designed to answer the longing for the primary caregiver, chooses the path of denial along which she/he expects eventually to find (or re-find) the original, perfect merger—Paradise, the Garden, the prelapsarian universe. Then what? To implement the regressive agenda, actually to stand reality on its head, actually to obliterate the facts, our New Age shaman locates a "hole," enters it, travels through a "tunnel" whose "ribbed" sides he can feel, passes through a "crack" or a pair of "doors" (the vaginal lips), and discovers himself looking out upon a beautiful landscape. In this mysterious, awesome, "new" but "anciently famil- iar" world, he acquires powers, insights, and joys that he did not pos- sess in his former, ordinary state. And when he returns (through the tunnel) to the place from which he descended, he brings these powers, insights, and joys with him—which is to say, he returns in a *changed* condition.

What we have here is a *backwards birth*, a *backwards borning*, complete with "hole," tunnel, "crack," and a brand new world to look out on at the completion of the trip down the "tube." The unconscious, regressive aim of our New Age shaman is to go back and get *born again* and thereby to deny one's *actual birth*, which led (tragically, as he sees it) to the separation, smallness, and mortality that comprise the ordi- nary condition, the fate, of all human beings everywhere. Because the reality one discovered through one's *real birth*—and I mean here the birth of the ego, perceptual consciousness, the awareness that comes as one traverses the stages of human development described in Mahler— was loaded with disappointment, anxiety, anger, and frustration, one will go ahead and have *another* birth, a birth that discovers *another* "mansion," another landscape, another reality, namely the joyous, marvellous, limitless, *paradisal* reality in which one's omnipotence is not relinquished, in which one's vibrational attunement (mirroring) and primal companionship (fusion) are not diminished, in which one's "ineffable joy" may continue uninterruptedly forever. In a nutshell, one will have another birth that *gets it right*, a birth that grants one all that one craves in his deepest unconscious wishes and longings, a birth that *cancels out* what happened the first time around.

This, precisely *this*, is the motivational scheme, the motivational picture, the motivational *press* and *urgency* that forges what Harner (1990) calls "shamanic reality" and the "shamanic state of conscious- ness." One can *reverse* what has occurred in one's life, and one can *do* this by taking off one's shoes, eating a light supper, banging on a drum, going into a pleasant trance, visualizing a hole, and indulging oneself in a mild, wish-fulfilling hallucination or "dream" involving tunnels, cracks, and pretty landscapes. What the crystal-user does when he/she lies down in an array of coloured stones and senses the maternal "vibes," the happy, regressive glow of the before-separation-world, the shaman does when he picks up his rattle and heads for the "mansions" of shamanland.

But let's be more precise and expansive about what the individual actually finds in shamanland, the nature of the place, the symbols and metaphors used to describe and characterize it. We've already heard Harner's (1990, 21) talk of marvellous landscapes and magnificent hidden universes. Now let's listen carefully to what his students have to say, those who have followed the master's instructions and, upon their return, reported the essentials of their journeys. Let's pay attention to those "middle-class Americans" to whom Harner is directing his wisdom. Let's get it from the proverbial horse's mouth.

"I chose a cave that was familiar to me," writes one of Harner's narrators (1990, 34). "It's in a wooded forest . . . You go down into a large room with several passages . . . I had to go over some crevices that were pretty deep, and there was one spot where I got to a place where you *literally have to squirm your way through* . . . I went further and came out at an exit onto a *tropical island* with a nice big shore . . . tropical birds . . . vegetation . . . *paradise!*" (my emphasis). Another subject states, "I felt myself getting *very small* as I went under a big rock. I entered a *tiny little wet channel* and it went uphill for quite a while . . . *It was very dark in there* . . . I didn't know where I was going. *I felt myself sliding down* . . . and ending up in a very big space where there was *a pool of water* . . . Across this water was a *tiny light* . . . I went through the water and came out into *a meadow that was very green and shaded by a huge oak tree.* I sat down under the oak . . . I was feeling very comfortable when it was time to come back. *I felt annoyed at having to come back*, but being a good student I followed the instructions" (34, my emphasis). Here's a third example: "I went to a hollow tree trunk . . . I crawled in there and *went down through a small opening just barely big enough for me.* I crawled through on my stomach and . . . came out on a hilltop. I had really good feelings looking out from the top of the hill in all directions. *I could feel the wind* coming through behind me . . . *It filled me up with a really nice feeling*" (35, my emphasis). And a fourth: "I visualized a cave . . . Concentric rings of dark and light opened up around me and seemed to *carry me along.* It was not so much a sense that I was moving through a *tunnel but that it was moving along me* . . . The tunnel seemed to go on and on, giving way to a dimly lit landscape—*an underground sea* . . . I was surprised to hear myself being called back and reluctantly I allowed myself to return . . . The sense of discovery and awe remain" (34, my emphasis).

Paradise, warm winds, green meadows, underground seas—one does not have to puzzle very long before detecting the *magna mater*, the bliss-giving, awesome maternal object of the early period, in these shamanic accounts. As for the *way* to the object, it too speaks eloquently for itself: wet channels, small openings, dark tunnels that "move one along"—images and symbols inextricably bound up with human birth. As I suggested a moment ago, because *going forward* (as most of us do) through the stages of development described in the writings of Mahler and others has led the New Age shaman to the anxiety-laden world of separation and smallness, he chooses to *go backwards* in an effort to recoup the "ineffable joys" of prelapsarian existence. Once again in Harner's (1990, 57) words: "While the mythical paradise is lost in ordinary reality, it still remains accessible in nonordinary reality to the shaman." Harner (32) also declares in relation to the shamanic journeys we have just proffered in abbreviated form that his subjects not only believed their experiences to be "real" and "profound," but that the subjects were in all cases "carried along by the drum," which is to say from the analytic angle *loaded with vibrational attunement* when they entered their "holes" and discovered their "tropical islands." Harner (32) then addresses the reader directly, telling him/her: "You should be able to have a comparable experience by using the simple method just outlined." Whether Harner's subjects were "carried along" by the "drum" or by the suggestions of Harner and others who were putting all sorts of ideas into their heads is, of course, a moot question. Yet the images and symbols of Harner and his subjects, not to mention the other anthropologists and actual native shamans that we've presented in this study, remain as striking projective witness to the regressive fascinations inherent in the shamanic enterprise as a whole. There is simply too much language, too much metaphor of a certain kind, to ignore. The *words* of Harner, his protégés, and the others included in the context disclose an unconscious emotional interest in not only *re-finding* the before-separation-world but in *staying there.* As Harner's (34) narrators declare, "I felt annoyed at having to come back"; and "reluctantly I allowed myself to return." What, after all, can compare with the bliss of paradisal fusion, particularly when it has been idealized through comparison with after-separation reality?

Yet shamanic regression does not lead automatically to the paradisal features of the early time. Like all regression, it can reactivate the negative or "bad" side of the before-separation-world, as well as the agonies of separation itself. Psychoanalysis, and the theory of object relations in particular, traditionally associates this painful early affect with what it calls the internalization of the *bad object,* the caretaker in her/his frustrating or rejective aspect. Most self-help groups know this intuitively, by the way, and often ask customers to sign release forms protecting the group (EST, for example) from lawsuits over nervous breakdowns. Customers are also routinely asked whether they have spent time in a mental facility; an affirmative reply usually begets an invitation to *leave* the group. No regression to the realm of the bad object for these folks, thank you very much. An excellent example from Harner (1990, 37) goes as follows: "I went down through a hot spring in the middle of a river. It kind of erupts from the bottom. I went down ... and ended up at a sheet of lava or magma ... I was just stuck there and I didn't know what to do." Or again, and this time much more graphically: "I went down but immediately after the entrance there was a left turn and suddenly all went black, just black. To the right just before the blackness, there was an incredibly disgusting kind of slimy laocoon-mass, intertwined snakes, and spiders whose legs were black, blue, and red" (124). A moment later the writer of this account declares, "I found myself in a long cavern, fairly bright and oval, which I later identified as the *inside of my own torso*" (124, my emphasis). In the final analysis, the shamanic journey, or "trip," is into *one's own inner world*, the emotional *and bodily* being into which the object of the early period has been internalized. The materials we take in during life's initial stages root themselves not merely in the psyche but in the human organism as a whole precipitating what we can think of as the psycho-physiological reality in which we have our own existence. The object of the early time is ultimately a facet of *one's own body*, of which one is always aware in his *head*. The shamanic journey, then, is designed to annul what happened originally to one's *organism:* one got *born;* one got *separated* from the *breast*, from the *mama;* one got differentiated, isolated, *anxious*. So what does one do? As we've seen, one uses *magic* to get out of the *bodily* and psychic reality in which one discovers himself. One restores symbiosis, fusion, omnipotence, "ineffable joy"—a better "reality" than the post-lapsarian one; and one tries to *stay there*, or to get the *power* to *go* there whenever one wishes ("dropping out," as the old lingo has it).

Examining "shamanism" through the writings of Carlos Castaneda and others during the 1970s and 1980s, New Agers eventually "got it"; that is, they eventually realized that "shamanism" was a good method for cancelling out the facts, reality, ordinary consciousness—all of which terms are merely ways of expressing the emotional, bodily, and perceptual legacy of human growth and development *away* from symbiotic fusion and toward separation, differentiation, and autonomy. And of course the New Agers who eventually *got* the meaning of shamanism characterize perfectly the essence of New Age thinking as a whole, which searches hungrily for any and all methods or disciplines that offer the practitioner a cleverly disguised and therefore egotically justifiable means of denying the facts and running to the past. In this way, New Age shamanism gets all dressed up in anthropological, mythic, and native trappings designed to conceal the devotee's regressive, infantile purpose. The New Age shaman "goes native," attacks science and reason, extols the "wisdom" of South American and Siberian medicine men (for the most part drug-dependent psychotics or near-psychotics), proudly presents himself as politically correct (which means intellectually or "spiritually" fashionable), and thus gathers to his ranks all sorts of men and women who are desperate to find their way back to the Garden of Infancy, the Paradise of Vibrational Attunement. Meadows (1991, 3) makes this perfectly clear when he writes in one place that shamans exist on special "wavelengths" of existence and that they are "carried" on their "journeys" by the "Life Force," or in another place (28) that shamanic reality is on a "vibrational wavelength" different from the "wavelength" on which ordinary reality occurs. It is the "vibrations" of symbiotic merger, the "wavelength" of before-separation-experience that our New Age shamans are seeking in their "holes" and "tunnels." This is the "mysterious world" that "opens before them" (Harner 1990, 21) on their regressive voyages. The point of the last two paragraphs has been simply to remind the reader that *bad* as well as *good* materials may be encountered on the way. Here, as everywhere else, there are no guarantees.

Guardians and Guides

Having journeyed to the other side, having reached the "mansions" of the "magnificent, hidden universe," the shaman sets about discovering what the literature calls his "guardian spirit" or "guide" (Harner 1990, 65). As we'll now see, these "spirits" or "guides" usually assume the shape of *animals* such as the buffalo, reindeer, eagle, wolf, or bear. As we'll also see, these "spirits" or "guides" usually provide the voyager with a variety of advantages and rewards that alter considerably his given or ordinary condition in the world. Finally, we'll perceive in the arguments and the explanations presented for this facet of the shaman's quest certain illogicalities, or, from the psychoanalytical angle, certain *projective assumptions*, which may render more intelligible the underlying nature of the business.

"The most famous method of acquiring a guardian spirit," writes Harner (1990, 64), "is the vision quest or vigil conducted in a *solitary wilderness location*, as among the Plains tribes of North America" (my emphasis). Again from Harner (73): "The best magic words [for summoning the guardian] are those which come to one when one is out *alone among the mountains.* These are always the most powerful in their effects. The power of *solitude* is great and beyond understanding" (my emphasis). Meadows (1991, 154) takes a similar position: "First, determine the purpose of the Quest ... Next, decide the location ... Choose a location which is *isolated ... some distance from home*" (my emphasis). Meadows (154) also suggests that one "fast" during the course of one's search for a "guide," a point with which Harner (76) agrees. The purpose of this *solitude,* this *isolation,* this *aloneness* is *not,* as it turns out, "beyond understanding." On the contrary, the purpose is made clear by the context of our discussion as a whole: it is to trigger powerful feelings of *separation,* feelings that will, in turn, trigger the wish for merger, fusion, dual-unity; it is to catalyze precisely those regressive longings that stand behind the shamanic enterprise in general and the trance-state in particular—the emotional gravitation toward the object of the early period, the before-separation-world, which comprises "shamanic reality." The more powerfully, the more painfully the subject feels his isolation, separation, aloneness, the more vividly he/she will recall at the unconscious level the primal terrors (including hunger) that provoked him in infancy and early childhood to cling to the caretaking figure. What shamanic tradition, shamanic methodology, shamanic "wisdom" has sensed intuitively here is what all individuals involved in systems of torture sense: the more *discomfort,* the more *regression;* the more *suffering,* the more *regression.* If we can get our subjects truly alone, truly cut off, truly "spooked," we can also get them to see things, and hear things, and *believe in* things, like "guardian spirits," for example. To put it in brief compass, *crisis begets belief,* crisis begets conversion, crisis begets faith and miracles by reactivating old terrors and fostering a desperate need to cleave unto magical beings, imaginary companions, totems, saints, gods, angels, space visitors, and spirits of all kinds.

When Harner declares in one place (1990, 49) that the "vision quest," the search for the "guardian" or "guide" who exists disguisedly on the "other side," often occurs spontaneously at the "climax of a serious illness," he corroborates strikingly the thesis just put forward. As one senses the proximity of *death,* as one apprehends in his mind and body the biggest and most frightening *separation* of all, he suddenly finds himself in the midst of a revelational experience. Here, in a flash, is one's "guardian spirit" or "power animal" or companionable "guide," come to assist one, to *join* one, at this perilous hour. It is the *crisis* that provokes the out-of-the-ordinary experience, that triggers the reactivation of those infantile defences against separation and loss which originally got one through the crises of the early period, the time when one's fluid ego boundaries were able to bring the all-important *other* into the sphere of one's own vulnerable, terrified being.

We don't have to wonder why someone would *do* this in the first place, why someone would be willing to go through the pains of isolation, separation, and hunger in his quest for the "guardian." We've established that already, in the context. New Agers are discontent with the normative or ordinary substitutes for the caregiver which most of us are able, more or less, to accept: spouses, friends, possessions, mainstream religious affiliations, national loyalties, art, literature, music—the list goes on. Accordingly, New Agers offer us a variation on Freud's theme of "civilization and its discontents," where the individual's unhappiness is caused by the repression of his instinctual aims (sexuality, aggression) in society. It is the dissatisfaction with *substitute objects* that causes unhappiness among New Agers. Anxious, restless, finding the world an insecure place, they crave the "real thing," the actual dual-unity, the actual paradise, the actual narcissism and omnipotence that they left behind as they negotiated the developmental stages (Mahler), which led to separation and differentiation. They want actually to *go back,* and they are attracted to ideas and systems that tell them they can do that. One may wish to interject that traditional or normative substitutes are dropping away swiftly these days and thus contributing to the rise of problematic alternatives. We live in a postmodern world of disintegrating families, divorce, urban impersonality and alienation, declining religions, declining communities—a world where the shopping mall serves as the home-away-from-home and the television set as the surrogate parent: fast cars, fast food, fast track to mental disturbance. There may be some truth in this, as we'll eventually see. But as I stated in chapter 1, the wish for fusion, re-union, the past, the desire to refind the before-separation-world, the belief in a "lost paradise" (Harner 1990, 57) and the longing to regain it are ancient wishes, longings, and beliefs predating our own civilization by thousands of years. For many, the ordinary substitutes for the original caregiver have *never worked,* and the hunger for omnipotence and narcissistic grandiosity has *always* been compelling. For many, the call of the past has *always* been the central call of life.

Harner (1990, 65) confirms much of this when he writes an incredible passage that harbours the kind of irrationality or projective assumption to which we referred a moment ago: "To a shaman it is readily apparent that many Westerners have guardian spirits, as evidenced by their energy, good health, and other outward manifestations of their power. It is tragic, from the point of view of such a shaman, that even these power-full people are nonetheless ignorant of the source of their power and thus do not know how to utilize it fully. A related tragedy is that lethargic, ill, and dispirited Western adults have obviously lost the guardian spirits that protected them through their childhood.

Worse, they do not even know that there is a method to regain them." What can this possibly mean, may I inquire? Can Harner actually be asking the reader to accept these ideas? Am I to *believe* what some shaman finds "readily apparent"? Why? Surely the "view" of, say, a South American medicine man, on or off drugs, should be no more authoritative to me than the view of, say, Dr. Spock. I have "guardian spirits" because I'm healthy and strong? I have "guardian spirits" even though I'm "ignorant" of them? Why should I attribute my well-being to "spirits," or consider myself "ignorant" because I fail to communicate with supernatural beings? I don't utilize fully my "power" because I don't do magic, don't visualize holes and tunnels, don't go into trances and shake rattles, don't squirm through "cracks" in search of talking animals? Is Harner mad, one almost wonders? I am "dispirited" because I've lost a "guardian"? Is that really the explanation for my "lethargy" and "illness"? Is that what I, as a "Westerner," need to hear? My guardian spirits are "lost" but there is a method to "regain" them? Regain what a medicine man says is lost by dancing about and imagining another "universe"? Guardian spirits "protected" me during my "childhood"? Are not my parents good enough? Are not my identifications and internalizations good enough? What about my own capabilities? Or the police? Must I believe in *projective images* of guardians as opposed to the actual people, including myself, whom I encountered along the way? Can we not achieve adulthood through our own power, with the aid of other human beings, of course? Is this not a case for the application of *Occam's razor*? Isn't it *simpler* to use *what's there* in explanation rather than create a world of *unseen entities*? My tragedy if I am feeling down, says Harner (65), is that I cannot find a way to recover my "guardian spirits": is not the "tragedy" here that New Agers are unable to live maturely in the world, to grow up and be men and women without resorting to magic, without sacrificing their intellectual and emotional integrity in their search for an idealized past?

In another place, and in a similar vein, Harner (1990, 43) declares, "As the Jivaro point out, whether an adult knows it or not, he probably has, or has had, the aid of a guardian spirit in his childhood; otherwise he would not have had the protective power to achieve adulthood." Again, what can this possibly *mean*? What does "probably" mean? And how does "probably" stand in relation to the rest of the utterance, particularly "has" and "or has had"? What kind of *thinking* is this? Where is the *rigour* in the reasoning? As I inquired a moment ago, why must one's "achievement" of "adulthood" be attributed to "spirits"? Are not the actual forces verifiably present in one's experience sufficient for creating a developmental scheme? Can't we use *Occam's razor* on this passage too? I believe Meadows (1991, 101,128) gets at the essence of the matter when he writes of the "guardian" or "guide" (which usually takes the form of an *animal*, remember): "A power animal is an *energy-pattern* that provides abilities ... It is the Life Force in animal form ... By *connecting* to this *power source* one can *draw upon it* and enhance *one's own energy*" (my emphasis). Or again, "A guide is an *energy-pat-tern* that *supplies information vital to your growth and development.* It operates *beyond the range* of ordinary physical perception" (my emphasis). Exactly. What the New Ager is after as he seeks magically for his "guardian spirit" or "guide" or "power animal" is the "energy pattern" that he shared with the caretaking figure during the time of affective or vibrational attunement. It is precisely this marvellous, blissful, protective *energy* that is projected into the "guardian," thus creating the *complexity* of shamanic explanation where the simplicity of one's actual life will do. The questing New Age shaman wishes regressively to make the *energy*, the *power*, of the *other* once again *his own*. He wants to *feed* off the fantasied object as he once did, before *separation*, when he and the object were *joined in attunement*. For that is, after all, what an infant *is*, one who feeds off the energy, the power, of the mother. The infant does that and mostly that until he begins to get an ego of his own.

The Big and the Powerful: Back on Daddy's Shoulders

Harner (1990, 57) titles his fourth chapter, in which he discusses "guardians" and "guides" at length, "Power Animals," and he makes it clear and explicit within the chapter itself that the "guardian spirit" and the "power animal" are *one*. "The connectedness between humans and the animal world is very basic in shamanism, with the shaman utilizing his knowledge and methods to participate in the power of that world. Through his guardian spirit or power animal the shaman connects with the power of the animal world, mammals, birds, fish, and other beings" (58). Again, "Shamans have long believed their powers were the powers of the animals, of the plants, of the sun, of the basic energies of the universe. In the garden Earth they have drawn upon their assumed powers to save other humans from illness and death ... Millennia before Charles Darwin, people in shamanic cultures were convinced that animals and humans were related [but not "related" in the sense Darwin intended!]. In their myths, the animal characters were commonly portrayed as essentially human in physical form but individually distinguished by particular personality characteristics [the mischievous coyote, the clever raven, etc.]" (57). As we just saw, Meadows (1991, 101) agrees with this, claiming that the guardian spirit or power animal is the "Life Force," and that our energy and power are enhanced as we enter into the sphere of this magical entity. As for the animals themselves, we can follow (very briefly) Meadows's typical presentation in which the *bear* signifies inner strength, the *beaver* the power to work, the *cougar* the will to take charge, the *crane* the power of knowledge, the *weasel* the power of intuitive insight, and so forth (Meadows, ch. 8).

Let's get to the gist of it: the shamanic subject contacts the power animal in the midst of a regressive trance during which the monotonous rhythm of the drum and the semi-hallucinatory visualization of holes and cracks and tunnels takes him/her to the other side, to the prelapsarian world where the unity of humans and animals is restored. "While the mythical paradise of animal-human unity is lost in ordinary reality, it still remains accessible in nonordinary reality to the shaman" (Harner 1990, 57). In this way, the shaman's regressive journey to "nonordinary reality" culminates in *his convergence with a source of power.* He goes to the other side through a kind of backwards birth and he finds there a marvellous, numinous, magical being who assists him, guides him, succours him, and *empowers* him in a thousand ways. From the psychoanalytic perspective, the shamanic subject is restored to exactly what he had as a neonate: a powerful, significant other at his side. Indeed, the shamanic literature on this theme gives us a precise picture of infancy, of *dual-unity*, in which the little one is joined to and blends with the big one, the one who *guards, guides,* and creates the illusion of *omnipotence.* The "power animal," then, is a projective version of the parent as fantasied by the baby. Conversely, the "adult" fantasy or myth of the power animal harbours the regressive, "adult" longing for the *earlier relation* which lives on in memory and desire. "Power animal" comprises the *way* the infantile unconscious of the grown-up recalls the early period and the dominating creature who resides at its centre. Thus the *separation* of animal and human, the centrepiece of the shamanic worldview, is a projective, symbolic version of the separation of infant and parent that transpires traumatically during life's developmental stages (Mahler 1975). It is not *the animal* from whom we were all separated long ago, it is *the parent.* What else, after all, could it be? We never *were* with the animals, but we *were* with the parents, the actual *guardians* (both legal and diurnal) who possessed all the *qualities* the *animals* possess in the *myth:* power, energy, uncanny vibrations, the capacity to aid us, protect us, succour us, and "boost our confidence" (Meadows 1991, 103). All of this is hinted at *broadly* in passages of Harner (43, 65) already examined wherein he states that we *had* "guardian spirits" in childhood and then "lost" them.

In the present, in the now of our lives as New Age shamans, we employ trances, rattles, drums, the visualization of holes and tunnels, and psychic journeys to hidden worlds—in short, *magic*—to undo reality and *get that big animal back*. We will have it again. We will have its protection, we will have its omnipotence, we will have the narcissistic glow that comes with attachment to so grand a creature. Not only are we not *alone* now, we have the "power animal" *all to ourselves:* it is *ours*, our *special one* whom we have found again and restored to the centre of our lives. Meadows (1991, 102) offers explicit information on what our "power animals" *do* with us and for us as we join together: they "convey words" to us "telepathically"; that is, they engage us in pure communicational *attunement* exactly as mother and baby are engaged early on; they give us "energy, vigour, strength, and enthusiasm"; they "supply" us with "ideas" for "projects"; they "fight off intrusions" in our bodies; they "speed our recovery" from illness and injury (make boo-boos better); they "protect us from harm"; and so forth. Surely even the non-psychoanalytic reader can recognize in all this, as it emerges from the context, the magical restoration of the parent-child relationship, the parent-child interaction, the parent-child *dependency*. And perhaps even the non-psychoanalytic reader will recognize, too, that there is something just a little pathetic in it all, in the New Ager's obsessive search for the parental figure, in his inability to stand on his own two feet, in his purblind attempt to dress up his regression, his longing for the past, as arcane wisdom, native profundity, the living legacy of awesome "medicine men." Harner (1990, 61) writes in one place of the aspiring shaman's "desire for unity with animals of power," and he goes on to describe the "dancing, rattling, drumming" and "frenzied condition" in which the shaman "imitates the actions and cries of the animal." He may "even wear the actual bear paws" over his hands in "his effort to become one with the animal." For that indeed is the aim: to fuse with the powerful being one knew long ago in *infancy* (the source of the "mythic past"). The Osage Indians refer to the buffalo, "in whose thighs there is strength; in whose humped shoulder there is power" (Harner, 62). This is the *infant* talking about the big "beast," Mama's strong legs, Daddy's massive shoulder on which the New Age shaman wants to ride through life again. May I say that the individual's *genuine* strength will emerge only when he honestly confronts his weakness, alone?

The Transformational Animal

The shamanic animal's power to guide, succour, energize, and protect the voyager is only one of its extraordinary or uncanny characteristics. Its capacity to *change its nature*, to alter its outward and inward qualities—in a word, to achieve *transformation*—may well be considered an even more wondrous and magical feature. The context, particularly chapter 2, afforded us insight into transformation's central role during the early period. The infant's experience of his first object, the mother, is fundamentally transformative in character. "It is undeniable," writes Christopher Bollas (1987, 13–14), "that as the infant's other self, the mother transforms the baby's internal and external environment ... [She] is less significant and identifiable as an object than as a process that is identified with cumulative internal and external transformations." Just as evoked companionship and affect attunement never disappear, so this feature of early existence "lives on in certain forms of object-seeking in adult life." The object is sought for its "function as a signifier of transformation." The quest is not to possess the object but to "surrender to it as a medium that alters the self," that promises to "transform the self" (Bollas, 14). In a section (15) titled "The Search for the Transformational Object in Adult Life," Bollas declares that psychoanalysis has failed to take notice of the "wide-ranging collective search for an object that is identified with the metamorphosis of the self." For example, in religious faith, when a person believes in God's potential to transform the environment, he "sustains the terms of the earliest object tie within a mythic structure." How does such transformation *look* during the early time? If the infant is distressed, the "resolution of discomfort is achieved by the apparition-like presence of mother" (33). The "pain of hunger" is "transformed by mother's milk" into an experience of "fullness." This is a "primary transformation": emptiness, agony, and anger become fullness and contentment. Now, as I suggested a moment ago, the power animal's transformational capacity is at the heart of the shamanic lore devoted to its nature. Crucial to remember, however, is the animal's ability to transform not only *itself, but the practitioner too.*

Writes Harner (1990, 59), "The capability of the guardian animal spirits to speak to a human or to manifest themselves sometimes in human form is taken as an indication of their power." And then, in a decisive utterance, "When its transformation into human form occurs, it is a magical act of power. When possessed by a shaman, the power animal acts as an alter ego, imparting to the shaman the power of transformation, and especially, the power of transformation *from* human to the power animal as well as back again" (59). Let me stress that this is not the quirk of a particular shaman or two; it is the general picture: "The belief by shamans that they can metamorphose into the form of their guardian animal spirit or power animal is widespread and obviously ancient" (Harner, 59). So strong, in fact, is the interest in transformation that it appears frequently to be hallucinatory or psychotic in nature: "In the course of the initiation of a shaman of the Wiradjeri tribe in Australia, the shaman had the nonordinary experience that feathers emerged from his arms and grew into wings" (Harner, 59). That certainly seems "nonordinary" to me. Here are a few more striking examples from Harner (60–62): "In northernmost Scandinavia, Lapp shamans changed into wolves, reindeer, and fish ... Eskimo shamans transformed themselves into wolves ... The Yuki Indians of California transform themselves into bears ... Shamans, in dancing their guardian spirits, commonly not only make the movements of the power animals but also the sounds ... As Eliade notes, this is 'less a possession than a magical transformation into that animal.'" Our business, of course, is to *analyze* "magical transformations," not simply to take them at face value. As for the *persistence* of this theme in our own Western culture, Harner (60) observes: "The ancient shamanic belief in the ability to transform oneself into an animal survived in Western Europe until the Renaissance. The Christian Church, of course, considered persons engaged in animal metamorphosis to be wizards, witches, and sorcerers, and persecuted them through the Inquisition. Yet a colleague of Galileo, the alchemist and scientist Giovanni Porta, in 1562 still possessed the ancient knowledge of how to experience such a metamorphosis and published the information in his famous book, *Natural Magick.*" We are currently experiencing the reappearance of this "ancient knowledge," this "natural magick," in New Age thinking.

Meadows (1991, 2) gives us essentially what Harner does on this score, stressing, as usual, the "energetic" or "spiritual" side of the business. "A shaman," he writes, "recognizes that man is very privileged, for he has the power to change or shape things at will." He goes on: "'Shaman' is derived from the language of the Tungus people of Siberia. It can be translated as meaning 'to work with heat or fire; to heat or burn up.' So the word as applied to a person may be taken to mean 'a transformer of energy' because fire is not only energy but an agent of change ... A shaman was considered to be one who was able to make the greatest transformation of all—from the physical to the spiritual." As Meadows sees it (155), the "spiritual" in shamanism usually takes the *form* of "a bird, an animal, or an insect." To *become* the creature, to enter into the creature's "energy," is to experience the essence of "shamanic transformation."

Here is a brief excerpt from an article by Jimmy Weiskoff (1993, 43) which describes eastern Colombian Indians getting stoned on *yaje* (a hallucinogen derived from a local plant) as they graduate toward shamanism. The excerpt, I believe, takes us to the heart of the matter concerning transformation, and also gives us additional insight into what middle-class New Agers are reading these days: "While we were waiting for the session [that is, the ingestion of the drug] to begin, my friend Humberto took me aside and explained that *yaje* visions come in progressive states which lead up to the formation of a shaman. First, he explained, you see the boa, whose appearance is always traumatic and accompanied by fear and pain. The boa swallows you, bringing on terrible vomiting. When these sensations disappear ... it means that you are through the first stage of purification and are ready for the higher levels. Next you see the dragon, which is the spirit of fire. The last and crowning level is when you see and become *transformed into a tiger*" (my emphasis). Harner and his followers do not, of course, sanction the use of hallucinogenic substances in their pursuit of sha-manic wisdom. In all likelihood, however, they would at least enter-tain the possibility that these poor, drugged Colombian Indians are attaining "high, crowning levels" of insight as they feel themselves "transformed" into "tigers."

The explanation for this, or better, the psychological factor that makes such confusion possible, should be clear enough: the longing for transformation, the belief that it is *occurring* and is *good*, arises from the infantile unconscious where transformational experience is stored as a central and wondrous feature of the early interaction with the care-giver. In shamanic practice, the persistent attempt to *achieve* trans-formation bespeaks a powerful, regressive wish for the before-separation-world in which one was not merely *joined* to the parental figure (here expressed projectively as the power animal) but *undergoing transformation all the time*, as, in Bollas's (1987, 13) words, the mother went about "transforming the baby's internal and external environ-ment." What interests the New Age shaman is "surrendering" to the power animal as a "medium that alters the self." He wants to "sustain the terms of the earliest object tie within a mythic structure." In this way, a transformational feature of early existence is allowed to "live on" in the "object-seeking of adult life" (Bollas, 14). As the shamanic subject feels himself transformed into the totem, as he *becomes* the power animal and as the power animal becomes *him*, he re-participates emotionally in the *mirror relationship* during the course of which fu-sion, evoked companionship, and affective attunement found their original and irresistible expression. For that is, after all, what *mirroring* is and does: one *reflects* the other, *becomes* the other psychically and emotionally, and the other reflects and becomes the one. When we re-call once again that the power animal is a version of the parent we begin to see the way in which shamanism has figured out a method for restoring several key features of early psychological life: one is *trans-formed* through *mirroring* into the parent, into the omnipotent, magi-cal caretaker; as one undergoes transformational mirroring one also re-experiences the fusion, omnipotence, affective attunement, and primary narcissism that accompany the blurring of ego boundaries in which the significant other and the self continually blend and merge, continually exchange biological and emotional being. Just as baby and mother comprise a *transformational unit*, so do shaman and power animal become such a unit. To *get* there, or, better, to get there *again*, the subject undergoes a transformational ritual which, at the "top," commences a process that will gratify the regressive wish at the "bottom," the underlying, unconscious, pressing urge to restore the past and have done with the imperfect present, the after-separation-world of *the gap*, the "fall." It does not matter, of course, that one does not "really" become the power animal. To be *doing* this, *feeling* this, is to be sniffing once again the emotional flowers of the prelapsarian realm. As Meadows (1991, 101) reminds us, the power animal emits non-ordinary energy, non-ordinary vibrations, which is to say, it emits the vibrations and energy of the early period when the caretaker transforms the infant's universe over and over again—pain to pleasure, loneliness to merger, hunger to fullness, anxiety to security. Now all of this happens afresh "in magic" as one recreates the initial transformational interaction by *becoming* the "power animal," *a creature with a transformational capacity*, a creature with the power (parental omnipotence) to *change* one, and to *keep on changing one.* We must also bear in mind that affective attunement and transformation often *work together*; that is, affective attunement often *results* when mother transforms baby's dissatisfaction into pleasure. This is the combination that ignites the unconscious longing for the early, transformational time. For example, when baby is hungry, mother and baby are not on the same "vibrational wavelength." The mother feeds baby and affective attunement occurs. We have here a "primary transformation," in Bollas's terms, and it results in affective attunement. Indeed, I suspect such attunement is experienced most forcefully just after transformation has taken place, just after the parent has turned the whole world of the infant around, changing the "empty vessel" into the full. The psychoanalysis of religious change, of religious transformation in general, is rooted in these early, fundamental happenings. The *empty sinner* will be *changed* when he sits down to supper with the Lord.

Transformation, needless to say, is one of the weirdest, most mysterious, and most inexplicable aspects of shamanism. Thus it is a bribe to the unconscious. One can't understand it, can't "figure it out." It appears uncanny, mythic, symbolic, the perfect "Jungian" moment, and so one is drawn in. But psychoanalysis, and in particular the psychoanalysis of early object relations, unpacks the myth and allows us to *see* what is occurring here: the simple wish for the before-separation-world and the complex rigmarole that disguises the wish and makes it acceptable to ego and superego. One's arms sprout feathers as one becomes the power animal: one wants the early time. One echoes the grunting bear during the transformational moment: one wants the early time. One leaps like the deer as the drums and rattles roar: one wants the early time. The sacred mystery, the uncanny, weird religious ceremony turns out to be the projection of an infantile wish, the primitive trace of what happened long ago when the infant's universe was the infant's parent. As New Age thinkers began to recognize the transformational obsessions of shamanism, as they came to spy a chance to magically become the animal of power, they jumped. Here was a path to the past, to the prelapsarian realm. Let me at it! I want to be a shaman too! I want to be in the old transformational relation once again! That New Age shamans understood why they were jumping is doubtful, of course. Perhaps now they will understand, and undergo another kind of "transformation." Harner (1990, xix), developing certain notions of Carlos Castaneda, writes in one place that "dragons, griffins, and other animals that would be considered 'mythical' by us in ordinary consciousness are 'real' in shamanic consciousness. The idea that there are 'mythical' animals is a useful and valid construct in ordinary consciousness but superfluous and irrelevant in shamanic experience. 'Fantasy' can be said to be a term applied by a person in ordinary consciousness to what is experienced in shamanic consciousness. Conversely, a person in shamanic consciousness may perceive the experiences of ordinary consciousness to be illusory in shamanic terms. Both are right, as viewed from their own particular states of consciousness." No, Dr. Harner, both are *not* right, and your banal retreat into relativism, the notion that anything goes as long as we fiddle around with the context, is a cop-out. The "illusions" of "shamanic consciousness" are projective expressions of unconscious desire regressively indulged in by those who have yet to confront themselves honestly. Such confrontation, and only such confrontation, will allow these individuals to grow up and gain the self, the autonomy, and the strength that characterize women and men in the true, full sense of those words.

Magical Stones, Magical Plants, and Synchronicity

The companions, guardians, and guides of the shaman do not always assume an animalistic shape. Plants and stones also figure in. We looked intensively at stones in the previous section, of course. It will be interesting to see how our conclusions apply to the shamanic realm. "While there is potentially an almost infinite variety of power objects,"

writes Harner (1990, 109), "there is one kind in particular that is regularly found in the keeping of shamans. This is the quartz crystal. In
North and South America, Australia, southeast Asia, and elsewhere,
shamans ascribe a singular importance to these pointed, six-sided
stones that are usually transparent to milky-white." Harner continues,
"The quartz crystal is considered *the strongest power object of all*
among such widely separated peoples as the Jivaro in South America
and the tribes of Australia. Peoples as distant from one another as the
aborigines of eastern Australia and the Yuman-speakers of southern
California and adjacent Baja California consider the quartz crystal 'living,' or a 'live rock'" (109, my emphasis). Meadows (1991, 74) contends,
similarly, that "natural crystals, particularly quartz, have a special relevance to shamans. Shamans employ the help of crystal allies to serve
as links between the inner world of the spirit and the outer world of
material manifestation ... Crystals reflect into being something that
was only a potential within the shaman." Meadows reasons as follows
on this score: "Everything around us may be considered a reflector of
some kind. Even people we meet, whether we like them or not, are in
some way *mirrors* of our own selves ... Crystals are particularly *powerful reflectors* for they are light-bearers. They receive, store, and transmit light. They can help us most by enabling us to discover our inner
light that connects us with the Light of All That Is" (74, my emphasis).
Like the "guardian animal," then, the crystal is a source of power, of
omnipotence, to the shaman. Through it, he unites regressively with
the energetic object of the early period whose unlimited capacities
become *the infant's* by means of primary, symbiotic *fusion*. Joined to
the object, the infant participates in the object's prepotent nature,
which is *internalized* and *never forgotten.*

Harner (1990, 110) informs us, for example, that "among the Australian Wiradjeri, shamans in training had a piece of quartz 'sung' into
their foreheads so that they would be 'able to see right into things.'"
Also among the Wiradjeri, "crystals were put into water for shaman
trainees to drink so that they 'could see ghosts'" (110). "'When you
carry a crystal in your pocket,'" say the shamans of western Yuman,
"'it tells you everything and it gives you everything'" (111). According
to Meadows (1991, 73), "by having a crystal ally, a shaman is able to
integrate its power-energy—its 'medicine'—into his own unconscious
potential which can then be used." For what? Meadows (73) tells us: to
"see into the past, find lost things, gain wisdom, and heal." Could the
regressive, magical wish for human omnipotence be expressed more
unabashedly, more ingenuously? I don't think so.

Because fusion and omnipotence are aspects of the *mirror* relationship (remember Meadows's comment that crystals are "reflectors"),

we would expect the shamanic "line" on magical stones to be loaded with "vibrational" meanings, for, as we have seen, the mirror relationship thrives during the time in which mother and infant share affective or vibrational *attunement*, a single, empathetic, emotional "wavelength." Informing the apprentice shaman how to treat his crystal, Harner (1990, 111) writes, "Leave it eight days in the sun to re-charge before putting it in the medicine bundle . . . Wake-up its power" so that it may eventually "diffuse through the bundle" and "energize" your "power objects." Thus does this "live rock," this "living," *psychological object*, send its magical vibes into and through the *objects* to which the shaman's *power* is linked. The transference of omnipotence characteristic of the symbiotic stage plays itself out disguisedly among medicine bundles and pieces of quartz as the infantile unconscious engenders still more shamanic rigmarole. "A crystal projects quite a powerful force field around itself," writes Meadows (1991, 74); and he goes on: "A crystal tends to raise the vibrational level of anything in its vicinity. That is why we feel uplifted or energized in some way when close to crystals." In some way? In a very specific way, I would suggest, a way that is integrally and *regressively* related to the energy and euphoria we experienced long ago when we were "close to the *original* vibrational object. When Meadows observes on the following page (75) that "people" strive assiduously to "attune" themselves to their stones, he simply makes explicit the ancient, underlying wish that drives the shamanic subject toward the quartz in the first place: attunement *means* mirroring *means* fusion *means* omnipotence. This is the magic circle of motivation in which the shamans gather; this is the psychoanalytic *underbelly* of their practice. "To find out why a particular stone has come to you," instructs Meadows (73), "lie down and hold the stone to your navel. This is the centre of your energy-system and where you are able to establish contact with anything in existence." Omnipotence, then, comes from the *belly*, the *navel*, the "centre" at which one originally "established contact" with the *parental* object who is projected into the crystal.

Transformational meanings? Meanings that tie the shaman's stone, his "strongest power object of all," to the transformational object of the early period, the inspiration of the power animal's wondrous capacities? They emerge, as we might suspect, very readily. "Crystals are primarily allies for self-transformation," writes Meadows (1991, 74); they "influence vibration and thereby manifest required change." The Australian Wakka shaman, writes Harner (1990, 110), "journeys with many crystals in his body down into the deepest water holes, where the rainbow spirit lives." While there, he "receives more crystals." Such a shaman, declares Harner, "would arise full of life and be a medicine-man of the highest degree," which is to say would arise *transformed, changed, altered,* an exceptional individual harbouring the power of the stone. Indeed, so "helpful" is the quartz to the "spirit" of the shaman that it becomes a source of life, a kind of *breast.* "The western Yuman shamans enter into a special partnership with their quartz crystals and must 'feed' them," states Harner (109). "This is reminiscent of Jivaro shamans feeding their spirit helpers with tobacco water to keep them." We have here what psychoanalysis calls a *concealment through opposition:* the actual relation is the one in which the magical stone *feeds* the energies of the infantile unconscious *to* the shaman, thus preserving his illusory omnipotence with its accompanying sense of fusion and narcissism. We have here materials rooted in the "oral stage" during the course of which the baby is attached to the breast of the vibrational caretaker from whom he sucks his energy, his power, his very being. It is hardly surprising from this perspective that shamans associate the loss or destruction of their stones with *absolute catastrophe:* "If the crystal [were] shattered," writes Harner (112), "the world would end." Here is the helplessness, the fragility, the *emotional dependency* that underlies not only shamanic omnipotence but New Age thinking as a whole. It is always that way, of course. When one's strength derives from magic, one has no real strength.

In the light of this, Harner's (1990, 110) "explanation" for the crystal's central place in shamanic practice becomes especially captivating. How are we to understand "its unique importance as an object involved in the shamanic manipulation of *power,*" he asks? And then, "The answer may lie in a most curious coincidence. In modern physics the quartz crystal is also involved in the manipulation of power. Its remarkable electronic properties made it a basic component in radio transmitters and receivers (remember the crystal set?). Thin wafers sliced from quartz crystals later became basic components for modern electronic hardware such as computers and timepieces. While this all may be coincidental, it is one of the many synchronicities that make the accumulated knowledge of shamanism exciting and often even awesome." If there is an "explanation" in these remarks I'm afraid I can't find it. In fact, I can't find anything here that one might take seriously even for a moment. Shamanic *lore* about quartz is "knowledge"? Has it ever been *demonstrated* that the tools in one's "medicine bundle" are more efficacious because the bundle contains a coloured stone? Or that a shaman who dives into a river with crystals in his pockets comes out of the river "transformed"? What, one wonders, can Harner possibly have in mind here by "knowledge"? Does he really go about with *this* idea of "knowledge" in his head? If so, heaven help his pupils at the Foundation for Shamanic Studies. True, crystals make watches go, but what is the *connection*—and I mean by that a connection that we can witness, demonstrate, and verify in the most rudimentary, modest way—between making a watch go and "seeing right into things," or "gaining wisdom," or "spying ghosts," or other such powers claimed by shamanic heroes in the jungles of Colombia and on the plains of Siberia? Moreover, what is the connection between making a watch go and feeling emotionally devastated, nay *dead*, if one's "crystal" is, in Harner's (112) words, "shattered"? Surely the shaman's emotional dependency on his omnipotent stone has more to do with his undeveloped, infantile psyche than with the properties of quartz. Thousands of years ago Druids regarded the lightning as a manifestation of godly power; when they came upon a forest bough struck down by a bolt they seized it, treasured it, performed magic with it, and called it "golden." New Age Druids today do much the same thing. Yet I know of no one who is going about in the belief that having an electrical generator in the house, or perhaps in the garage, gives him the power to "see into the past" or "gain wisdom." Lots of things—nuclear bombs, for instance—have *power*, but we don't ascribe *magical capacities* to them because they do; and we surely would not regard such an ascription, were it made, as "knowledge" even in our wildest intellectual moments, fuelled by generous draughts of Chardonnay.

When Harner proffers the use of quartz in shamanism and the current employment of crystals in computers as an example of "synchronicity" he merely reflects from still another angle the New Age obsession with affective attunement, masked in shamanic lore by the practitioner's belief in the crystal's magical, vibrational capacities. The human sense of *duration* commences as the frustrated infant anticipates the fulfillment of his needs (see Hartocollis 1974). In this way, the first and the most significant *synchronicity* that we experience as humans is rooted in the caretaker's ability to *be there* (in *time*), as the infant expresses his discomfort. When the caretaker *meets* the infant's needs, answers the infant's frustration, affective attunement results: the baby and the caretaker are on the same, wonderful, "vibrational wavelength," the original source of transformational magic. Thus the *sensation of synchronicity* in adult life (very common among New Agers and often attributed to some occult power or Jungian "archetype") comprises a *mnemic trace* of affective attunement projected onto the *temporal* world as uncanny coincidence (Harner's sense of "awe" in the passage just cited). The psychological bedrock of "synchronicity" as it is used in New Age thinking is the reactivation of the infantile unconscious. "Synchronicity" is a kind of regressive *déjà vu*; it triggers the fantastic conviction that events in the environment (originally the mother) are occurring in a way which coincides meaningfully, *relationally*, with one's own psychological wishes and needs.

When Harner (1990, 113) declares that "the shaman uses the power offered to him not only by the animals, but also by the plants of garden Earth," and, further, that the "vast majority" of these "plants" are "wild, undomesticated species," he provides us with the analytical way into the topic: like all shamanic magic, the plant-related or "garden variety" is linked unconsciously to the *first garden,* the *first paradise,* here projected onto the earth as *magna mater.* What peeks through the metaphor is the original, prelapsarian relationship that resides at the core of the before-separation-world, the relationship in which mother and baby share their "wild," fresh, "undomesticated" energies in mutually blissful exchange. In comparison with guardian animals, plants are mild, tender, sweet, and comforting "spirits." They "do not have nearly as much power as the power animals," Harner (113) informs us, "but a shaman can come to possess hundreds of them, so that their cumulative power can in many ways match that of his guardian spirit." Plant helpers become in this way gentle, *transitional companions* that call to mind the concept of "evoked companionship" detailed earlier by Daniel Stern as one of the basic methods we employ to cope with the problem of separation from the caregiver. We can *surround* ourselves with our plant helpers, *heaps* of them, just as the toddler heaps his bed with stuffed frogs. Harner (114) instructs us: "As you stroll through the wild area, keep conscious your mission: to encounter a plant to be your helper. When one plant attracts you, sit down with it and become familiar with its details. Explain that you have to take all or part of it for your work, and apologize to it before picking part of it or pulling it up." Here is the regressive, childish babble we frequently overhear as parents when we come upon our children at play with their teddies and rag dolls. The New Age shaman talks to his "friends" from the "garden," gets cuddly and intimate, just as the little one does with the caretaker and his/her *substitutes.* Meadows (1991, 77) offers us much the same thing: he calls the "plants" and "trees" to which we turn as "helpers" our "spiritual *relatives"* (my emphasis), and claims their roots "penetrate into the darkness of the earth"—an "earth" that Meadows characterizes, following an American Indian myth, as our "grandmaster." Also like Harner, Meadows (78) asks us to "talk" to our plants and trees, to "communicate" with them and "establish a working partnership." We are to go to nature, or, more specifically, to the fruitful earth, and discover *familial* ties that bind and empower us. Instructing the apprentice shaman who has had the good fortune to purchase his book, Meadows (80) writes, "Go to a place where [your] plant grows naturally and spend time there. Let the plant know how precious it is to you. Voice your thoughts ... Ask the plant to reveal to you something of its spiritual nature." Here is more of the childish babbling we discovered in Harner: "Raggedy Ann, you're so precious to me; tell me all your secrets. What's behind those big button eyes?" Meadows continues: "Explain to the plant that you need its help and you want to take a small cutting from it ... Take your cutting and smear a little spittle from your mouth over the wound on the plant. If it is possible, lie down on the grass nearby and relax, *holding the cutting to your navel.* Close your eyes and ask the plant to reveal its 'medicine' to you" (my emphasis). I believe we have the essence of the business right here: just as the shaman holds the crystal to his navel to get "power," to rediscover and utilize the "energy centre" of his existence, so he holds his little plant friend to his navel to get its "medicine." Such gestures disclose uniquivocally the regressive urge to reunite with the *original object* of protection and power, the "belly-object" from whom we derived our being-in-the-world and who we now project onto the *earth* as a *garden of magical helpers.* We hold the plant to the place to which *we* were tied, and through such holding we strive to fill it with maternal energy and succour which we can then *use.* To "thank" the tree or plant for its "power," for its ability to change "our weakness into strength," Meadows (80–81) advises the shamanic reader, "pull out a few strands of your hair and leave them tied to an appendage of tree bark, or prick your thumb and deposit a spot of blood on the trunk. Even a little spittle will serve the same purpose. It is simply an expression of an *exchange of energy*" (my emphasis). We have in this an explicit attempt to re-establish through bodily fusion the affective, vibrational attunement with the object, or the "exchange of energy" with the object, that was both savoured and deeply internalized by the child during life's initial stages. The "helpers" of "garden earth" are avenues back to such attunement, to such "exchanges of energy," and we begin to understand why New Age thinking as a whole is so preoccupied with this sort of thing.

Exchanging energy with the universe, with the objects therein, provides the practitioner with the illusion of dual-unity, with the regressive, fantastic version of the mirror relationship where mother and baby flourish on the same vibrational "wavelength." New Agers want to "exchange" their "energy" with everything around them in a kind of *emotional pantheism* wherein objects—plants, trees, stones, animals—are worshipped as items upon which one may lovingly *feed.* If it is the "beech" we are after, it will give us "well-being"; if it is the "holly," we get "potency" and "growth"; ivy offers "tenacity and persistence"; and the pine, "emotional strength" (Meadows 1991, 79). The entire issue is well summed up by Meadows (79) in another arboreal passage: "Sit under the tree with your back firmly against its trunk ... Concentrate your mind on sensing the aura of the tree and being energized by it ... Ask the tree, 'please help me to sense your aura and to share its energy' ... Then relax. You will recognize the feeling when it comes, like soaking in a bath, a comfortable, warm, glowing sensation as your aura merges with that of the tree. Be patient ... and the response will come." The tree's "aura" is of course the tree's *vibration* with which we want to *merge* so that we can get from the tree its vibrational *response* and *bathe* in it, for it is precisely *this* kind of "response" from the world that signifies *the end of separation.* And it is precisely this kind of "response" from the world that fills the practitioner with feelings of *transformation*, feelings of *change.* Declares Harner (1990, 114): "Keep studying the plants until they change into a nonplant spirit form. Almost any form is possible, but insects, serpents, birds, and even stones are common. As soon as you see the change, *eat them* in their nonmaterial form in the shamanic state of consciousness just as you ate their ordinary material aspect that day; but this time take in the whole entity" (my emphasis). Here is the *orality*, the unconscious, psychic *hunger* that underlies the transformational quest in all New Age thinking, including shamanism. *We eat the vibrations*, the "nonmaterial form," the inward essence of the thing, and we *get that into us* until we *feel* its transformative effect, just as the infant *feeds* upon *both* the mother's milk *and* the mother's loving vibrations, the mother's "nonmaterial form"; the baby, too, takes in, as Harner puts it, "the whole entity." This is supping in the Garden, supping on the old, symbiotic vibrations which originally energized us and which are now *projected* into the magical "helpers." As the *plant changes*, and as we *internalize* it in its changed condition, *we* change; *we* enter more fully, more profoundly, into the "hidden universe," the "awesome" prelapsarian realm where "unity" is restored and the ancient, tragic "fall" undone. There is no *rapprochement* in this shamanic behaviour, no cordial (or relatively cordial) reconcilement with the facts, with the realities of separation and smallness. We *change* the world with our minds, we *alter* it, and then we "eat" it so that *we* can be changed too. Now *there* is an example of what psychoanalysis calls the omnipotence of thought.

The Healing Journey, Sucking Style

Shamanic practice, both ancient and modern, culminates in healing the sick; for who, after all, are more in need of *magic* than those whose lives are deteriorating because of illness? We see how it goes in Harner (1990, 117) where we get detailed instructions for the shamanic healer's attempt to suck out—that's right, *suck out*—the patient's sickness, or disease. Harner dubs this "sucking work" and declares that to accomplish it "successfully" the shaman "must alert and marshall his spirit helpers to help him in the extraction of power intrusions from a patient. For this, the shaman uses one of his power songs: 'Come, come, spirits of magic ... Spirits of magic, arise from sleep.'" Harner (119) goes on to observe that a "qualified sucking shaman," on his "knees" and leaning over the supine patient, "starts to sing his power song, calling his spirit helpers to aid him in the sucking ... He also pulls toward him a basket or bowl containing sand ... in which to spit that which he extracts from the patient." Shaking a "rattle" over the patient, or perhaps passing a "feather" over to "pick up any vibration," the shaman "sings powerfully" as he strives to "locate the harmful, intrusive power" and "suck it out." When he "senses the location" of the "intrusion," he "wills it into his mouth" with the aid of his magical helpers; he can do this by "sucking with all his might through clothing" or by "physically sucking the skin." He must be careful, states Harner (121), not to allow the "voracious creature he saw" to "pass into his throat"; indeed, he must "expel it into the container" and then "dry vomit" to make sure he is rid of it. Finally, he must "pass his hand back and forth above the patient" to be certain that "he [the shaman] no longer feels any localized emanations of heat, energy, or vibration." Harner (122, 126) supportively includes pen and ink drawings of a shaman (bearded, bald, and Caucasian) kneeling over a patient and sucking and spitting, as well as tales from the writings of one Essie Parrish, a famous North American Indian shaman known as "the sucking doctor." From such materials, the psychoanalytic meaning emerges irrepressibly.

By locating the *bad vibrations* of the patient, and then by *sucking them out*, the shaman replaces the bad vibrations with *his own vibrations.* In this way, he *merges* his vibrations with those of the patient in a regressive re-establishment of dual-unity, the *good*, security-inducing *fusion* of the early period. Let me develop this: the patient's "illness," his bad "energy," is a psychosomatic expression of his *anxiety*, his absorption into the *bad object* of the *inner realm* with its accompanying sensations of separation, rejection, and loss. The shaman takes this object *away.* Thus he *restores affective attunement*, the shared, *vibrational* well-being in which a powerful caregiving figure and a dependent, helpless baby come to comprise a mutually supportive, life-giving unit. Psychoanalysis regards sucking in and spitting out as among the first and most basic ways in which human beings express acceptance and rejection, yes and no, good and bad (Spitz 1965). Shamanic healing returns to precisely this primal world and enacts its magical, placebo effects *right there.*

Harner (1990, 123) presents an example drawn from the writings of a "beginning shaman" in the midst of a healing journey: "I got up on my knees . . . and started examining the patient's body from the outside with my hands. I could not get a clear sensation at first. It felt like it was covered with spider webs. I brushed them off with my fingers and then clearly felt a focus of energy . . . around the stomach/ovary/bladder area. I sucked out what I could and got rid of it down the wash basin. It was very disgusting. After rinsing my mouth clean of whatever it was, I returned to my lying position next to the patient." Harner (123) comments on this episode: "The student was not trained or prepared to suck out intrusive creatures, but he spontaneously did a creative job of removing the 'dirtiness.'" As for the supine *patient* who underwent the procedure, Harner's "student" writes: "She later explained she had been feeling a loosening in her abdominal area. When I told her what I had found, she confirmed that she had digestive and ovary problems. In a letter six weeks later she reported changes for the better. The feeling of being stuck had gone and concrete conflicts were coming out into the open" (Harner, 125). Could we have a more vivid corroboration of the thesis? The "intrusive, disgusting, dirty creature" removed by the shaman's sucking is a projective expression of *bad* internalized or inward contents, the *psychic object* whose negative "powers" or negative "vibrations" have *converted* the patient's abdomen from wellness to illness. She carries the bad object in her "guts." By sucking on her belly, by magically replacing her "bad vibes" with his own "good vibes" (of succour, care, concern), the shaman has returned the patient psychically to the world of the good object, affective attunement, evoked companionship, positive fusion—the source of one's strong, vibrant approach to existence. Restored to life as a matrix of hope through her regressive union with a "sucking doctor," the patient no longer feels "stuck," repressed, defensive. Her conflicts are beginning to emerge into awareness, and her belly feels better, too. What New Age healing shamanic-style has accomplished here is exactly what New Age thinking as a whole is always striving to accomplish, namely, a return to the garden of dual-unity, a return to the before-separation-world in its good or benign aspect, the magical restoration of symbiotic merger with a nurturing, soothing presence, the removal of all stress-inducing, discomfort-inducing elements from one's being—in a word, paradise. What is of special psychoanalytic interest in this particular configuration is the reversal of the normative dynamics of *feeding* as they transpire during the early period. That is, instead of sucking *in* the milk of paradise as the baby does in the before-separation-world, the patient allows the shamanic healer (who comprises half the patient-healer dual-unit) to suck *out* the bad elements that vitiate her life in the after-separation-world, indeed, that trigger her regressive longing for the prelapsarian realm in its idealized aspect. The bad object, or the intrusive power, which Harner (121) calls in one place the "voracious creature," is sucking the patient's life away until the "healer" comes along as *good object* and sucks that object, or power, or creature away. The shaman's sucking *out* of the bad object is empathetically and by transference the patient's sucking *in* of the good object. Thus the *patient's sucking* is done *by* the parental shaman. This is the patient's *ultimate dependency*. In precisely this elaborate disguise of opposi- tions and reversals is the paradisal, feeding union of mother and baby reconstituted in the now of after-separation reality.

Essie Parrish, the famous Indian "sucking doctor" we mentioned, claimed that her "sucking" was "like a magnet," that it possessed the "power" to "pull out" the patient's "dirt" (Harner 1990, 128). Her hands, in her view, contained "electricity" or the capacity to "see" the location of the offending agent: "That is my hand power" (128). Parrish goes on, "While the disease is coming to me, I'm in a trance ... That disease flies and sticks to a certain place in the mouth. Our shaman's teeth have the power ... I spit out the dead disease ... Whoever picks the disease up, into him it would enter" (129). The entire emphasis, note, is on power, energy, electricity—in short, on the *vibrational* as- pect of the procedure. At the surface, the shaman is the "big" vibra- tional presence, the parental healer, the good object of affective attunement who uses his/her power, his/her *omnipotence*, to alter the patient's vibrations, to rid the patient of his/her bad, internalized, psy- chosomatic materials. Beneath the surface, however, the shaman, in a *trance*, is participating in the dual-unity situation and deriving a re- gressive, infantile satisfaction from it. This is disclosed, of course, by the central and overwhelming fact that the shaman *wants to suck*, wants to suck on the body of the supine, passive patient, wants to be in a trance-like, sucking relationship (the "stoned" baby at the mother's breast). The shaman's omnipotence, then, is an *infantile feature* of his mentality; it is adjunctive to and indicative of his urge to suck. Thus shaman and patient are *interchangeable*: the shaman sucks while play- ing omnipotent parent, while dominating the patient, and the patient sucks through the transference relation, through an identification with the shaman and a participation in the dual-unity equation. Accord- ingly, the shaman is also a patient in need of healing, in need of address- ing his own emotional illness, and the patient is also a shaman in need of a sucking union. Just listen to Harner (132): "When the shaman feels power-full, he and the patient slowly take off their clothes and ex- change them with each other. As the shaman puts on each article of the patient's clothing, he concentrates on taking on the patient's hurts and afflictions and on assuming the patient's personality. By the time the shaman puts on the last piece of clothing, the shaman should now begin to feel he *is* the patient." While the patient's wish to be sucked *on* may be a one-time expression of his "personality," the shaman's urge *to suck* is a persistent, lifelong compulsion. He/she goes about re-locating the good object through the patient and getting rid of the bad object, the "voracious creature," also through the patient. It is a projec-tive game in which the "healthy" one *uses* the "sick" one to act out *his own* disease," his own inner "dirtiness." Shamanic healing sucking style is a kind of vampirism, and the shaman is a kind of vampire. It is the shaman who is the "voracious creature," and his persistent spitting out of that "creature" (taken *projectively* from the patient) is his per-sistent *denial* of its dominating presence in his own personality.

Nor can we overlook the central role of *isolation* here. Writes Harner (1990, 132): "First the shaman discusses with the patient the nature of the pain or illness. He finds out everything he can about how the illness or pain feels ... When the shaman is satisfied, he is ready to undertake the critical phase of the healing work ... The shaman and the patient *go to a wilderness location devoid of human habitation.* The shaman, with his rattle and power song, wakes his guardian spirit to help him" (my emphasis). It is at *this* point, declares Harner, that shaman and patient *exchange clothing*—immediately after which the "sucking work begins. Just as isolation triggers the regressive need for fusion during the "vision quest" when the apprentice shaman discov-ers his "animal guide," so isolation catalyzes an identical need here, as patient and shaman exchange identities, indulge themselves in the re-turn of infantile omnipotence, submit to the longing for a relationship based on sucking, orality, the mouth. It is the *reclusion* of the pair, their "wilderness location," that helps to break down the scaffolding of the personality, that allows *both* to enter the realm of magical transfor-mation in which *symbiosis* is savoured once again as an antidote for separation anxiety.

Meadows's (1991, 166) corroboration of all this is indirect but very striking: "Some shamans believe that a sense of separation, and a feel-ing of being cut off, alone, will ... cause illness. In such cases the sha-man endeavours to revive the sense of belonging and of being wanted." From the psychoanalytic angle, however, the wilderness location is *chosen to bring out* the "illness," to focus it, to capture it, so that it can be *used* for the central, unconscious purpose involved in the "healing" ritual. And it is, of course, precisely the sense of "belonging," of "being wanted"—in other words, dual-unity and psychological merger—that "revives" *both* the patient and the healer. We may note in this light Meadows's (166) observation that the most common causes of "sick-ness" from the "shamanic point of view" are "fear, anxiety, and stress." Meadows (166) goes on: "The shaman does not use his own personal power to effect harmonization. Energy from his own energy-system would be speedily depleted, and in certain cases he might fall prey to the very condition he is endeavoring to alleviate. Instead he goes to a source of inexhaustible energy on a spiritual level to provide the necessary power, and is not afraid to touch it and be touched by it." Thus the healing is *vibrational*, as we've suggested all along. The shaman "touches" the patient in a manner that restores affective (or vibrational) attunement, that takes away "fear, anxiety, and stress," that reestablishes the mirroring tie to the good object. Needless to say, such behaviour constitutes unconsciously a powerful version of the *transformational* exchange which characterizes the early, caregiving period when the maternal figure turns discomfort into satisfaction. The patient once again experiences the transformational object in his life, and it is *this* experience that enters integrally into effecting his "cure." Meadows (169) states that "participants," as they undergo their "healing," experience a "transformation of their lives." They "emerge with a new sense of direction and purpose." Yet the shaman, too, participates in a "healing," I mean *his own*, by *becoming the transformational object*, by experiencing transformation from *his* side of the dual-unity equation as he gets rid of his bad materials *through the patient*. The "healing" ritual gets *him* back to the before-separation-world of magical change—over and over and over again. For thousands of years shamans and patients have been playing this game. It may be New Age thinking now, but it is an old story.

The Theoretical Picture

With all of this behind us, and on the verge of the next section, let's look briefly at the theoretical arguments which Harner and Meadows offer us in support of shamanic experience, shamanic reality. Let's get into some "New Age *thinking*. Meadows (1991, 4) writes in his opening section, "The New Frontier": "Shamanism has nothing to do with the so-called supernatural because it is essentially a natural and holistic activity ... It rests not on faith but on the acquisition of experienced knowledge—that is, knowledge that can be attained by the individual. A difference between a religionist and a shaman is that a religious person's concept of truth is based upon faith in the word or authority of another and depends upon the interpretation given to those words ... A shaman's concept of truth is based upon personal experience. For instance, a religious person believes that realms do exist beyond the normal physical existence ... A shaman knows such realms exist because he has experienced them for himself, in an altered state of consciousness." What we have here, in essence, is the enormously popular and deeply influential New Age notion of *anything goes:* anything achieves philosophical, or, better, epistemological status if I "experience it for myself"; and if I "experience it for myself" in an "altered state of consciousness," why, then, so much the better. It would be difficult, of course, to over-stress the vapidity, the vacuity of such a notion, yet it is a notion that resides at the theoretical centre of New Age thinking. Imagine the poor wretch at the inquisitorial stake, on the verge of incineration, crying out his innocence to the hooded executioner and receiving in return the reply, "Silence, sinner; I *know* you're the Devil; I've *experienced* you personally as the Devil on several occasions, and once when I was in an altered state of consciousness." Not only is such thinking philosophically bankrupt and undeserving of professional respect, it is *dangerous.* It closes debate before debate can get started: "I experienced this for myself, baby, so shut up!" Only the *converted* can participate—*one at a time.* Each "theoretician" inhabits a self-contained, monadic capsule from which he determines the authenticity of his own experience, and by extrapolation the truth of the world or the nature of reality, without logical or epistemological or informational *criteria* beyond his own subjectivity, without intermeshing social, communicational, observational materials, without rigorous discussion and dialogue—in short, without any standards for *judgement.* The result: epistemological kick-the-can, a philosophical world in which every position is of equal value and therefore no position is of any *particular* value—no matter how diligently, how skilfully it is presented. "Well, man, I think I see what you mean about the many ways an experience can be interpreted, but this was still *real* for me, OK?" This is among the very worst aspects of New Age thinking—I mean from an ideational angle, and it attests *psychoanalytically* to the New Ager's absolute unwillingness to probe the meaning of his wish-fulfilling thoughts and sensations, the ones that restore him to the before-separation-world of symbiotic fusion and omnipotence. Any fool is free to jump in with his "story," and no one dare challenge its "personal" veracity. This is the tyranny of "doctrine" *in reverse,* the tyranny of "doctrine" from the *other side:* "I experienced this, so f—-off!" Every person, every egomaniacal guru, every mystic, every doper, every "beginning shaman," every borderline schizophrenic in every borderline cult becomes a shaper of reality, a pronouncer of the truth.

Meadows gets even more problematical, if that is possible, when he writes a few pages later (1991, 11): "spirit *is* the Life Force. It is the invisible essence of whatever is manifested. It is the power that is flowing through every living thing and which provides energy for it to express its separate identity. But although spirit flows through all forms it is largely 'unknown' because it is hidden behind the apparent physical appearance of things. Modern science has no knowledge of the true nature of spirit because, unlike matter, it cannot be seen or measured. It is so elusive that it cannot be dissected by the logical mind either, because it transcends the intellect. Spirit is 'nothing' yet, paradoxically, it is in everything and everything is in it. Modern science has an inadequate and incomplete understanding of the nature of man and of life itself because it tends to be concerned solely with the physical, and ignores the spiritual ... Yet spirit, and how to live within it, was known to shamans before any organized religion or man-made philosophy determined what was and was not to be believed." Think about this for a moment—I mean, about what Meadows is actually *saying*. We don't *know* what "spirit" is, at least in the usual sense, because we can't *see* it or *measure* it; it is ungraspable by the "logical mind"; indeed, it "transcends" the very intellect itself. Yet Meadows knows all about it, or at least enough to know that it is the "Life Force," that it is the "invisible essence of whatever is manifested," that it is "in everything and everything is in it." Quite a series of claims, I should say—a series, in fact, that purports to reveal fundamental aspects or facets of the universe around us, "everything." If spirit is so *elusive*, one wonders why it has made itself so accessible to Meadows. Would it not be more consistent on his part simply to admit that he hasn't a clue as to what exactly "spirit" *is*, if it is *at all*, and let it go? I say "at all" because one also wonders here how Meadows found out about this elusive spirit in the first place. If it can't be seen, measured, dissected, or grasped, if it transcends the intellect itself, how did *anyone* discover it? And not only discover it but discover enough to make it the foundation of "everything"? As I say, think about it: the world is founded on something which we can't see or measure or know with our intellectual intelligence—*the same* intellectual intelligence which, somehow, brought *Meadows* to know it (spirit) comprised the world's foundation. Yet the old shamans knew all about spirit, too, says Meadows; and not only knew about it but how to "live within it." How did *that* come about? What gave *them* such pre-eminent insight? And why is *their* belief, shamanic belief, more compelling than any *other* old belief, the materialism of Lucretius, for example? Is not *all* religion, *all* philosophy, just another push toward belief, like shamanism? What makes a shaman's claim that this or that is "true," more valid, or more engaging than the claim of an ardent priest or rabbi or Platonist? I don't *get* it; I don't get the *privilege* that underlies shamanic claims and apparently doesn't underlie *other* claims. And if everything boils down to my "personal experience" anyway, as Meadows says earlier (4), why is *any* philosophical or religious claim less or more valid than any other? What if my personal experience tells me there is no such thing as "spirit"? Wouldn't that mean, according to Meadows, that spirit does *not* exist, at least for *me*? But if spirit does not exist for *me*, how can it be the foundation of "everything"? Does that mean everything except poor me? Surely what Meadows says on one page should fit in with what he says on another.

Harner, in spite of his reputation as "the world's leading authority on shamanism" (see the opening paragraphs of this section), takes us no further than Meadows does. He writes in his Introduction to *The Way of the Shaman* (1990, xxi): "In the shamanic state of consciousness the shaman not only experiences what is impossible in ordinary consciousness, but does it. Even if it should be proven that all the shaman experiences in the shamanic state is purely in his mind, that would not make that realm any less real to him. Indeed, such a conclusion would mean that the shaman's experiences and deeds are *not* impossible in any absolute sense." Shall we apply this to any experience which anyone might have in any state of consciousness? Indeed, are we not *obliged* to do that? For the shamanic state is not a *privileged* one. Although it may go *further* than other states, it is no more or less *valid* than other states. Well, what do we discover when we do this, when we extrapolate Harner's position? Just the following: "Even if it should be proven" (I will follow Harner's very words) that a lunatic's "experience" of, say, two hundred elephants performing Haydn's *Creation* upside down "is purely in his mind," that would not make the experience "less real to him ... Such a conclusion would mean" the lunatic's experience is "not impossible in any absolute sense." Or perhaps, "even if it should be proven" that a religious mystic's visionary "experience" of the ticket-takers at Gate 19 of Yankee Stadium as Jesus and the Disciples "is purely in his mind," that would not make the experience "less real to him or impossible in any absolute sense," etc. What Harner is saying here in support of "shamanic reality" boils down to something so obvious, so trite, so *useless* that one wonders why he bothers to say it at all: if I am thinking something, or imagining something, or fantasying something, it exists to the extent that I am thinking or imagining or fantasying it. Yes, that's right. That's *all* Harner is saying. Yet he tries to dress it up as insight or philosophical polemic by gesturing toward the "absolute," by suggesting that we have here, are *confronting* here, some compelling sort of logic with epistemological overtones. *Of course* a mystic's visions are real to him; and they are real to us *as his visions.* So what? Are we supposed to jump from this to entertaining their possibility in the world *out there?* Why should we do that? And even if we *do*, what difference does it make? OK, one of the ticket-takers may be Jesus. Surely we do not have in this a philosophical stand of any great urgency. Were I to rush into the Philosophy Department at Columbia University and announce that Jesus may be a few blocks away because, in Harner's words, that is "not impossible in any absolute sense," I doubt seriously that it would have much effect on next year's curriculum. The only thing it would affect, I suspect, would be my continued presence in the Philosophy Department. What Harner's position amounts to finally is just another variation on the ubiquitous New Age theme of *anything goes*. Anything is possible as long as it isn't impossible, and nothing is impossible ("absolutely") because anything is possible to the extent that it is "experienced."

Think of Descartes struggling to get *past* this sort of thing nearly four hundred years ago and finally discovering a cornerstone with the *cogito:* I think, therefore I am. That is all Descartes can be certain of when it comes to his "experience." The rest, all the rest, is doubtful. Even his most elaborate fantasies and philosophical ruminations may be simply a dream occurring in another being's mind. Descartes, at one point, turns to the notion of God in his efforts to achieve some certitude, maintaining that He would not set out to trick His children. Harner (1990) writes as if all this hadn't even occurred in Western thought. Indeed, he goes the *other way, doubting nothing* and declaring the possibility of everything in a typical New Age philosophical moment, one that glibly sweeps aside the blood-and-sweat efforts of not only Descartes but of thinkers such as Plato and Aristotle and Hume and Locke and Kant and Hegel and Husserl. All that philosophical rigour, all that philosophical sophistication and exactitude, goes straight into the dustbin as we lurch forward with our nugget of wisdom, our pearl of insight: nothing is "absolutely" impossible to the extent that it is "experienced"; anything goes, man, anything *goes.*

There is no philosophical radicalness or revolution here, just in case someone is wondering. Philosophical revolutions, the kind we associate with existentialism or postmodernism, rely on strong, genuine intelligence, often of the very highest order. What we have in Harner and Meadows is just plain shallowness, the sort that results from inborn limitations, or lack of education, or paucity of application and effort, or all three working happily together. Note the final paragraph of Harner's (1990, xxiv) Introduction in which he "states" the following: "I practice shamanism myself; not because I understand in ordinary consciousness *why* it works, but simply because it *does* work. But don't take my word for it: truly significant shamanic knowledge is *experienced*, and cannot be obtained from me or any other shaman." Shamanism "works"? Harner "practises" it because it "does work"? And we can verify that it "works" *only* through our own "experience"? Here we are again, back in Harner's solipsistic capsule, back to Harner's shallow reasoning and shoddy philosophical presentation. Yes, by all means, shamanism "works," but so does TV evangelism, and cultic manipulation in Jonestown and Waco, and crystal-gazing and snake oil, and past-life regression, and communication with the dead through a medium, and a thousand other "experiences" in which people get themselves involved. Behold New Age *pragmatism* in all its pathetic inadequacy: shamanism "works." What *doesn't* work for those who are eager to believe, to buy in, to rediscover their long-lost omnipotence and narcissism and symbiotic fusion through some master or some ritual? What *doesn't* work for those who are longing for the transformational object, for those who, in their discontent or perhaps desperation, are already half convinced? There is not one scrap of proof, *not one scrap,* in Harner or Meadows or Castaneda or anyone else, that *any* of this "works," apart from the subjective *claim* that it does, which is precisely the point: the individualistic *anything goes* is theoretically inseparable from the pragmatic *it works.* Indeed, the former is the *prerequisite* of the latter. I and only I am the judge; I and only I happen to know; hence, I and only I can declare what "works" and what doesn't "work." Harner (45) keeps it up: "A true master shaman does not challenge the validity of anybody else's experiences ... The master shaman will try to integrate even the most unusual experiences into his total cosmology, a cosmology based primarily on his own journeys ... The master shaman never says that what you experienced is a fantasy. That is one of the differences between shamanism and science." Again, *anything goes.* Nothing is "challenged." Everything is "valid," capable of demarcating and defining the reality of human participation in the world, as well as the nature of the world itself. There are no bases for judgement, no psychological theories or guidelines for the analysis of one's "experience." There is just the individual and whatever the individual happens to present. *Of course* the shaman never "questions" the "validity" of another person's experience, for if he *did* it might call his own experience, on which his "total cosmology" is "based," into question by creating an interpretative or analytic perspective capable of unpacking experience and tracing it back to specific projective (fantasying) tendencies in the individual. To "question" might open the door to the kind of psychological probing that would end the free-for-all. In a metaphoric word, to question might trigger the burglar alarm in the house of truth. And that is why the "shaman" is such a popular figure among New Agers. Because he "questions" nothing, he encourages the participant to believe whatever he wishes to believe about himself and the world around him. No one ever has to come to terms with his own inner reality. Instead of bravely confronting one's problems and working them through, instead of bravely facing up to the quality of one's own character and striving for constructive, analytic change, one is allowed to indulge his omnipotence, his narcissism, his regressive desire for symbiotic fusion, his longing for the before-separation-world. By never "questioning" anything, the shaman permits his New Age admirers to skirt the supremely real issue of growing up.

Yet Harner (1990, 45) won't let "science" go, even though he "puts it down" at the end of the last citation. "There are similarities between the shaman and the scientist," he writes; "the best of both are in awe of the complexity and magnificence of the universe ... and realize that during their own lifetimes they will only come to observe and understand a small portion of what is going on." Both "shamans and scientists," Harner continues, "personally pursue research into the mysteries of the universe, and both believe that the underlying causal processes of that universe are hidden from ordinary view ... Neither master scientists nor master shamans allow the dogma of ecclesiastical or political authorities to interfere with their explorations. It was no accident that Galileo was accused of witchcraft (shamanism)." And finally, "The shaman is an empiricist. One of the definitions of empiricism is 'the practice of emphasizing experience esp. of the senses' ... The shaman depends primarily on firsthand experience of the senses, to acquire knowledge. Still, the master shaman is humble. After all, none of us really knows what is going on. Everyone is limited to his own small window onto the universe." Thus shamanism pushes science away when it comes to the issue of "fantasy" (there is no such thing), yet snuggles up to science when it comes to the "complexity" of the "universe" and the urge to penetrate its "mysteries." What Harner *fails* to mention (let alone italicize) are the enormous and decisive *differences* that underlie shamanic as opposed to scientific *empiricism*. These differences, in my view at least, *sunder* the scientist and the shaman for ever and ever.

Scientific empiricism does *not* make individual "experience," sensorial or otherwise, the sole or even the chief criterion of truth. On the contrary, it regards individual experience as merely the *inception* of a rigorous, methodological, observational, and mensurational process of *testing* to determine what is actually occurring in the world out there, which includes the realm of psychological functions. In even stronger terms, scientific empiricism *abhors* the sort of individualistic perceptual emphasis on which Harner and Meadows base their theoretical presentation of shamanic reality. It considers such an emphasis the *enemy* of scientific endeavour. The subjective position, the cornerstone of shamanism, is the *danger zone* of science. When Harner pulls in Galileo and offers him to us as a kind of shaman, he is guilty of obscurantism in the very worst sense of the word. Galileo was accused of Witchcraft by a pack of ecclesiastical bigots and fools who had not the slightest idea of what he was up to—I mean, of course, in terms of the scientific empiricism that Galileo was striving to develop. How can their accusations be of any significance here? Moreover, Galileo used his "experience" as a *preliminary to making rules* about the exploration of nature, rules that would perforce *invalidate, annul, cancel out* the "experience" of others who ignored them. Is it your "experience" that dissimilar falling bodies such as a flower and a brick do not fall side by side as the density of the medium through which they pass decreases to nearly zero? Well, you're *wrong*. Your "experience" is *not valid*. Scientific empiricism *negates* it, something that "master shamans" never do, according to Harner. Or perhaps it is your "experience" that the Earth is the centre of the solar system, rather than the sun. Well, once again, you're *wrong*, and it's just too bad for you and your "experience." The point is, scientific empiricism, such as Galileo's, strives to *monitor* sensorial experience until it gets what it considers to be an accurate reading of it—*one* accurate reading—which it then calls "true." All the remaining "experiences" are *thrown out*. This is the very *opposite* of the shamanic creed by which *nothing* is "questioned," and by which *anything goes*. Harner maintains that both shaman and scientist are awestruck by the universe and eager to probe its mysteries—a superficial analogy which has no genuine value. Pretty much everyone, at least in the developed world, is in awe of the cosmos and wants to know the answers to the big questions: this hardly makes them all intellectually compatible. True, both scientist and shaman resent religious and political interference with their activities, but so do the Hell's Angels. Again, Harner's analogy is superficial, unproductive, useless; it covers too wide a range to have any bite. As for Harner's remark that none of us really knows what is going on, it is a mere rhetorical gesture. The scientist *really knows*, or believes he does, and he puts forth his theories when he is feeling reasonably certain about it. Those theories are designed not only to *validate* his "experience," but to reject *other* "experience" which stands behind *other*, oppositional theories. It was by *really knowing*, and by *not* considering all experience to be of equal value (the shamanic view), that empirical scientists got people onto the surface of the moon. And yes, as Harner asserts (in another spate of banality), we all have one small window on the world from which we peer out. Yet one window in a specific context such as empiricism may provide a sharper outlook than another, and science claims that *its* window is the *best* window. Surely that's the essence of the matter. Harner would do well, in the final analysis, to drop the analogical comparison between the scientific empiricist running his data in his laboratory and the "master shaman" dancing about the tundra with his rattles and feathers. To call shamanic goings-on "research" in the scientific sense is, quite simply, absurd.

Harner's expression "master shaman" alerts us for a final time to the authoritarian-permissive seesaw which resides at the heart of the shamanic creed *anything goes*. On the one hand, anything goes because the "master" says so; his word is sufficient to arrest one's critical faculties, to smooth the path of one's narcissism and omnipotence, to justify the indulgence of one's regressive, infantile predilections. On the other hand, anything goes because one takes on the mantle of the master oneself: by following Harner's (1990, 30) simple instructions any "middle-class American" (32) can become "in a few hours" (xii) a kind of mini-guru or mini-magician able to reside in whichever reality he happens to prefer, and that includes of course the reality of one's symbiotic urges, one's thirst for narcissistic enhancement, for those psychological states that so *masterfully* push down and conceal the residues of early conflict, the inward stuff which prevents one from achieving an honest, mature relationship with oneself. What is "hidden" in all this is not the "other side," the "shamanic reality" that ostensibly emerges as one attains "shamanic consciousness," but the deep unconscious aim of never confronting one's infantile anxiety again, of never facing up to one's limitations as a person, of never tracing back to their origin those behavioural traits that defeat the evolvement of one's character and that make the other people around one very, very miserable. Needless to say, it may feel gratifying in the glow of one's self-love and/or dependent devotion to the "master" to don a shamanic outfit and journey to Cloudcuckooland, but the price one pays in forestalled psychological growth is staggeringly high, as it is with all New Age undertakings. Meadows (1991, 2) writes, "A shaman recognizes that man is very privileged, for he has the power to change or shape things at will." Anything goes means *my will* shapes reality, *my will* shapes the world. To hell with science or philosophy or logic or psychology or any other discipline that calls for standards of judgement, for the stringent analysis of personal motivation. Shamanism New Age-style is a variation on the old theme, "the will to power," the rejection of everything that stands in the way of my wishes as they are dictated by the press of my unconscious longings and fears.

We will probably never see the advent of an actual Shamanland, a Walt Disney-like theme park where one pays, enters, and gets an "animal guide" (a college kid dressed up as a toad) who takes one to see the Raven Display, or Coyote, or the Shaman on the Butte, or perhaps the Shamanic Fun House that duplicates with distorting mirrors the bizarre perceptual shifts one experiences while on peyote or some other type of cactus button. But Harner's book, and Meadows's book, and the "scholarly" papers in *Shaman's Drum*, and countless other New Age writings, surely move us in that direction as they popularize this particular version of *anything goes*. For that is the New Ager's goal, to have all things easily conform to his all-encompassing regressive wishes. Make it simple, accessible, and *mine*—including the truth of the world and the nature of reality. My ultimate advice to the reader (if I may be so bold and parental at the close of my little analysis) goes like this: if you want to learn about shamanism go to the appropriate section of a good research library or perhaps take a course at a solid, accredited university, say, Oxford or McGill. Study hard, keep your feet on the ground, and don't believe *anything* for at least ten years. And oh, if there is a New Age bookstore near your library or campus, stay out of it; consider going in only *after* you've tucked some quality education under your belt.

Part 3

Channelling: Transmitters, Receivers, Masters, and Guides

That old literary expression "point of view" can help us to understand the nature of New Age literature on channelling. On the one hand, we have what I will call straightforward texts which present the author's ideas in his/her *own voice*. Thus far in our study of New Age thinking we have dealt *only* with works of this kind. Harner's *The Way of the Shaman* (1990) or Bowman's *Crystal Awareness* (1992) might serve as examples. On the other hand, we have texts that are *themselves* the result of supernatural intervention. They come to us not in the author's voice, but in the voice of the beyond, the voice of the spiritual entity for whom the author serves simply as a *channel*. Needless to say, when a New Ager merely *goes along with* such a book he is already having a non-ordinary experience; he is already in contact with the other side, which means psychoanalytically that he is already *regressing*. During the course of what follows I will offer a detailed analysis of each kind of text, and I will try to disclose the psychoanalytic significance of materials that are ostensibly channelled. First, however, let's indulge ourselves in a brief, scholarly digression on the subject of channellers and channelling. A little background information will be helpful.

Channelling has been with us for a long, long time—thousands of years, in fact. It enters integrally into the prophecies of the Bible, the oracular pronouncements of the ancient world (Oedipus will slay his father and wed his mother), and into the variegated goings-on of the-fortune-tellers, seers, sibyls, shamans, and spiritualists of all ages. What exactly is it, from a non-psychoanalytic perspective, I mean? Suzanne Riordan (1992, 105) defines channelling as "a process in which information is accessed and expressed by someone who is convinced that the source is not their ordinary consciousness." As for the channeller, Phillip Lucas (1992, 196) defines him/her as "a human vehicle through whom beings from other dimensions of existence can address persons in this world." With regard more specifically to channelling as an aspect of New Age thinking, several items might be underscored as preliminaries to our psychoanalytic study.

"If the sheer volume of New Age literature is any indication," writes J. Gordon Melton (1992, 21), "channelling is possibly the single most important and definitive aspect of the New Age. It is certainly the activity which has had the greatest success in mobilizing support for the movement as a whole. It also provides an excellent illustration of the manner in which the movement has interacted with the older esoteric groups already established in the culture." Channelling, Melton (21) goes on, "is simply another name for spirit contact, no different in form than that practiced in Spiritualism for the last 150 years. However, channelling, a term derived from the extraterrestrial contact movement of the 1950s, distinguished itself from Spiritualist mediumship in its purpose and content. What is now termed channelling made a definitive appearance at the end of the nineteenth century." Throughout Spiritualism's history, we learn (Melton, 21–22), "its mediums have specialized in contact with the spirits of the dead for the purpose of demonstrating the continuance of individual life after death. Its typical format was the seance." Once the believer was convinced of spirit survival, however, he "was often led to the further conclusion that spirits should be able to tap extraordinary and authoritative sources of information about the great questions of human existence." Edgar Cayce was probably the most widely known channel of the era preceding the New Age. During the 1970s, "two selections of channelled material heralded a new wave of spirit contact. In 1970 the first volume of *The Seth Material* appeared. Seth was an entity who spoke through Jane Roberts, a housewife who lived quietly in upstate New York. The unexpected response to her first volume led to a sequel, *Seth Speaks*, and more than ten others" (Melton, 22). In 1975 *A Course in Miracles* appeared. It was channelled by a New York psychologist named Helen Schucman and supposedly came from Jesus Christ. Its popularity eventually equalled that of the Seth materials.

Of particular interest to us here is what Melton (1992, 23) calls the "redirection" of channelling's goals: "Within the New Age movement channelling has been redirected to the goal of facilitating the personal *transformation* of the channeller's clients. The Spiritualist concerns of proving life after death ... have been swept aside. Channelled entities developed their variations of New Age philosophy, and the only criteria for their value have been their internal consistency and their ability to resonate with the audience of seekers after transformation." Private meetings with a New Age channel "become more of a counseling session for the discussion of personal problems than the traditional seance, which offered the possibility of a continuing relationship with those now dead" (Melton, 23, my emphasis). From a psychoanalytic angle, we have here an early indication that New Age channelling will evince an interest (as do all New Age practices and beliefs) in "recontacting" not the "spirits of the dead" but the transformational object of the early period whose ministrations continually resolved the infant's "personal problems," continually changed his dissatisfaction into pleasure, or relief. As we will see, what the New Age channeller channels comes not from the "other side" but from his own "inner spirits"—that is, from the internalized objects of his unconscious mind.

If we take the enormous New Age literature on channelling as a whole, writes Suzanne Riordan (1992, 110), it "offers an analysis of the human condition and a set of prescriptions designed to assist humanity in discovering its true destiny. The argument is based on certain assumptions about the nature of reality which the authors present from their presumably enhanced perspective." In essence, Riordan continues (111), "they seek to convince us that we are not who we think we are and that much of our suffering can be traced to our mistaken identity; they are here to 'awaken' and 'remind' us." As for their tone, it is "passionate and imploring, sometimes angry, ironic, or admonishing," but also "tender and reassuring," as a "parent would comfort or admonish a misguided child." One of the "basic assumptions" of these "disembodied luminaries," declares Riordan (111), is that "humanity has drifted into a deep sleep, has severed its connection with its source and fallen under a 'spell of matter'—forgotten its origin and identity." It is therefore "separated from the whole" (113). Only when the "last soul" on earth remembers to "choose love" will humanity be able to overcome its "alienation" and "return home" (119). Here, then, are further contextual hints of a psychoanalytic nature about channelling's projective, unconscious preoccupations: like shamanism, it buys into the myth of a tragic fall from paradisal union and the possible restoration of bliss, which is to say, it laments the advent of the after-separation-world and longs to rediscover, somehow, the before-separation-world of dual-unity, the so-called "golden age," characterized simply and symbiotically in Riordan (119) as "home." When Riordan points out (115) that channellers also characterize this restored perfection as being "filled to the full with the energy and power of life," we recognize immediately the obsessive New Age interest in affect attunement (Stern,

1985), the vibrational, energetic union of mother and baby which begets endless projective expressions in New Age literature identical to the one at which we are looking here. We will, of course, keep a close eye on these themes as we go.

Of the various esoteric or occult activities that earmark the New Age, channelling is the one that has received the most attention (often of a ridiculing nature) from the media. Some New Agers regard it with suspicion, others obviously with wholesale devotion (Riordan 1992, 105). According to a number of scholars, channelling probably peaked in the 1980s with the writings and telecasts of the movie personality Shirley MacLaine. According to other scholars, however, it is still going strong. The question of the life and/or death of New Age channelling is moot (Lewis 1992, 10). In the words of J. Gordon Melton (1992, 28), "given the withdrawal of New Thought [roughly, Christian Science and the Church of Jesus Christ of Latter-Day Saints] and the Eastern religions, the New Age movement has been left with its base in theosophical and channelling groups. The older theosophical groups are continuing with their set agenda. That leaves the channelling groups as the remnant of the movement most likely to survive." With all of this in mind, let's turn to a concrete instance of this "likely survival"; let's turn to the first of the texts that will assist us in suggesting the psychoanalytic core and essence of that spiritualism which we now call channelling, New Age-style.

Wisdom from the Beyond

Sanaya Roman and Duane Packer are the authors to whom *Opening to Channel: How to Connect with Your Guide* (1987) is attributed on the title page and on the cover (pink, with a large mandala of orange, red, and blue shining out kaleidoscopically from the centre). As it turns out, however, Sanaya and Duane (they put themselves on a first-name basis with the reader, and I'll go along) are related authorially to the volume in an indirect, even ancillary way. They are merely the vehicles, the transmitters, the *channels* through whom the beings or powers or spiritual guides who *ultimately* stand behind the book have chosen to communicate their wisdom to those of us who dwell down here, among the ordinary reading public. How do Sanaya and Duane indicate to the reader when they are passing along messages from the other side, when they are not just *writing* but *channelling* the profundities of Orin (Sanaya's guide) and Da Ben (Duane's)? Simple: they present the channelled materials in italics and their own, ordinary ideas in boldface. As Marshall McLuhan might say, the typography is the message. Also,

Sanaya and Duane preface each italicized section with the names of
Orin and Da Ben to make sure the reader knows that what follows
comes from the spirit world.

Now as it turns out, the channelled materials in *Opening to Channel* are similar psychoanalytically (and metaphorically and ideation-
ally) to those aspects of New Age thinking which we discovered in our
earlier investigations of crystals and shamanism. What comes from the
other side is what comes from Catherine Bowman (1992), Melody
(1992), and Michael Harner (1990). The explanation for this does not lie
in widespread divine inspiration but in J. Gordon Melton's (1992, 23)
shrewd remark that "channelled entities develop their variations on
New Age philosophy" for the many "seekers after transformation." As
I suggested a few paragraphs earlier, what the channeller channels
arises *projectively* from the psychic presences of his own inner world,
as opposed to the inhabitants of the supernatural realm. The channelling is simply the "gimmick," the *magical action* through which the
channeller pursues the infantile goal of re-establishing the mirror
relationship, of rediscovering the affect attunement and evoked companionship ("How to Connect with Your Guide") which emotionally
suffused the first years of life. Because this infantile goal supposedly
derives from a numinous, spiritual source, from a channelled entity
who is larger-than-life and associated with wisdom and power, it becomes not only acceptable at the level of the channeller's ego but compelling at all levels of his personality, both conscious and unconscious.
Standing reality on its head, transforming regress into progress, the
channeller declares, in effect, my aims of symbiotic merger and affect
attunement, my longings for evoked companionship, omnipotence,
and narcissistic inflation, are divinely inspired; they come not from my
obsessive hunger for maternal attachment but from the higher powers
of the universe. In the actual words of Roheim (1955, 11–12): "Magic
[is] rooted in the child-mother situation because in the beginning the
environment means simply the mother." Therefore "wishing or manifesting the wish is the proper way to deal with the environment." The
mother "is not only known by the fact that she gratifies the wishes of
the child. In truth, she would never be discovered were it not for the
fact that there is a gap between desire and fulfillment." And then, more
specifically: "Magic originates from the child's crying when he is abandoned and angry; it is not merely the expression of what takes place in
the dual-unity situation, but is also a withdrawal of attachment from
the object *to the means by which the object is wooed*, that is, from the
mother to the word and back again to the mother" (my emphasis).
While the "magical omnipotence fantasy is part of growing up, magic
in the hands of an adult means a regression to an infantile fantasy." It

is from this perspective that we must view the *voices*, the *words*, which the channeller hears and utters: they are "from the mother to the word and back again to the mother." Channelling, in short, is the "means by which the object is wooed," the "means by which the gap between desire and fulfillment" is overcome.

We must also note carefully that channelling involves a magic which transpires entirely *within* the individual practitioner. There are no crystals here, no rattles, no drums, no objective, tangible means to employ in the process. It is the practitioner's *own body* and *bodily manifestations*—his mouth, throat, voice, words—through which the numinous "guide" reveals its behests and its wisdom. This means that the channeller will magically become both himself and another "supernatural" being (the object) in the same psychological moment, or place. As we shall see, not all practitioners feel psychologically comfortable with this arrangement; indeed, some experience considerable anxiety as they strive, in the terminology of Duane and Sanaya, to "open the channel." Allow me to underscore here, too, the omnipotence, the grandiosity, the narcissistic inflation that are available to one through whom supernatural powers make themselves known. The channeller presents himself to his followers or clients (if he has them) as considerably *more* than an ordinary mortal. He is prophetic, momentous, unignorable, surrounded by the glow of divine inspiration. Needless to say, many worldly advantages and opportunities open up for the person who is perceived in this manner by others.

The Spirits Speak

"Welcome to channelling," write Orin and Da Ben most hospitably (and of course in the *italics* of the spirit world). They then get down to the business of inducing the channelling state in the novice practitioner. It goes like this: one begins by "turning his attention inward" so that he may "receive messages from the higher realms" (Roman and Packer 1987, 27). The "channelling space" is "reached" by accomplishing an "internal focus" (27). Some people, Orin and Da Ben inform us from the supernatural realm, "have described this as a state of intense inner listening" (56). One leaves the world of ordinary perception, sets aside all thoughts and ideas, concentrates, and self-induces a powerful *trance:* "Channelling involves consciously shifting your mind and mental space in order to achieve an expanded state of consciousness that is called a trance" (13). It is in this "receptive state" of inward listening, focusing, and concentrating that one becomes the "vessel for bringing through the higher energies" which are integrally associated with—indeed, which are a direct manifestation of—one's guide (13). Thus the trance state is designed specifically to facilitate the connection with the being whose wisdom, power, and *energy* the practitioner will be channelling: "A trance state," declare Orin and Da Ben, "is a state of consciousness that allows you to connect with a guide" (25). It is "somewhat like finding a doorway where you link with your guide" (28). Essential to remember here is that all this inward listening, concentrating, and focusing aimed at discovering the guide is consistent psychoanalytically with the conception of the guide as an *internalized object*, an inward presence or psychological entity. As Orin and Da Ben themselves disclose from the other side, "the wise teacher you seek *comes from within* rather than without" (14, my emphasis). For some people, we are also told (28), the trance state, or channelling state, is so intense that they become "unconscious channels" who do not recall the messages they utter. The trances of others are lighter. "The experiences of most people fall somewhere between deep unconscious trances and alert states" (29). For everyone, however, some sort of *trance* is essential if the *connection* with the guide is to be made.

How does one know when he has in fact entered into a facilitating trance? "When a very clear internal voice tells you things that seem to come from a higher level than your normal thoughts," maintain our spirits (we're in the midst of italics here), "when you are teaching others and suddenly feel inspired, when you feel an impulse to say unexpected and wise [!] things or touch in unusual and healing ways, you may be experiencing elements of how a trance state feels" (Roman and Packer 1987, 26). And then, "trance states feel as if you have suddenly become very wise" (26). Psychoanalytically, we have in this the sensations of omnipotence and narcissistic grandiosity which typically attend the regression to dual-unity, or symbiotic fusion with the object. Trance states may also involve the feeling of "heat in your hands" or "an increase of body temperature." Some individuals experience "sensations along the spine or a band of tightness or energy around their foreheads" (26). During the actual channelling, "the rhythm and tone of your voice may be different from normal, perhaps much slower and deeper" (26). Certain channels have the sensation of "floating in space" (55); others "see lights and colors" (55). But it is when Orin and Da Ben underscore the *alignment*, the *attunement*, that is involved in successfully connecting to one's guide that the psychoanalytic essence of the matter begins to emerge in earnest. These are very rich passages: "With a *good alignment of energy fields between you and the guide*, it is possible to go into a trance without a lengthy period of transition ... As you achieve *attunement* and harmony with your guide, the veil between the realms which *separate* you becomes thinner ... As you continue channelling you will be able to feel the *vibratory presence of your guide* as different from your own. Guides have a vibration beyond your normal range of perception ... Your guide will *deepen the connection* as he becomes aware of your ability to *handle his energy ...* Every time you channel there is a deeper and stronger link to your guide" (55–57, my emphasis). And finally, "Most people say, 'I have experienced that feeling before—it's so familiar'" (57). Let's pull these various quotations together now and make a preliminary psychoanalytic picture of channelling, a preliminary psychoanalytic interpretation of our instructions from the beyond.

The novice channeller takes up his "intense inward listening," his "intense inward focusing," because at the unconscious level from whence his most urgent motivation arises he is eager to refind and reconnect with the internalized caregiver of the primary years (the object). In the syllables of our supernatural masters, Orin and Da Ben, the entity one seeks emerges "from within" (Roman and Packer 1987, 14). By inducing a deep, meditative trance, by entering into a kind of self-hypnotic dream zone, the novice channeller shuts out the external world so that his entire organism, his entire being, his body and his mind, may be directed toward the inner realm where the object—or, better, the fantasied version of the object—resides. The channeller's self-induced trance is pure, unadulterated regression. He is seeking dual-unity; he is seeking re-attachment to the magical, caretaking figure with whom he was *entranced* early on, the figure who induced *in him* the omnipotence, narcissism, and symbiotic fusion of the mirroring period. At the level of conscious processes, of course, all this is dubbed simply "attracting your guide" (53). To facilitate the re-attachment to the magical caretaker, or, alternatively, to facilitate the successful operation of the trance, the channeller must strive to "align" his "energy" with that of his guide; he must work to create an energetic "attunement" through which the "separation" between his "realm" and the "higher" realm of his guide will disappear (57). Here, the novice channeller is psychically and emotionally orienting, adjusting, squirming, as it were, to re-locate the affect attunement with the object that he enjoyed during the early time; he is striving to re-attain the *energetic, vibrational* relationship through which the sweetness of mirroring and merger came to him toward the inception of his existence. In a word, he is after the old, magical *wavelength* of dual-unity. "Attuning with vitality affects," writes Daniel Stern (1985, 157), "permits one human to 'be with' another in the sense of sharing likely inner experiences on an almost continuous basis. This is exactly our experience of feeling-connectedness, of being in attunement with another. It feels like an unbroken line. It seeks out the *activation contour* that is momentarily going on in any and every behaviour and uses that *contour* to keep the thread of communion unbroken" (my emphasis). This is what is occurring, says Stern, "during an average mother-infant interaction" (156). It is also what is occurring at the trance-like level of unconscious regression as the channeller seeks to "connect with his guide"—the subtitle of the book through which Orin and Da Ben treat us to the benefits of their supernatural wisdom.

The result? Well, if the regression works, if the old, vibrational attunement is caught in its sublimated, onanistic expression, or, in the language of Orin and Da Ben, if the channeller is able to handle the "energy" that comes from the other side, then the guide is inwardly discovered—one feels his presence—which means from the analytic angle, one feels omnipotent, omniscient, precious, *connected*, rescued from the gap of separation and loss, restored to the bliss of primal companionship and merger, the delicious *union* of the before-separation-world. When we hear the successful channeller cry out, "I have experienced that feeling before—it's so familiar" (Roman and Packer 1987, 57), we think to ourselves, of course it's familiar, of course you've experienced it before, during the period of your own infancy and childhood as you attuned vibrationally to the caregiver and basked in the power and narcissism that affectively accompanied the attunement. Your "guide" is "familiar" to you in the same way that "shamanic reality" is "familiar" to the apprentice shaman who, in the words of Michael Harner (1990, 21), "gains access to a whole new and yet familiarly ancient universe." For the fact is, what you are doing emotionally and psychologically in your regression to the energetic guide is exactly what the crystal-user and the shaman are doing in their regression to the vibrational stone and the power animal. The variations are peculiar to each facet of New Age thinking; the theme is the same.

Loving Vibrations from the Beyond: The Thirst for Affect Attunement

Let us deepen this preliminary psychoanalytic picture by noting, first, the manner in which our supernatural presences characterize themselves, and, second, by noting the emphasis they place upon the *vibrational* or *energetic* nature of the relationship between channeller and guide. "The qualities you will find in your guide," go the italics, "are constant love, perfect understanding, and unending compassion ... Your guide is a friend who is always there to love, encourage, and support you" (Roman and Packer 1987, 14). And then, "We, Orin and Da Ben, are beings of light. We exist in the higher realm ... We have great love for you and it is our concern that you grow and move upward as easily and joyfully as possible" (15). And finally, from a later passage (55), "Your guide is totally accepting of you, protecting, caring, supportive, and wise." We do not have to ponder long on such citations to discover their psychoanalytic meaning. The guide is purely and simply the loving internalization of the parent as the child would wish the parent to be: devoted, constant, protective, totally accepting, eager to see the child "grow upward," and above all, ever-present, always there, always (as the expression has it) front and centre in the service of the child's biological and emotional needs. The unconscious cry here is the cry we detect in New Age thinking generally—to undo the separation stage, to deny the reality of the parent's withdrawal from the child's world, to close the gap that yawns as differentiation gets underway (Mahler, 1975), to restore the past as one knew it in the Eden of infant-parent bonding. When Orin and Da Ben disclose to the novice channeller that they are "beings of light" they put the accent overwhelmingly on their *vibrational* or *energetic* essence, for that is what the channeller is seeking, and what Sanaya and Duane are projecting into the made-up figures of Orin and Da Ben—I mean, the *wavelength* of the early period, the *frequency* on which the mother and the baby mirror, merge, and vibrationally exchange their inner selves through affect attunement. This may well be the psychoanalytic significance of *light* in all religious and occult imagistic expression. The guide "assists" the channeller by "boosting" his "energy" (14) because *energy* is what the channeller wishes to be channelling. Indeed, to channel in this context *means* to fill oneself up with the vibrational, energetic traces of the early period as they are elicited concentratively and regressively through the trance which summons the guide in the first place. One is looking for the hum, the buzz, the hit one knew long ago during his "contour activation" with the object.

Thus, in the convoluted projective design that Sanaya and Duane have set up here to induce regression in the novice channeller, "guides are certain beings who are highly skilled at transmitting energy from their dimension into yours" (Roman and Packer 1987, 36), which means psychoanalytically, you, the novice channeller, will not encounter very much difficulty in regressively calling up once again the vibrational attunement you internalized and treasured in your before-separation merger with the parent. Guides are "nearly pure energy" (38), because the symbiotic union of infant and caregiver is predominantly affective or vibrational in nature. "To channel," declare Orin and Da Ben, "you step up your frequency and we lower ours to match. It is not an exact energy match but a complementary one. We create electromagnetic fields in our dimension that are similar to yours in your dimension. As we align both our energy fields, transmission can take place" (45). They continue: "Our ability to match your frequencies for accurate transmission is also important. As you continue to channel we learn by feedback how to monitor our transmissions and you learn how to track our fields more accurately ... We can come through to you only when we set up frequencies that can match yours and thus open the doorway" (46). With a little bit of tinkering here and there, this could be Dr. Daniel Stern (1985) describing *clinically* the way in which mother and baby interact to form RIGs during the first year of life. As for the notion of dual-unity, the notion that mother and baby comprise one existential world during this crucial period, Orin and Da Ben are perfectly forthcoming: "To help you understand this extremely complex matter, imagine that there is only one universe. Think of us not as existing in a universe apart from yours, but in the same universe at a different frequency" (46). Sanaya and Duane, the "authors" of Orin and Da Ben, appear to have as good a "feel" for mother-infant dual-unity as does Dr. Stern, and they *project* that "feel" for us through their manufactured supernaturals right here.

When Orin and Da Ben point out that "guides may appear as either male or female although in the realms of pure energy there is no polarity, so guides are not truly male or female" (Roman and Packer 1987, 37), they not only capture still another crucial aspect of the symbiotic stage, they indicate unmistakably the level at which the projections and reifications of *Opening to Channel* originate. I mean, we are dealing here with *pre-verbal, pre-conceptual* wishes, regressive longings that arise from the realm of symbiotic attunement ("pure energy"). The guide has no gender because in the phenomenology of the infant's experience the object of the early period has none. There is simply no gender awareness *as such* on the infant's part. Indeed, what the infant knows and internalizes during this time are affects, feelings, emotive mutualities. Such empathetic awareness of connection is of course facilitated vibrationally as the infant and the caregiver attune to each other on the affective, energetic level. "We can come through to you only when we set up frequencies that can match yours and thus open the doorway," state Orin and Da Ben (46). And when Orin announces (36) that he "appears to Sanaya as a radiant shimmer of light that sits around her body when she channels," he merely renders the way in which the vibration of the caregiver, the energy of the caregiver, or, in New Age lingo, the "aura" of the caregiver, surrounds the infant's being and wraps him in the delicious wavelength of affect attunement, the frequency of loving symbiosis, the garden of the pre-verbal, before-separation-world. Once the channeller has re-connected himself to the object vibrationally, he can begin to let the object move into him, possess him, *use him* at all levels including of course the egotic levels of cognition and conceptualization; or, alternatively, once the channeller has re-connected himself to his source of inspiration and power, he can begin to *use the object*, which means he can indulge his omnipotence and narcissistic grandiosity. In a word, once the primary *fusion* has been accomplished through the trance, the channeller can begin to *do magic.*

Rebirth Channelling Style: Easy for Some, Not So Easy for Others

The emotionally delicious rediscovery of dual-unity is only the beginning of the novice channeller's supernatural adventure. He does not rest passively on the vibrating breast of the caregiver, as it were; his goal is not merely the nirvanic sleep of psychological regression. On the contrary, the novice channeller wants to be changing the reality in which he exists, wants to be altering the world in a way that fulfils his wishes and, longings, wants to be doing the magic that is the ultimate aim of his activities. As it turns out, the first and the most remarkable of the changes that he strives to bring about is the transformation of the object itself and, concomitantly, the transformation of the separation stage of development (Mahler 1975) and the transitional attachments (Winnicott 1974) which arise therefrom. We've observed these magical processes at work already in relation to crystals and shamanism; the channelling version of the business has a flavour all its own.

The reader will recall the passage in which our spiritual guides, Orin and Da Ben, offer the following insight to the practitioner: "As you continue channelling, you will be able to feel the vibratory presence of your guide as different from your own. Guides have a vibration beyond your normal range of perception, and it may take awhile for you to distinguish between yourself and your guide. You may notice subtle changes in your body, in your posture, or in your breathing. You may observe a subtle change in the rhythm, speed, or pattern of your voice ... Every time you channel, there is a deeper and stronger link to your guide" (Roman and Packer 1987, 55). The emergent psychoanalytic implications here shed light not only upon the nature of channelling but on the nature of mystical, occult, and religious activity generally. As the child engages himself in the mirror relationship, as he undergoes the sensations of dual-unity, as he "locates" the object vibrationally through affect attunement, he is continually *internalizing* his experience. He is taking the object inside of himself as the very scaffolding of his developing personality. As the separation stage deepens, as the object has increasingly to be relinquished in reality, the child relies more and more upon its internalized presence, which becomes *a part of the self*, indeed which becomes the "companion" (Stern 1985, 113–116) that can be "evoked" (ibid.) whenever the child (and subsequently the adult) wishes to "be with" the other. For most of us, luckily, to be alone is also to intuit the inward presence of a companion. The child also *projects*, during the separation stage, the internalized presence of the caregiver into the external and usually cultural objects that surround him, thus creating what Winnicott (1974) calls the "transitional realm" of experience made up typically of stuffed animals, blankets, story-books, and toys, and later, for the adult, of churches, nations, and works of art. The *gap* of separation is filled, then, by inward presences and by cultural (or symbolic) substitutions. Now, as the practitioner's channelling commences, what was *a part of the self* and indistinguishable *from* the self is relocated once again vibrationally and made, in a very special psychoanalytic sense, *external to the self*: the channeller regresses to the realm of vibrational fusion in order to find the object again *in the form of the guide.*

As our supernaturals inform us, the guide "comes from within rather than without" (Roman and Packer 1987, 14), yet the guide *comes, appears, emerges;* in spite of his inward origin, the guide is ultimately apprehended only to the degree that he is *separated off* from the other internalized contents of the subjective realm. In this way, the channeller's *aim* is to "feel the vibratory presence of the guide as *different* from [his] own" (55, my emphasis), and it may "take awhile" (55) for the channeller to bring this about. "Keep pretending that your guide is there," instruct Orin and Da Ben (55), keep trying, and "eventually you will be able to sense your guide as more than your imagination" (55): you'll find him. The channeller is being directed, from the standpoint of psychoanalysis, to regress to the period of dual-unity when the object *was* distinct from the self, indeed to regress to the time when the object was in the process of being *internalized* or *integrated* into the self, and to *split it off again*. He is being directed to *dis-integrate* the integration he formerly achieved when he internalized the object fully and then experienced the object as the "evoked companion," as a self-object no longer distinguishable from the self, no longer *dual* in the accord of a two-way mirroring. Yet every time the practitioner *does* this, every time he splits the object off and then relocates it vibrationally, there is a *stronger connection*. As we are told, "Every time you channel, there is a deeper and stronger link to your guide" (55). And again, "Your guide will deepen the connection as he becomes aware of your ability to handle his energy" (55), which is simply a projective turning around of what the channeller is doing as he strives to "align himself with his guide" (55). Thus one splits off, externalizes, *severs* a "connection" at the same time that one strives to "deepen" a "connection." This curious and somewhat paradoxical feature harbours the psychoanalytical core of the channelling game and of course the psychoanalytical core of its magical bent. Why is the channeller attempting to do this? He wishes to locate the object for a *second time* because he wants to *undo* the object-relation and the corresponding psychological reality that resulted from his *first*, actual contact, from his original experience in the world.

The novice channeller strives (through his trance) to get back to the early period and, this time, to get it *right*. He wants on the one hand to magically transform the original, imperfect object into an angel, into a flawless protector, succourer, and companion with whom he may enjoy all the advantages that attend supernatural assistance. To put it another way, the novice channeller strives to *isolate* the positive, transformational side of the original imperfect object, the side that routinely changed discomfort into pleasure or relief, and to make that side the object *in its entirety*. In the words of Orin and Da Ben (or the *projections* of Sanaya and Duane), "you are surrounded by a powerful and loving being who is totally accepting of you, protecting, caring, supportive, and wise" (Roman and Packer 1987, 55). On the other hand, by externalizing the object, by splitting it off and then finding it again *after* the separation stage has passed, the channeller puts himself in a psychological position *to hang on to it forever in its idealized form*. Thus does he *undo* the separation stage. Once again in the words of our supernatural helpers, "your guide is always there" (14); your "guide," or "guardian angel," is "with you for a lifetime" (43); "your guide is always present when you call" (59). Orin and Da Ben also declare on this page (59), "We experience no time between our sessions with you. To us, there is no start or stop, but only a continuous thread consisting of our time together." We may note here that psychoanalysis finds the origin of the time sense in those periods of frustration and anxiety when the neonate is longing for the caretaker's ministrations or coping with the caretaker's real or imagined absence (Hartocollis 1974). In this way, what happened in the past as the infant and very young child internalized the flawed, ambivalent, inconsistent caretaking presence, and then *lived* with it inwardly as a part of the self, *is erased*. The separation, loss, loneliness, rejection, and pain of one's real, actual life are *denied* as the split-off, angelic guide is *re-internalized* to become the foundation of one's character. The novice channeller will rise from his ashes, as it were, a shining New Age thinker, freshly blessed. No longer will he have to make do with mere feelings of evoked companionship: he has the real thing. No longer will he have to put up with the limitations of his human nature: he is assisted by a powerful divinity and may achieve *all* his goals, whatever they are. No longer will he have to endure living in the gap left by the withdrawal of the caretaker: the caretaker is back. How does that old song go, "Love is better the second time around"?

The novice practitioner's rediscovery (and re-internalization) of the good object as the "guide," as the "guardian angel" (Roman and Packer 1987, 43), is New Age channelling's version of *rebirth*. One is born again, and this time into a perfect psychological world where the good object enfolds one forever. The channelling clients of Sanaya and Duane, newly hooked up with their guides, "feel as if they have just arrived on earth" (160). A "whole new world opens up for them" (160). It is "as if they are seeing the world for the first time" (159). "Enjoy the process of getting to know your guide," advise Orin and Da Ben; "you are like a child learning to walk" (200). Sanaya's own biographical description of her connection with Orin captures the matter unforgettably, particularly in regard to the guide as the transformational object who changes the world back into its prelapsarian mould (we will soon examine Sanaya and Duane's personal experiences in full): "When Orin comes in," states Sanaya (105), "my whole view of reality changes. I feel an incredible love and caring for others. When I see people through Orin's eyes, they are wonderful. To him people look like unique, beautiful, and perfect creations [Hitler? Stalin? serial killers?]. He sees each person working as hard as he or she knows how and growing as fast as he or she can. Through Orin's eyes everything becomes positive [the Inquisition? the Holocaust?] ... He will show people what they are learning and explain how they will be more powerful and evolved by going through those experiences." Pollyanna herself, one may safely say, could hardly keep up with Sanaya when it comes to finding good (that is, the good object) in everything. Orin "comes in" and, presto-changeo, it is paradise regained.

Once the novice practitioners have experienced Edenic perfection, once the regressive hit of wholesale denial has seeped into their minds and emotions, they want nothing else. Feeling "letdown" as their "trance" subsides, "they don't want to come back" (Roman and Packer 1987, 158). For "back" means the after-separation-world, the gap, the fall, ordinary awareness, the good and bad contents of one's inner realm—in short, *reality*—the very thing their channelling activity has set out to erase. No matter that one has sacrificed his rational faculties in the accomplishment of all this; no matter that one is denying, negating, expunging the actuality of his participation in the world; no matter that one is throwing away the experience, the knowledge, the pain, the suffering that makes him fully human, indeed that forges him as a *person*, puzzling, complex, perhaps tragic; no matter that one has stood his psychological universe on its head and gravitated, to a greater or lesser extent, toward *delusion*. Because having the good object forever means having symbiosis, omnipotence, and unlimited narcissism forever, the practitioner is willing to make the move; he is one for whom anything goes; that is, when a magical transformation of his existence is on the line.

According to Sanaya and Duane, things proceed smoothly for the "majority" of those who choose to play the channelling game (Roman and Packer 1987, 163). They "start off verbally connecting with their guides and just keep improving and strengthening the connection each time they channel" (163). Some practitioners, however, run into problems, and it will be instructive for us to look closely at a couple of instances.

"A woman artist who ran a successful fashion design company," we are informed (Roman and Packer 1987, 150), "came to learn channelling to open her creativity. Her biggest fear was that she would lose control or be taken over by the guide. She was very independent and strong-willed." Our authors continue (151), "She tried very hard to do everything the right way at the course, and yet a part of her was holding back, worried that her guide might take her over and control her. She was afraid of losing her identity and being 'swallowed up' in the guide's identity . . . She was in a quandary; she was afraid of being controlled." Well, what happened? We learn the following: "She reported several months later that she had some very successful channelling experiences . . . and had more confidence in accepting that her guide was really present . . . She says that, bit by bit, she is trusting her guide more, although she still wants to make certain that she is in control of her own life and not dependent on her guide. After she receives her guide's advice she checks it out very carefully with her own inner guidance, and only acts on it if it feels right at a deep level" (152). Having regressed through trance to the early period, and more, having attempted to split off and project outwardly the object that was originally integrated into her personality through the internalizing process, this "artist" brings home vividly the psychological dangers of channelling, New Age-style.

To go straight to the heart of it, she is in danger of losing the autonomy, the independence that she has achieved through her successful negotiation of the separation stage. She struggled early on to *differentiate* herself from the object, to get separate, to escape the object's control so that she might live her own life and not that of another. She moved toward the cultural realm, the realm of *art* and religion, and she found there transitional substitutions which permitted her to maintain a certain emotional connection to the caregiver at the same time that she worked out a style of existence for herself. She was "on her own." Now, striving to connect with her "guide," indulging in wholesale regression through her trance, she risks re-establishing the old dependency that she worked so hard to relinquish; she risks returning to the old symbiosis, the old psychological merger, the old system of dependent, inward control out of which she formerly *grew*. It is as if a part of her is saying, I can't make it on my own; I want my big, idealized version of the caretaker, my "guardian angel" on whom I may depend for assistance forever; let my infantile wish come true! And it is as if another part of her is saying, nonsense! What Sanaya and Duane have on their hands here (*in* their hands?) is a woman who struggles mightily against her own regressive proclivities, who doesn't *want* to return to the orbit of the object, who senses the danger of channelling and works to extricate herself from her developing delusion. Anxious and ultimately *confused*, she is paying the price of dis-integrating her character, of re-opening an agonizing conflict that had already been successfully resolved.

The question arises of course, *had* it been successfully resolved? Is not this artist's involvement in channelling witness to the boundary issues (i.e., issues of distinguishing self and other) that remain alive in her personality? Perhaps. Indeed this may well be a general, underlying feature of the individual's interest in channelling as that interest begins to express itself. Yet what Sanaya and Duane have to offer toward the resolution of such a conflict is precisely the opposite of what the individual requires. Analytic understanding along with sharper and more confident *differentiation* from the presences of the inner realm is what is called for; not, of all things, a regressive, dependent, semi-delusional re-blending fraught with magical expectations.

The second instance may not be quite as dramatic as the first but it is no less instructive. "A sophisticated, well-educated woman came to learn to channel because she felt that she had been guided to do so by a whole series of events," report Duane and Sanaya (Roman and Packer 1987, 149). "She said that two years ago she was a firm disbeliever in phenomena like channelling, but now she was eager to make the connection. She was quite concerned, however, that she might be the only one who wouldn't connect with a guide. When her guide was instructed to come in, she reported that she didn't feel anything." Sanaya and Duane go on (149): "Through Da Ben, Duane could see that her guide was fully present in her aura. Sanaya channelled Orin, who talked to her, as it was apparent that she was intellectualizing about the process and blocking her ability to channel. [Thus do

Duane and Sanaya work on the client.] She kept reporting that after every sentence spoken in a voice other than her normal one a part of her would say, 'That's not really a guide, it's just me' ... Although at the time of channelling she sometimes felt that she might have a guide, when she came out of trance she again doubted that it was real. *Her mind was standing in her way*" (149, my emphasis). And finally we have this: "She called several months later to report that she was feeling physical sensations while channelling and was admitting, even to herself, that she was connecting with a guide. A year later she still reports doubts and says she has not channelled as frequently as she hoped she would ... She says she is still working with her doubts" (150).

Sanaya and Duane have captured for us an individual whose good, strong sense of reality stubbornly impedes her regression. Perhaps less immersed in boundary issues than the "artist" at whom we just glanced, this "sophisticated, well-educated" woman tries and tries to "connect," yet keeps saying to herself, this is *me*, there is no "guide," or, in psychoanalytic terms, I'm just projecting, fashioning a psychic entity out of my own inner world. Duane and Sanaya (through their made-up supernaturals, Orin and Da Ben) work hard on their client, trying to break her down, or bring her over, but she resists. When our authorial reporters observe (149) that "her mind is standing in her way," we suppress our laughter and declare, you bet it is! For it is precisely this woman's "mind," her good perception, her sense of reality, her healthy, no-nonsense attitude toward the world around her, that keeps her from sliding down toward delusion, toward the "spiritual entities" with whom her instructors go about chatting out loud on a daily basis. Indeed it is precisely the sort of "mind" this woman has that comprises the *enemy* of channelling, and of New Age thinking as a whole: it must be gotten rid of, or set aside, so that infantile wishes can get going, so that "higher" (read regressive) faculties can take over, so that unconscious agendas may come into play. Thus we have before us here another confused, troubled soul whose solid perceptual grounding or, as the idiom has it, whose "grip on reality" is being *undermined* by her association with people bent upon substituting their projections and magical wishes for the actualities that surround them. Yet this "sophisticated, well-educated" woman's "doubts" are by no means exceptional among channellers. As Duane and Sanaya inform us, "By far the most common initial block people have is the fear that it is not the guide who is speaking but themselves ... People who have continued to practice channelling have eventually been able to feel the difference between themselves and the guide" (Roman and Packer 1987, 155). In other words, when people are asked to split themselves up, to projectively externalize inward contents, to dis-integrate, to put the object back *out* there after making it a part of themselves, they have problems, or, as Duane and Sanaya put it, "fears." They don't *want*, at least in a part of themselves, to *do* this at all. That they eventually can, that they eventually do find their "guide," that they eventually do get hooked on this rigmarole, merely speaks for the power of the infantile wish, the unconscious, regressive longing for symbiosis, omnipotence, and narcissism, the second coming of the caretaker in perfection ever-lasting. It may also speak for the commonality of boundary issues among intelligent (and unintelligent) adults. For Sanaya and Duane, of course, such a second coming is good, not bad; it attests to "spiritual progress," not psychological regress. This is what makes their game so disturbing, and, for some, so dangerous.

Conscious Motivations, Unconscious Implications

The clients of Duane and Sanaya, when asked why they have chosen to channel, do not, obviously, make reference to their unconscious aims as we have described them in our psychoanalytic context. Thus the questions arise: What do these people offer in the way of explanation? Might that be of interest to us here?

"Many," write Sanaya and Duane (Roman and Packer 1987, 141), came to channelling "in a period of personal transition, leaving long term relationships or thinking about leaving them, or quitting jobs they'd had for years and moving on the new areas" (141). "One woman had tears streaming down her cheeks. All morning she had been clenching her hands and reporting trouble relaxing. She said her boy-friend had just broken up with her and that all week she had been hav-ing strong feelings of being abandoned, rejected, and not being good enough. She had wondered whether she would find a guide because she didn't feel special or deserving" (144). "Many were successful," con-tinue our authors (141); "they had achieved their goals and gotten what they wanted, and still had the feeling something was missing in their lives." They were experiencing "large internal shifts" and "question-ing things they had taken for granted" (141). Still others "had read the Seth books by Jane Roberts and wanted to be able to connect with a higher wisdom and intelligence themselves" (141). As soon as these people "decided to learn more about channelling," declare Duane and Sanaya (141–42), "one coincidence after another began reinforcing their decision. Only days later a book on the subject would come their way, or a friend would give them additional information ... It was as if some unseen force was directing them ... Over and over again people spoke of being on a quest they hadn't consciously chosen." And when the channelling actually commences, when the guide is actually discovered, feelings of uncanny coincidence give way to feelings of transformation. The world looks bright and new (159); the sense of "something missing" fades off (162); fresh insight into intellectual and practical issues emerges (146). As Sanaya and Duane express it in relation to one particular client: "When she made the link with her guide she felt as if she had come home" (158).

We cannot make of all this a precise, rigorous theory—that is, unless we force such soft, informal "data" into our psychoanalytic framework. Not only might all three of the motivational factors at which we have just looked be working in particular individuals to varying degrees of intensity (a person, for example, may be reacting with grief to the loss of a relationship, feeling considerable "free-floating" anxiety, and experiencing the urge to prophesy, all at the same time), but there may well be, and undoubtedly are, ten thousand other consciously announced and idiosyncratic reasons that bring people to the channelling parlour of Duane and Sanaya. At the same time, such loose, informal "data" do permit us to make a few psychoanalytic suggestions that may turn out to be useful.

We have, first of all, people in *crisis*, people who have lost or are about to lose relationships or jobs, people for whom separation, divorce, or unemployment looms, people who are undergoing the grief and the anxiety that typically attend such painful change. Daniel Stern (1985, 116) writes of "evoked companions" that "never disappear. They lie dormant throughout life, and while they are always retrievable, their degree of activation is variable. *In states of great disequilibrium such as loss, activation is very manifest*" (my emphasis). Our individuals in crisis or "disequilibrium" here are unable or unwilling to make do with the evoked companionship available to them in their ordinary consciousness. Channelling draws them because it offers not to "activate" the old "companion" but to create a new idealized and projective version of the caretaker with whom *direct and powerful contact can be made in the now of the crisis*. In New Age terminology, it offers a *rebirth* in which the object not only achieves perfection but is actually *there*—directly present, directly accessible forever. This is "activation," which conjures up *the entity itself*. This is "activation" as delusion. The novitiate in crisis does not fully grasp, at the deepest psychological level, where his being ends and external reality begins (the boundary issue).

Second, we have ambitious, goal-directed individuals who have fulfilled their aspirations and who still have the feeling that "something is missing." This group of potential channellers includes, in a manner of speaking, everyone. I mean, our postmodern, capitalist world contains countless millions of people who cannot live by bread alone. Their material success is unable to provide them with an inner satisfaction sufficient to gratify the self in its entirety. So broad and multi-motivated is this group that it defies monistic analysis, yet I believe I can say with impunity that it consists in some measure and probably in significant measure of individuals who are coping with the legacy of the separation stage. What is "missing" for these folks is quite simply the transformational bliss and perfection of the before-separation-world, the original symbiosis of caretaker and infant whose relinquishment created "the basic fault," the gap, the wound, the inner emptiness and disappointment that no material substitute can ever take away. Again we must be careful of generalizing, but many people who come to channelling in search of the guide, the all-loving, all-protecting angel of symbiotic rebirth, are people for whom the pain of early separation and of the related demand (both biological and social) to go off and be on one's own has never subsided. For these people something will *always* be missing because nothing can ever take the place of the original Eden with the original caregiver at its centre, among the blossoms. They come to channelling *to fill the gap directly*, to get the original Eden *back*, the original caregiver *back*, both of course in an entirely idealized and gratifying form. A measure of this, I suspect, is at work for *all* who come to channel, and for some it is a sizeable measure indeed.

Third, we have individuals who are attracted to channelling for its prophetic flavour, its association with arcane and esoteric knowledge, its promise of supernatural power and wisdom. These are the "readers of the Seth books by Jane Roberts," and we sense in their quest a narcissistic thirst for all-encompassing sagacity, a swelling toward the *omniscience* which is a direct outgrowth of the *omnipotence* that the infant experiences through his interaction with the caregiver. The channeller's putative connection to higher, immortal entities and mighty, spiritual beings (the guardian angel) is a regressive screen for reunion with the omnipotent object of the early time, the gigantic and limitless parent with whom the neonate and very young child merged and identified for many impressionable months and years. With its grandiose and magical claim of offering the practitioner a direct line of communication to the transcendent realm, channelling transforms its followers into little individual popes, into very special, numinous persons who can easily reap the egoistic reward of other people's regard: just look at him/her channelling down the voice of heaven itself; just listen to the mysterious, spiritual powers speaking through his/her throat. What a fantastic man! What an incredible woman! Awesome! It would appear that Sanaya and Duane have a good number of such characters among their motley clientele.

The sense of uncanny coincidence or, to use the Jungian buzzword, "synchronicity" that infuses novitiates as they make up their minds to channel marks the reactivation of the transformational object in the unconscious. We went into this earlier, but another word or two on the subject might be a good idea now. In what can be termed the transformational phenomenology of the infant and very young child the following routinely occurs: baby is hungry and cries out for food when, lo and behold, here comes mother to relieve him; what a synchronicity! Baby is wet and uncomfortable; he needs to be changed; lo and behold, here comes the caregiver with a fresh diaper, just at that *time*! Because infancy is consistently transformational, and because the caregiver is exquisitely sensitive to the infant's requirements, it (infancy) appears in the phenomenology of the neonate and very young child to be loaded with happy, meaningful coincidence, indeed with the sort of coincidence which tells the baby that he is in a special and magical relationship with the world. His needs and desires are miraculously met, over and over again, by the "apparition-like" appearance of the mother (Bollas 1987, 33). As our novice channellers approach their return to the object, as they gravitate toward the appearance of the guide—the numinous angel who is to transform their lives—this early material and this early phenomenology resurface: one uncanny, coincidental, synchronous thing happens after another, and there is *meaning* in it. A person decides one morning to channel and, lo and behold, he spies that very afternoon a book in a shop window that deals with channelling! A person contacts Sanaya and Duane with an eye to signing up and, lo and behold, he discovers a moment later that a TV show about Shirley MacLaine is on that very evening! It all *means* something. Fate is speaking. The external world is hugely bound up with one's own personal agenda. What it *really means*, of course, is regression and magical thinking, the psychological return to the time of transformational "coincidence" (simple maternal care) when one existed at the centre of the mother's universe and took that universe for the whole of reality.

As for the novice channeller's sense that some "unseen force" is directing him, that he is on a "quest" he has not "consciously chosen," it speaks, obviously, for the infantile unconscious pressing forward with its agenda, urging its special needs, its wish for symbiosis, omnipotence, and narcissistic inflation, its desire for the restoration of before-separation reality. And when the guide appears, when the succouring, supportive angel actually becomes manifest, the "spiritual" transformation itself occurs: the world is bright and new, a matrix of hope and wonder; the gap is gone, the nagging, awful sensation that "something is missing." Loaded with inspiration and insight, the novitiate has the sensation, as one of Duane and Sanaya's customers puts it, that he is "home" at last (Roman and Packer 1987, 158).

As Sanaya and Duane spell out for us the rewards and achievements of their successful clients we appreciate more fully why people take up channelling, or "what's in it" for these "seekers after transformation," to use J. Gordon Melton's (1992, 23) apt expression. We have indicated this all along, of course, from the psychoanalytic standpoint, and it is time now to see how the words of Duane and Sanaya support our theoretical context. Successful channellers, declare our authors (Roman and Packer 1987, 182), "bring more light into their cells," alter "the molecular and cellular structure" of their bodies as they "open" to "higher vibrations" (the regression to affective or vibrational attunement, recapturing the affective wavelength of the mirror relationship, the "thrill" of rediscovering the object); they find themselves (187, 193) experiencing sudden, "deep insights" and "new levels of wisdom" (the restoration of infantile omnipotence); they "radiate more light" (203) and "begin to attract people" (the narcissistic glow of the caregiver shining on the neonate during the early period, here restored by the delusion of the "guide" or "guardian angel"); no longer do they "struggle" with the problems of "life" (95), as the "guide" is there to assist them at all times (symbiotic re-attachment to the parent, as well as narcissistic empowerment); they are protected (188) from "crisis or upset" by the unfailing ministrations of their "guide" (symbiosis and omnipotence); they experience "peace," "contentment," and inward satisfaction (158) with things generally (symbiosis); the numinous guide at hand, they find that life is fulfilling and rewarding (201) just in itself (the young child's contentment simply to *be* with the caregiver); they have a sense of being "at one with the universe" (172, 195), unseparated, fused (symbiosis projected onto a grand scale); and finally (167), many undergo the "telepathic" sensation of being "linked" to others, "even miles apart" (omnipotent projection of affective or vibrational attunement in the effort to create a symbiotic environment). These rewards and achievements obviously reflect the age in which our channellers are living and remind us of Melton's (1992, 23) observation that "channelled entities" today "develop their variations of New Age philosophy"; the "only criteria for their value," states Melton (23), is "their internal consistency and their ability to resonate with the audience of seekers after transformation." Had Genghis Khan channelled a thousand years ago he would presumably have discovered more effective ways to subdue and torture his enemies, as opposed to "feeling at one with the universe." In our fragmented, postmodern world of computers, urban sprawl, and divorce courts one gets peace, protection, telepathic union with others, and a better sense of self.

Sanaya and Duane Open to Channel

Sanaya

As our authors work toward their prophetic pronouncements on the future of humankind, as they near their philosophical arguments for the authenticity and validity of channelling, they treat us to a vignette of their own personal experiences, their own "opening to channel," their own "connection with the guide" (Roman and Packer 1987, 127–35). Let's explore this material for a few moments, focusing a psychoanalytic light upon it at what I will judge to be the appropriate, significant places.

"People often ask me how I first met Orin, and if I knew beforehand that I could channel," writes Sanaya (Roman and Packer 1987, 127); and then, "I had not really thought of being a channel until I had a reading by a woman, Betty Bethards, who told me I would be a channel by the time I was in my mid-twenties and that channelling would be my life's work . . . I was 18, going to college." Sanaya continues (127), "I finished college and got caught up in practical things . . . I worked in an office for several years, and later started a small marketing business of my own. I loved the business world, but it seemed as if something were missing. About that time Jane Roberts channelled several books by her guide, Seth, which I read and loved. Several friends and I began to get together to discuss the books, and got a Ouija board to connect with our own guides . . . That was how I first met Orin in 1977. Orin came through the Ouija board, announcing he was a master teacher and that we would be hearing more from him as I grew more able to receive him" (127). We come now to a crucial passage: "Later that year, I was in an automobile accident. A car pulled out in front of my VW Bug, causing me to slam on my brakes, which then locked. As my car was turning over on the freeway, time was greatly slowed and doorways seemed to open onto other dimensions. It was as if I could see into the future and know I would be all right. When I ended somewhat dazed and right side up, I knew a shift had taken place inside me. That night I put away the Ouija board and began channelling directly through my voice" (128). Thus Sanaya's brush with death, her sudden glimpse into the void, her confrontation with total separation from everyone and everything—in a word, her *crisis*, precipitates an emergence of what Daniel Stern (1985) would call "evoked companionship." Stern (116) writes (and we have seen these important words before), "Evoked companions never disappear. They lie dormant throughout life, and while they are always retrievable, their degree of activation is variable. In states of great disequilibrium such as loss, activation is very manifest." For Sanaya, time is "slowed" and "doorways" open onto "other dimensions" as she begins to move regressively toward the infantile unconscious and the internalized presence (or evoked companion) which tells her at the feeling level that she will be "all right." Sanaya's "other dimension" is quite simply the "timeless" dimension of infancy, of symbiotic fusion with the other. This reactivational experience, provoked by crisis, triggers in turn an inward "shift" wherein Sanaya "puts away" her Ouija board and begins "channelling directly" through her "voice." In a word, she responds to her trauma by going "directly" after the guide, the "master teacher" for whom she has been vaguely questing for several years. What might be termed the normative evoked companionship as in Stern is, for this woman in this crisis, insufficient. Having stared at nothingness and having "tasted" once again the sublime security of infantile fusion (her uncanny sensation that she will be "all right"), Sanaya wants *more;* and she *gets* more by bringing in her version of the object "directly," through here voice, her *throat.*

When Sanaya channels her guide, he does not come through her in some diffuse, spiritual way, but in a way that actually takes over a specific part of her body. His presence is manifested through Sanaya's physical organism. In this way, the practice of channelling is designed *to get the caregiver back into the body of the practitioner,* to have her/ him dwelling therein once again. During the early period, as we saw in chapter 2, the infant and the caregiver are locked in a kind of "organ" relationship; the mother or mothering figure serves as a symbiotic organ of the baby, and the baby is attached to the mother as a neotenous, dependent facet of the *corpus maternum.* This is the dual-unity situation in which bodily (and egotic) boundaries do not yet exist, in which two human beings are physiological and emotional appendages of each other. It is precisely when this unique situation ends, when dual-unity gives way to differentiation, when one becomes two and the child moves toward the cultural realm, that the self-other polarity of human existence begins to emerge in earnest. And it is precisely this polarity that Sanaya wishes to erase as she strives to channel the "master teacher" through her throat. As for the master teacher's *voice,* it is, of course, the parental voice, the voice (as Sanaya projectively arranges things) of admonition, care, protection, and love. While the infantile ego is content to feel the return of affective attunement at the vibrational level, other, later facets of the personality—facets integrally tied to and emanating from infancy—want communication through words, through the verbal system which is formed in close connection to the parental presence. Channelling offers the practitioner the miracle, the impossibility, as it were, of being with the parent on the infantile level *as an infant,* and on subsequent, more egotically developed levels as well, *all at the same time.* This is the essence of magic: it defeats time. It allows things to transpire as they did *not.* In short, it denies reality. Thus the crisis on the freeway deepens considerably the boundary confusion in Sanaya's character. Such confusion has been there for some time, needless to say (since college, the reading of the Seth books, and the days of the Ouija board). As she rolls over and over on the concrete in her Bug with the traffic swirling around her, the doorway to delusion (or the collapse of ego boundaries) swings wide open.

As it turns out, the first supernatural entity to appear in that doorway is not Orin but Dan. Writes Sanaya, "The ease of channelling ... messages depended upon my energy and the amount of validation and belief I was willing to give to what I was bringing through. By focusing on receiving the first word or two and imagining that they were coming from the Ouija board, I was able to make the successful transition to channelling. Once I received the first words the rest of the message would flow ... The gestures and the voice were a part of Dan, who was speaking through me. Dan explained that he would step-down Orin's energy until I was able to receive Orin's *higher vibration* directly. Orin explained that *my body was like an electrical wire that could only handle twenty volts, and Orin was more like fifty volts*" (Roman and Packer 1987, 128–29, my emphasis). Such metaphors have an unmistakable psychoanalytic meaning which echoes strikingly the context of our discussion as a whole, right back to the material on crystals. What Sanaya is attempting to do through Dan (and subsequently through Orin) is to rediscover the vibrational attunement of the early period, the affective, energetic connection to the caregiver that marks the symbiosis or the mirroring of the before-separation-world. Sanaya is trying to recapture the *wavelength* of dual-unity, to hook up once again with the Big One, the "master guide," the "fifty-volt" powerhouse of infancy, as she discloses her unconscious wishes through her projective imagery. As for Dan, he is a way station on the regressive, delusional road, a figure who represents a temporally later (or vibrationally lower) version of the object, from the age of perhaps three, who is still "humming" with the vibrations of the early years and who can take the subject through mnemic associations to the earlier, more regressive levels, or Orin's "higher vibrations" (remember, higher invariably indicates regressive symbiosis or merger in New Age thinking). Sanaya needs Dan as a "step-down" because anxiety often accompanies delusion ("at first the messages I received sounded like a tape recorder going too fast ... I would lose the connection" [128]), and Sanaya wants to take it gradually, or relatively so. Evidently she experienced some security through her tie to this later internalized object and feels safe in approaching the original, high-vibrational powerhouse through "Dan."

In the end, of course, Sanaya achieves her regressive, infantile goal. "Channelling required tremendous concentration," she writes

(Roaman and Packer 1987, 129), and then in further striking metaphors that capture the psychoanalytic meaning of "energy" and "vibration" not only in this particular instance but in New Age thinking as a whole: "It was like finding a station on TV that I could bring in as long as I held the thought steady in my mind." As the delusion grows so the vibration grows, for that is the aim of channelling, to get to the vibrational time of symbiosis and mirroring, the time of omnipotence and primary narcissism that *transforms* the after-separation-world and restores the practitioner to Eden. Hence (129), "Orin suggested many things to help me increase my vibration and make it possible to receive him" (receive in a triple sense: vibrational transmission, interpenetration, and sacramental merger). Orin proceeds to "counsel" (while Sanaya is in a deep trance) that she "practice" her channelling "with a metronome set at the speed of a heartbeat" (129). Having reached the object through trance, the practitioner can attune to its presence through heartbeat, just as baby attunes to caregiver (and caregiver to baby) by pressing himself to the breast. In this way, Sanaya returns to the fusion of the before-separation-world and more specifically to the "energy," the "vibration," of the object's beating heart. Orin's "counsel" is Sanaya's projective revelation that she wishes to be dependent "upon" him.

At this point Sanaya can drop the less regressive figure of Dan, who accordingly leaves, "saying that his purpose has been accomplished" (Roman and Packer 1987, 129). Orin "takes over from then on" (130) and Sanaya is right where she wishes to be, forever. She has rediscovered her original symbiosis with the caregiver as it is delusionally projected into the "master teacher." That Sanaya wishes to *remain* in her delusion, to undo or deny the traumatic reality of separation by enjoying her regressive merger on a permanent basis, is perfectly clear from the text. As Sanaya herself declares (130), she "prefers being with Orin over anything else." Not surprisingly, then, Orin becomes the centre of Sanaya's life; she "quits [her] other work" and "devotes all [her] time to [her] work with Orin" (131). Yet Orin is not content with Sanaya alone; he enters Duane's life, encouraging him to develop his "clairvoyant sight" (131). In other words, and from a psychoanalytic standpoint, Sanaya manipulates Duane through her delusional behaviour so as to get him also into the orbit of regression where they might share as co-dependents a symbiotic union similar to the one they both relinquished during the painful separation stage.

Duane

"My first experience with Da Ben," writes Duane, "occurred during bodywork sessions. As I worked on people's energy, I found myself doing things that didn't seem to stem from any previous training or knowledge, and these movements and techniques produced amazing results. People found that injuries or pain they'd had for years went away in as little as an hour ... I simply couldn't explain how I was producing these results. I seemed to 'know' when I had truly finished a certain procedure, and *I sensed an unseen presence that seemed to be assisting me* ... This unseen presence was helping me to know what to do, giving me methods of healing I had never been taught" (Roman and Packer 1987, 131–32, my emphasis). Thus does Duane disclose to us his tendency to confuse his own powers, his own capabilities, his own intuitive insights with self-created, projective "presences" in the world around him. We've suggested in the context that such boundary confusion, such splitting and projecting of the internalized object, characterizes psychoanalytically the practice of channelling. Here, the object's influence is revealed through Duane's feeling of omnipotence, disguised as a miraculous ability to heal.

Duane's delusional tendencies increase as he continues in his healing endeavours, but he also has certain misgivings rooted in his educational background and, of course, in his own intelligence. He tells us (Roman and Packer 1987, 132), "As I worked on people's injuries, I realized that I was sensing energy that was in and around the body, but not of the physical body itself. The sense of a presence nearby was growing stronger when I worked, but I rejected the idea of guides and psychic healing because they didn't fit in with my scientific training. Being the scientist, I began methodologically researching every body-work technique I could find—from Eastern to Western approaches" (132). Duane reminds us in some ways of that "sophisticated, well-educated" client (150) who came to Duane and Sanaya's channelling parlour, tried to connect with her guide, and could not get past her "mind," her persistent conviction that *she and only she* was speaking during her channelling sessions, as opposed to a supernatural presence. Indeed, what we have in Duane is a striking "case" of a rational, sincere, scientifically oriented individual wrestling with his own powerful regressive tendencies and experiencing a good deal of confusion, doubt, and discomfort in the process.

Now, it is precisely in the midst of this struggle that Sanaya enters the picture and commences her manipulation. Writes Duane: "A friend who was familiar with channelling and had had readings from many guides gave me the gift [certificate] of a reading with Orin ... That is how I met Sanaya and Orin. The reading really made me re-examine the way I thought about my life. I didn't believe Orin when he told me I would probably quit my job, nor was I convinced that channelling itself was real. I deferred judgment, however, because I hadn't found any answers to my new experiences in bodywork [his near-delusional sense of omnipotence]. As I continued working with Sanaya, I noticed a shift in her energy and aura when she channelled [her delusional re-discovery of vibrational attunement]. I also realized that Orin's love and wise perspective exceeded that of any human being I was aware of. So I found myself faced with many contradictions between what I believed and what was occurring before my eyes" (Roman and Packer 1987, 133). It is not Orin, of course, but Sanaya who is telling Duane he'll probably quit his job; it is not Orin but Sanaya who is declaring that channelling is "real"; it is not Orin's "love and wise perspective" that Sanaya is managing to get through to Duane during these meetings but her own grandiose presentation of herself as perfect parent, complete with narcissistic glow. Thus Sanaya is entering actively into Duane's conflict and striving to get him over to her side. She is looking for something; she is "up to" something. She works on Duane just as Duane and Sanaya later work together on the sceptical customer, moving him into an orbit of regression which confirms their own perspective and establishes their own professional, financial success as channellers.

Duane's conflict deepens: "A series of psychic experiences intensified the growing contradictions in my belief structure. One day as I was running in the hills, everything became moving patterns. The trees no longer looked like trees but like vibrational patterns, and I could see right through them. *I was immediately concerned about my sanity.* Not only did I not want to tell others about it, I didn't even want to admit to myself that these things were happening. A few days later, I pulled up along side a car at a stop light. I glanced over at a woman driver and, to my shock, instead of seeing a person I saw a cocoon of light and energy lines all around her body. I was so concerned that I asked for these experiences to stop, which they did. It was a while before I could bring them back when I later wanted to develop this clairvoyant sight" (Roman and Packer 1987, 133, my emphasis). What we have here, obviously, is not "clairvoyant sight" but a growing nervous breakdown, an eruption of radical dissociation prompted by the widening gulf between Duane's solid, healthy sense of reality and his regressive, delusional tendencies. He wants to put a "stop" to "these experiences" and pathetically asks himself to do so because they *harrow* him in his psychic core, in his very *identity* as a mature, grown-up, independent man. Duane made it through the separation stage (Mahler) into adulthood. He is now very close to restoring an infantile dependency on a projective, supernatural version of the original object. The discordance is tearing him apart.

Once again he begins to "see the energy in and around people's bodies" (Roman and Packer 1987, 133); the "unseen presence" about which we heard at the outset "seems to be all around" him once more. "I was beginning to feel a deep split," he writes (134). "My scientific self would tell me *I was going off the deep end* if I pursued bodywork ... My intuitive self was telling me it could no longer stand going to work and denying my experiences with superconscious reality" (134, my emphasis). And then, focusing for us perfectly the struggle with his regressive, infantile dependency: "I certainly didn't want to turn my life over to a guide; *I wanted to handle it myself*" (134, my emphasis). The crisis is at hand. Duane knows that "something" is about to "happen" (134).

So what does he do? Instead of "handling it" himself he decides "to resolve the conflict" by spending a "whole day with Sanaya and Orin" (Roman and Packer 1987, 134). Sanaya, needless to say, is ready to assist him in the "resolution." Duane writes, "Weeks earlier the name Da Ben had come to me while driving. I heard [it] as if it had been whispered in my ear ... I still wasn't sure I believed in channelling, although I could see the shift in people's auras as their guides came in" (134). This is Sanaya's cue: "That day Orin had me say the name Da Ben and invite the presence closer" (134). The invitation to delusion takes Duane to the breaking point itself: "I began to get hot and cold ... I started seeing Sanaya in colors and layers, and I could see right through her [an ironic observation]. The entity [Da Ben] seemed to come closer and become more real ... My lower diaphram was vibrating uncontrollably [the wavelength of infancy ambivalently restored] and I was gasping for breath [regressive re-birthing]" (134). Such is Duane's anxiety, such is his *terror*, as he stumbles toward "superconsciousness." We see here a man who is losing not only his reason but his grown-up, *differentiated* self, his identity as a separate person, forged in the trauma and turmoil of the early period. And we see in Sanaya, of course, a full-fledged *version* of the original object who is, for her own urgent reasons, pulling Duane into a world of regressive magic that she has already chosen for herself.

Duane's "opening to channel," as he puts it (Roman and Packer 1987, 135), is by no means the end of his story, or his struggle. He writes, "I had to confront all the years of scientific training that had ignored or laughed at metaphysical phenomena. Channelling and guides were definitely not topics one discussed around fellow scientists!" (135). Then, in a crucial utterance, "I knew that *for my own sanity* I needed to find some logical, scientific explanations for channelling so I set about studying it as I had studied science and bodywork" (135, my emphasis). Duane maintains (135) that his "relationship" with "Da Ben" is becoming increasingly "firm," increasingly "trusting," yet one cannot help wondering what the final outcome will be for his precarious "sanity." As for his union with Sanaya, it moves along steadily on the road to regressive, symbiotic fusion, or, in the parlance of the day, co-dependency. Not only do Duane and Sanaya "start channelling together," but it turns out that their guides "seem to know each other" (135). Duane declares, "They often want to talk about the same topics, one taking up where the other left off. We received much guidance that helped us make some major changes in our lives" (135). In this way, the regressive move toward the object of the early period is *between* the channellers. They begin to communicate within a shared unconscious orbit of infantile merger, each becoming for the other the wished-for, caretaking figure of the before-separation-world. It is Sanaya, as parent, who channels Orin for Duane, allowing him to indulge his powerful dependent urges, and it is Duane, as parent, who, by channelling Da Ben for Sanaya, allows her to indulge her longing for the dissolution of ego boundaries and the restoration of infantile merger. Duane becomes Sanaya's master and little child alternately, and Sanaya becomes Duane's master and little child in her turn (imagine them doing this, I mean channelling together with their altered voices). Such a regressive symbiosis, we may safely guess, was Sanaya's unconscious *aim* when she commenced her manipulation of Duane. She saw in him one with whom she might accomplish this purpose, and she went for it. And Duane, needless to say, went for it too, after he began to sense emotionally what Sanaya was trying to do. Duane was interested in re-uniting with the object of infancy quite as much as Sanaya was, in spite of his higher levels of anxiety. Thus Duane and Sanaya manage to purchase their projected version of the caregiver *in three areas simultaneously:* on the inside as "companion" (Stern 1985), on the outside as spirit, and in *each other* as magical substitute. It is paradise regained all 'round!

So goes what we can describe, finally, as the disappearance of Duane, a rational, sensitive, educated, scientifically oriented man with mildly delusional tendencies toward the omnipotence of thought (as it arises from the early identification with the caregiver), who puts in the place of his mature, masculine identity this channeller, talking aloud with spirits and locked in a co-dependent symbiosis with his delusional partner. New Age thinking continually trumpets its transformational potentialities. There is nothing very inspiring about the transformation we witness here.

Philosophies and Prophecies:
A Few Closing Remarks on *Opening to Channel*

It is Duane who takes up the philosophical challenge, presumably because of his "scientific training" (Roman and Packer 1987, 132).

What he gives us, I am sorry to say, is "more of the same"; that is, more of the intellectual lameness and naïvete that we experienced in our crystal and shamanic contexts. Duane writes, "Proving that guides exist and that the process of channelling is valid presents a number of far-reaching difficulties. We have learned that, *in the end, the proof of anything is whatever constitutes proof to the individual . . .* We accept things in our lives every day as proven without examining the underlying assumptions . . . *We accept the existence of atoms without ever having seen them ourselves . . .* We accept it without asking for proof . . . Ultimately, our own experiences as individuals mean the most to us" (204–5, my emphasis). Here is the familiar, persistent New Age theme of *anything goes* dressed up in still another individualistic costume. If the "proof of anything" is "whatever constitutes proof to the individual" then we have no general, *communal* need, no need as a *society* searching for intellectual integrity, for arguments, or proofs, or methods, or ideational frameworks of any sort at all to begin with. Why is Duane even writing this? If an unfamiliar and mysterious light in the sky "proves" the existence of UFOs to *me*, well, there's an end to it. My proof is just as good as yours because my proof constitutes proof to *me*. It all boils down, by the assumption that underlies Duane's position, to a subjectivity so radical and uncompromising that it simply corrodes proof and method, even *thought itself*, away to nothing.

True, we accept the existence of atoms without ever "seeing" them, in the usual sense of "seeing." For Duane, this means analogously that we can accept the existence of guides, and guardian angels, and all manner of supernatural entities whom we also cannot "see." Duane fails to mention, of course, that an enormous amount of indirect empirical evidence has been brought forward for several decades which establishes irrefutably the existence of atoms (or quanta) on the concrete, physical, experimental level where such existence can be tested and re-tested to the heart's content. Just ask the citizens of Hiroshima about the reality of atoms. At the same time (Duane doesn't mention this either), there is no direct or indirect empirical evidence of any kind whatsoever that can be tested which establishes the existence of guardian angels, spirits, guides, supernatural entities, and so forth. *Were* there such evidence, and were it as empirical and as substantial as the evidence for the existence of atoms (the charts from bubble chambers, for example), we would be living in an *entirely different world* than the one in which we find ourselves right now.

Duane states (Roman and Packer 1987, 205) that channelling "challenges people to examine their beliefs about the nature of reality and offers great potential for expanding mankind's view of what is possible. It brings people in contact with ideas that are on the frontiers of what mankind can 'prove' at this point in its evolution." All of this may be true, of course; channelling may well challenge people to examine their beliefs about reality, and it may hold the potential to expand our views of what is possible; it may also contain "far out" ideas on the "frontiers" of thought. Yet none of this, *none of it*, constitutes an argument for the existence of guides or angels, indeed for the validity of the *channelling* that is at issue here. What Duane is maintaining can be applied to countless other activities and pursuits. Trying to get chimpanzees to read *King Lear* or attempting to turn clay bricks into platinum might also encourage people to examine their beliefs and expand their views. So what? The veracity of channelling is not going to be established by suggesting that it has useful spinoffs. The spinoffs, in fact, become attractive only *after* the veracity is there, or *any* wild-goose chase goes—and I mean goes as in *anything goes*.

Duane brings his philosophical discussion to a close by remarking (Roman and Packer 1987, 206), "I began to realize that although my experiences could not be scientifically explained or proven, they were valuable and, surprisingly, consistent and reliable enough to use. In short, they produced results." And then, "I have stopped trying to prove channelling is real, and now use it in a more business-oriented approach: if it works, use it." The question arises, to what is Duane referring when he writes of his "experiences" and their "results"? Does Duane have in mind his panic attacks, the confusion and doubt which he so graphically described and which obviously continue to plague him, the "clairvoyant sight" which caused him to wonder whether or not he was losing his mind? Are these included? That his "experiences" were "valuable," who would deny it? All "experience" is "valuable," just as all experience produces "results." As is so often the case with New Age thinking, what is supposed to be *thinking* boils down in the end to a series of clichés, commonplaces, old saws. I can't prove it, but I sure got somethin' out of it! Yes sir! Tell me what such a pedestrian position can *not* be applied to? As for Duane's final point (if channelling "works" then "use it," and don't worry about questions of truth), it does indeed speak for "a more business-oriented approach," as Duane phrases the matter. It calls to mind, in fact, the narrow, superficial pragmatism that characterizes modern "business" in its most ignorant and egoistic expression. What Duane is contending here—that validity is irrelevant as long as one gets results—can serve to justify *any* social practice or belief, from TV evangelism to the marketing of snake oil as medicine to the contacting of the dead for the benefit of inconsolable mourners. Who cares whether or not devils exist if believing in them, and I mean really believing in them, keeps one from the bottle? This is, of course, still more of the New Age's *anything goes*. It does not *close* the philosophical issue, as it pretends to do, it simply *abandons* it. It concedes failure and frustration in the process of trying to make its position look respectable to people. But we can also regard Duane's comment as an invitation to lobotomy. It asks us to take our minds away, to remove them, and just *do* things without worrying about their trueness, their grounding in reality, what they *mean*, what they *are*. Duane's comment reminds us once again of that "well-educated," doubting woman (149) whose active, critical intelligence kept getting in the way of her channelling. Well, Duane the channeller, and New Age *thinking* as a whole, isn't going to let *that* happen when it comes to accepting the *actuality* of supernatural occurrences. Such are Duane's wise philosophies on the validity of channelling. We assume their profundity comes in part from his contact with the great Da Ben and the great Orin—guides from the beyond—as well as from his interaction with the other channelled presences visiting in the parlour with him and Sanaya.

Certainly that is where the prophecies of *Opening to Channel* come from. "As all of you think and act in new ways, you are spreading higher, more loving thought forms throughout the world," assert Orin and Da Ben (Roman and Packer 1987, 208). "Form follows thought. Real changes will happen on earth as more and more of you open and refine your channel to higher dimensions and bring that increased light through to your daily lives" (209). Is this not hugely ironic—I mean from the psychoanalytic angle that we have established here? One goes about believing that he is "spreading higher thought forms" when in reality he is spreading regressive, magical thinking. One goes about with the conviction that he is bringing "increased light" into his "daily life," when he is in fact bringing into it wholesale denial, the failure squarely to confront the facts of separation and differentiation from the object. One speaks grandly of "higher dimensions" as he vigorously pursues symbiotic fusion with the internalized caregiver of infancy projected into a supernatural being called "guide" and "guardian angel." Pronounce Orin and Da Ben: "There is a great plan of mankind's evolution, and each of you has a part in it" (209). Maybe there is, but it has little to do, I suspect, with this way of thinking and behaving. Channelling takes us *backwards* to a world of superstition and cultic mumbo-jumbo rooted in the participant's inability to deal maturely with very specific anxieties stemming from life's early stages. It is *acting-out*. It is *regress*, not evolutionary progress. "The golden age of man is coming," announce Da Ben and Orin prophetically (220); "more and more people will be opening to channel" (218); "the time is now for mankind" (217); and then, refining the matter down to the details of what all this means: "There is a continuing step-up in the *vibration* of the earth ... There are many *electromagnetic frequencies* that are just outside of the range you detect with your eyes. Some of you are developing the ability to sense subtle *frequencies* beyond the range of your normal senses. It is in these *frequencies* that you become aware of guides" (218–19, my emphasis). We don't need to be fooled any longer— that is, if we were ever fooled. Psychoanalysis enables us to see these "vibrational step-ups" and "electromagnetic frequencies" for what they are: unconscious, metaphorical expressions of the longed-for affective attunement which characterizes the interaction of mother and baby during the early period, the period that stands (in its idealized expression) directly behind channelling's prophetic vision of the "golden age." I suppose we all have a bit of the prophet in us, so let me make a prophecy here, as we say farewell to Duane and Sanaya (and, of course, to Orin and Da Ben) and move on to the next section of this book: I don't know about the world becoming "golden," but it may become a tad more tolerable when people stop trying to change it through magic and develop the courage to look at it directly and honestly. The only "evolution" that most of us need to concentrate upon at this point in the world's adventure is simply growing up.

Channelling on the Grand Scale: The Universal Masters

In contrast to Duane and Sanaya's *Opening to Channel*, Benjamin Creme's *Transmission* does not come from the realm of immortal guides and angels but from a mortal channeller whose methods are designed to make the will of the cosmos known to the inhabitants of earth. Creme always speaks to us directly, in his personal terminology, or, to use the expression we introduced at the outset, his *point of view* is invariably his own. The sharpest contrast between these texts, however, emerges not from the communicative angle but from the *tone* of the discussion, its *mood*, and above all its *aim*.

For the most part, and with the exception of a few prophetic pronouncements at which we've just glanced, the emphasis of *Opening to Channel* is on *individual* goals. People are encouraged to channel individually, to find their individual guides, to pursue those individual purposes which hold importance for them. One channels because one wants to improve his performance in the marketplace, or increase his wisdom, or discover a more rewarding relationship with his spouse or lover. As J. Gordon Melton (1992, 22) expresses it, "Within the New Age movement, channelling has been accepted and redirected to the goal of facilitating the personal transformation of the channeller's clients ... Private meetings with a New Age channel become more of a counseling session for the discussion of personal problems than the traditional seance which offered the possibility of a continuing relationship with those now dead." *Opening to Channel* is a perfect illustration of Melton's point. Creme's (1992) *Transmission*, on the other hand, gives us channelling on the grand, cosmic scale. The transformation Creme is after has very little to do with one's personal problems; he couldn't care less that one's mate is cold in bed. Creme is interested in the spiritual transformation of the whole planet, indeed the whole universe, and, as we'll see, he believes that his collective (as opposed to individual) sessions are actually in the process of bringing this transformation about, now, as I'm writing this sentence. Freud ([1914] 1971, 54–55) once remarked that philosophers and paranoiacs have in common the tendency to create elaborate "systems." Creme's book calls Freud's comment to mind. The hints of delusion, the suggestions of madness that one detects in *Opening to Channel* swell to arresting proportions here. One reads *Transmission* with a growing sense that its author has broken with reality, that he dwells in a delusional world of wholesale distortion. Again, Duane's "business-oriented approach," as he announces it in *Opening to Channel* (if it works, use it and don't ask questions), while inadequate philosophically, gives that volume a certain practical atmosphere. When one finds Creme (97) declaring that certain heavenly masters (including Christ) are in the process of taking control of the earth's "energy," including yours and mine, and that they are watching us "clairvoyantly" (43) at all times to see whether we are fulfilling their spiritual purposes, one realizes he is in another sort of mental realm entirely. Yet the psychodynamics that underlie *Opening to Channel* and *Transmission* are very similar, and that is what is so remarkable and so fascinating about the matter. Both works are unconsciously absorbed in the *same* infantile aims. Both seek the transformational object and affective (or vibrational) attunement; both long for symbiotic fusion and omnipotence, for the restoration of the before-separation-world. Such aims call to mind, of course, the writings of Melody and Bowman on crystals, of Harner and Meadows on shamanism. The point is, New Age thinking as we have experienced it thus far comprises one sharp outcry in what its adherents perceive to be *the dark*, namely, the after-separation-world, the disruption of symbiotic fusion, the disappearance of mother-infant bonding, of the vibrational mirroring which determines the emotional nature of life's first years. And, needless to say, New Age thinking as we have experienced it thus far seeks to restore through its magical practices the precious, truncated connections. So forcibly, so irresistibly, does all this emerge in Creme that it is, if the reader will pardon my enthusiasm, unforgettable.

Mr. Creme and His Symbiotic Vision

Benjamin Creme is among the most famous and influential New Age channellers, attracting worldwide attention to his lectures and writings (Poggi, 1992). I'm not suggesting that Creme is "popular" in the sense that Jane Roberts and Shirley Maclaine are, but that his work is taken very seriously by large numbers of very serious spiritualists and occultists.

Born in Scotland in 1922, Creme claims that in 1959 he received a telepathic message from his personal master, a member of a celestial hierarchy, telling him that he would play a role in Christ's return. A telepathic link was established with this master enabling Creme to receive precise and current information about the momentous event. In 1974, Creme formed a group to prepare for the coming of Christ (also known as the Lord Maitreya). According to Creme, messages from and contacts with Christ have already transpired. He writes in his pamphlet *The Reappearance of the Christ and the Masters of Wisdom* (cited in Shepard 1987, 13), "There now lives among us a man who embodies in Himself the hope and aspiration of the religious groups as well as the aspirations of the political and economic thinkers for a better life for all ... On July 19, 1977, Maitreya, the Christ, entered the modern world. Since then, he has been living as a member of the Asian community of East London, an ordinary man, not known as the Christ ... A number of TV and radio programmes in which the Christ has taken part have already been broadcast. The Plan was that through media coverage of His public meetings He would gradually become well-known ... As part of a contingency plan, Benjamin Creme was allowed to disclose the Christ's location at a press conference in Los Angeles on May 14, 1977." In spite of considerable interest on the part of the media, however, the Christ has thus far not appeared. Creme asserts that certain "materialistic forces" both "seen and unseen" have been interfering with the appearance, and he has therefore decided to postpone the Second Coming to a later date. There is no disputing Creme's sincerity. He has spent a great deal of his own money and time promoting his message, which appears to stem from the theosophist Alice Bailey whose booklet *The Reappearance of the Christ* also announces an imminent incarnation.

As I have indicated, the work of Creme on which I'll concentrate here is called simply *Transmission,* a title that vividly expresses the act of channelling in the "electrical" or vibrational terms which have engaged us all along. As for Creme's subtitle, it is aptly fitted to our purpose: *A Meditation for the New Age.* Creme's definition of the New Age takes us straight to the heart of his symbiotic purpose, his vision of connectedness, his longing to see all of humanity melded together in one common spiritual bond. He writes (1992, 108), "The New Age is the age of group consciousness, not simply working together as a group, but *thinking and feeling and experiencing together* in group consciousness, *total oneness*. This is unknown to humanity as yet. The Masters of Wisdom, on the other hand, have only group consciousness. *The separate self does not exist* in their consciousness. Working together in groups gives humanity experience in developing that group consciousness ... There is a world out there to save" (my emphasis). For Creme, this is the planet's ideal destiny: millions—nay, billions—of people all existing together in a state of universal connection—connected to each other and connected to the Masters of Wisdom, the higher powers, which is to say connected to the religious or spiritual *version* of the parental object. Reading Creme, one gets the feeling he does not want a single person on earth *out* of this collective tie because that would create in him a reminder of the dreaded separation stage (Mahler 1975), the time of differentiation and commencing autonomy. If and when *everyone* is merged together, Creme can relax. God's "city" will be at hand. All will have been "saved." What Creme calls the "transmission group" is his preferred means for bringing this worldwide merger about. There, the channelling is collective and intense: "When you have a Transmission group as the basis of all activity, you have an *inflow of energy* which is constant. It is like being *tuned in to the electricity* the whole time, so you always have the fire on if you need it" (my emphasis). We note at once of course the emphasis on *energy, inflow, electricity, tuned in*, the ubiquitous New Age metaphors for the unconsciously remembered affective attunement of the early period, the vibrational frequency, the *wavelength* of the mother-infant mirroring. But let's look more closely at Creme's discussion of *energy*, its transmission, its transformational potential, and its origin in his own life. Let's begin at the beginning as we analyze, and savour, these remarkable materials.

The Obsessional Pull of Affective Attunement

"As a child of four or five," Creme (1992, 1) tells us, "I became consciously aware of and extremely sensitive to energy currents; so much so that eventually I could tell when an atomic bomb had been exploded in the Pacific or anywhere else in the world. Across thousands of miles I registered the shift in the etheric currents caused by the explosions. Inevitably, a day or two later would come the report that America, Russia, or Britain had tested a device of such and such a size." From the standpoint of psychoanalysis, what Creme is disclosing may be described as an intense unconscious preoccupation with and emotional interest in the preservation of affective or vibrational bonding, a propensity and a need to exist in a psychological space where uninterrupted regressive contact at the vibrational or affective level may be maintained with the environment generally. As we know, the infant's first environment is the mother, and, as the infant develops, he tends to project that maternal influence onto the world around him. Creme displays at "four or five" (a time of growing separation from the caregiver) a tendency to transform his universe into a version of the maternal figure in her vibrational, affective, mirroring aspect. That is why he finds himself so "sensitive" to "energy currents." Separation makes him anxious. He is continually "listening" to the world around him in an effort to detect (through projection) the wavelengths of symbiotic fusion. When he does so he feels reassured: the original attachment to the object is still there. So great is Creme's need on this score that he eventually creates an elaborate delusional system of cosmic proportions designed to block out, negate, erase, deny the realities of the separation stage. He will *not* be alone, ever.

Creme (1992, 2–3) continues with his story: "Towards the end of 1972, when I was rather in the doldrums and least expecting it, that Wise and Wily One Whom I have the privilege to call Master, pounced. He took me in hand, and subjected me to the most intensive period of . . . training and preparation. For months we worked together, twenty hours a day, *deepening and strengthening the telepathic link until it was two-way with equal ease* [Creme is attempting to re-establish dual-unity with the parental object, or "Master"], requiring the minimum of His attention and energy [the parent's ever-present subliminal awareness of the baby]. He forged in this period an instrument through whom He could work, and which would be responsive to His slightest impression . . . Everything I see and hear, He sees and hears [dual-unity re-established]. When he wishes, a look from me can be a look from Him; my touch, His [Creme as God; omnipotence regained] . . . He Himself remains, in a fully physical body, thousands of miles away . . . He has asked me not to reveal His identity for the time being . . . In March 1974 He gave me a list of fourteen names of people to invite to a talk at my home . . . They all came. I talked about the Hierarchy of Masters . . . and presented them with the following offer: I invited them to take part in a group work in which their occult meditation [channelling] would proceed under the guidance of a Master of Wisdom, in exchange for which they would act as *transmitters of the Hierarchical energies*, thus forming a bridging group between Hierarchy and the disciples in the field . . . Twelve of the fourteen agreed" (my emphasis). Thus Creme needs a *group*; he needs others to sit with him and to act as "co-transmitters" of the "Hierarchical energies," the vibrations, the frequencies, the wavelengths which come from the "Masters of Wisdom" (the parental gods of the nursery projected onto the universe) and which re-establish the original, infantile bond. In this way, what Creme calls a "bridge" is formed between the "Masters" and the "disciples" in the field, a bridge that comprises from the psychoanalytic angle a kind of psychic umbilicus, an unconscious attachment to the objects of the inner realm. Creme's group not only provides him with followers who reinforce and reconfirm his view of reality as symbiotic (the "disciples" want symbiosis too), the group provides him with a measure of actual symbiotic attachment to others in the now of his existence. Additionally, the group gives him influence, power, authority, all of which gratify and absorb the feelings of omnipotence and narcissistic grandiosity that accompany his radical regression to the early time.

"The group was formed in March 1974 to *channel* the spiritual potencies," Creme (1992, 4, my emphasis) goes on: "We met twice weekly, at first, for about one and a half to two hours ... At the same time, the Master gave me a blueprint for building the transmitter-transformer instrument which we use in this work, and which I also use in healing. It is a tetrahedron in form and is based on the principle that certain shapes have inherent energetic properties ... Nowadays we meet regularly three times a week to transmit the energies from Hierarchy for anything from four to seven or eight hours on end ... In June 1974 began a series of ... transmitted messages by Maitreya [Christ] inspiring us and keeping us informed of the progress of his externalization ... Towards the end of 1974 the Master said, 'you must take all this to the public' ... On July 7, 1977, Maitreya Himself informed us that his body of manifestation was totally complete, that he had 'donned' it ... the Descent had begun ... Maitreya had now arrived in a well-known modern country [England] ... Many, many times since ... I have made this announcement but never again with the sense of having ... shared in a great planetary event. The tears of joy on the faces of the group around the table showed that they, too, felt the same ... Their [that is, Christ and the Masters] reappearance will lead us into the Aquarian Age" (4–5). Thus Creme is, as the expression has it, *on his way:* he is re-attached to the Master, he has his group of channelling disciples, and he is ready to change the world, to lead it straight into the Age of Aquarius, "as it is written" (5). Once there, everyone will be connected to everyone else, with Creme at the centre of the gigantic symbiosis, of course. In keeping with his unconscious, regressive longing, Creme is out to transform the earth into a humming, channelling, vibrating mass of worshippers, all tied energitically to the body, the "fully physical body" as Creme (3) emphatically puts it, of the cosmic giant from whom we all derive, Maitreya. So unacceptable to some human beings is separation from the object of infancy, or disruption of the vibrational, affective tie which marks the symbiotic stage, that they cook up the sort of delusional magic (and madness?) we witness here. But what exactly is this instrument, this "transmitter-transformer," this "tetrahedron" that Creme mentions?

We are shown a picture of it toward the end of *Transmission* (Creme 1992, 144), in the Appendix, actually. It appears to be a one-metre-high, four-sided glass pyramid with a chunk of quartz crystal sitting inside on a gilded, disc-shaped pedestal located directly below the pyramid's apex. Creme (61, my emphasis) writes of the thing: "The pyramid was an instrument of Atlantean times. *It was built specifically to draw astral energy ... The instrument which draws mental energy is the tetrahedron.* It does two things: the quartz crystal in the centre blends the incoming energies, and the magnetic field potentizes them [the "energies" emanate from the Master, of course]. The sending is never of just one energy but of several. The instrument transforms the energies downward—brings down the voltage just like a transformer in electricity—but potentizes them at that lower voltage. They are sent out through the gold disc into the world, directed not by us but by the Masters to wherever they are needed, at a voltage that can be used, experienced, and *assimilated by humanity in general ...* The tetrahedron does not itself bring in the energies and it does not ... improve their reception. It does improve the *transmission* of the energies. These come *directly from the Masters to us* through the chakras ... The tetrahedron further transforms the energies, brings them lower than we can, and at the lowered voltage, it gives them in the end a final boost—potentization." When we blend the electrical, energetic, vibrational implications of Creme's term "transmitter-transformer" with his explanatory remarks just cited, and when we take the admixture in the context of his overall symbiotic purpose, we realize the tetrahedron is designed *to facilitate projectively and omnipotently an outflow* of frequencies that will re-create in "humanity" the vibrational bond Creme and his disciples experienced with the caregiver during the period of symbiotic fusion, the period *before separation.* Channelling the Master's "energies" into their organisms, Creme and his followers sit next to their vibrational powerhouse much as the ambitious general sits next to his favourite cannon. Here is the item that will help us do the job. Here is the baby (pat-pat) that will bring about the final victory. With the crystal-bearing tetrahedron's assistance (it's *loaded*), we'll have all of humanity linked up to Maitreya, hooked up to the "vibes" that emanate from his real, divine body. We'll change the whole world into a humming, vibrating version of the first relationship, and then we'll *merge* ourselves with it, creating as Creme puts it (108), "total oneness." Also, the word *transformer* calls to mind our discussion of the *transformational object* as it asserts its influence unconsciously in the regressive wishes of the religious or spiritual adult. Bollas (1987, 14–16) writes, "Not yet fully identified as an other, the mother is experienced as a process of transformation, and this feature of early existence lives on in certain forms of object-seeking in adult life, when the object is sought for its function as a signifier of transformation. Thus, in adult life, the quest is not to possess the object; rather, the object is pursued in order to surrender to it as a medium that alters the self, where the subject-as-supplicant now feels himself to be the recipient of enviro-somatic caring, identified with metamorphosis of the self." And again (15), "I think we have failed to take notice of the phenomenon in adult life of the wide-ranging collective search for an object that is identified with the metamorphosis of the self. In many religious faiths, for example, when the subject believes in the deity's actual potential *to transform the total environment*, he sustains the terms of the earliest object tie within a mythic structure" (my emphasis). And finally (17), "The search for symbolic equivalents to the transformational object, and the experience with which it is identified, continues in adult life." Creme's tetrahedron is intended to assist in the accomplishment of precisely such purposes: through it, the entire surrounding world will reflect "enviro-somatic caring" (remember, Maitreya's is a *real* body); Creme and his followers will "surrender" meditatively, as "supplicant" channellers, to the "object that alters the self"; they will "sustain the terms" of the "earliest object tie" within their "mythic structure." There is no delusion *in infancy* when the neonate perceives the caregiver as a "transformational process." She/he *does* transform the baby's world, over and over again. The delusions arise when the adult who refuses to accept the fact that symbiosis is over goes about changing the items in his environment into versions of the original transformational figure. It is sheer projective magic, of course, that allows him to do this.

Transmission Meditation and New Age "Evolution"

Creme develops his metaphysical theory, his "mythic structure," his view of "humanity" and its supernatural destiny in response to a direct question posed in the text of *Transmission* (1992, 7): "What is transmission meditation?" Declares Creme in response, "Transmission meditation is a form of meditation which is also a transmission of energy. We would not be human beings if we did not knowingly or unknowingly act as transmitters of energy ... This is because the human kingdom (as do all kingdoms) transmits energy, albeit in a unique fashion. Whether we know it or not, we are transmitters." He then goes on, in a particularly vivid utterance, to announce that we are essentially "a clearinghouse for energies received from the kingdoms above us. These energies are transformed by passing through us to the lower kingdoms" (7). Thus human existence and the human beings who manifest it are there to facilitate the passing on or passing along of *vibrations*, which Creme calls "energy." Sitting concentratively in our little groups of fourteen people, perhaps with the tetrahedron in our midst, we close our eyes and transmit "vibes." We enter a powerful trance-state, a "transmission meditation" (Creme offers us a picture on page 58 of people who are doing this), and we direct the "energies," the frequencies, the wavelengths of the Master(s) toward the other human beings (and lower creatures) in the world around us, and this is *all* we do—I mean, this is all we do of any real significance. Our chief function on the planet, our chief purpose, is, as Creme (7) says, to be a "clearing-house" for "energies" from "higher" (read regressive or infantile) sources: "We are transmitters" (7). Creme continues a few pages later (11), "In a transmission group you simply let yourself be an instrument, while the energy is put through your chakras by the Masters. You act as a channel through which the energy is sent." What Creme has created here is a *scheme*, an unconsciously cunning *method*, for keeping himself and his disciples (and everyone else if he could manage it) in the dual-unity situation, in the affective or vibrational attunement which characterizes the symbiotic stage and which is relinquished to varying degrees by the developing child only with the most intense reluctance and in an emotional state of genuine shock and trauma (Mahler 1975). Concealing his regressive purpose in the robes of spiri-tual prophecy and supernatural mystery, transforming his infantile aim into religious theory, Creme has set out to undo intrapsychic separa-tion once and for all by returning behaviourally to a condition that dis-guisedly recalls the mirroring period in which mother and baby go about the world as an affectively intertwined symbiotic unit. "There is nothing in all reality but energy," Creme writes (14); "our planet is a chakra in the body of the great cosmic being who ensouls this solar sys-tem" (14); "we live in an ocean of energies" (14). And then, in terms that recall explicitly Stern's (1985) concept of affective attunement, "transmission meditation is a simple *aligning* meditation—the align-ment of the brain and the soul [read object] by the act of holding atten-tion" (11, my emphasis). Finally, reflecting the narcissism, the grandiosity, that accompanies the move toward the internalization of the caregiver, Creme asserts, "This is how we become divine" (14). "Every single one of us is divine" (9). For Creme, then, the vibrational object of the early period is still the whole world, the whole universe, the whole environment, just as the caregiver is for the infant and very young child. The planet earth becomes in Creme's eyes a mere chakra, a mere vibrational hole for sucking in and re-distributing the frequencies which emanate from the parental internalization as that internalization is projected outwardly or "cosmically" into the "great being" who "ensouls" us.

In typical New Age fashion Creme (1992, 8) gives all this an evolutionary spin: "The evolutionary aim is that we shall be bound together by the energy of Love ... Unfortunately, humanity as a whole does not demonstrate this as yet, but in the coming Age of Aquarius we shall manifest the quality of Love ... Humanity will become one." At the conscious level, of course, "evolution" means for Creme and his followers (as well as for New Agers generally) the attainment of spiritual progress, the movement in the direction of the Masters, the "higher" beings of "Love" and "total oneness". At the unconscious level, however, where the emotional realities reside, "evolution" means the promise of reunion with the *transformational object* of the early time (evolution equals transformation, alteration), the one who *changed* the infant's discomfort into relief/pleasure over and over again on a daily basis as part of the symbiotic arrangement. Evolution for Creme and his disciples (who equate *discomfort* with *separation*) signifies the re-attainment of the Garden, the restoration of prelapsarian bliss (universal "Love"), the persistent transformational ministrations coming from the caregiving figure. Thus Creme's evolutionary spin, like his notion of transmission, conceals an unconscious agenda, a regressive purpose that is made palatable to the ego by virtue of its "higher," conscious designation. Long the *enemy* of religious and spiritual practice, "evolution" becomes in *Transmission*, as in all New Age texts, a powerful ally of the author because evolution implies the kind of *change* the author regressively *craves*. Oblivious to evolution from a scientific angle, oblivious to evolution's dependency on the genetic system, oblivious to the conservative, trait-preserving nature of evolution's workings, Creme latches on to the term and uses it in a soft, informal manner that turns it into an emotional promise: the transformational object for which you seek is just around the next psychological corner.

The Master's Eye, the Invocation, and Om

As noted, Creme considers the group meditation, or channelling session, to be the ideal means of achieving his evolutionary, transformational purpose. He writes, "The beauty of group formation is that more energy can safely be put through a group than through separate individuals"

(1992, 27). As he develops this idea, what might be termed the paranoiac aspect of his thought, also noted earlier, emerges with unmistakable clarity. "Once the group is established," he asserts (29), "the
Masters know exactly who you are and where you are. They see you
clairvoyantly. They then send the energies through the group. It is a
highly scientific process. They know what the group can take. They
know which particular rays or types of energy make up the group,
which rays are governing the individuals, and the manipulation of
energy is in accordance with that fact. Some people will take one set of
energies and some another. In this way, the Masters can pour Their
energy into the world. They need such transformers to do it." And in
another place (43), "The Masters know when a group is ready to be used
as channels ... Once the group is formed, the Masters know the individuals connected with it. They can see you clairvoyantly. They see
exactly the state of the centres, chakras, the light that each individual
and therefore each group radiates, and They can find you." Like the
vast majority of paranoiac systems, Creme's is one in which the subject
is watched, observed, kept track of, and judged by the all-powerful,
unseen "Masters" who are themselves unreachable in any ordinary
sense. One is reminded of Tausk's (1919) classic paper on the "influencing machine" which stands centrally behind the psychoanalytic literature on paranoia and which offers the reader the fantasy of a deeply
disturbed patient who feels his existence is being controlled by a complex mechanical device that works upon him secretly from a distance.
Yet paranoiac fantasies and the systems they contain usually reveal to
the investigator an aggressive, harrowing component, a sinister, perhaps life-destroying agency which transforms the disturbed carrier of
the fantasy into a pathetic, helpless victim. Creme's system of
entranced channellers gathered together around the tetrahedron to
receive and redistribute to humanity the energies of the Masters,
including Maitreya, or Christ, appears to be, by contrast, a rather
benign sort of thing, loaded with sweetness and light, with the infinite
"Love" of supernatural spirits. The Masters are "good," the channellers
are "good," and their aim is "good." What sort of system is this, then?

I believe the answer emerges from the following related citations:
"When the Masters measure advancement, they look clairvoyantly
into the world. They do not look into your thoughts to see if you are
thinking good or bad thoughts—not at all. They see an individual's
inner light, a dim light or a bright one. *When They see a steady, brilliant light, They take an interest in that individual.* They look at the
state of the centres to assess his or her exact point in evolution. They
can tell at a glance which centres are open or activated ... They can
then evaluate the individual accordingly. In Transmission Meditation,

the Masters choose the amount of energy for a particular person and they send it through you. You can understand how potent the transmission of energy from Them can be" (Creme 1992, 77, my emphasis). And again: "The coming together of the group adds a dimension of vitality to the Transmission ... It adds a dimension to the identity of the group as a group. It contributes to the growth of the group soul ... *It creates a bond of love among the group members* ... It is very important to come together in this way, from the energetic and psychological point of view, *for the nurturing of the group as a unit* ... Transmission Meditation is a pure act of service to the world" (36–37, my emphasis). What Creme has fashioned here is a kind of *ideal familial situation* which offers each individual the opportunity to successfully "plug into" (37) the loving vibrations of the projectively created parental figures. Each of Creme's practitioners can do his very utmost to become the Master's *favourite* with nothing but his own individual desire, longing, *wish* to determine his divine, supernatural status in the Master's eye, which, as Creme (77) says in a fascinating image, "can tell at a glance" who among his devoted, serving children is radiating "brightly, steadily, brilliantly" (77). Thus each member of Creme's transmission group can strive *successfully* to interest the Master, to beget his attention, and ultimately of course to beget his "potent" (77) vibrations, his "potent transmission of energy" (77). Each member can strive *successfully* to be the best, the most devoted and concentrated channeller, the one who draws unto himself a huge, humming portion of the Master's frequency, for in Creme's cosmic system of supernatural observation, *only the Master* can see and judge the individual, only the Master knows where each individual channeller belongs on the scale of dispatched vibrations: the channellers cannot see, the channellers cannot know *what is going on amongst themselves; they cannot measure each other* in relation to the Master's eye. In this way, each individual member of the group can nourish his private fantasy of parental bonding, parental fusion, perfectly achieved dual-unity with the all-powerful celestial giant, which means of course that the group as a whole can *reverse* emotionally the all-too-common familial situation of siblings striving rivalrously to beget the interest of and the affection from the coveted parental figure (for the "only children" in Creme's group it is either more of the desirable same, the reversal of hated neglect, or the sudden presence of wished-for, loving siblings). All the members of the group become the parental favourite, the actual parental favourite, *simultaneously.* Hence, as Creme says (37), transmission meditation "creates a bond of love among the group members" and "nurtures the group as a unit." All are "saved," all are "chosen," all rediscover prelapsarian bliss as everyone channels together, receives divine vibrations together, and redirects such vibrations in his or her "act of service to the world" (36). And when the *whole world* is doing this, when the *whole planet* is doing this, the whole world, the whole planet, will have been *transformed* into the perfect, loving *family*, with the children bonded forever to the perfect, loving parent (Master). In the meantime, on the way to such perfection, each member of the group can receive from the *other members* the kind of symbiotic bonding and fusion that he craves in his infantile unconscious, the unconscious that got him involved in this regressive, vibration-seeking, affect-seeking, parent-seeking activity to begin with, for when all the siblings are treated equally by the loving, perfect parent there is nothing to interfere with their emotional support of each other. If there is an aggressive, paranoiac aspect to Creme's system in the way in which we usually understand paranoiac thinking, it resides partly in his grandiose intention to see the Master's will take over the world, in his belief that supernatural forces such as Maitreya are actually in the process of doing that, and partly in the implied threat to the unsuccessful meditator (or non-meditator) that he will *not* get very much parental vibration directed toward him.

The efficacy of transmission meditation, Creme (1992, 17) tells us, is increased significantly by two central features of the practice. First, there is the meditator's, or channeller's, prayer, which Creme calls "The Great Invocation" and which goes like this:

From the point of Light within the Mind of God
Let light stream forth into the minds of men.
Let light descend on earth.

From the point of Love within the Heart of God
Let love stream forth into the hearts of men.
May Christ return to earth.

From the centre where the Will of God is known
Let purpose guide the little wills of men—
The purpose which the Masters know and serve.

From the centre which we call the race of men
Let the Plan of Love and Light work out.
And may it seal the door where evil dwells.
Let Light and Love and Power
Restore the Plan on Earth.

Once again the writings of Roheim (1955, 11, 46) on the magic of words and thoughts turn out to be very helpful. "Magic must be rooted in the child-mother situation," he declares, because in the beginning the environment means simply the mother. Therefore, wishing or manifesting the wish is the proper way to deal with the environment." Roheim then goes on to say, "The mother is not only known by the fact that she gratifies the wishes of the child. In truth, she would never be discovered were it not for the fact that there is a gap between desire and fulfillment." More specifically, "Magic originates from the child's crying when he is abandoned and angry; it is not merely the expression of what actually takes place in the dual-unity situation, but it is also a *withdrawal of attachment from the object to the means by which the object is wooed*, that is, from the mother to the *word* and back again to the mother" (my emphasis). While the "magical omnipotence fantasy of the child is part of growing up, *magic in the hands of an adult means a regression to an infantile fantasy*" (my emphasis). Magic says, in the end, I refuse to give up my desires. Creme's "Great Invocation" is the verbal cry that summons the object, that expresses the primal aim of terminating the anxiety which attends separation by restoring the symbiotic bond in which the child feels secure and happy. When Creme (18–19) writes that the Invocation "forms a telepathic conduit between yourselves and the Hierarchy" through which "the energies thus invoked can flow" and that it should be uttered as the practitioner "visualizes a great sphere of white light" projecting its "brilliant beams into the world," he merely describes the dual-unity situation as it is sought and conceived by the regressive adult. The "telepathic conduit" which carries the Master's "energies" to the channeller is a magical version of the vibrational mirroring that exists between mother and baby during the early period. It renders exactly the kind of uncanny, intuitive, communicative link that characterizes the caregiver's interaction with the infant and the infant's interaction with the parental presence. Indeed, here is the origin of "telepathic" phenomena generally, of the belief that human beings can communicate with each other (and with supernatural powers) in an inexplicable, mysterious, mystical way. People believe this because they have *experienced* it; they have *known* it during the early time, and they have connected it emotionally with the deliciousness of dual-unity, with the bliss of loving merger, with the transformational object's continuous conversion of the baby's discomfort into pleasure, or relief. That is why they want it and wish for it again. The after-separation-world with its anxiety and isolation will be "traded in" for the before-separation-world and the "telepathic conduit" that magically fuses the vulnerable neonate to the all-powerful caretaker. As for "the great sphere of white light" that one tries to visualize as one woos the inner parent with the Great Invocation, it is of course a metaphorical representation of the vibrating, radiating, parental body itself: it is *the object* that sends its "brilliant beams" streaming toward the entranced, receptive subject. The most popular recent expression of this is probably the great, awesome, omnipotent and omniscient Oz as he first appears to the mesmerized Dorothy in the children's classic.

The second enhancing feature of Creme's meditational program turns out to be a mantra, a sacred, magical word intended, like the Great Invocation, to summon the absent object. I am referring to the now famous syllable Om, or Aum. Creme (1992, 31–32) writes, "When you sound OM aloud, you are really saying A-U-M. As you say A it is *vibrating* the base of the spine; as you say U it is *vibrating* in the heart centre, or between the solar plexus and the heart; and when you say the M it is *vibrating* in the head. If you say AUM you are bringing all three *vibrations* together from the base of your spine to the top of your head. That is the power of AUM. The *inward-sounding of the OM* is not used to ground energy, but simply to help send the energy into the world. The OM is used to put our attention at the mental plane level where the energy can then go out . . . If your attention wanders off, sound OM inwardly to bring your attention back to the mental plane" (my emphasis). I often wondered during the 1970s and 1980s when New Age thinking began to take root why OM had developed into such a popular mantra, such an integral part of the "scene," so central in fact that it was often treated comically on stage and screen (including the television screen). The answer emerges clearly from Creme's comments: as one *says* this word, as one pronounces it over and over again, as one projects it through one's throat and voice, it *vibrates* through one's organism, from "spine, to heart, to head"; it allows the practitioner to "bring all the vibrations together" at the "mental plane," to *resonate* with the sonorous extension of the uttered syllable. In short, *saying* this particular word *recreates in actual, physical reality the vibrational tie one experiences during the early period as one interacts vibrationally, affectively, with the object.* One sits in a trance, seeking the Master, believing that one is *in contact* with the Master (through the telepathic conduit), and all the while one is *vibrating himself* from head to toe *with his own voice.* Om is popular and finds its way into Creme because it appears to be a particularly good syllable, or sound, for engendering vibrations, for permitting the practitioner to reproduce in himself the affective attunement, the vibrational dual-unity, that he actually felt in his organism as he experienced the frequencies, the wavelengths, the "energies," of the primal symbiotic fusion. Thus the New Age subject has figured out a way to be both object and subject *in himself;* he has figured out a way to get the object back, to get dual-unity back, to get symbiotic fusion back, *in the absence of the original object.* Accordingly, he has figured out a way to *deny separation,* to deny differentiation, to undo the traumas of the early time when the object began to *withdraw* her/his parental attention from the developing child. He has figured out a way *in himself* to suspend the after-separation-world and restore the before-separation-world. He will "sound Om" and "hold it on the mental plane"—that is, on the "plane" where he can regressively re-fashion the vibrational merger he had to give up long ago. Like so much else in New Age thinking, a mysterious, esoteric, mystical practice—the sounding of Om—turns out to be, quite simply, a way to cling on to the past, to the security, the dependency, the perfection, the bliss that growing up happened to impair. New Age thinking rhythmically rocks between the themes of paradise lost and paradise regained.

Nourishing the Little Ones

We come now to one of Creme's most vivid and revealing metaphors, from the psychoanalytic angle at least. As Maitreya streams his energies, his "vibrations," toward the members of the transmission group he is, in Creme's (1992, 64) words, "nourishing the little ones," nourishing the "babes" who have come to prepare the world for its "transfiguration" into a "network of light." Further, by "touching each other" or "holding hands" (65), group members can "transfer" the Master's "nourishing" vibrations between themselves, thereby increasing the group's overall power to change the world. As Creme (121) puts it in another place, "The vibration which the group soul itself generates ... can be utilized by Maitreya" as he works to transform the world into a "radiant" and "magnetic" condition (122). Thus do the members of Creme's group get *fed* by the Master, *fed* with vibrations, just as the "babe" gets *fed* the affect, the mirroring frequency, the emotional wavelength of the "nourisher" during the early time. Maitreya feeds his entranced devotees *psychically* in a manner that restores dual-unity in both the individual feeder and the group of symbiotic co-dependents who comprise the regressive, newly discovered "family." The group reconstitutes in explicitly *oral* terms what was dissolved during the separation phase. Accordingly, the "energy," the "vibration" that resides at the centre of Creme's discussion, is also ultimately a psychological metaphor recalling the "telepathic" exchanges of the first relationship, which brings Creme's use of such figures into harmony with other such usages in New Age thinking generally. Further still, as the group becomes a vibrational "hothouse" (77), "a forcing process" (forced feeding?) with the Age of Aquarius as its goal, the individual members manifest their "evolutionary" (77) significance. Creme (78) declares, "Every inflow of higher, spiritual energy produces change in the recipient." And then, using "evolution" and "mutation" in the pseudo-scientific fashion characteristic of New Age discourse, "That is how evolution proceeds: by the nourishment of the kingdom above of the energy which produces the mutation, which produces evolution itself" (78). What this finally means psychoanalytically can be stated very simply: as one sits in his trance and delusionally receives Maitreya's vibrations one re-experiences the presence of the transformational object, the numinous, primal caregiver who continually converted one's discomfort into pleasure, or relief, during infancy and very early childhood. The "evolution" of the channeller is in reality a *regression* to the time of transformational interaction with the parent. The only "change" here, the only "alteration," is the advent of actual regressive delusion in the channeller, who with each "transmission meditation" sinks deeper into his/her distorted psychological world.

Creme (1992, 79) employs the phrase "holding the mind steady in the light" to describe from yet another perspective the process of connecting to the transformational vibrations of Maitreya. He writes (79), "Through meditation correctly carried out, the channel of light between the physical brain and the soul is gradually built and strengthened. By means of that channel the soul is anchored in the head of the disciple. This is seen as a brilliant light within the head during meditation. *With the attention drawn inward* . . . the mind is held steady, that is, without thought or movement . . . *In that condition of thoughtless, focused attention* the intuitive levels of mind can come into play" (my emphasis). Creme captures here the vibrational "stone," the vibrational *trance* of the channeller, or, psychoanalytically, the channeller's attempt to turn his mind and body into a version of the dual-unity situation wherein mother and infant *hold* and *fix* each other "steadily" in the strength of their affective attunement, the mirroring linkage which nourishes *both* during the symbiotic stage. "Holding the mind steady in the light" expresses metaphorically the object holding the neonate in the light, in the *life* of her devoted ministrations, and the neonate reciprocating affectively. Creme's channeller becomes a self-gripping, self-bonding monad of psychological regression, magically fulfilling his wish to undo and deny separation long *after* separation has transpired. He "holds his mind steady" to erase the past as it disappointed him and to restore the past as it comforted him. It is paradise lost and paradise regained once more, and it calls to mind another line of Milton that applies wonderfully to New Age thinking: "The mind is its own place, and in itself/Can make a Heaven of Hell, a Hell of Heaven" (*Paradise Lost*, I, 254–55). Such is the power of regressive mental *magic.*

However, "holding the mind steady in the light" (Creme 1992, 79) does not connect the regressed, monadic disciple only with the object of his inner realm; it connects him also with the members of the group. "When you can attain and hold steady a certain vibration, you can be brought closer to the group and closer to the Master, until you can work closely with and be really useful to Him. But the most important thing for the disciple to know is that he is a member of that group soul and can draw on the energy of the group" (137). In this way, the delusional dual-unity of the self-monad is reinforced and validated by an "energetic," vibrational bonding with the group, the supportive, re-constituted family that surrounds the practitioner as he receives the nourishment of the parental Master. Eventually, says Creme (80), this state of "focused, thoughtless attention" becomes "instinctive" and "fixed," needing "no formal meditational going within to bring it about." That is, the regressed, delusional "disciple" gets *conditioned into his trance state*, his habitual, vibrational "stone." He holds "his mind steady in the light" over and over again until it is *fixed* there, until he is able to go around that way *all the time*, needing no medita-tion to induce the delusional condition. His obsession takes him over. His longing for dual-unity rules his life. And when this occurs, accord-ing to Creme, the "disciple" is "saved"; he has "mutated" and "evoked" himself into "perfection," into divinity itself (108–11). He has "ser-viced" the kind of "network" Creme would like to see controlling the planet. It is, of course, a horrid, chilling picture—a world of fixated zombies spending their days in a regressive, delusional trance—yet it appears to be Creme's unconscious wish, elevated into religious proph-ecy and spiritual enlightenment.

Something of a guru himself, Creme (1992, 83) is supportive of the guru's role in the vibrational nourishing of the world. He writes: "Transmission meditation does not work against any other form of meditation. Indeed, it will enhance the quality and effectiveness of any other meditation you may do" (83). And he goes on: "All true gurus *are members of the Hierarchy* at some level ... These gurus are themselves *centres of force* who act as *transmitters of energy* from their Masters. Usually gurus are from the Indian tradition in which there is a direct lineage from guru to guru to devotee" (my emphasis). The guru, then, is an *externalized*, fleshly version of the delusional transference figure, Maitreya, whom the channeller conjures up from within. In the guru's presence, the practitioner's need to split his own ego and outwardly project into delusional space the idealized good object is obviated. Here is the object *in reality*, simply waiting to be loaded up with the practi-tioner's regressive longing. Accordingly, the guru *holds* the practitioner in the power (energy, vibration) of a *transference relationship*, thereby creating a version of the original fusion, the original attunement, that resided at the centre of the *first* relationship. Creme's interest in and recommendation of such transference, such "force," is perfectly con-sistent with his interest in and recommendation of "transmission med-itation" as the inward, monadic expression of the bond between "disciple" and "Master."

Creme's use of the terms *higher* and *lower* also illustrates well his consuming interest in regressive, primal nourishing, or feeding. "How can we distinguish higher level guidance?" he asks. And then: "You will know by the quality of information given—whether it is really impersonal or very personal. If it is personal it is certainly not from a high level. If it is impersonal it may be. The higher the guidance, the more impersonal it is. People from all over the world present to me guidance from their guides, their Masters, sometimes Maitreya. Without exception all these messages are from some level of the astral plane. For the most part they are totally trivial and have no value ... All lower psychism comes from the astral plane" (1992, 94–95). Creme's "trivial, lower messages" call Duane and Sanaya's clients to mind, their concern with romance, profit, personal popularity, and the rest—as well as their attempt to channel from their guides the method for achieving their "trivial" egotic aims. We might call this "channelling for worldly improvement." Creme, by contrast, has but one goal in mind, namely the spiritual transformation of the planet, to be accomplished by the reception and re-transmission of the Master's "higher," transfiguring vibrations. From the psychoanalytic angle, of course, Creme's goal translates into regressive, symbiotic fusion with the object, a return to primal merger, wholesale denial of reality. "Higher," in short, means more serious illness, sharper distortion, deeper delusion. "Lower" means a magical thinking that at least has some realistic connection to the world. As Creme declares (105), "Transmission meditation is a method for bringing the man or woman into contact and eventual at-one-ment with the Higher Self or soul." And again, "All those who have engaged in meditation will have been engaged, whether they know it or not, in aligning the physical brain with the soul, the personality vehicle with the Higher self" (106). As I have indicated all along, this dichotomous usage of higher and lower, with its underlying psychoanalytic significance, is characteristic of New Age thinking.

As for *soul*, it is the ubiquitous New Age term for the internalized object, the internalized caregiver of the early period upon whom one depended almost entirely for his feelings of merger, wellness, and security. We will take this up more fully in a subsequent section, but we might note here Creme's assertion (1992, 111) that those who have succeeded in "aligning" their "brains" with their "souls" (the monadic version of dual-unity or affective attunement) lose their "sense of separation" until "they and the cosmos are one." They become "perfect as the Masters are perfect." Here, evoked companionship, vibrational attunement, omnipotence, and narcissistic grandiosity all blend together in the regressive movement toward symbiotic fusion, the golden age of the transformational caregiver, the dispenser of "perfection." The channeller is home at last, absorbed into the "group soul" (116) at last. Creme (117) tells us in a remarkable but inadvertent delineation of psychological dual-unity as it transpires during the early time: "This is not a one-way process. The work of groups themselves often stimulates a development of the Master's plan. I know, for instance, that my Master is doing work which He never planned to do, answering questions, writing books, and giving ray structures of initiates with their points of evolution [these are things that *Creme* is doing, by the way]. However, groups around the world have evoked from me responses which have in turn brought responses from the Master." Creme was probably a delightful, loving, clinging baby involved in a delightful, loving, clinging relationship with the parent; yet something occurred that prevented him from getting free, from becoming autonomous, from being genuinely on his own. He spends his life going in and out of a regressive, delusional trance and attempting to transform the world into a version of the symbiotic object. "Are we not all together a Transmission Group as a whole?" he asks (143). We will probably never know the exact nature of Creme's infancy and childhood, but we can recognize in his resulting existence a steadfast, fanatical refusal to give up the past, to accept his condition as a separate, and limited, person. In this, Benjamin Creme is a representative New Age thinker.

Part 4

Goddess Worship in the New Age: Neo-Pagan Witchery

To read Margot Adler's (1986) definitive study of Neo-Paganism (of which the Craft, or Wicca, or Witchcraft is by far the most sizeable offshoot) is to come away with a variety of arresting facts: During the past three decades North America, Europe, and Australia have witnessed a "population explosion" within paganism, an "extraordinary proliferation of Witches' covens" that has culminated in the foundation of the Witches' International Craft Association with headquarters in New York, the Wiccan Church of Canada with headquarters in Toronto, Wicca Française with headquarters in Paris, and, finally, to round out the picture, the Pagan Anti-Defamation League with headquarters in London. This last group is dedicated to correcting misconceptions about "Wicca," the "natural faith of Britain" (51, 455, 529).

According to Adler, there are approximately one hundred thousand active, self-identified pagans or members of Wicca in the United States alone, and many thousands more (both in and out of the closet) throughout the world. What Adler calls "the Witchcraft movement" is experiencing more and more acceptance in the larger culture. Books on "the Goddess" have entered the mainstream of religious and philosophic thought. Serious scholarship is taking place both inside and outside the universities. There is less persecution. There are more children in Wiccan communities, and more attention is being paid to their needs. More older people are getting involved, as well as more highly skilled people such as computer programmers, doctors, lawyers, architects, anthropologists, accountants, welders, machinists, nurses, market analysts, and scientists. One can easily come away from Adler's book believing that Witches are taking over the world. That is, of course, a long way from the truth; but "the movement" has unquestionably achieved a certain influence, and the future will probably see that influence increase. Witchcraft may still be a cult, but it is rapidly becoming a prominent one whose cultic status could be outgrown by the end of the century.

The Craft as we know it today has a maddeningly complex, disputatious history capable of discouraging the most sanguine investigator. Some adherents point to Sir James Frazer (1890) as the founding father, others to Margaret Murray (1921) as the founding mother. Still others would give the nod to Robert Graves (1946), or Aleister Crowley (1930), or Gerald Gardner (1959). The list could be easily extended to include not only more names but whole mystical societies such as the Golden Dawn Rosicrucians or the Theosophists. Because the Craft contains a wide variety of sects (Gardnerian, Alexandrian, Georgian, Dianic), it abounds with claims and counter-claims of ritualistic authenticity, with accusations of apostasy and/or betrayal, and with endless explanations of why this or that belief or rite or tool is the key to the acquisition of enlightenment, or power. In spite of all this, I will endeavour in the next few paragraphs to hack my way through the underbrush and give the reader some idea of what probably occurred.

With the repeal of the Witchcraft Acts in Britain in 1951 the relatively small number of Frazerian and Murrayite Witches in England and North America began to come out of the closet and proselytize for the Craft. Notable among these was Gerald B. Gardner (1884–1964), a British civil servant who had immersed himself in the religious practices of the East while on duty in Malaysia and who had been converted to Witchcraft during the 1940s in England by the renowned and mysterious hag Dorothy Clutterbuck. Setting up a museum of Witchcraft on the Isle of Man in 1951 and ensconcing himself therein as the resident Witch, Gardner began to generate a good deal of newspaper publicity. He relied upon the *Book of Shadows* (ostensibly a sixteenth-century guide to the Craft but in fact a home-made forgery) to offer the world a version of Witchcraft considerably different from that which appears in the work of Frazer and Murray. Adler (1986, 62) writes of it as follows:

> To Gardner, Witchcraft was a peaceful, happy nature religion. Witches met in covens, led by a priestess. They worshipped two principal deities, the god of the forests and what lies beyond and the Triple Goddess of fertility and rebirth. They met in the nude in a nine-foot circle and raised power from their bodies through dancing and chanting and meditative techniques. They focused primarily on the Goddess; they celebrated the eight ancient Pagan festivals of Europe and sought to attune themselves to nature.

With the publication of *Witchcraft Today* in 1954 and *The Meaning of Witchcraft* in 1959 Gardner managed not only to spark a revival of the Craft based on his own conceptions but to establish himself as a kind of guru, or founding father.

Gardner's life and work are surrounded by controversy; some regard him as a genius, others as a dangerous fraud who may have been overly fond of flagellating his female initiates (cf. Farrar 1984, 33). Still, there is no denying his influence. What is more to the point, there is no denying the spread of Witchcraft during the post-war years: by the mid-1960s, Robert Graves (1964) could write in the *Virginia Quarterly Review* that the "old religion" was "growing fast," and that the next few decades might well witness an even more dramatic increase in both coven members and solitary practitioners. This is, of course, exactly what happened, as I indicated in my opening paragraph. In North America, Europe, Australia, and New Zealand many thousands of people, from all walks of life, have found their way to Wicca.

The rise of the Witches has resulted from far more than the activities and writings of Gerald B. Gardner, of course. It may be attributed in large measure to the alignment of Witchcraft with such popular modern causes as feminism and the environment, to the declining family structure that we witness everywhere around us, to the advent of an increasingly impersonal technological order, and to the appearance of extraordinarily influential recent books by such authors as Margot Adler, whose work we have already cited, and Miriam Simos (or, as she modestly calls herself on her title pages, Starhawk), whose work we will take up now.

The Magical System of Modern Witchcraft

At the centre of the system stands the Goddess. As Simos (1988, xxvi) has it, connection with the Goddess *is* Witchcraft. While it is true that

Witches routinely announce the importance of the God in their scheme of things, even claiming an equality between the God and his female counterpart, it is impossible to read the texts of the Craft, or to talk with Witches, or to attend coven meetings, without realizing the God's predominantly formal or doctrinal significance. When one comes right down to what Witches read and say and do, it is the Goddess, not the God, who is central. However, I do not mean to exclude Him from the analysis and will bring Him in at the appropriate place.

The Goddess of the Witches is a version of the omnipotent mother as she is perceived by the infant during the symbiotic stage. She is limitless, ubiquitous, all-encompassing, all-enveloping, all-controlling; she is also the source of everything. As the old expression has it, the Goddess is the be-all and the end-all of the world. Roheim, you will recall, stated that the mother is the first environment. In Witchcraft this is explicitly pronounced in a way that focuses unforgettably on not merely the aims of the early period but the manner in which those aims persistently find their way to the surface in the later worship of a substitute object. The core wish is to overcome differentiation, the stage in Mahler (1975) where fusion and omnipotence are lost. To overcome differentiation is to regain union, to deny separation, and to recapture omnipotence. Differentiation is the enemy to be wiped out by magic. According to Simos (1979, 8), "The Goddess is not separate from the world"; She is not *in* "reality," or a part of "reality"; the Goddess "*is* reality, *is* the world, and all things in it," including "woman and man." Becoming a Witch is a matter of "relinking" with Her endless "manifestations" (9). Simos asserts, in a striking phrase that has become a canonical feature of modern Witchcraft, "One thing becomes another in the mother." Thus the Goddess, the mythic Great Mother, is ultimately and explicitly the great source of non-differentiation, the great abolisher of boundaries, the great blender of beings. Through Her we can collapse precisely that separateness which was accomplished with such agony during the early years and which has streaked our lives with painful undercurrents and with a continuous search for fusion through substitute objects.

Let me offer a few more examples of this theme from Simos's (1979) *Spiral Dance*. The Goddess "dissolves separation" and "glues the world together" through Her "love" (25). Each of us is "the Goddess' child, the Goddess' beloved, the Goddess' self" (15). There is no deity who stands apart from the world, an object of fear; for the world is the Goddess, whose "laughter bubbles and courses through all things" (14). She manifests herself in "ordinary tasks"; no matter what you are doing, in the kitchen, in the yard, at the store, She is with you (62). Each stage of life is an aspect of Her nature; She is the moon waxing as life grows, the moon waning as life fades; She is the end of life, the way to reincarnation (65). The rain is Her "menstrual blood" (26). The "earth" is Her "body" (57). The rivers and oceans are Her "overflowing breast milk" (64). You are "one drop," Simos instructs us, in the "primal ocean," which is Her "womb." When you worship the Goddess, you "merge" with all that is of earth: grass, fruits, beasts, stones (64). Your very susceptibility to gravity is a pull to Her bosom (64). When you breathe, it is Her breath that you take in. When you step in the oozing "mud," it is Her body that you feel (64). The four seasons are aspects and expressions of Her being. She is the "wheel of the year" (169), the "vaginal passage of rebirth" (82). As you worship Her—and here is the key metaphor—"the drought of separation is over" (71).

But it is not only the planet earth that Simos transforms into a version of the Goddess; the whole universe becomes the Great Mother. The "cosmos is modeled on the female body" (85), she writes, blithely projecting away, and everything in the cosmos, including you and me, is "charged" with the Goddess's "power." Accordingly, the most important contribution of Witchcraft to our "spiritual" perception derives from its capacity to make us see that "all is one," that the Goddess is our "cup," our "wine of life," and that She has "never been separate from us" (Simos 1979, 196–99).

Again and again in reading texts of the Craft one comes upon similar notions. It is a veritable endless flood. "All things come to fruition through the Goddess," writes Cunningham (1988, 71). She is "the earth, the sea, the moon, the stars," and we are part of her endless domain, joined to her "creation."

The "primordial Mother" was "bequeathed to us before the dawn of time" (that is, before the dawn of the ego, or the end of the autistic stage), declares Warren-Clarke (1987, 3). She "answers our cries," and "acknowledges Her children." We "fuse" with Her and "are one" with Her. She is the "corn, the oceans, the dew, the rivers ... All things are in Her, and we are in Her too" (3).

"She is the Great Mother of All," states Gerald Gardner (1959, 132). All life comes from Her, and all people and things are Her "children." What are her gifts? "Magic and inspiration ... She is the Goddess of Magic and Magicians" (133).

The Goddess is "continuous with the heavens," writes Farrar (1984, 37). She is the "giver of life," the "Mother of all creation," and the Witch is "her secret child" (20). She is "in all women" and "all women are in Her" (75). She exists now, and she existed "before the earth was formed" (100). She is "the sea, the tides, the earth, the heavens," the

"Mighty One" who "governs all" (199). Farrar then goes on to state in a fascinating expression that each individual is a "part" of the Goddess' "central nervous system" (269), a part of her body. Underscoring this notion in another place, Farrar (1987, 3) writes that the "cosmos" is an "organism," namely the body of the Great Goddess, and that we as human beings comprise that organism's "individual cells." Clearly, to discover the Goddess is to rediscover dual-unity.[1]

Magic at Work

Wiccan ceremonies invariably commence with what practitioners call "casting the circle." Here is the way it goes (in abbreviated form) in Simos (1979, 55–57):

> The room is lit by flickering candles ... The coveners stand in a circle ... The High Priestess, her consecrated knife [athame] unsheathed, steps to the alter and salutes the sky ... Raising her knife the High Priestess calls out, "Hail, Guardians of the Watchtowers of the East ... Come! By the air that is Her breath, send forth your light" ... The High Priestess, knife held outward, traces the boundaries of the circle, and cries, "Lady of the Outer Darkness, come! By the earth that is Her body, send forth your strength, be here now!" The High Priestess traces the last link of the circle and says, "We are between the worlds" ... The ritual is begun.

Although Simos, "for literary convenience," has the High Priestess casting the circle, "any qualified covener, female or male, may take her role" (55). Also, a solitary practitioner may commence his/her magical activities by casting a circle in the privacy of his/her own room.

Having created a sacred space and positioned herself "between the worlds," the Witch proceeds to "grounding and centering." According to Simos (1979, 49, my emphasis), this is a "basic technique of magical work" and consists of "establishing an energy connection with the earth" by "visualizing *a cord* extending from the base of your spine to the center of the earth" and by "aligning your body along its center of gravity." The Witch then "breathes from her center," from her "abdomen," and "feels the energy flowing up from the earth to fill her." Grounding is "important," writes Simos (49), "because it allows you to draw on the earth's vitality rather than depleting your own." What is the psychoanalytic significance of all this?

The circle is cast to facilitate the accomplishment of various magical ends; consecrating a tool, initiating a new member of the coven, protecting one's home and family from enemies, healing a sick friend, and so on. We must note immediately, however, that none of these ends can be achieved without power, the power to influence—indeed, to alter—reality. "The main function of a circle," writes Farrar (1984, 82), is not "protection"; it is "to preserve and contain the power that is raised within it—in other words, to concentrate and amplify the psychic efforts of the group." We must also note here the endlessly repeated Wiccan tenet that the earth is the body of the living Goddess, the Great Mother, a huge female organism with both a "nervous system" and "awareness" (Farrar 1987, 16). In this way, power is raised in the circle by establishing a psychic link between the Witch's imaginary "cord" and an "earth" that is explicitly regarded in Craft theology as the Great Mother's living, breathing body.

There is an integral psychoanalytic connection, then, between the raising of power to do magic and "relinking" with the Goddess in the circle. Just as omnipotence, or power, was taken by the child from the symbiotic body of the mother during the early period, so is it now taken again from the sacred space where the Witch bonds psychically, *vibrationally,* with the all-powerful Goddess. Let us note Cunningham's (1988, 158) definition of Witchcraft as "magic," along with Simos's (1988, xxvi) definition of Witchcraft as "relinking with the Goddess," and let us appreciate the full unconscious meaning of the relation: Having regained fusion through the circle, the Witch immediately regains omnipotence too. They go together automatically as what we might call psychic epiphenomena. Thinking back momentarily on the work of Roheim and Malinowski, we would suggest that the Witch has attained the dual-unity Roheim spied as magic's chief end and is therefore in a mental-emotive position to accomplish those mundane purposes Malinowski singles out as magic's goal. With the power of the Goddess in hand (or, as we shall see, in wand), the Witch can remould the world closer to her heart's desire.

Circles of Power

The main function of the circle, we discovered in Farrar (1984, 82), is to raise, and to contain, power. Note the extent to which this idea is echoed and amplified in the texts of the Craft: "as we gather in the circle, join hands, and breathe together," writes Simos (1979, 43), we "suck in the power" as if "through a straw." Becoming "one, one circle, one breathing, living organism," we "breathe the breath of the belly, the breath of the womb," and are "revitalized" and "renewed" through our bond to the "earth" (44–45). The circle is our "place of power," our "reservoir of power" (58, 150), and its centre is our "point of transformation" (67).

The circle is not "cast" to keep out "demons," writes Gardner (1988, 25), but to keep in "power." It is the "domain of the gods," of expanding "energy" and "will." It is the place to which we are "summoned" to hear "mighty words."

According to Cunningham (1988, 103–04), the circle is the "sphere of energy," the "temple of magical energy," the "power construction of energy." It opens us to the world of transforming ritual, and the casting of it "precedes nearly every [magical] rite."

Warren-Clarke (1987, 20) suggests that we envision the circle as a "fruit" and then, in our minds, "chew on it for power."

In the view of Margot Adler (1986, 109), the circle is "the container of raised energy," a "sacred space" where "contact with the gods is possible." Indeed, says Adler, when a Witch is in the circle, she/he may become the God or Goddess, the "archetypal force" itself.

All of this allows us to make psychoanalytic headway in grasping the manner in which energy or power is characterized by Witches in their depictions of the universe. "Energy flows in spirals," declares Simos (1979, 130); its motion is always "circular, cyclical." The universe does not simply "move," it "dances," and as it does so it creates a "swirl of energy" (20), a "spiral dance," which is itself the manifest Goddess releasing her power into the cosmos (14). Accordingly, the Goddess is both the galaxy in the heavens (spiral nebula, etc.) and the cycle of the seasons on the earth, the "wheel of the year" (169), winter, spring, summer, autumn. "The wheel turns," writes Simos; "on and on" it goes in its never-ending spiral expressions. From this perspective, the Witches' circle itself becomes a "living" entity, a "living mandala" (58), and not merely a line on the ground.

Farrar (1984, 83) underscores this last notion when she reminds us that casting the circle is merely putting a trace around what is actually a sphere, a sphere that is full of pulsating energy, a kind of "glowing, transparent, electrical globe" or ball (84). This living, vibrating entity gives us not only power; it gives us protection too. We can "zip ourselves up in it" when we feel threatened by a "psychic attack from the outside" (84). In fact, maintains Farrar, we do not even have to "cast a circle" on the ground if and when we wish to "zip up"; we can simply do it "mentally, often without giving any outward sign that we are doing so." Can there be any doubt at this juncture that the circle which is the dancing galaxy is also the protective womb, *that* glowing, vibrating sphere?

Power is circular in Witchcraft because the circle, in all its manifestations as symbol and coven group, is psychically bound up with the mother as symbiotic, transformational, and transitional object. It makes no difference at which conscious level the projection is operating—from the cosmos, to the Earth, to the group, to the womb—the obsessive need to undo the traumas of the early period, to terminate separation and smallness, to recapture symbiosis and omnipotence, makes the unconscious tie between fusion and power automatic and inextricable, exactly as it was in the beginning, and exactly as it began to be wished-for when separation, with all its agonies and longings, got underway. To maintain with the Witches that the circle's main function is to raise and contain power is affectively equivalent to maintaining that power is circular. Each notion is simply a version of the mother's body, the glowing, *vibrating* entity from which the practitioner was cut off at the onset of differentiation. Thus to "zip up" in the circle, either mentally or in the coven group, is to use the symbolic realm, or culture, as a substitute for the original source of narcissistic supplies and protection. It is to go back inside the omnipotent object of life's first years.

With this in mind, we will not have any trouble understanding the psychoanalytic significance of what the Witches regard as their most coveted and highest accomplishment, namely "ruling the circle." According to Farrar (1984, 19), when a Witch has been fully initiated into the "secrets" of the Craft, where she/he has been "consecrated" and made a "priestess of the Art," a sword or "athame" is placed into her hands with the words "now thou art ruler of the circle." When we recall that the circle is the body of the mother (Goddess), the place of fusion, power, and magical achievements, we begin to spy the very essence of Witchcraft today: it strives to control the object of the early period and by doing that to reverse the course of development during which such control was lost. To become a Witch-Priestess and thereby to "rule the circle" is to be in a psychic-emotive position to do whatever one wishes with the mother's body: one can fuse with it, zip up in it, suck its power up through one's "cord," and use that power magically to fulfil one's desires. What more can magic do? What more could one want from a cult? Surely we comprehend now the meaning of Simos's statement (1979, 2, 9), common to Witchcraft, "*You* are the Goddess ... *you* are divine." [2]

I suspect we also comprehend now the meaning of Simos's words (1979, 55), equally common to Witchcraft, that the practitioner, after "casting the circle," exists "between the worlds." We have, on the one hand, the world of ordinary reality, ordinary consciousness, ordinary autonomy—the world in which we confront, and live with, the facts of our separation and smallness, our differentiation from the environment and in particular the caretaker, our limitations as people, our mortality. We can think of this as the after-separation-world, or the world that emerges after the struggle toward individuation and object constancy has occurred. On the other hand, we have the before-separation-world, the world of fusion and omnipotence, of dual-unity and magical-autistic thinking, the world from which the child is torn as the drive for separation and the demands of the environment make themselves powerfully known. This is the world in which "one thing becomes another in the mother" (Simos 1979, 9), and the goal of Witchcraft, to express it from still another angle, is to cross psychological boundaries and get these worlds together so that the emotional features of the before-separation-world can be worked back into the after-separation-world. As Simos (1979, 57) declares, "in witchcraft, we define a new space and a new time whenever we cast a circle." In other words, in Witchcraft we undo precisely those perceptual categories (space and time) that are established, or fixed, as the child moves toward differentiation and the attainment of an individuated ego. There is nothing "new," ultimately, about the space and time Simos refers to; we knew them before, during infancy, as paradisal merger and eternal bliss. It is an old story.

Patriarchal Concerns

Witches constantly pronounce their purpose of defeating the old, patriarchal "values," of terminating the aggressive, exploitative era of masculine domination and war, of restoring the mother and the Goddess to their rightful place at the centre of society and the world. "Since the decline of the Goddess religions," writes Simos (1979, 8), a "male God" has "ruled the cosmos from the outside" and "shaped our perceptions unconsciously." Because of this, we passively accept not only the "oppression of women" but a host of damaging "cultural pressures" that lead to "self-hatred," aggression, and the "plundering of the earth" rather than to "nurturance" and "creativity." According to Warren-Clarke (1987, 66), "an overpowering masculine force" has dominated the West for nearly three thousand years. "Ideology" has become "patriarchal and male," and this has "tipped the balance to the side of war, greed, ownership, bigotry, anger, power for power's sake, and the subjugation of women." A return to the Goddess will restore the balance and lead to "compassion, freedom, love, and wisdom." But with the context of this study firmly in mind, we immediately recognize such ideological pronouncements for what they are, namely rationalizations for the unconscious, regressive need to get back to the mother, to restore the before-separation-world with its delicious fusion and omnipotence—in a word, to get rid of the gap that yawned when symbiosis came to an end. After all, can a "religion" that encourages again and again, in a thousand glowing, passionate metaphors, the dissolving of the practitioner into the huge, breasty body of the Great Mother, that presents a view of the universe in which the individual human being comprises but a cell in the *corpus maternum*—can such a religion actually expect one to believe that it seeks to place the Goddess at the centre of the world for ideological and ethical reasons?

I am not denying, of course, that Witches can have ideological and ethical concerns; nor am I denying that these may play a role in the activities and beliefs of the Craft. I am denying only that they are paramount, or exclusive. In other words, I am suggesting that the ideology sits, as it were, on top of the basic, underlying needs and wishes, concealing them in a cloud of rationalizations and noble, humanistic purposes. Patriarchy is the enemy of the Witches because patriarchy speaks for separation, for loss of fusion and omnipotence, for the individuated world of the father that succeeds the symbiotic world of the maternal figure. Witches pine nostalgically for the putative matriarchate of old because matriarchy means mother, and mother means, at the deep, regressive level, the restoration of merger, power, and bliss. Unless Witches see this, unless they acknowledge honestly their unconscious agenda, they will have no chance whatever of achieving maturity as human beings.

This all-pervasive longing for the maternal figure explains the persistent tendency of Wiccan texts to play up, or highlight, the benign, loving aspects of the Goddess and to play down, or soften, Her negative, harrowing features. For if fusion with the Goddess is the aim of practitioners, She must be presented in a way that will encourage them to fuse with Her. To express the matter in psychoanalytic terms, we would say that Witchcraft endeavours to collapse the splitting that transpires during the early period, to get rid of (deny) the "bad object," the side of the mother that enforces separation, terminates dual-unity, ends symbiosis and omnipotence. The Goddess "swells with love" for Her children and Her world, writes Simos (1979, 26). Because Her "law is love," namely the "protective love of mother for child" (83), we may "invoke" Her "in perfect trust" (75). The Goddess's love for us is "constant unchanging, unconditional," Simos continues (84, 138), employing precisely those descriptive terms which characterize the perfect, idealized caretaker.

She is the "gracious, blessed Mother of all things," declares Cunningham (1988, 71), our "refuge" and our "healing." In the expression of Warren-Clarke (1987, 135), we "walk in peace upon the breast of our Earth Mother." Everything that happens to us, claims Gardner (1959, 132), is ultimately attributable to the Goddess, yet She always proceeds "in a sweetly loving way." She is the "mother who lovingly spanks and kisses her children" (132). Even the Goddess as Crone, Old Age, Winter, Death is presented in these texts in a manner that denies finality, "softens the blow," makes the reality (the "spanking") a desirable, supportive one: for winter always leads here to spring, and death always leads to rebirth. "Worship Me as the Crone," writes Cunningham (1988, 71, my emphasis), "tender of the unbroken cycle of death and rebirth." To "die" is to be "reborn," writes Simos (1979, 170), who, like Witches generally (cf. Farrar 1984, 115), expresses a belief in reincarnation in her works. To "behold the circle of rebirth," or the "cord of life," correctly, is to realize that "you will never fade away" (180). The fear of death is unconsciously associated with separation from the caretaker: the Witches work hard to mould *their* Caretaker in a way that will diminish this fear.

We are in a good position now to understand the role of the God in modern Witchcraft. Simos (1979, 26) writes in one place, "The view of the All as an energy field polarized by two great forces, Female and Male, Goddess and God, which in their ultimate being are aspects of each other, is common to almost all traditions of the Craft." As I suggested earlier, this is the official line: Goddess and God are equal and inextricably joined together as they manifest themselves in the world around us. However, as I also suggested, such formal, doctrinal equality is belied at the level of practice. When we come right down to what Witches do and say, we recognize at once that this is a Goddess-centred (or mother-centred) cult in which the God plays a fascinating but decidedly subordinate role. The following passage by Farrar (1984, 169, my emphasis) summarizes the matter for us as well as we could wish: "Wicca is matriarchal, and the High Priestess is the leader of the coven—with the High Priest as her partner. They are essential to each other, and ultimately equal (remembering that the immortal Individuality, the reincarnating monad, is hermaphroditic), but in the context of Wiccan working and of their present incarnation, he is rather like the Prince Consort of a reigning Queen. He is a channel for the God aspect, and there is nothing inferior about that; but Wiccan working is primarily concerned with the gifts of the Goddess." To capture the psychoanalytic meaning of this we must move momentarily to the Oedipal level of analysis.

Modern Witchcraft reconstitutes the Oedipal situation in a manner that prevents the paternal figure from impeding the mother's "gifts" of fusion and omnipotence. To be sure, the Father-God is there, and his presence allows the practitioner to participate, along with his coven siblings, in an ideal (or, better, idealized) family gathering. In an age when intact, traditional families are crumbling all around us, the attraction of such an opportunity is not to be underestimated: here is the great male God, the handsome Prince Consort, and here is His wonderful Queen. "Come," says Wicca, "join the family circle and relive your Oedipal journey in perfect safety and security. Was there danger and disappointment in your Oedipal past? Well, erase them now. Make the world conform to your Oedipal, as well as to your pre-Oedipal, wishes." The Father-God's presence may also provide the practitioner with an opportunity to resist psychologically too complete, too total an engulfment into the mother's sphere. Obviously such attractions and fears will vary from one adherent to another. But what Wiccan ritual and text disclose at the bedrock is a wish to remove the Father from the centre of the picture, to "take care of him" in a way that permits the Witch to stay with, and in, the *corpus maternum*. For, we must remember, it is fusion with the Mother-Goddess that returns the Witch to the symbiotic stage and thus provides her with the power (omnipotence) to perform the magic in which her vocation is rooted.

Offering us a typical Wiccan creation myth, Simos (1979, 17, my emphasis) declares, "Alone, awesome, complete within Herself, the Goddess ... floated in the abyss of the outer darkness before the beginning of all things ... The Goddess became filled with love ... and gave birth to a rain of bright spirits that filled the world and became all things ... As She moved out from the Goddess, She became more masculine. First she became the Blue God ... then she became the Green One, vine covered ... At last she became the Horned God, the Hunter whose face is the ruddy sun and yet dark as death. But always desire draws Him back toward the Goddess, so that he circles her eternally." Here, then, is the heart of the matter: in the beginning is the Mother, not the Father, and the Mother remains at the centre of the magic circle with the male figure revolving around her forever, like a planet orbiting a sun. In this Oedipal universe, it is the "awesome Queen" who reigns.

Initiation and the Meaning of Rebirth

A "normal Gardnerian" initiation ritual includes the following, as depicted in Farrar (1984, 10): The candidate is carried "bound and naked in torchlight procession into a cave by a group of naked women" who withdraw and "leave her terrified in pitch darkness." She gradually "conquers her fear and becomes calm," at which point the women return. They "stand in line with their legs astride," and the candidate is "ordered to struggle, bound as she is, through the vagina-like tunnel of legs," while the women "sway, howl, and scream as though in child-birth." When she is "through," she is "pulled to her feet and her bonds are cut away." The Leader then faces the candidate and offers the latter "her breasts." This "symbolises that she would suckle the candidate as she would her own child." As for the "cutting of the bonds," it "symb-olises the cutting of the umbilical cord." Finally, the candidate "kisses the proffered breasts, is sprinkled with water, and told that she has been reborn into the priesthood of Moon Mysteries."

In Simos (1979, 161), one of several descriptions of initiation ritu-als begins with a "death cycle," an "enacted dissolution" or "symbolic annihilation and purification." Taken to an ocean beach or lakeside, the blindfolded candidate is told to "walk trustingly into to the waves" where, eventually, "protective hands will pull her back" and guide her to a nearby "tub" around which a "circle is cast." Helped into the water, the candidate is "washed and chanted over by other coveners . . . She is told to meditate, purify herself, and look for a new name." After being dried, and having one of her ankles bound with a "cord" by a Priestess, the candidate kneels in the centre of the circle, vows loyalty to the Craft "on her mother's womb," and undergoes a "cutting of the cord." With this, "coven members grab her, lift her up, and carry her three times around the circle, laughing and shrieking."

The inclination of Wiccan texts to regard initiation as a symbolic death and rebirth is perfectly explicit: "Every initiation," writes Farrar (1984, 10), "is a symbolic death and rebirth," a preparation for a "new life." The initiate, writes Vivian Crowley (1989, 64, 69), is "like the child in the womb who has not yet been exposed to the light of day." She/he is "unborn," and her former life "but a dream." Coven members "await her entry into the circle of light." An initiation is a "symbolic death and rebirth," writes Simos (1979, 160), a "new beginning." As initiates, we "strip ourselves and go through the open door bound by cords." What is the psychoanalytic significance of all this?

The "rebirth" of the Witch is her second coming. She is permitted through magic to do everything all over again, and this time to get it *right*. Instead of losing omnipotence and fusion as she lost them during the course of her original development, the Witch attains the emotive, psychic capacity not only to gain them but to retain them forever. The old, bad "dream" of ordinary autonomy, and the old, bad reality of sep-aration, smallness, and death, are expunged as the "new beginning," complete with new umbilicus and name, gets underway. Does the Witch desire to stay fused with Mother-Goddess? Well, then, she *will*.

Does the Witch desire to sustain her omnipotence and her special narcissistic identity? Well, then, she *will*. For it is the Witch who is now in control, not the parent. It is *her* will that now governs the emotive, existential picture, or, as the religious terminology has it, the "new life." It is *she* who becomes, with the assistance of ritualistic magic, the agent of her own *transformation* (Bollas 1987).

Witches are fond of citing Aleister Crowley's famous definition of magic as "the Science and Art of causing change to occur in conformity with Will" (cf. Adler 1986, 8). We see now exactly what this means. It isn't "change" in "conformity" with "will" in some *general* sense that the Witch is seeking. She doesn't crawl through "a vagina-like tunnel of legs" and undergo "rebirth" into a power-giving cult for *that*. The magic Witchcraft brings is precisely the magic of *reshaping one's psychosexual development*, of denying the smallness and separation that comprise one's ordinary autonomy. It is separation and smallness that do not "conform" to the Witch's "will." Indeed, the Witch's will to power is her wish to enter the powerhouse of the mother once again and to manage the controls forever. Simos (1979, 7) asserts in one place that a Witch becomes a "shaper" who "bends the unseen into form." We may translate: a Witch becomes a wisher who believes in her omnipotent ability to change her ordinary, actual development (achieved through the caretaker) into a shape more pleasing to her anxious, demanding ego. When a Witch says she has the "ability to bring about anything she wants," and that her "life holds infinite possibilities" (Gardner 1959, 37), we can be very sure of what it is she "wants": the "infinite" that she knew, and lost, during the early period of her existence when the transformational object was the "Goddess."

Tools and Invocations

Having been "reborn," having regained the security and omnipotence of the idealized caretaker, the Witch wants to be doing things, wants to get on with the business of being a Witch. Hence, it is time for us to examine more closely the details of her craft: the tools she employs during the course of her rites and spells, the words she uses as she invokes the supernatural powers that are now available to her.

Among the items the Witch frequently employs may be numbered the wand, the cup, the cauldron, the cord, the pentacle (five-pointed star), and the athame (sacred knife). The psychoanalytic significance of these objects emerges readily from the literature. Simos (1979, 61) tells us that the "tools" of Witchcraft are "tangible representatives of unseen forces," and that to use them is to "augment the power of the mind." According to Farrar (1984, 41), the Witch's tools carry an "invisible and powerful spiritual charge" that may be traced to "bodies" on "other levels" of the universe and that may be tapped by the Witch during the course of her practice. In Farrar's view, the "power" of the object increases the more it is used.

To get the spiritual power lurking in the tool to work for her, the Witch must participate in a ceremony of consecration that entails a particular kind of transference, namely infusing the energy of one's body and mind into the already-charged physical object. When this is done, the power of the object joins with the power of the individual to create the instrument of magical change. As Warren-Clarke (1987, 72) puts it, the "power of our will" enters the tool to "complete its charge" and to make it capable of assisting us "in directing the course of events." According to Simos (1979, 69), the "tool" becomes a viable instrument of Witchery when and only when it is "charged" with our "psychic energy" during the moment of consecration.

Here is the way it goes in Simos (1979, 63) with regard to the wand:

> Hold your wand in your strongest hand. Breathe deeply, and feel the power of Fire, of energy. Be aware of yourself as a channel of energy. You can change spirit into matter . . . Feel your own power to create . . . Be in touch with your *will*—your power to do what you must . . . Let your will flow into your wand.

Here is the way it goes with regard to the athame, or sacred knife, used to demarcate space and draw circles:

> Hold your athame or sword in your strongest hand . . . Feel the power of your mind to influence others and the strength of your responsibility not to misuse that power . . . Let the power of your intelligence flow into your tool. (63)

Here is the cup:

> Hold your cup cradled in both hands. Breathe deep and feel the power of Water, of emotion . . . The cup is the symbol of nurturing, the overflowing breast of the Goddess that nourishes all life . . . Let the strength of your emotions flood the cup. (64)

And finally the pentacle:

> Hold your pentacle in both hands. Breathe deep and feel the power of earth, of the body. The pentacle is your own body, four limbs and head. It is the five senses, both inner and outer . . . The pentacle is the four elements plus the fifth-essence. And it is the five stages of life, each an aspect of the Goddess. (65)

Let us recall at this point the manner in which objects are used transitionally as a way both toward the caretaker and away from the caretaker during the crisis of separation that follows the symbiotic stage of development. As the traumatic diminution of omnipotence and fusion takes place with the passing months and years, the child turns to substitutes—teddy bears, blankets, story-books—that facilitate his transition away from the relationship with his mother, and that also enable him to continue in that very relationship at the level of fantasy and emotion. Such items (Winnicott [1974] calls them "transitional objects," as we saw in chapter 2) attest to our distinctive, paradoxical capacity as humans to move in two opposing developmental directions at the same time. In this way, the child learns to use the objects around him in the culture to preserve his security, his tie to the maternal and/or paternal figure, while he struggles to achieve a measure of his own power, his own control.

So it is with the Witch's tools: note that she takes them up after she has been reborn, after the commencement of her "new existence," her "new life," her new bonding with the Mother-Goddess. Just as the original transitional object recalls the mother's omnipotence, just as it must be invested projectively with qualities of the mother which the child has internalized along the way, so must the Witch complete the tool's transformation by "breathing" her "power," her "energy," into it and by uttering magical words of consecration which explicitly recall the "overflowing breasts" of "the Goddess," the "unseen force" that comes not from "other levels of the universe" but from the nursery. The magical formula for the tool's tranformation is, then, perfectly obvious from a psychoanalytic perspective: after consecration the tool is reinternalized to become part of the Witch's new identity, part of the new existence in which her will, and not the parent's, controls the course of events. As a new transitional object, the tool moves the practitioner back to the Goddess and away from the Goddess in the same psychological moment. It both relinks her with the omnipotent mother and grants her fresh, autonomous power, exactly as the original objects of transition did.

What we see in regard to the pentacle is especially fascinating here, for when Simos (1979, 65) declares that the pentacle represents the body—the four limbs and the head—she reminds us of the Craft's insistence that the body of the practitioner is the Goddess and the Goddess the body of the practitioner. "She is the body," writes Simos (1979, 78), "womb, breast, belly, mouth, vagina, penis, bone and blood … Whether we are eating, sleeping, making love, or eliminating body wastes, we are manifesting the Goddess." The reborn Witch experiences not only her "tool," but her whole body as a transitional object—

tied to the Great Mother and a manifestation of Her, and yet a wilful, magic-working entity in its own right. Thus, in a very special psycho-analytic sense, the Witch's body itself becomes a "tool," a link to the past and a means to the attainment of omnipotence in the present and future. Can we miss, now, the significance of Farrar's (1984, 45) instruc-tion that the Witch, to get power into the athame, "should press it against her body for a time" and thereby "impregnate" it with her "aura"? We have here the early, primitive, transitional dynamics acted-out all over again in symbolic disguise. The Witch gives to her tools the "vibes" she originally derived from the parent.

Much the same reasoning may be applied to Wiccan invocations. As the Witch takes up her consecrated wand, or cup, or pentacle, or athame, she calls upon the Goddess to come and assist her in the per-formance of a particular rite. Here is an example from Simos (1979, 56):

> Hail, Lady of the outer darkness!
> We invoke you;
> Center of the sky,
> Fertile field,
> Come!
> By the earth that is Her body,
> Be here now!

Or again:

> Hail guardians of the watchtower,
> Rain on us,
> Help us to remember
> The ocean womb from which we come.
> Now let all of us be connected.
> Let our moods be flowing . . .
> Until all is one.
> Let the drought of separation be over.
> Blessed be. (71)

And finally,

> Nameless One,
> Eternal,
> Open our hearts!
> That we may live free at last . . .
> Mother of all life,
> Engulf us with your love,
> Breathe with our nostrils,
> Touch with our hands,
> Kiss with our lips! (105)

As Roheim (1955, 9) reminded us earlier, "More than anything else, magic consists of incantations or of mere wishes which have been uttered. The child utters sounds and the mother reacts to the cry or the call or the babbling." And as we noted in chapter 2 while discussing the onset of symbolization, the word serves the child as a way both toward the emerging culture and back to the maternal object during the developmental crises of separation and rapprochement. Indeed, language may well be goaded into existence by the trauma of separation, by the anxiety that arises as the mother gradually but persistently disengages herself from her offspring (Faber 1981, 64). In this way, the invocation or magical word is, like the magical tool, a means of relinking with the Mother-Goddess after one's "rebirth," and a means of drawing on the energy of the Mother-Goddess to accomplish omnipotently one's newly discovered ends. The internalized power of the original caretaker is once again projected, but this time into an image, a verbal embodiment of the *corpus maternum*, as opposed to a physical item, or "tool." It is the passionately uttered word, the semantic equivalent of Roheim's "cry," that will make Mother-Goddess "react." It is the grown-up, syntactic "babbling" that will make her "come" and "bless" her Wiccan children.

The eager activity of the Witch, her enthusiastic employment of tools and invocations, must not prevent us from appreciating the ultimately regressive nature of her conduct. True, she moves away from the Goddess as well as toward the Goddess with her pentacles and wands and cups and magical utterances. But she moves away as a reborn child, as one who chooses to deny and expunge her actual birth and development, her actual separation from mother, her actual smallness and mortality. We don't have to wrack our brains to figure out who and what is behind the Witch's invocational cries. "Let separation be over"; "remember the ocean-womb from which we come"; "mother of all life, engulf us." It isn't the "mother of all life" but the mother of *this* life, *her* life, upon whom the Witch is calling; for that is the only mother she knows, and that is the mother she unconsciously projects into her tools and her prayers. In all of this, we see the past repeating itself compulsively and obsessively, which is precisely what is wrong with this "religion" and with all New Age thinking: it doesn't truly move us forward, perceptually or intellectually or emotionally. It leaves us floundering in current versions of old issues. Like the little child of scriptural prophecy, the reborn Witch enters the kingdom of heaven through her magical endeavours, but it is a heaven of denial, a heaven of omnipotent, narcissistic wishes, a heaven in which dependency is pathetically acted out in rituals that ostensibly speak for independence and strength. Witchcraft does more than remind us of the extent to which the early period of our lives can govern, can dictate, our present behaviour; it allows us to perceive a measure of heroism in all those actual little children who underwent the developmental crises of their actual lives and who refused to deny reality when they grew up.

Omnipotence: The Limitless Self

Linked with the Goddess, possessed of wondrous tools and invocations, the Witch is now in a position to manifest her belief in her own omnipotence. The way this goes in the literature is unforgettable and calls to mind Malinowski's fundamental insight that magic is purely and simply an expression of emotion, a desire, a wish that something might be brought about or be otherwise than it is. "A child," writes Simos (1979, 23), who discloses more than she realizes by the analogy, "makes-believe that she is a queen; her chair becomes a throne." A Witch "makes-believe that her wand has magic power, and it becomes a channel for psychic energy." Lifting her wand into the air and invoking the Goddess (we may call this, officially, the posture of omnipotence), the Witch concentrates upon achieving a particular aim. This is termed, among Wiccans, "raising a spell," and may be regarded from a psychoanalytic point of view as a kind of projective identification or psychical transference and the nodal expression of omnipotence in action. When she feels that her "spell" has been attached to the person or item upon which she has been concentrating (wand in air), the Witch completes the transferential change or alteration of the environment by saying, simply, it is so—in other words, by verbally insisting upon the efficacy of her concentration and the corresponding result.

Here is an example from Simos (1979, 122, 134). We may imagine the following words spoken as the Witch concentrates upon "healing a broken heart," helping a coven member succeed in business, "attracting love" or "money," or any such task:

Source to source
Flow through me . . .
As I will
So shall it be.
Spell make it so!
[Lower hands as you speak until wand touches ground.]

Thus do we behold the omnipotence of thought in all its pathetic, naked simplicity: a person wants something, wishes for it, and believes he will get it. What was learned so deeply during the early period, namely that all one had to do to achieve one's end was will it and express it, is never forgotten. And no wonder; for how could such a marvellous situation ever be relinquished in the unconscious? As Simos (1979, 132) states, capturing for us once again the simple-minded essence of the business, Wiccan "magic teaches us" that our powers, our "energies," are "unlimited, infinite ... Our voices carry power, the power to create, to change the world ... Our voices are sacred ... Open your eyes and look about you ... Feel your strength sparkling through your body. This is power." The reborn Witch, her eyes newly "opened," feels regressively once again the emotional, bodily "sparkle" experienced by the omnipotent child in his magical, vibrational fusion with the caretaker.

Is the Witch afflicted by loneliness? Well, how does she deal with this dilemma, one of the banes of human existence? She adopts the posture of omnipotence (wand raised on high), recalls her link to the Goddess, concentrates her energy into a "spell," and says, "Loneliness, be gone!" That is all there is to it. In Simos's (1979, 118) words, the Witch will now "feel free of loneliness." Does the Witch have an enemy? Well, what does she do about it? She casts a circle, takes a doll in her hand, visualizes a net falling over the doll, adopts the posture of omnipotence, and says, "So be you bound, as I desire" (126). Her enemies haven't a chance.

According to Farrar (1984, 238), the "best spells" are created by "using your own imagination and devising them." Does a friend suffer from paranoia? Well, adopt the posture of omnipotence, invoke the Goddess, and repeat the word *paranoia* over and over again. This will "build up a thought-form," or "raise a spell," which one can then "activate" and "discharge" toward the sufferer by "focusing" it into its "quasi-independent existence" (240). If all goes well, the result will be as one wishes: the paranoiac will experience a diminution of his malaise. If we are gathered in a coven and have a magical aim, we can employ "linked-hand magic." This "limbers the psychic muscles and builds up a cone of power." When we have decided on our objective, when, in Farrar's (239) words, "our wishes have been named," we wait for the coven leader to cry, "Let go!" and then we "visualize the power flying outward to achieve its various objectives." I could cite dozens of similar examples from the Wiccan texts.

The reader may be wondering, of course, how Wiccans go about explaining such omnipotence of thought. After all, we live in an age of science, of empiricism, experimentation, and debate, and we would expect Witchcraft's appeal to the primitive unconscious to be supported by some sort of argument. As we saw in our opening section, the ranks of the Craft are currently filled with people from all walks of life—with lawyers, doctors, engineers, nurses, cooks, couriers, and computer programmers. Surely among these motley practitioners are some who find themselves unwilling simply to take things at face value.

Wiccan texts offer the reader a continuous stream of intellectual self-justification that takes the form of metaphysical claims (by analogy and of a general nature), reminders of the mysteries of modern physics, and references to the work of C. G. Jung. "There is a power in the universe," writes Cunningham (1988, 19) in what turns out to be a typical Wiccan intellectual moment. It can be used for both good and evil, and it can also be "roused, concentrated, and programmed to effect a specific result, as in a spell." Such a process, continues Cunningham (21), "may entail creating and holding certain images and concepts in the mind." True, we cannot at present "explain how this works," but "fringe physics is coming close to this achievement" (23). I leave it to the reader to judge the value of this kind of thinking. In another of his books, Cunningham (1989, 5) informs us that "the physical world is one of many realities" (a ubiquitous cliché among Wiccans). He then proceeds to declare that "the only difference between the physical and the spiritual is that the former is denser." May I say with impunity that such a statement begs a few additional questions?

"Witches are not fools," says Farrar (1984, 105); they live in "the twentieth century, not the Middle Ages," and there are a good many "scientists and technicians" among them. The "working power of the Craft arises from the emotions, from the vasty deep of the Collective Unconscious" as described by Jung. The "Gods and Goddesses" of Witchcraft "draw their forms from the numinous Archetypes which are the mighty foundation-stones of the human racial psyche." Exactly how this occurs is never explained by Farrar, any more than it is by Gardner (1959, 43), who makes a similar claim. But then, the matter was never fully or satisfactorily explained by Jung, who struggled throughout the course of his life to understand the nature of what he chose to call "archetypes."

Farrar (1984, 107) proceeds to declare that "reality exists and operates on many levels," that "each of these has its own laws," and that "these sets of laws are compatible with each other and govern the interaction between the levels." When a Witch raises and casts a spell she has simply discovered a "point and area of interaction between the levels" (109). Magic "does not break the laws of nature"; it "obeys laws that the observer has not yet understood." Thus Witchcraft is "the philosophical framework into which every phenomenon, from chemistry to clairvoyance, from logarithms to love, can be reasonably fitted." Needless to say, it would be wonderful to behold "every phenomenon" (including spells) fitted into Witchcraft's "philosophical framework"—I mean, in a detailed, specific, systematic way. But, alas, this never occurs in Farrar, or in the work of any other Witch. What we get in the end is a wide variety of unorganized, unsupported observations and general, overall claims—in other words, a farrago of pseudo-scientific and occult speculations.

Psychology is simply a branch of magic, writes Simos (1979, 192), as both "psychology and magic purport to describe and change consciousness." Although Witchcraft's "testing" of magical rites to see if they work is somewhat more "subjective" than scientific procedure (is this, perchance, an understatement?), science and religion are ultimately on a par in that each "is a set of metaphors for a reality that can never be completely described or comprehended" (190). That many kinds of "psychology" exist, some of which are given to rigorous experimental methodology and the systematic compilation of clinical data over decades; that "science" comes by its "metaphors" in ways that are entirely different from the "testing" of Wiccan rites and spells—all this is of little concern to Simos and, apparently, her followers. Witchcraft, psychology, and science: they are all essentially similar; to believe in Witchcraft, psychology, and science really amounts to the same thing. There isn't much difference, ultimately, between Gerald Gardner running around the Isle of Man with his cords and wands and Albert Einstein sitting down to his desk at Princeton.

Simos (1979, 129) writes in one place that the Witch's power to "shake the world" is "most perilous, dangerous." Hence, it must "follow knowledge, serve need," and be employed in a "cleansing, healing" fashion. But the real danger here, I would submit, is the belief in one's omnipotence, the unwillingness to acknowledge one's limitations—in short, the refusal to grow up and join the human race; for in this denial, in this infantile, narcissistic imperviousness to the facts of one's development, there resides a major threat to the welfare and advancement not only of the individual psyche but of the social realm as well: a good measure of the violence, havoc, and general suffering that people have had to endure in this world has stemmed from those grandiose characters who have regarded themselves precisely as our prophet Simos (1979, 13) urges her followers to regard themselves, namely as "manifest gods," as "divine" and "sacred" (9). The "knowledge" that is needed here is the knowledge of the early period of existence when problems of separation, along with Oedipal rivalries, awaken the taste for omnipotence and self-aggrandizement. This is the knowledge that has a "healing, cleansing" potential. The working of Wiccan spells ultimately calls to mind Harold Searles's (1984, 38) observation that disturbed individuals struggle to mature and become fully human *without* relinquishing their infantile omnipotence.

Six Wiccan Rituals

1. Drawing Down the Moon

Adler (1986, 19) calls this ritual "one of the most serious and beautiful in the modern Craft." The Priestess "invokes the Goddess or Triple Goddess, symbolized by the phases of the moon and known by a thousand names ... In some Craft rituals the Priestess goes into a trance and speaks; in other traditions the ritual is a more formal dramatic dialogue, often of intense beauty, in which, again, the Priestess speaks, taking the role of the Goddess. In both instances the Priestess functions as the Goddess incarnate, within the circle." Adler then describes the "feeling of power and emotion" that comes over her as she "listens to the words of the Great Mother."

In Simos (1979, 166), the rite goes (in abbreviated form) like this:

Waxing Moon Ritual
(To be performed after the first visible crescent has appeared.)

On the altar, place a bowl of seeds. Fill the central cauldron with earth, and place a candle in the center. When the coven gathers, begin with a breathing meditation. A Priestess says, "This is the time of the beginning, the seed time of creation, the awakening after sleep. Now the moon emerges, a crescent out of the dark; the Birthgiver returns from death. Tonight we are touched ... She changes everything She touches."

Purify, cast the circle, and invoke the Goddess and God. A covener chosen to act as Seed Priestess takes the bowl of grain from the altar, saying, "Blessed be, creature of earth, moon seed of change, bright beginning of a new circle of time. Power to start, power to grow, power to make new, be in this seed" ... Going sunwise around the circle she offers the bowl to each person ... Each person visualizes a clear image of what they want to grow ... One by one, they plant the seeds in the cauldron ... Together, they raise a cone of power to charge the seeds and earth with energy ... Share cakes and wine, and open the circle.

Full Moon Ritual
(To be performed on the eve of the full moon.)

The circle gathers, does a breathing meditation, and a Priestess says, "This is the time of fullness, the flood tide of power, when the

Lady in full circle of brightness rides across the night sky ... This is the time of the bearing of fruits ... The Great Mother, nurturer of the world pours out her love and her gifts in abundance ... Purify, cast the circle and invoke the Goddess and the God" ... One covener moves to the center of the circle and speaks her name. The others repeat it, and chant it, raising a cone of power as they touch her, earthing it into her and filling her with the power and the light of the moon. She returns to the circle and another covener takes her place ... A final cone can be raised for the coven as a whole ... Share cakes and wine and open the circle.

Dark Moon Ritual
(To be performed on the waning moon. A crystal or scrying bowl should be placed in the center of the circle.)

Gather and meditate on a group breath. A Priestess says, "This is the ending before the beginning, the death before new life ... The moon is hidden, but the faintest of stars are revealed and those who have eyes to see may read the fates and know the mysteries. The Goddess, whose name cannot be spoken, naked enters the Kingdom of Death" ... Cast the circle ... The Leader leads a chant:

Leader: She lies under all, She covers all.
All: She lies under all, She covers all ...

Continue as long as there is energy and inspiration ... Build into a worldless power chant ... Crystal gaze together, sharing what you see. Share cakes and wine, and open the circle.

Warren-Clarke (1987, 86) offers practitioners the following instructions as they perform this rite: "Extend your arms out and up, and with your Will proceed to Draw Down the Moon. Breathe deeply and visualize a stream of force entering into you from the Moon's light, the Essence of the Goddess."

Psychoanalytic Notes. This metaphor reveals the underlying purpose of the Craft as a whole. The moon is of course a projective version of the maternal figure, and the fantasy embedded in the rite is to pull the mother back into the psychological orbit of the individual. As we have seen, the onset of differentiation marks the loss of fusion and omnipotence. The mother moves away, into "outer space," as it were; she is no longer directly in the sphere of the child's will. Thus to "draw the moon down," to bring it back or near with one's wilful effort, is to deny and to reverse the central, traumatic event of infancy and childhood. The rite expresses, on the one hand, the individual's belief in his own omnipotent capacity to undo the past, to get the mother back; and it expresses, on the other, the individual's wish and need to have the mother's power, that "stream of force" which "enters him" as he basks in the "light" of the Moon-Goddess. This is, surely, the way the child feels as he participates in the mother's omnipotence, in her magical, immaterial energy, or, as Warren-Clarke puts it, her "essence."

Drawing Down the Moon also constitutes a fantastic attempt to allay unconscious anxiety by mastering the maternal object in several of her "phases." These correspond, at their metaphorical core, to aspects of developmental interaction as described in Mahler (1975) and in object relations generally. When the moon is "slim," when it does not shine upon us with the radiance we require, when, in short, it metaphorically harbours a facet of the bad object, we do not have to be afraid or anxious: the mother is slowly getting full, slowly coming to birth, or seed. Soon we will have our emotional nourishment, our narcissistic supplies; soon we will be "blessedly" included in a "new circle of time." The full moon celebrates the maternal figure in her idealized form, replete with life and power. Here is the full breast, the loving, nurturing object for which the practitioner yearns most deeply, and the aim of the rite, quite simply, is to draw this down to the mouth, to get the love and the power inside. Once again in Simos's words, each covener is to be "filled with the power and the light of the moon." When the moon is absent, or "dark," when the mother is not there at all, we are also comforted. For we are told, first, that her absence is not permanent. Just as the babysitter reassures the child who wakes up and finds the parent gone, so does the ritual reassure the Witch. Second, and perhaps more significantly, the ritual informs the practitioner that the absent mother is actually present; although she cannot be seen, she's there: "She lies under all, and she covers all," says the Leader, and the coven members repeat the words. Here we see echoed the child's first, primitive efforts at internalization of the maternal image and the object constancy that such internalization brings. We also see echoed early efforts at specifically transitional phenomena: like the baby's blankie, the Goddess "lies under all and covers all." Finally, as coveners move to the circle's centre to gaze into the crystal ball, they collectively allay anxiety about the future, the time during which the absent object is scheduled to return. Taken as a whole, Drawing Down the Moon acts-out obsessively several major conflicts of the mother-child relationship.

2. The Mirror Ritual

In Warren-Clarke's (1987, 45) version of the ritual, one sits in front of a "fairly large mirror" and, with open eyes, "goes into meditation."

Rocking back and forth and chanting his "own name," the practitioner "every now and then" interrupts the chant with the words "I am." Warren-Clarke insists that one "does not lose eye contact with himself" during the course of this rite, which concludes with the words "I am who I am and I am one." Cunningham's (1988, 55) rendition has the Witch "gazing at his reflection in the mirror" and pronouncing these words: "Love is before me, behind me, beside me, above me ... Love flows from me, love comes to me, I am loved." For Cunningham, a "small mirror" that enables one to "see his face within it" is sufficient for the purpose.

Psychoanalytic Notes. We have here another striking example of modern Witchcraft's endless preoccupation with issues of separation and union, and in particular with the mirror stage of development during which the child begins to establish an identity distinct from the mother's. So persistently does the loss of symbiosis and the trauma of differentiation echo in the unconscious of the practitioner that he must act the matter out over and over again, reassuring himself that he has survived and does in fact exist. What the child apprehends as the loss of the mother during the onset of differentiation is often accompanied by feelings of rejection. Cunningham's version of the mirror ritual strives to reassure the Witch that he can still love and be loved in spite of his differentiation from the original object. The emergence of a separate identity during the mirror stage depends upon mutual face-gazing activity between mother and child. Such activity is indeed one of the earliest ego-formative interactions between humans. The Wiccan rite focuses intensely upon staring at one's own face—a new version of the old, primal relation and an attempt to transform one's countenance into a transitional object on which one can depend emotionally in the present, post-maternal environment.

3. The Openings of the Body Ritual

Described by Farrar (1984, 85) as a "time-honored method for the psychic protection of an individual," the rite can be performed "either by oneself or by one's working partner." For "obvious practical reasons," the "person to be protected" undergoes the ritual naked, or, as Witches are fond of saying, "skyclad." Here are Farrar's instructions: "Moisten the index finger of the right hand with a consecrated salt-and-water mixture, and touch each of the openings of the body in turn saying each time, 'Be thou sealed against all evil.' Strongly visualize the seals which you are creating ... On a man: right eye, left eye, right ear, left ear, right nostril, left nostril, mouth, right nipple, left nipple, navel, tip of penis, anus ... On a woman [the same, with the female sexual parts indicated]." As to whether this ritual is preferable to the casting of a protective circle, Farrar contends that an individual who is on the move will find it particularly useful: "A cast circle can be carried with you as you move (we have often cast a circle round a moving car, for instance), but it requires deliberate and continuing visualization." The openings of the body ritual, by contrast, "accompanies you like a suit or armor wherever you go."

Psychoanalytic Notes. So salient is the omnipotence of thought here that it may easily obscure the ritual's transitional purpose. One wishes to be protected and one therefore indulges in simple magical thinking in order to fulfil one's wish. But underlying the wish for protection is the unwillingness to face danger (or what is perceived as danger) alone—without the protective presence of the parental figure. Naked, the practitioner returns to the early period during which the mother's omnipotence enclosed the child permanently within its protective "armour." As we earlier demonstrated, the circle in modern Witchcraft is a symbolic expression of the primary caregiver, and, as Farrar's work makes clear, the Openings of the Body Ritual is psychologically equivalent to casting a protective circle. Thus it strives omnipotently, like Drawing Down the Moon, to refind the symbiotic mother, the good object who seals one off from invasion by the "bad" or "evil" forces of the world. In most cases, of course, these forces are the projective expressions of one's own psyche (the bad object) and hence the source of obsessional conduct, such as we witness here.

4. The Circle of Stones

Used to "raise energy" for the working of magic, the rite requires, in Cunningham's (1988, 105) words, "four large flat stones" and a lengthy piece of "white or purple cord." After "cleansing the area" with a "ritual broom," one places the first stone to the north, and the second, third and fourth to the east, south, and west. "This square," says the author, "represents the physical plane on which we exist: the Earth." One then takes his length of cord and lays it out circularly around the stones. "Now you have a square and a circle, the circle representing the spiritual reality. As such, this is a squared circle—the place of interpenetration of the physical and spiritual realms." The next step is to "set up the altar" and get hold of one's "tools": wand, athame, pentacle, censer, and whatever else one requires for a particular magical purpose. When one has completed his "consecrations," he "stands facing north at the edge of the cord-marked circle and summons up his power, readying it to be projected during the circle-casting." It is through one's "visualization" that the circle is created. One "walks slowly around the circle's perimeter clockwise" with feet inside the cord and with one's "words and energy charging the area." Let the "power flow out of your knife's blade," instructs Cunningham; "stretch the energy out until it forms a complete sphere around the working area ... Then say, 'Here is the boundary of the Circle of Stones ... Charge this by your powers, Old Ones' [a reference to the Goddess and God]." Moving to the north, one holds his wand "aloft" (the posture of omnipotence), and says, "O Spirit of the North Stone, I call you to attend this circle." One behaves similarly at the eastern, western, and southern points, until "the circle lives and breathes about you. The Spirits of the Stones are present. Feel the energies. Visualize the circle glowing and growing in power." Magic, Cunningham declares, may now be "wrought."

Psychoanalytic Notes. The purpose of this rite is to re-create and to re-enter the mother's body. As we have seen, the Earth in Witchcraft represents the Great Goddess, and the stones in this ritual represent "the Earth." We do not have to struggle to grasp the underlying significance of the "cord" that surrounds the stones. Having refashioned symbolically the *corpus maternum,* and having equipped himself with magical tools, the practitioner literally steps inside the "sphere," charges it with "energy," and thus erases the primary psychological boundary that was established between mother and infant during the differentiation phase of development. It is not the "physical and spiritual planes" that "interpenetrate" here, but the past and the present, and more specifically the before-separation and after-separation worlds. The practitioner of this ritual, like the practitioner of Drawing Down the Moon, believes that he has the power to reconnect with the omnipotent object, to rediscover the wondrous vibrational union of the early period. At the same time, he performs the rite to gain the omnipotence he associates with the parental presence. Wand "aloft," he calls upon the "Old Ones," the "Spirits of the Earth," to cause the circle of energy in which he stands to "glow and grow in power" so that his "magic" might be "wrought." To consider the Circle of Stones in its entirety is to realize that modern Witchcraft comprises a war upon human limitation. Accordingly, it attracts to its ranks individuals who simply cannot or will not relinquish an infantile demand that might be stated this way: I must be joined with my omnipotent mother forever; I must continue to possess the special, unlimited powers that I enjoyed during the initial stages of my life.

5. The Doll or Stuffed Animal Ritual

After casting a circle and lighting a candle, one takes a doll or stuffed animal in his hands, sprinkles it with consecrated salt water, and gives it a name. Then, according to Simos (1979, 121), one holds it in his arms, coos to it, rocks it, and tells it "everything one would have liked to hear" as a child. "Playing" thus, one "raises energy" through "visualization" and "pours it into the doll." This "creates an image of one's child self as one would have liked it to be." When the doll is "glowing with white light and love," the practitioner concludes the ritual by kissing it, wrapping it in a white cloth, and "laying it to rest on the altar."

Psychoanalytic Notes. Playing with substitute objects is one of the chief methods through which the child attempts to resolve the crisis of separation that confronts him/her during the early period. The doll, the blankie, the teddy, moves the child away from the mother and toward the cultural realm at the same time that it allows him to stay with the mother emotionally. Psychoanalysis, following the lead of D. W. Winnicott, terms such behaviour "transitional," as we noted in chapter 2. The practitioner of this rite has failed to resolve transitional problems satisfactorily. He is therefore attempting (here is the omnipotence) to "do it all over again" *without* the separation and loss that of necessity attend the onset of differentiation. "Raising energy" through "visualization," he projects it into the substitute object, which is immediately transformed into an idealized version of himself as neonate. Thus he resolves the transitional dilemma by magically becoming both mother and child at once. He is born again, named again, cooed again, and rocked again by himself. There is no parental figure here to push him away, to demand that he exist on his own as a separate, differentiated creature. Once again we behold modern Witchcraft's obsessional longing for the good object, for the never-never land of eternal fusion, for that place over the rainbow where we are perfectly loved, perfectly secure, all wrapped up in white and resting blissfully on the Great Mother's bosom (the altar).

6. The Great Rite

This is, quite simply, sexual intercourse Wiccan style, which means sexual intercourse that is linked symbolically to the body of the Great Mother. "Sexuality," writes Simos (1979, 195), "is a manifestation of the Goddess." Indeed, "all the acts of love" belong to the Goddess who says "they are mine." When an individual achieves "orgasm," it is not only his own "pleasure" that he/she feels, but also the "moving force" of the "mother" (79). As Cunningham (1988, 131) conceives it, "sex" is a union with another person and with the Mother-Goddess who created us. In the words of Farrar (1984, 32), it is the "Great Rite" that celebrates our "holy, divine" connection to the "Goddess and the God."

Psychoanalytic Notes. The appeal of all this is twofold. There is, on the one hand, the sheer titillation that derives from associating sexuality with the parent, with the forbidden, incestuous object. The "feeling of incredible erotic intensity" referred to by the Witch Alara Bretanne (1989, 10) in her review of Qualls-Corbett's *The Sacred Prostitute* is a good example. By relinking our sexual behaviour to the "sensuality of the Goddess," writes Bretanne, we can reconnect our "passion" to the "depths of our unconscious minds" and thereby renew our "spiritual natures." Permit me to suggest that there is nothing very "spiritual" about this. Indeed, the putative "spirituality" is merely a screen behind which one's incestuous proclivities can be indulged in relative safety. Bretanne gets it right when she brings in the connection between "passion" and the "unconscious," but she gets it wrong when she tries to make the unconscious religious or spiritual. It is the familial, personal unconscious that is at work here, troublesome as that may be for the ardent practitioner. On the other hand, there is the transitional appeal of the "rite." I mean, by linking sexuality to the Goddess, by going to bed with our partner and the Great Mother too, we remain in the protective circle of the first relationship. Our genital behaviours harbour the soothing and reassuring overtones of the oral stage. We enjoy the kind of fusion, the kind of merging and blending of boundaries, that we associate with the early period and with the good object who resides at its centre.

But Wiccan sexuality can also be put to magical purposes which allow us to behold the coital partners indulging both their sensual nature and their psychological omnipotence. A "couple" who wishes to use "sex magic" for a "worthwhile objective," writes Farrar (1984, 171), will "cast a Circle around themselves" and make "love" therein. "Building up sexual tension-in-unity to the highest possible peak … they will aim at simultaneous orgasm, at which point they will hurl the whole power of the vortex into the achievement of their magical objective." In modern Witchcraft, then, we can "screw" our way toward the achievement of our goals. The "circle" in which we indulge ourselves is a magical provider not only of the security we seek but of the power we aspire to as well. Yet how could it be otherwise? For as we have seen repeatedly, the circle in modern Witchcraft turns out to be the body of the Great Mother herself. Reunited unconsciously with that body, we transfer our infantile omnipotence of the sphere of our sexual conduct.

Several of the rites at which we have glanced can be performed by solitary practitioners. When a rite unfolds in the context of the coven, however, it will be enhanced by the psychological dynamics peculiar to such gatherings. As members join hands around the circle, writes

Simos (1979, 41–45), they feel "close," secure, bound together by their practice. They "breathe one breath" and "become one," inhaling the "odor of the womb." The coven has many significances, of course, but the foundational one is captured by Ashbach and Schermer (1987, 6) when they observe that "the group often takes on the qualities of the maternal object," and that "group fantasy and ritual are simultaneously ways in which the membership defends against primitive anxieties." Where Wiccans are concerned, such primitive anxieties have a great deal to do with separation from the caretaker and the loss of omnipotence that attends the onset of differentiation. In a fascinating phrase (slip?) Simos (1988, 134) declares that the coven comprises "one nation indivisible," thus disclosing the extent to which the group can absorb those emotions ordinarily transferred to the nation—one's "motherland," one's "fatherland," the macroscopic *home*. Finally, when a meeting has concluded and members are free "to go their separate ways," they all say together, "The circle is open but unbroken" (Simos 1979, 45). In other words, coven members are *never* obliged to be separate; they carry each other (and the Goddess) around on the inside even while they are "on their own," just as the child carries around his internalized image of the mother.

Trance and the Astral Journey

Induced through a kind of meditative visualization, trance is the extreme instance of the persistent imaging Witches do in their transitional quest to rediscover and hold on to the caretaker. Simos (1979, 144) discloses the essence of the business when she writes that "in trance we find revelation. We invoke and become Goddess and God, linked to all that is. We experience union, ecstasy, openness. The limits of our perception dissolve ... We dance the spiral dance of existence." Simos also observes here that trance can be "dangerous" because it "opens the gates to the unconscious mind." As we noted earlier, the "spiral dance" is one of Witchcraft's chief expressions for the ubiquitous, all-encompassing, all-powerful Goddess. Hence the appeal of trance (that it permits us to re-enter the *corpus maternum*) harbours a measure of anxiety: we may regressively "dissolve" into the mother's body, become engulfed in it, as we were long ago.

The astral journey (or astral projection) commences with the practitioner casting a protective circle around himself. He then induces a trance-like state by imaging, say, the "temple of Isis" with its "great halls and pillars" (Simos 1979, 143). As the trance deepens and the "astral vision takes charge," the practitioner undergoes a "separation of his astral body from its physical housing." He then "projects" that "astral body" into the vast, endless "realm" of "energy and thought forms," which underlies and somehow gives rise to the crude, "physical universe." The separation of the practitioner's astral body from its physical "housing" is not, however, total. A "connection" is "retained" by means of an "etheric cord" (Simos also calls it a "raith") through which the practitioner "feeds" while on his cosmic travels.

Other Wiccan accounts of the astral journey are essentially similar to Simos's. According to Warren-Clarke (1987, 41), the practitioner's ability to project his astral body "from one place to another" may be enhanced by a rigorous training of his imagistic powers. Farrar (1984, 214) informs us that we have "no cause to eat or drink" as we go, but "if we did drink ritual wine during astral projection it would be astral wine, manifested on the astral plane" by the traveller's "own will-power." Farrar remarks that astral projection is ultimately a kind of "bilocation," or the "gift of being able to be in two places at once." In helping us to see this, he offers a drawing of a naked woman lying on her back while another woman just like her but of a slightly different colour arises out of her body and floats into the air.

What is particularly striking about astral projection is the degree to which it strives to actually reproduce and regain dual-unity. One *was* "bilocated" at the inception of his life, existing in and through the mother as much as in and through himself. In a very special psychoanalytic sense, one was two. Here, one casts a magical circle around himself, goes into a trance, leaves the "physical housing" of his body, and psychically floats into a huge cosmic sea of primal energies to which he is connected by a "cord," an etheric, wraith-like umbilicus designed explicitly to "feed" him during the period of his projective altered state. And, needless to say, one can do this over and over again, every day, for hours on end, should one wish to do so. The repressed, in this case the obsessional longing to refuse with the mother's body, has returned thinly disguised as a manifestation of one's "higher" or "spiritual" nature. Astral projection is, of course, practised by occultists generally, not just by Witches, and it was indulged in long before the modern Witchcraft movement commenced (Carrington and Muldoon 1929). It found its way to the Craft (and the New Age) simply because it offered Witches a splendid opportunity to deny their separation from the caregiver. Ultimately, astral projection says to the Witch, "Do you want dual-unity? Do you want to exist again in the sphere of the all-encompassing mother? Well, lie down, close your eyes, and go for it!" When Simos (1979, 151) declares that we must return from our astral journey "slowly and gently," that "coming out" of our trance-like state is just as "important" as "going in," she merely touches upon the other side of the dual-unity equation. Having engaged in re-fusion with the object, or, in Mahler's (1975) terms, having "refuelled" emotionally through our psychic umbilicus, we return to the "real world" secure in the knowledge that Mother-Goddess is there, dancing galactically in space and awaiting another visit from her charge when his affective hunger wells up within him again. Like all dual-unity games (going to church on Sunday, talking with God in prayer, etc.), astral travel is both toward and away from the object, a rhythmic regression and return to reality. The toward part of this game happens to be more fascinating and more challenging to us psychoanalytically because it stands at the edge of mental disturbance.

Visualization: Magic and Its Ends

Visualization, states Cunningham (1989, 82), "is the most basic and yet advanced technique called for in magic and Wicca, for it "reprograms the power" raised by the Witch "to create changes in this world" (84). More specifically, when the Witch feels himself "bursting with power," power that has been raised by "rubbing his palms together for twenty minutes, tensing his muscles, and breathing deeply," he "holds out his right (projective) hand, and directs his energy from his body, through his arm and out his fingers," all the while "using his visualiza-tion." "Really see and feel it streaming out," writes Cunningham, as you go about, say, sealing your house from evil. Simos (1979, 151) regards visualization as the means to discovering one's "place of power," a "new space" of being in which one feels "safe, protected, in complete control, and in touch with one's deepest sources of strength." In the words of Warren-Clarke (1987, 18), "those who choose the path of magic" will find visualization to be "the most important technique of all." This brings us to a pivotal assertion.

As we consider the psychoanalytic significance of these passages, we must not make the error of confusing the working of magic with its ends. I mean, it is tempting to regard the end—protecting a house from evil, recouping lost wealth, etc.—as the essential item in the activity, much as Malinowski (1925) does when he declares that all magic is a kind of emotional wishing for something, or Roheim (1955) (by impli-cation, at least) when he asserts that magic originates in infancy and is devoted to accomplishing unconscious purposes of an oral or Oedipal nature. But the end, the wish, the purpose is merely a kind of secondary bribe, and an ancillary consideration. What the doer of magic most deeply desires is to be in the position of doing magic, *to be in that state*, for it is *in* that state that he experiences re-fusion and the omnipotence of thought that accompanies re-fusion. It is *in* that state that he establishes, or, better, re-establishes, the lost and longed-for link with the object. In a very real sense, it makes no difference to the Wiccan magician what the aim of his magic is; anything will do, anything will interest him (barring, of course, obviously immoral requisitions), as long as he is able to be magical, as long as he is able to engage in activities that will give him the delicious, ecstatic feeling he knew formerly in the dual-unity situation when he was fused, omnipotent, and ever, ever so precious. That is why a Wiccan fortune-teller can appear to take an interest in the trivial affairs of ten thousand ridiculous clients; each time he goes to work he gets, in addition to his fee, the drug-like "hit" of feeling omnipotent and fused.

This applies to an enormous range of magical practices but is perhaps most vividly exemplified in scrying, or crystal-gazing. As the Witch stares into her crystal ball she experiences power, power to master time and space, to know the secrets of the past and future both in the immediate location and far away. Moreover, the act of staring recalls unconsciously the primal, mutual face-gazing activity between mother and infant through which the latter's ego, with its rudimentary perceptions of space and time, was formed. Here is the dual-unity situation, with its fusion and omnipotence, all over again. Here is the mother-infant bond with its wondrous feelings of connection and power. No wonder Witches are traditionally hooked on staring into their crystal balls. To put the matter as bluntly as possible from the psychoanalytic perspective, and to recall the final sentence of our section on magical stones, the crystal ball of the Witch is the mother's face.

Polarity and Channelling

Magic is ultimately rooted, say Wiccans (Farrar 1984, 33), in the "polarity" of the universe. Positive-negative, female-male—when these interact we get power. On the higher, transcendent "levels," it is the union of "the Goddess and the God" (33) that dramatically puts to work polarity's creative potential; on the "level" of human interaction, polarity manifests itself in a thousand ways, from sexual congress to rubbing one's palms together in preparation for magic. Yet no matter what "level" is involved in producing power, the principle is the same. In Farrar's (1984, 33) words, which are echoed endlessly in the literature, "as above, so below." Thus, in the Wiccan view, all "levels" of existence, from spiritual to mundane, are ultimately connected as manifestations of a polarized cosmic design. What we do "down here" not only echoes but actually expresses what Goddess and God do "up there." And what Goddess and God do "up there" discovers its way to the human "level," *is* the human "level" to the eye that can penetrate the core.

Certainly the production of energy in the world has something to do with what we choose to call positive and negative charges, or particles. We've all read simple descriptions of electrical devices. But to say these have something to do with the working of magic, or with the behaviour of deities, or with the ultimate nature of the universe (if there is such a thing), is nothing more nor less than facile analogizing and fantasizing. Witches do not know the answer to such mysteries and so they make up "theories." Their projections, however, are not without interpretative value. Indeed, when we examine them from an analytic perspective we find that they guide us quite nicely to the essentials of the matter. The "poles" from which magic arises are, quite simply, the before-separation and after-separation worlds, the "positive" feelings one has during the stage of omnipotence and fusion, and the "negative" feelings one has during the period of separation and differentiation, as described by Mahler (1975). It is when these "levels" interact, it is when the urge to recapture the limitlessness of the early time meets the traumatic reality of one's separation and smallness, that the "energy" to do magic, or to be magical again, arises. The "power" of the Witch is a projective manifestation of the dynamic, conflicting objects of his inner world, the "positive" and "negative" forces that clash therein.

Nor is it a coincidence that Witches locate the cosmic powerplant in the male and female "poles" of Goddess and God: when fusion subsides, when omnipotence ends, when separation and differentiation loom, it is the symbiotic world of the mother that the child must give up for the more socially oriented world of the paternal figure. *This* is the primal conflict. The Goddess and the God are simply the mother (the before-separation-world) and the father (the after-separation-world) "writ large," metaphoric or mythic expressions of the gods of the nursery. Witchcraft projects the parental influence on a cosmic scale (as the small child is wont to do) and then turns to its own projection in a grandiose effort to explain its power-seeking, its thirst for omnipotence and fusion. In short, the Wiccan "theory" of polarity, rooted explicitly in the figures of Goddess and God, comprises a fairly obvious "Freudian slip." As for the Wiccan notion of "levels," and the traditional Wiccan causative formula, "as above so below," it merely discloses, through an additional slip, the manner in which the unconscious spins the plot here. What is happening "above," at the conscious level, in the projective metaphors and myths of the Craft, is indeed related integrally to what is occurring "below" the surface, at the "level" where old wishes and aims, tied to the parental figures or the gods of the nursery, will not be relinquished.

Note how the idea and practice of channelling perfectly illustrates the point. As the Priestess "draws down the moon," writes Farrar (1984, 67), she becomes the actual, physical "channel of the Goddess," who comes through her not in some diffuse, spiritual way but really takes over a specific part of her body and manifests divine power through that. "Anybody who has witnessed Drawing Down the Moon regularly," states Farrar elsewhere (1987, 65), "must agree that it works. Time and time again, an 'ordinary' human woman seems transformed by it, so that the coven has no difficulty in reacting to her as the voice and the presence of the Goddess ... Nor is it just the matter of the tone of delivery. Many times we have known the familiar words of the Charge to be unexpectedly replaced by something quite different." And then, in words that beget our full analytic attention, "In either case, the delivery is not usually determined by the Priestess' conscious decision. Every experienced Priestess is familiar with the strange feeling of observing from a corner of her own mind, *of listening to the Goddess using her vocal cords*, and wondering what will come next" (Farrar 1987, 65, my emphasis). Clearly, as we maintained in the previous section, the practice of channelling is designed to get the mother—in Wiccan terms the Goddess and in psychoanalytic terms the object— back into the body of the practitioner, to have her dwelling therein once again. During the early period the infant and the caretaker are locked in a kind of "organ" relationship; the mother serves as a symbiotic organ of the baby, and the baby is attached to the mother as a neotenous, dependent facet of the *corpus maternum*. This is the dual-unity situation in which bodily boundaries do not yet exist, in which two human beings are physiological and emotional appendages of each other.

It is precisely when this unique situation ends, when dual-unity gives way to differentiation, when one becomes two and the child moves toward the cultural realm, that the "polarities" of human existence begin to emerge in earnest. Astral projection witnesses the Witch leaving the physical "house" of her body to join the Great Mother in the heavens; channelling, by contrast, draws the Goddess down into the "house" of the Witch, where she proceeds to inhabit or take over a specific bodily part. In this way, both practices deny polarity (or pursue dual-unity), but from opposing psychological directions. As for the coven members in attendance while the "channelling" proceeds, they undergo the powerfully transitional experience of beholding the Priestess in the grip of the Great Mother, of witnessing a bodily organ of the Leader being usurped by a mythic version of the original caregiver. The

Priestess's delusional conjuring up of the object into her own throat says to those who sit in awe around her: dual-unity can be recaptured; polarity can be collapsed; we can feel the mother back in our bodies again; we are fused with the object in the most primitive, fundamental way—body with body, cell with very cell.

Even when an instance of channelling takes a form somewhat less intense than that which we witness in Farrar, even when the Goddess makes her presence felt in a more general way, the underlying psychodynamic configuration will be very much the same. The Witch will experience her being, her body, her "soul," as the expression has it, under the sway of the object, in the control of the object, and it is precisely that experience, that seductive, infantile experience, which the practice of channelling aims to induce.

Auras

Our bodies evidently give off some sort of electrical field that has been captured photographically by the Russian inventor Semyon Kirlian. We do not know exactly what this field consists of, let alone what it means. The entire matter is currently under investigation and the investigations (to put it mildly) are not leading us in any obvious direction (cf. Drury 1985, 143). All of this does not deter the Witches, however. They plunge right in with a variety of explanations and applications, and they do so because the so-called aura, like the so-called astral body, extends itself invitingly to the unconscious as a version of the dual-unity situation. A fine example emerges from a ritual that consecrates the athame, or sacred knife.

The athame "serves the Witch as a strength and defence in all magical operations against her enemies visible and invisible" (Farrar 1984, 44). It can be "conjured" by the names "Abrach and Abracadabra," and it can be consecrated through the "Great Gods and Gentle Goddesses." Having been conjured and suitably consecrated, the athame "should be handed to its new owner with a fivefold Salute." In turn, the new owner should "press it against his body for a time to get the aura." The athame "should be in as close connection as possible to the naked body for at least a month, i.e. kept under the pillow, etc.," and must not come into contact with anyone else until it has been "thoroughly impregnated" with the owner's "aura." However, "a pair working together may own the same tools, which will be impregnated with the aura of both."

Farrar's "scientific" explanation for all this is straightforward enough. "Power is latent in the body and may be drawn out and used in various ways by the skilled" (Farrar 1984, 53). It "seems to exude from the body via the skin and possibly from the bodily orifices." Yet "unless it is confined in a circle it will be swiftly dissipated." Now, as we have been told over and over again by the Wiccan texts, the power of the body, like that of everything else in the universe, is ultimately an expression of the Goddess, indeed *is* the Goddess manifesting Herself energically on the physical plane (Cunningham 1988, 20; Simos 1979, 138). Just as the Goddess can touch us and change us (Simos 1979, 175), so we can touch items to our bodies in which the Goddess dwells and experience a mighty change in those very items. The sword or athame gets power when pressed to the subject's skin because the subject still feels the omnipotent object residing beneath it. The transformation or empowering of the athame, then, is an expression of the subject's belief in his own omnipotence, derived from the object of infancy extant in his inner world and assuming the projective form of "aura."

It is not only through an invisible transference of "power" that the aura expresses itself. On the contrary, it can be seen, and it is Simos (1979, 137), among others, who tells us how to see it. The "exercise," she writes, "is best practised in a group. Each of the members can take turns being the subject. All should be proficient at sensing the aura." Having set up a plain dark background, and having situated the naked subject against it, we dim the lights, relax, and in a "light state of trance . . . scan the space around the subject in search of a glowing line." To some, Simos continues, the aura will appear as a "cloudlike astral body," to others it will appear simply "like a shadow, oddly lighter than the background"; and to others still it will manifest itself only as a "subtle difference between foreground and background." Yet all of us will see it as we "accustom ourselves to our astral vision" and "learn to see energy move." Simos concludes by reminding us that the "energy" of the aura is ultimately derived from the "great dance of the universe," which is to say from the Goddess. Indeed, she closes her projections on this topic with the following words, addressed of course to the reader: "Thou art Goddess, eternally linked, connected, at one with the moving spirit of All" (138). What does this mean from a psychoanalytic angle?

Surrounding the Witch as a kind of psychic halo, the aura is, quite simply, a delusional version of the maternal object. Linked explicitly with the Great Goddess, it radiates the omnipotence and narcissistic admiration that the mother shined on the infant during the early period (affective attunement). Standing in front of her fellow coveners, who, of course, validate the thing's existence through sheer group suggestibility (only those who are predisposed to finding auras should do this, Simos states), the subject is given the chance to luxuriate again in the wondrous, inward "vibes" she knew toward her life's inception, when the object resided at the centre of her emotional and perceptual world. Equally significant, the aura's visibility, its "factual" presence, gives subject and coven members alike undeniable proof that separation and differentiation never really occurred. Not only is the Goddess present but She is attached to, blended into the subject (or vice versa). As Simos puts it, "Thou art eternally linked to the All; thou art Goddess." Once more we see Witchcraft's obsessional effort to collapse ego boundaries, to unite the subject with a version of the caretaker, to restore dual-unity, to deny separation. When God became flesh in the person of Jesus, He afforded Christians the opportunity to see Him and know Him. Witchcraft goes one step further. Not only does it permit the adherent to see the Goddess in her divine form of radiating energy; it also permits him to fuse with Her, to be Her: once again, "thou art Goddess."

Numbers

Modern Witchcraft is awash in numbers. It ascribes them to the heavenly bodies, and to all manner of magical and/or ritualistic behaviours in an effort to increase their effectiveness. During the course of a healing ritual, for example, one might invoke the Goddess three times instead of once, in keeping with the notion that the number for healing is three. Simos (1979, 207) tells us that the "number" for "Mars" is "2, 3, 16, or possibly 5." Accordingly, if Mars appears to be influencing one's chances for success during the performance of a particular rite, one might consider repeating specific aspects of that rite "2, 3, 16, or possibly 5" times, thus exerting a measure of control upon the planet.

The Wiccan "mood" in regard to numbers is captured by a passage from Gardner's *Book of Shadows* cited in Farrar (1984, 52):

> It is not meet to make offering of less than two score lashes to the Goddess, for here be a mystery. The fortunate numbers be 3, 7, 9 and thrice 7 which be 21. And these numbers total two score, so a less perfect or fortunate number would not be a perfect prayer. Also the Fivefold Salute be 5, yet it be 8 kisses; for there be 2 feet, 2 knees and 2 breasts. And 5 times 8 be two score. Also there be 8 Working Tools and the Pentacle be 5; and five eights are two score.

The phoney, "archaic" English of this passage is, by the way, entirely Gardner's invention. Although Warren-Clarke (1987, 47–50) does not have the space to give us "a full layout of numerology," she does manage to show us how we may through numbers discover the "key" to our "destiny," as well as a way to bring about personal "change." For the most part, it is a matter of writing our names down, assigning specific numbers to the letters, figuring in our date of birth, and then adding and subtracting in the light of a "Numerology Chart" that guides us toward the spiritual realm. "Because all things are vibrational," writes this author, "they can be reduced to numbers," numbers that "have connections with all other aspects of the occult."

Discussing patients who suffer a "disturbance of the time sense," Arlow (1984, 15) notes that the "dissynchronous patterns of the child's needs and the mother's availability inevitably introduce the factor of frustration." Time becomes a "representative of realistic necessity" and of the "frustrations experienced at all levels of subsequent sexual development." Thus the "roots of rebellion" against the "tyranny of the clock" extend far back into the individual's past. Indeed, notes Arlow (16), our "notions of time follow inexorably from early experiences with word concepts." The child "hears that time flies, flows, marches, crawls, and stands still. Time brings and time takes away." Now, "during the same period, the child also learns to count." Numbers, like time, "bind the child to reality and help to further the process of socialization. The child soon learns that each moment of time is assigned a specific and unalterable number in the history of eternity." However—and we come here to the crucial insight—"while time and causality are irreversible, numbers are not. Numbers can be moved in either direction. They can be extended, contracted, fractioned, and reversed. The fact that numbers can be manipulated at will endows them with a special appeal in the endless quest for omnipotence." It is "not surprising to see," Arlow concludes, "how prominent a role numerology plays in systems of magic." These remarks guide us nicely toward the psychoanalytic essence of Wicca's interest in numbers.

The "key" to the Witch's "destiny" is precisely the same as the "key" to everyone else's, namely what happened to her during the course of her development when symbiosis, with its attendant omnipotence and fusion, gave way to separation, differentiation, the rapprochement struggle, and the subsequent Oedipal and adolescent periods. What we can call the Wiccan numbers game is an attempt to set all this aside, to claim that the tie to the omnipotent object is still intact, still functioning, still endowing the Witch with the power to determine not only the course of future events but the very meaning of planetary motion. As Arlow makes plain, numbers take the Witch back to the time when symbiosis was disrupted and lost. To the extent that the numbers game ties the Witch to the internalized object, it comprises, like the channelling game, or the astral travel game, or the visualization game, but another version of the dual-unity game played out obsessively in an effort to restore an idealized, longed-for version of the past. As far as "destiny" is concerned, if one chooses to persist in the numbers game, or in any of the dual-unity games that characterize modern Witchcraft, one's destiny will be, quite simply, to remain fixed in regressive behaviours that give expression to unresolved infantile conflicts—in short, to never grow up. Of course the Witch may regard the numbers game as something new and remarkable in her life, but there is really nothing new or remarkable about it. The concerns it addresses and the manner in which it strives to handle events and issues are an old story, reaching back into the initial stages of the Witch's existence. What appears new is old, what seems fresh and exciting is ultimately stale and neurotically obsessive. How did F. Scott Fitzgerald express it on the final page of *The Great Gatsby*? "So we beat on, boats against the current, borne back ceaselessly into the past."

Some Wiccan (and Human) Paradoxes

Everywhere in the literature of the Craft one comes upon statements that indicate a passionate concern with ecological, political, and feminist issues. "Witchcraft can be seen as a religion of ecology," declares Simos (1979, 10). Its goal is "harmony with nature, so that life may not just survive, but thrive." We must "save" the earth from destruction, writes Farrar (1987, 111); we must "watch over it, protect its fruits, and guard it against those who would lay it waste." Witches hate "commissars and fascists," asserts Gerald Gardner (1959, 130); "there is no room for this sort of spirit in the Witch cult." According to Simos (1979, 7), Witchcraft stands on the side of American democracy; it is devoted to protecting freedom of speech, and to promoting both decentralized government and individual rights. Witchcraft opposes "discrimination" in any shape or form, including of course discrimination against women, states Warren-Clarke (1987, 134). One of its chief purposes is to forge a society in which women may "liberate themselves" from old, patriarchal prejudices and enjoy full equality and wholeness as human beings (Simos 1979, 57). Indeed, Witchcraft urges women to forge their own identities aggressively, to gain their fair share of power and respect, and to heal the wounds inflicted upon them by men over the centuries (Simos 1979, 189). The question is, how does all this jibe with the regressive, magical thinking, the longing for fusion and omnipotence, the narcissistic grandiosity and outright mumbo-jumbo—in short, the infantilism that we have been exploring in this chapter?

Like cults, religions, and cultural institutions generally, Witch-craft appeals to all the levels of an individual's psychosexual develop-ment. It is both toward and away from the object of the early period. As we know, the Craft's magical systems speak powerfully to pre-Oedipal and Oedipal wishes, to the longing for fusion and omnipotence, to the hunger for a harmonious, reconstituted family. In its cultic status and fringe, rebellious nature, Wicca manages to address significant adoles-cent concerns. It "stands aside from the mainstream of society," writes Simos (1979, 19), scorning the "fruits of monetary success," and inden-tifying with "artists, poets, shamans, mystics, and visionaries." At what we can call the adult level of realistic biological and social respon-sibility, Witches express genuine, ego-syntonic concern with environ-mental and political issues, with the need for careful stewarding of the planet and with the widespread, growing call for the just and decent treatment of all human beings, regardless of race or gender. Thus a sec-ond question arises: if Witches are able at one level of their psycho-sexual development to work constructively for the good of the world, why should we bother about their regressive, obsessive, infantile behaviours? Why not leave the Witches alone?

First and most obviously, there is the normal intellectual respon-sibility one feels to point out superstition, irrationality, and hokum when he believes he has come upon them. To discharge this responsi-bility is to afford devotees of the Goddess a chance to view their con-duct from a fresh perspective, but that is only a happy spin-off of the central purpose. The writer can no more ignore what he considers to be regressive, infantile behaviour on the part of a group claiming religious and philosophical legitimacy and working to establish a foothold in the cultural scheme of things than he can pretend not to notice a full eclipse of the sun while out walking on a bright summer day. Second, to live in the shadow of the object, to pursue omnipotence, grandiosity, and fu-sion, to go about the planet in the belief that one is magical, limitless, wondrous, special, is to increase the potential for disorder in the world. It is to keep all the old, irrational, mad forces alive and available to those who know how to use them for their own grandiose, egotistical ends. This is not to suggest that the ancient, patriarchal, Judeo-Christian setup is preferable to Wicca. It is not. But that does not make Wicca a desirable alternative. Indeed, *both* of these schemes come from indif-ferent aspects of the same psychological place. The Judeo-Christian setup is tied neurotically to the father. The Wiccan alternative (matri-archy, etc.) is tied neurotically to the mother. What the world needs is detachment from the objects of the inner realm, detachment from those inward energies that seek to actualize the impossible, infantile aims of the early period, detachment from the unconscious agenda that is born aggressively and passionately in the crises of separation and differentiation through which all of us are fated to go. If we are capable of improvement as human beings, it will come as we see, clearly see, the degree to which our present "magical" goals are unconsciously connected to developmental events that transpired toward the inception of our lives, and accordingly give them up. For it makes no sense, to this writer at least, to work realistically for social and political progress on the one hand and to deny reality on a broad, massive scale on the other.

Much the same thinking may be brought to bear on the morality of Witchcraft, for here too we see the mix of reason and unreason, maturity and infantilism, acceptance and denial of reality, that characterizes Wicca as a whole. For example, the most popular moral maxim of the Craft, often expressed in a defiant fashion, states that one is free to do whatever he wishes as long as he does not harm anyone else. Farrar (1984, 135) puts the matter this way, echoing the bogus, antique style of Gardner's *Book of Shadows*: "Eight words the Wiccan Rede fulfil, And it harm none, do what you will."

Imagine the reaction of Socrates, or Aristotle, or Kant to this sort of simple-minded nonsense. For how can a morality be based upon a position which ignores the responsibility of the individual to himself? If one "harms" oneself might it not have a deleterious effect upon others? Are all people islands? Is not the individual a part of the community, and is not the community diminished when the individual behaves self-inimically? What, exactly, constitutes "harm" to another? And is the amount of "harm" always sufficient to curtail an individual's wish? Are not some things very harmful, and other things not so harmful? Where does one draw the line? If I am doing something important to me, and another person for neurotic reasons claims I am harming him, do I automatically desist? Who judges "harm"? Do not individuals, and groups, and societies need judges? How do we address this problem in terms of the "Wiccan Rede"? I won't continue. Not only does the literature of the Craft ignore such issues, but the reader has by this time, I suspect, recognized the inadequacy of a moral position that looks to others, as opposed to the self, for what we may term the moral foundation.

By contrast, the insistence of the Wiccan community that theirs is a morality based not upon the punitive, paternal superego but upon the nurturing and love associated with the figure of the Great Mother raises crucial considerations. "The model of the Goddess fosters respect of all living things," writes Simos (1979, 10); "it is not a parallel structure to the symbolism of God the Father." Hence "Wiccan ethics are positive rather than prohibitive. The morality of Witchcraft is far more concerned with 'blessed is he who' than with 'thou shalt not.' The extremes of masochistic asceticism and gross materialism seem to the Witch to be two sides of the same coin, because both distort human wholeness ... All living creatures are our siblings, different but related offspring of the same womb" (Farrar 1984, 135). Such an emphasis calls to mind the wholesale rethinking of moral issues that is currently taking place in the psychoanalytic community.

Questioning both the accuracy and the value of Freud's moral theory, Eli Sagan (1988, 9) observes that the "dependence of the superego on the *particular* society in which it exists underlies a fatal flaw in the theory of the superego as representing the *moral* function within the psyche." Far from carrying out the task of morality in the mind, Sagan continues, "the superego is essentially amoral and can be as easily immoral as moral. Within a slave society, the superego legitimates slavery. Within a racist or sexist society, the superego demands racism and sexism. And in a Nazi society, the superego commands one to live up to genocidal ideals." Throughout the course of history a corrupt superego has been the norm, not the exception. Indeed, "most of the worst troubles that humankind has brought upon itself, including warfare, are impossible without the functioning of the superego," which we must finally regard as a kind of psychological "disease" (13). Unlike the superego, however, the "conscience knows clearly which actions are moral and which immoral"; the conscience is "incapable of corruption and pathology. It may be silenced or paralyzed, but one can never accurately speak of a diseased conscience." Furthermore—and we come here to the key consideration—the conscience "does not have to wait until the child's fourth or fifth year to make its presence felt. *Conscience has its origins in the basic nurturing situation*, and identification with the nurturer plays an essential role in its composition. Traditionally it is the mother, not the father, who presides over the birth of conscience, over the beginnings of morality" (14, my emphasis). Because Freud was unwilling to look closely at the child's first relationship with the mother, he failed to extend his discussion of Eros to the place of its origin. Putting the matter in a nutshell, Sagan (176) writes, "Identification with the nurturer is essential for psychic health because it is the only effective defense against the destructive drives." To protect the world's environment, to foster respect for all living creatures "great and small," we must strive for what the Witches would call a Goddess-centred morality and for what Sagan would call a morality grounded in the pre-Oedipal, mother-child situation.

The point of the last distinction is that we do not *need* "the Goddess" and all the regressive, magical thinking that surrounds "the Goddess" to find our moral way. Just as we can shed this kind of baggage in the ecological and political spheres so we can shed it in the moral sphere too. We can spy the origins of morality in the actual circumstances and events of our own lives with our own mothers, as opposed to the supernatural realm with its mythic entities. We can have Witchcraft's wholesome moral emphasis without the narcissism, grandiosity, and omnipotence of thought that accompany the wish to re-enter the *corpus maternum* and that feed the world's troublesome appetite for irrational behaviour. In my view, our actual lives, our actual bodies, our actual experiences serve as a stronger, firmer foundation for morality than the projective expressions of the psyche. Moreover, to foster detachment from the objects of the inner world does not mean that we lose our capacity to love and nurture others. It means simply that we strive to see the origins and the significance of our emotional goals. It means that we stop identifying automatically with the passionate, narcissistic urges that well up within us, particularly when we are told by other people that we are Goddess-like and wonderful. Again in my view, our capacity for compassion and care can only be enhanced as we develop the courage to work through the crises of separation and loss in which our longing for fusion and omnipotence was born. Earlier we established Witchcraft's tendency to deny separation and loss. Perhaps we begin to perceive fully now the negative consequences of such a denial. Genuine confrontation with the self is the only true basis of morality.

Gender

"Through the Goddess," declares Simos (1979, 7), women can "reclaim their right, as women, to be powerful, to explore their own strengths and realizations." They can "enlighten their minds, celebrate their emotions, and move beyond their narrow, constricting roles." Indeed, "through the Goddess," women can become "inspired to see their aggression as healthy, and their anger as purifying." The Goddess is also "important for men," Simos (9) continues: "The oppression of men in Father God-ruled patriarchy is perhaps less obvious but no less tragic than that of women." Men are encouraged "to identify with a model no human being can successfully emulate: to be minirulers of narrow universes"; they are "at war with themselves" and "internally split"; they "lose touch with their feelings and their bodies, and become successful male zombies." It is "the Goddess," concludes Simos (10), who "allows men to experience the feminine side of their nature, which is often felt to be the deepest and most sensitive aspect of the self." The texts of the Craft abound with similar passages (cf. Warren-Clarke 1987, 66; Farrar 1984, 161; Cabot 1989, 15).

Carol Gilligan (1982, 6) observes in a crucial discussion of gender differences that the tendency of psychological theorists "to project a masculine image" onto human development "goes back at least to Freud, who built his theories ... around the experiences of the male child that culminate in the Oedipus complex." This tendency has of late been rectified in psychoanalysis by a variety of writers including Nancy Chodorow (1978), Robert Stoller (1964), and of course Gilligan herself. It boils down to the following: by the time a child is three, "the unchanging core of personality formation is with rare exception firmly and irreversibly established for both sexes" (Gilligan, 7). Given that for both sexes "the primary caretaker in the first three years of life is typically female, the interpersonal dynamics of gender formation are different for boys and girls." Female identity formation "takes place in a context of ongoing relationship since mothers tend to experience their daughters as more like, and continuous with, themselves." Thus girls, in identifying themselves as female, "experience themselves as like their mothers, fusing the experience of attachment with the process of identity formation." By contrast, "mothers experience their sons as a male opposite," and boys, "in defining themselves as masculine, separate their mothers from themselves," thereby "curtailing their primary love and sense of empathetic tie." Male development "entails a more emphatic individuation and a more defensive firming of ego boundaries." Girls emerge "with a stronger basis for experiencing another's needs or feelings as one's own ... Furthermore, girls do not define themselves in terms of the denial of preoedipal relational modes [fusion] to the same extent as do boys. Therefore, regression to these modes tends not to feel as much a basic threat to their ego." In this way, "male gender identity is threatened by intimacy while female gender identity is threatened by separation ... Males tend to have difficulty with relationships, while females tend to have problems with individuation, competitive achievement, and success." In a passage that summarizes the central thrust of her theoretical position, Gilligan (17) writes, "Women not only define themselves in a context of human relationship but also judge themselves in terms of their ability to care. Women's place in man's life cycle has been that of nurturer, caretaker, and helpmate, the weaver of those networks of relationships on which she in turn relies. But while women have thus taken care of men, men have, in their theories of psychological development, as in their economic arrangements, tended to assume or devalue that care." These stereotypes "reflect a conception of adulthood that is itself out of balance, favoring the separateness of the individual self over connection to others" and an "autonomous life of work" over "the interdependence of love and care." The bulk of Gilligan's subsequent discussion is devoted to exploring this "imbalance" in particular men and women.

It is precisely the rectification of this imbalance, in both females and males, that Witchcraft seems bent upon accomplishing. As we have just seen, Wiccan texts tell women not to fear competition and aggression, and not to believe that their capacity to care conflicts with the expression of so-called masculine traits. Men are told to develop their empathetic, caring, sensitive natures and not to succumb to the cultural stereotype of what constitutes a "real man." Can anyone fail at this juncture to see the ironic contradiction in all this? While Witchcraft asks women to be strong and independent, it also asks them to re-enter the *corpus maternum*, to merge dependently with an obvious, full-blown, projective image of the mother—the Great Goddess. While Witchcraft asks women to rely on themselves, to discover their genuine inner resources, it also asks them to rely on magic and magical invocations, to consider themselves gifted and precious because they have relinked psychologically with the *magna mater*. Surely it counts for something psychoanalytically that the texts of the Craft typically include invocations such as the following: "Come Mama! come into our circle, our womb, be with us now, Mama, be with us now!" (Simos 1979, 89). Thus the Craft takes women in two opposing emotional directions. No matter how cleverly its advocates rationalize and explain this antithesis, it must ultimately have a confusing, stultifying effect on the female psyche.

As for men, Witchcraft asks them to indulge their caring, sensitive, feminine side and to relax their fears of boundary violation at the same time that it plays upon those very fears by urging them to re-fuse with the Great Mother, to re-establish the pre-Oedipal symbiosis they strove so mightily, as males, to relinquish. "Mother of all life, engulf us with your love, sweep us away!" cries another Wiccan invocation (Simos 1979, 73, 105). Surely this goes beyond a mere increase of one's empathetic capabilities. What the Craft is encouraging in men here is precisely what it is encouraging in women, namely regression to an earlier stage of psychosexual development in which the symbiotic bond to the caretaker remains intact. I cannot see what good such a denial of separation and differentiation will do anyone, whether male, female, or a combination of both. But even more contradictory and ironic is the following: while Wicca asks men to rein in their lust for power, their urge to control others and to enhance their material wealth, it offers them a variety of magical techniques for increasing their power, for increasing their control over people and objects, indeed for actualizing their omnipotence. Again and again it reminds them, following Aleister Crowley, that "magic is the Science and Art of causing change to occur in conformity with Will" (cf. Adler 1986, 8), and that Wicca is the way to discover precisely that science and art. It is not only women that

Witchcraft is fated to confuse. Men must come in for their share of emotional befuddlement too.

A final word on the Wiccan texts. Of the many compelling psychological realizations they offer us, the most outstanding perhaps is this: the only real magic is the magic of honest self-exploration, the magic of no magic at all.

Notes

1. I am aware that Wiccan texts occasionally make a distinction between the Goddess and the particular items in her domain. Simos (1979, 25), for example, writes that "all things are one, yet each thing is separate, individual, unique"—a view that is echoed by Farrar (1987, 3). Such distinctions, however, mean little in the Wiccan sea of metaphors and symbols announcing the divine, salvational fusion, the termination of the old, dreaded separation. Indeed, such distinctions emerge ultimately as afterthoughts or qualifications engendered by the anxiety that must at one level attend the powerful impulse toward merger with, or engulfment into, the Great Mother's body. They are the exceptions that prove the rule.

2. During the course of the Dini Petti talk show televised in Toronto on October 13, 1989, Tamarra James, High Priestess of the Wiccan Church of Canada (Toronto), told her fascinated audience, "You are the Goddess, you are divine, you are perfection, if only you would realize it." High Priestess James also made it clear that initiation into the Wiccan community was an excellent way to bring this realization about.

3. Witchcraft's use of James E. Lovelock's Gaia Hypothesis is worth noting here. According to Tim Beardsley (1989, 35), Associate Editor of *Scientific American*, the hypothesis asserts that "all the animals and plants can be regarded as a single vast organism capable of manipulating the atmosphere, geosphere, and hydrosphere to suit its needs." What Beardsley calls "Lovelock's musings" were challenged by the scientific community upon their first appearance in the late 1960s, and they have now been thoroughly discredited and abandoned by all except "the scientifically innocent" (35). Wiccan texts routinely resort to Lovelock's hypothesis in an effort to prove that the Great Goddess is alive and well, and dwelling in our corner of the cosmos. "The earth," declares Farrar (1987, 16), "by occult theory and scientific fact" (i.e., Lovelock's musings), is a "living entity." The "frontiersmen of science" (i.e., Lovelock) are currently discovering the "coherence of that multi-leveled reality which occultism has always recognized." See Beardsley's essay for a delightful and trenchant presentation of the issue.

References

ADLER, M. 1986. *Drawing Down the Moon.* Boston: Beacon.

ARLOW, J. 1984. "Disturbance of the Sense of Time." *Psychoanalytic Quarterly,* 53: 13–37.

ASHBACH, C., and V. SCHERMER. 1987. *Object Relations, the Self, and the Group.* London: Routledge and Kegan Paul.

BEARDSLEY, T. 1989. "Gaia: An Overview." *Scientific American*. December, pp. 35–36.

BOLLAS, C. 1987. *The Shadow of the Object: Psychoanalysis of the Unthought Known*. London: Free Association Books.

BONEWITZ, R. 1987. *The Cosmic Crystal Spiral*. Longmead: Element Books.

BOWMAN, C. 1992. *Crystal Awareness*. St. Paul, Minn.: Llewellyn.

BRETANNE, A. 1989. "The Sacred Prostitute" [Review]. *Shared Vision* (Vancouver), 14: 10.

CABOT, L. 1989. *Power of the Witch*. New York: Delacorte.

CARRINGTON, H., and S. MULDOON. 1929. *The Projection of the Astral Body*. London: Rider.

CHITOURAS, J. 1992. "Chakras." *Gnosis: A Journal of the Western Inner Traditions*, 27: 38–40.

CHODOROW, N. 1978. *The Reproduction of Mothering*. Berkeley: University of California Press.

CREME, B. 1992. *Transmission: A Meditation for the New Age*. London: Tara Press.

CROWLEY, A. 1930. *Magick in Theory and Practice*. New York: Castle.

CROWLEY, V. 1989. *Wicca: The Old Religion in the New Age*. Wellingborough, England: Aquarrian Press.

CRUDEN, L. 1993. "The Changing Spirit of North American Shamanism." *Shaman's Drum*, 31: 10–13.

CUNNINGHAM, S. 1988. *The Truth about Witchcraft Today*. St. Paul, Minn.: Llewellyn.

———. 1989. *Wicca: A Guide for the Solitary Practitioner*. St. Paul, Minn.: Llewellyn.

DEAVER, K. 1987. *Rock Crystal: The Magic Stone*. York Beach, Maine: Samuel Weiser.

DE MILLE, R. 1985. *The Don Juan Papers*. Santa Barbara, Ca.: Ross Erikson.

DRURY, N. 1985. *Dictionary of Mysticism and the Occult*. New York: Harper and Row.

FABER, M. 1981. *Culture and Consciousness: The Social Meaning of Altered Awareness*. New York: Human Sciences Press.

FARRAR, J., and S. FARRAR. 1984. *The Witches' Way*. Custer, Wash.: Phoenix.

———. 1987. *The Witches' Goddess*. Custer, Wash.: Phoenix.

FERGUSON, M. 1980. *The Aquarian Conspiracy: Personal and Social Transformation in Our Time*. Los Angeles: Tarcher.

FRAZER, J. 1890. *The Golden Bough*. London: Macmillan.

FREUD. S. 1960. *The Ego and the Id*, trans. J. Strachey. New York: Norton.

———. 1971. "On Narcissism." Pp. 30–59 in *Collected Papers*, ed. J. Riviere. Vol. 4. London: Hogarth.

GARDNER, G. 1954. *Witchcraft Today*. Lakemont, Ga.: Copple House Books.

———. 1959. *The Meaning of Witchcraft*. New York: Magickal Childe.

GILLIGAN, C. 1982. *In a Different Voice*. Cambridge, Mass.: Harvard University Press.

GRAVES, R. 1946. *The White Goddess*. London: Faber.

———. 1964. "Witches in 1964." *Virginia Quarterly Review*, 40: 550–59.

HARNER, M. 1990. *The Way of the Shaman*. New York: HarperCollins.

HARTOCOLLIS, P. 1974. "Origins of Time." *Psychoanalytic Quarterly*, 43: 243–61.

LEWIS, J. 1992. "Approaches to the Study of the New Age Movement." Pp. 1–13 in *Perspectives on the New Age*, ed. J. Lewis and J. Melton. Albany: State University of New York Press.

LEWIS, J., and J. MELTON. 1992. "Introduction." Pp. ix–xii in *Perspectives on the New Age*, ed. J. Lewis and J. Melton. Albany: State University of New York Press.

LUCAS, P. 1992. "The New Age Movement and the Pentecostal Charismatic Revival." Pp. 189–212 in *Perspectives on the New Age*, ed. J. Lewis and J. Melton. Albany: State University of New York Press.

MAHLER, M., F. PINE, and A. BERGMAN. 1975. *The Psychological Birth of the Human Infant*. New York: Basic.

MALINOWSKI, B. 1925. "Sorcery as Mimetic Representation." In *Witchcraft and Sorcery*, ed. M. Marwick. Harmondsworth: Penguin.

MEADOWS, K. 1991. *Shamanic Experience: A Practical Guide to Contemporary Shamanism*. Rockport, Mass.: Element Books.

MELODY. 1992. *Love Is in the Earth: Laying on of Stones*. Richland, Wash.: Earth-Love.

MELTON, J. 1992. "New Thought and the New Age." Pp. 15–19 in *Perspectives on the New Age*, ed. J. Lewis and J. Melton. Albany: State University of New York Press.

MURRAY, M. 1921. *Witch-Cult in Western Europe*. London: Oxford University Press.

POGGI, I. 1992. "Alternative Spirituality in Italy." Pp. 271–86 in *Perspectives on the New Age*, ed. J. Lewis and J. Melton. Albany: State University of New York Press.

RIORDAN, S. 1992. "Channelling: A New Revelation?" Pp. 105–26 in *Perspectives on the New Age*, ed. J. Lewis and J. Melton. Albany: State University of New York Press.

ROHEIM, G. 1955. *The Origin and Function of Magic*. New York: International Universities Press.

ROMAN, S., and D. PACKER. 1987. *Opening to Channel: How to Connect with Your Guide*. Tiburon, Ca.: Kramer.

SAGAN, E. 1988. *Freud, Women, and Morality: The Psychology of Good and Evil*. New York: Basic.

SEARLES, H. 1984. "Transference Responses in Borderline Patients." *Psychiatry*, 47: 37–48.

SHEPARD, L., ed. 1987. *Occultism Update*. Detroit: Gale.

SIMOS, M. [Starhawk] 1979. *The Spiral Dance*. New York: Harper and Row.

———. [Starhawk] 1988. *Dreaming the Dark*. Boston: Beacon.

SPITZ, R. 1965. *The First Year of Life*. New York: International Universities Press.

STERN, D. 1985. *The Interpersonal World of the Infant*. New York: Basic.

STOLLER, R. 1964. "A Contribution to the Study of Gender Identity." *International Journal of Psychoanalysis*, 45: 220–26.

TAUSK, V. 1919. "On the Origin of the 'Influencing Machine' in Schizophrenia." *Psychoanalytic Quarterly*, 2: 519–56 (1933).

TURPIN, S. 1993. "Shamanic Motifs in Pecos River Rock Art." *Shaman's Drum*, 30: 32–39.

WARREN-CLARKE, L. 1987. *The Way of the Goddess*. Bridgeport, Conn.: Prism Press.

WEISKOPF, J. 1993. "In the Shadow of the Tiger and Boa: The Healing Gifts of a Siona Shaman." *Shaman's Drum*, 31: 41–50.

WINNICOTT, D. 1974. *Playing and Reality*. London: Penguin.

CHAPTER IV

HEALING IN THE NEW AGE

Nᴇᴡ Aɢᴇ thinking is everywhere preoccupied with matters of health (both psychological and physical) and healing (again, both psychological and physical). We touched on these matters earlier during our investigations of shamanism (Essie Parrish and other sucking shamans) and crystals (Melody's laying on of stones). It is time now to concentrate in depth on the work of a single, representative author. How does one come to live the full, wholesome life he is supposed to be enjoying? How can one transform his drab, commonplace reality into an existence of radiance and power? How can one cope with his anxiety, his depression, his divorce, his cancer? How can one achieve "psychological integration" and the enabling "lifestyle" that goes along with it? Of the many New Age writers who are answering such questions, Dr. Richard Moss is among the most famous and influential. He offers the world not only his books and articles, but also his lectures, workshops, tapes, and, last but certainly not least, his Three Mountain Foundation, a "nonprofit organization which invites people into greater aliveness, health, and wholeness." The advertisement continues, "The Foundation sponsors conferences and workshops for individuals, organizations, and hospitals, including transformational conferences led by Richard Moss ... Based on the work of Richard Moss, the Foundation is continuously unfolding in new directions. Its work is timeless and is the basis of a cultural and social evolution revealing new possibilities for life."[1] So goes a typical, "foundational" instance of New Age hype.

In 1977, while in his early thirties, Dr. Moss abandoned his main-stream medical career and took up the art, or practice, or perhaps trade, of spiritual healing. Behind this sudden and dramatic change in the di-rection of his life lay a profound transformational experience, or *expe-riences*, for Moss describes the upheaval twice in his writings and the two descriptions do not jibe very well, the significance of which I will touch upon eventually. However, before we get to the actual transfor-mation, we must look very closely at Moss's discussions of the issues and events that led up to it. I believe we will discover in the doctor's remarks a veritable key to the psychoanalytic nature of what follows.

According to Moss, "All human consciousness creates a kind of external authority, a veil or curtain upon which reality must be precip-itated in order to have a sufficient sense of contrast with itself" (IW, 184).[2] He continues, "The parental dynamic filters reality in an uncon-scious parent-child fashion. This begins as the infant gradually devel-ops a personal consciousness and distinguishes itself from the parents. Our very sense of reality carries a hidden authority over us, and the seemingly external situation we are in (the medical world) is held in consciousness as a parent" (184). And finally, in terminology that we have found to be inescapable in New Age discourse, "The veil is rela-tive and shifts as we grow and refine our awareness ... As each veil thins and eventually disappears, the human experience moves toward higher energy states. There one looks at existence and sees profound spaciousness and mystery" (184). Now, without offering us even one shred of evidential material (either clinical or theoretical) in support of this psycho-metaphysical view of just about everything, Moss proceeds to link his notions up directly with his departure from mainstream medicine: "One of the reasons I stopped practicing traditional medi-cine was that I began to realize I had found a very compelling role in which I was fundamentally safe and well-rewarded—a role in which *I was playing the parent while the patient was playing the child.* I had found a way to be safely defined in reality ... and I was no longer grow-ing ... I realized with astonishment that if my work as a physician was predicated even minimally on a subtle defense against a broader truth and range of experience, then I was in fact indirectly and subcon-sciously supporting the reality of disease. We reciprocally empower the very reality through which we know ourselves as real" (185, my em-phasis). Moss then asserts, in an utterance crucial to our purpose, "The moment I no longer wanted to shield my life from genuine growth, my whole sense of medicine and the role of the physician changed ... I made a commitment to explore life in a much broader sense and *not to allow my work to draw me into the parental dynamic* that medicine had become for me" (185, my emphasis). Needless to say, there is no denying the authenticity and the urgency of Moss's confession: as a "physician" he discovered the parent-child relationship, or the "parental dynamic," to be controlling his behaviour, holding him down, preventing his "growth" and development. Yet surely we may point out at this juncture that being a physician does not automatically re-create in every case the parent-child relationship, and even if that relationship does tend to colour the doctor-patient interaction, the doctor does not have to become absorbed in it, or encourage it, or allow it to govern his "role" as a doctor, as apparently Moss allows it to do.

If I am not mistaken, a doctor's first interest is, or should be, ministering to his patients, investigating their problems, and treating those problems medically when and if treatment is required. What has that to do with "playing a role," as Moss puts it, or "playing" *anything* for that matter? A doctor may also be interested, of course, in doing research, in exploring the origins of illness (and health), or in administering the services of hospitals and laboratories. Accordingly, I would think that "traditional medicine" offers ample opportunity for what Moss calls "growth," as doctors specialize, become absorbed in particular problems, take on new duties and responsibilities, and so forth. Is not the field in fact endless? And is there not plenty of "mystery" in its various facets and manifestations? To imply that doctors are apt to be held down by and trapped within the "parental dynamic" because "all human consciousness" and "most human activity," including "medicine," are "dominated by the parent-child energetic" (IW, 184) strikes me as arbitrary and idiosyncratic. I would submit that doctors, to speak of them generally, are busy being doctors, busy treating people in emergency rooms and cancer wards. They are not worried by or obsessed with "parental dynamics." They are perfectly capable of interacting with their patients on an honest and equal footing as fellow human beings. The point is, Moss sees the "parental dynamic" everywhere and postulates it as the ruler of "all human consciousness" and "reality," including "medicine," because he *projects* it everywhere, because he reads it into everyone and everything around him. He fashions a general psychological and philosophical model along *authoritarian* lines because the "parental dynamic" is, as he puts it, "very compelling" to him. Thus Moss is the problem, not "traditional medicine" or "consciousness" or "reality." Moss creates the dilemma, not the nature of his profession, or the nature of the mind and human society. To put the matter in a psychoanalytic nutshell, Richard Moss is obsessed with the *transference relationship*. He finds "very compelling" the authority and the power that adhere in it.

Of particular fascination in all this is that Moss, in the face of his departure from "traditional medicine" because of its "parent-child energetic," in the face of his determination to shed the "role of parent" with the patient as "child," in the face of his dramatic vow not to let his work draw him into the "parental dynamic" ever again, becomes as a spiritual healer *nothing other* than an all-powerful, god-like parental authority, a magical being more loaded up with "parental dynamic" than any mere doctor could ever hope to be; and more, as such an entity, as such a dispenser of endless spiritual wisdom and empathy— nay, endless "humility" and "unconditional love," to use his own terms—Moss is capable of frightening little children out of their wits by working his newly discovered "telepathic powers" upon them, of taking emotional and perhaps sexual advantage of his female patients, and of attempting to get rid of illness by exorcising it out of the patient's body, much as saints exorcise devils out of the bodies of the possessed. Moss leaves "traditional medicine" not because he wants to lessen his "authority," and the parental power that accompanies authority, but because he wants to *increase* it, because he wants to *transform* himself into a numinous, curative presence of proportions that are normally denied to "traditional," mainstream "physicians." Moss leaves "traditional medicine" not because it limits him by placing him in the parental "role," but because it limits him *in* that role. As is often the case with those who are driven by their unconscious aims, in this instance for power and narcissistic aggrandizement, the very *opposite* of what they offer us by way of explanation for their conduct turns out to be the truth. As soon as they begin to explain, one must begin to interpret.

The Power of Sainthood

"With the irreversible finality of an earthquake shifting plates, a profound shift in my consciousness occurred in early 1977 and the old Richard Moss, M.D., disappeared forever" (IW, 1). Thus commences Moss's auto-hagiography, a seemingly endless series of emotionalistic, self-glorifying passages (I will condense them radically here) describing his gravitation toward and ultimate "surrender" to "unconditional love" (27) as that love is thrust upon him by the divine. "The new me felt like an atomic reactor powered by energies so great that I could not have conceived them before. For awhile I even considered the possibility of possession, but there was also the love and inexpressibly uplifting joy when I realized that I was nothing and only existed by God's grace. Gradually I recognized that a fundamental transformation of my nature was taking place ... I was learning to live with sensitivities such as telepathic rapport, clairsentience (the ability to feel things not available to ordinary senses), and a powerful current of energy that seemed to move with varying intensity both within and around my body" (1–2). We note here, in addition to the strong suggestion of *omnipotence*, the *energetic images* (atomic reactor, current of energy), the tendency of New Age discourse to express affective states in physicalistic, *vibrational* terms. As we shall see, such images harbour the same crucial psychoanalytic significance in Moss's explanation of healing that they harbour in the other New Age areas we've explored: shamanism, crystals, Witchcraft, channelling.

In the grip of supernatural powers, Moss is at pains to tell us ordinary folks exactly what is happening to him: "Ego boundaries begin to dissolve into the realms of a greater Self. The personal me was being fostered by a force so incredible and seemingly alien that it defies definition." And then, in the purple prose of which he is so fond, "I was being shown directly—in the very cells and molecules of my fleshly existence—a whole other reality" (IW, 4). The "challenge," Moss continues, still struggling to help us understand, lies in the person's attempt to exist "with a part of Self that is infinite, total, and in one sense uncompromising," while he is still "in the world of relative experience" (5). To make sure that we have at least some sense of what he is going through on this particular score, Moss offers us a few lines from the poetry of T. S. Eliot: "Men's curiosity searches past and future / And clings to that dimension. But to apprehend / The point of intersection of the timeless / With time, is an occupation for the saint." And, sure enough, just as saints are apt to cry out "in the dark night of their trial," so Moss cries out, "Why me?" Why am I "being shaken to the core of my mortal nature?" (5). Eventually Moss gives up; he realizes that he cannot "articulate what comes from a place where there are no words ... The very effort and intensity of my commitment revealed to me the depth of my own transformation" (5). It is a wondrous business, to be sure.

The change continues apace, even as Moss finds himself in the midst of his medical duties: "One day in the emergency room, as I approached a frightened and pain-gripped man with injections of Demerol and Valium, a voice came into my head. The voice rang within me: 'You have nothing to give this man but love.' Handing the syringes to the astonished nurse, I approached the man [the emerging saint is about to perform a miracle] and placed my left hand on his groin and my right hand on the top of his head. Almost instantly I and the room became blazingly hot. Perplexed family members moved to the windows to let in some cool air. The patient's eyes rolled back and he went limp and fell into a deep sleep. Thirty minutes later free of pain and with only a mild limp, the patient rose, thanked me with tears in his eyes, and left the hospital. His pain and hysteria had stopped in seconds" (IW, 8).

Moss takes this "miracle" to be "a cosmic confirmation" of his newly gained powers (8). "It was one of the key experiences," he writes, "that led me out of traditional medicine" (8). And indeed, what would "traditional medicine" *do* with a healer-saint suddenly in its midst?

On the road to a "complete transmutation" of his "emotions," Moss has yet to "surrender" entirely, to "allow the gate to open" and the "love" and "compassion" for all "humanity" to "engulf" him (IW, 21). Eventually, however, the beatification occurs: leaving home in state of profound agitation and turmoil, Moss sets out on a journey "to resolve the powerful oscillation or polarization of my consciousness that had begun with the spontaneous awakening." He calls this, "the pilgrimage" (5) and notes that it took him to Europe, the Middle East, Nepal, and finally India where, "one day on a roof," the "resolution" occurs. Moss "embraces unconditional love" for everyone and "surrenders all emotion and thought" that might "separate" him from his fellow mortals. "In many ways," he concludes (29), focusing for us the humility that characterizes those who have been "guided" toward their own "unfoldment" by higher powers, "I am only an infant in the ongoing process of full human Beingness." Shall we say, amen?

The Black Butterfly presents us with essentially the same story, although here Moss plays up much more fully the emotional agitation, the *anxiety*, that grips him as he leaves the real world and comes to believe in his own saintly transfiguration. In some ways we are reminded of Duane, whose delusional tendencies emerge as he anxiously struggles with the issue of his guide's reality during the course of his gravitation to channelling. Moss, however, is not confronted with a projective, *external* other; his delusional bent emerges wholly from his convictions about *his own grandeur. The Black Butterfly*, in fact, offers us one of the clearest expressions I have ever read of an individual who is given to such delusions. Moss dresses all this up, of course, in expressions of humility: to be "At-One with life's mystery," he writes (BB, 4),[3] "is bequeathed equally by Grace as by effort." Yet this is merely the flip side of his narcissistic inflation. As Nietzsche was fond of remarking, he who is most humble seeks most to be exalted.

Alternatively calling his experience Realization, Enlightenment, and the Awakening (BB, 34), not an awakening or my awakening but *the* awakening—a world event—Moss declares that it is preceded by "nagging uneasiness and a sense of foreboding" (17). Such feelings arise just after he attempts to cure a patient of cancer by "sharing energy with him" (17). Moss confesses, "For the first time in my life after seeing a client I washed all the sheets, aired the room, and attempted to do a ritual purification of myself. But the foreboding persisted" (17). Moss gets rid of the guilt he feels in the face of his own hokum (not to mention his betrayal of "traditional medicine" and the "parental dynamic") by undergoing a self-induced mania: "Two days later I was sipping coffee in a restaurant and scanning Dr. Wolff's book *Pathways Through to Space.* All at once the words began to dance on the page. As I looked around everything seemed alive with energy. The very air itself was on fire with radiant light and my body felt like an atomic reactor gone wild" (18). Leaving the restaurant, Moss feels "nauseated, as though [his] body would explode. A shimmering brilliance pervaded everything . . . With a blink, my attention turned to a cow and at once I began to dissolve into it. I and the world out there were almost but not quite indistinguishable" (20). Moss struggles with his dissolving ego, with his loss of a stable identity, for several agonizing days. Finally, his delusional mania begins to engender in earnest the grandeur that will allow him to make a transition *away* from "traditional medicine" and *toward* the "energetic" healing about which he harbours such disconcerting, guilt-filled ambivalence. "I was . . . fighting for my life," he states (20), when "I visualized protective light" and "entered into invocations of the Christ" (20). Believing he has put "the devil behind" him (21)—that is, believing he has reconciled himself to the betrayal of his medical training and to his indulgence in spiritual cures—Moss begins to experience feelings of "the very Divine" (21). Yet he still cannot fully "surrender," fully open himself to "unconditional love." Thinking upon "Jesus and Buddha" (24), upon their timeless and exemplary struggles, Moss realizes that he must release himself "to a higher consciousness, to a higher dimension" of transcendence (24). "All that was left was acceptance" (24). It is in "this state" that Moss undergoes, at last, his beatification, which he presents to us as follows: "I observed two butterflies dancing in the air. One was predominantly black and the other white. They alighted on a branch and, to my amazement and delight, I saw them mate . . . Suddenly the black one flew to me and landed right between my eyebrows. At that moment life changed forever . . . It was a living bliss . . . All of existence stood before me in its totality with its secrets uncovered and revealed" (25). Such remarks, needless to say, are very arresting in their narcissistic, delusional significance. Yet they are actually mild in comparison to what follows.

Going about in his "transformational, apocalyptic" condition (BB, 27), Moss claims that people "spontaneously break into tears" upon seeing him, the godly man (29). "Some find their skin reddening as though they were being sunburned"—such is Moss's radiance (29). "I would simply speak," he writes, "and people" would "ask if I were reading their minds" (29); he has become omniscient. Moss "reads of the saints with a sense of brotherhood" (29). He understands "immediately the mystical statements in Handel's *Messiah*" (26). He "marvels at how the universe seemed to conspire to create the moment of awakening," the moment of his "opening" to "Grace" and "love" (28–31). Yet in all of this Moss feels profoundly "humbled" (29). The "son of man has no place to rest his head," he declares, following St. Thomas (29). He must go forth into the world to heal others through "unconditional love": "What Christ is to a Christian, unconditional love is to me" (45), and Moss claims to know "unconditional love directly" (47). Being a "saintly helper" (210), indeed, being one of his "generation's few awakened souls" (31), is by no means all peaches and cream: "For myself it feels like a crucifixion to come to another and offer energy for healing. I am drawn to the other in love, yet feel a subtle violence to my deeper nature in the very splitting from the other that this gift may be shared" (179). Thus Moss's "pilgrimage" toward "unconditional love" brings him finally to the cross.

I do not offer these materials simply to underscore the lengths to which human narcissism, and human confusion, may be carried. In ancient Rome, the emperor Caligula awakened one morning in the belief that he had been transformed during the night into a god, an actual god. My interest ultimately is in New Age healing and in Moss's writing as a guide to how New Age healing works. We must ask, accordingly, what is the purpose of his adoption of sainthood? What exactly is he up to, from the psychoanalytic angle? Moss becomes a saint because *as a saint* he will be in a position to exercise unlimited power and control over others, and specifically *over patients, the sick*. Such power and control over patients recalls explicitly the "parent-child relationship," the "parental dynamic" or "parental energetic" that Moss finds so "compelling" and so disturbing as a "traditional physician." Moss leaves mainstream medicine to heal *spiritually*, to work "miracles" (his own word, as in IW, 8), to awesomely transport his patients from a state of sickness to one of health, and what better way to *do* this than to become not merely a healer but a saintly one? More specifically, Moss's sainthood allows him to re-create with his patients an especially powerful version of the dual-unity situation; it allows him to engender a regressive fusion over and over again in which he, Moss, indulges the parental "role" and the patient the role of the child. The saint can dominate, awe, and finally fuse with the vulnerable, ordinary client. He can glory in his sainthood, glory in his power, glory in the love and attention bestowed upon him, and at the same time he can answer *his own need* for merger by forging a dyadic union wherein the significant objects of the early period are reactivated through wish-fulfilling illusion. In this sense, it does not matter that Moss gives us two dissimilar versions of his transformational experience, that "the awakening" transpires once "on a roof" in India, and again as a butterfly lands on his nose while he reclines in a meadow near Lone Pine, California. What matters is the "role" he wants to play, and does play, in healing, namely a role in which the *transference relationship* may be fostered—the father-saint over here and the child-patient over there. Let's look more closely now at how this system works.

The Magic of Energy

Toward the system's centre resides what Moss calls "energy," that ubiquitous New Age term which is just vague enough, just imprecise enough, just *imponderable* enough to serve as a psycho-physicalistic catch-all for pretty much anything and everything the New Age savant may want to establish about humanity and the universe. As it turns out, "energy" in New Age discourse is often bound up with matters of emotion, spirit, and soul—that is, with *subjective, feeling states, or states of being*; and as New Age discourse is overwhelmingly concerned with denying separation, with restoring infantile relationships as those relationships are *idealized* through regressive wishing (the utopian or paradisal urge), "energy" becomes the New Age's chief ruse for fulfilling its magical agenda in so-called reality. Note how the following citations from Moss (BB, 49–51) disclose the essentials of the business: the "exercises" that produce "openings," he tells us, "all involve energy." Indeed, "the concept and experience of energy is central to the understanding of transformation. It is one of the most difficult concepts to describe because of its esoteric nature. To appreciate energy one must have direct experience, and this level of experience frequently transcends the dimensions expressible with words. Energy is fundamental to existence; everything is energy. In its pure and unobstructed form it is consciousness ... Becoming aware of energy as the dimension of our psychophysical reality is crucial to ... the transformational process." This is perfect, is it not? Only one's "direct experience" can allow one to "appreciate" energy, and such "experience" turns out to "transcend" what we may express through language. Thus, as is always the case in New Age thinking, when it comes to "openings"—that is, to the regressive fusion with the *transformational object* who turns discomfort into pleasure and discontent into satisfaction—*anything goes*. My "direct experience" is all-determining, irrefutable, and final, because it is transcendent, inexpressible, and *mine*. I and I alone can "appreciate" it, so butt out. Energy is "fundamental to existence," writes Moss in a sentence that means precisely everything and nothing at all. "Everything is energy," Moss declares, in a sentence that has universal significance and no significance whatsoever, particularly when it comes to a person's underlying psychological nature as it is forged through his interactions with others. "Becoming aware of energy is crucial to the transformational process" (BB, 51)—of course it is, for Moss, like all New Age thinkers, will attempt to perform his regressive magic entirely in the energy realm and therefore needs the client to buy into that realm before anything can happen.

That Moss views the "energy" of transformation, the energy he will employ in his spiritual healing, in specifically *vibrational* terms is revealed by a dozen or so of his metaphors; this is crucial to an understanding of how his mind works and of course how his healing works, for it is in the area of *affective attunement*, in the area where caregiver and baby share the same affective *wavelength*, interacting as emotive, vibrational *mirrors* of each other, that the healing (such as it is) transpires. "Body energies course in strange *currents* and evoke incredible somatic phenomena" (IW, 10, my emphasis), writes Moss, as he describes his own "opening of the heart" (10). "Who is to interpret these phenomena?" Soon we will experience Moss's healing itself as one of these "strange, incredible phenomena," triggered in significant measure by his own idiosyncratic "interpretation" of energy. "Every cell can be alive and *vibrating* as if one were *electrical or atomic*" (53, my emphasis), he declares in a discussion of "awakening to higher energies." And then, focusing for us the *omnipotence* of thought lurking in all this, "If one comes into harmony with the *current*, the sense of strength and vitality can be nearly superhuman. But, even when there is inner peace the initial energy can simply be too much for the body— something like *putting too much current through a wire*" (53, my emphasis). As one develops the ability to "intuit deeper energy," Moss claims (62), one's own "self becomes the locus of *interpenetrating forces, or wavelengths, or vibrational frequencies* that seem to be coming from different dimensions" (my emphasis). The "refinement" of these "forces," Moss goes on, in a sentence that anticipates his own magical strategies for cure, "can be mastered consciously" as one "adjusts to the current" (63). In his chapter on "bridging psyche and soma" (73), we have this: "A human being is a multidimensional *receiver/transducer* whose consciousness determines how ... *forces* are recognized ... *transmuted*" (73, my emphasis). Moss continues, "There is an *energy body* ... which is directly experienced as a reflection of the level and quality of consciousness in any moment. At the same time, this *energy body* is a subtle manifestation of the physical self, so that *shifts in the energy* correspond to bodily transformation and vice versa. Thus *energetic dimensions* are clearly seen to bridge between the body and the consciousness" (74, my emphasis). As we will see, Moss's putative healing behaviours are tied inextricably to the particular, and peculiar, stance he adopts in regard to the "vibrational shifts" of this "energy body." A final instance of Dr. Moss's vibrational metaphors, this time from *The Black Butterfly* (91): "During the early period [of my transformation] there was so much energy moving through me, that when I contracted due to old psychical habits, it was like having *1000 watts in a 50-watt system* ... Energy not creatively engaged and radiated becomes morbid" (my emphasis). In the end, of course, the reader will judge for himself as to what is "morbid" in Moss's energetic "system."

Not content to rely entirely upon vibrational metaphors in support of his theory (I use this last word in the loosest possible sense), Moss drags in modern physics and endeavours to get it squarely behind his position. The reader may recall Scott Cunningham's (1988, 23) pathetic attempt to do this very thing for Wicca. "True," declares Cunningham, we cannot at present "explain" how Wiccan "powers" work, but "fringe physics is coming close to this achievement," and he lets it go at that. The efforts of Moss are just as pathetic, as he throws around his chosen terminology. Yet he thereby makes his way of thinking about "energy" and "healing" still clearer, and it is that kind of information which we are after here. "In Newtonian physics," Moss writes (IW, 17), "the word *energy* is no problem. A block slides across a table and we can measure the force needed for that movement to occur. We never question the energy represented by this action." In his own esoteric system of healing, however, we must make a "quantum leap" beyond Newton. We must enter a kind of "energetic-emotional" realm in which "energy becomes a living current," as elusive and spontaneous as "light" and capable of precipitating multiple realities at a variety of different "levels" (17). "In my work," Moss continues, "the important thing is to bring the awareness of self as energy into direct bodily experience" (18). Once this "force has been awakened in a human being, that person is gradually dissolved in it, or transformed by it" (18). Thus "the emotive dimension is a high-intensity realm" in which "oscillations of feeling" can be apprehended only by one who makes "a quantum leap of awareness" (119). Within this domain of intensity or "energy fields ... all human beings can be seen to be united in a continuum of consciousness." And then, "modern physics is drawing us toward an understanding of this" (163). That no such "understanding of this" happens to exist at present, particularly in regard to emotional and physical illness, let alone "all consciousness,"[4] does not deter Moss for one moment in proffering and *acting upon* his "theories," any more than it deters other New Age thinkers who have climbed upon the same bandwagon. How does that line from Pope begin? "Fools rush in ..." Allow me to cite a final example of this "scientific" gobbledygook: "We are all invited into direct experience, into a vibration, a quality, a poetry that is a continuum that helps us abandon our relative viewpoint. Where it is leading us we cannot know ... It is like the paradox of light, which seems to exist in or to obey a dual reality: In one reality we discuss discrete quanta, a unit of particles; in the other is a wave— uninterrupted—a continuum. The paradox is only in our perception. It is resolved by consciousness itself, in our very being and experience, as we lift to a higher level" (196). I wish I had a nickel for every passage *exactly like that one* which I have read in New Age books. The "level" on which Moss's curative activities transpire, I will maintain, is the level of *magic,* and in especial the magic of *regressive fusion.* As is always the case in New Age thinking, "higher" here means lower, means merger, dual-unity, the psychological movement toward the oceanic "continuum" of everyone and everything. As the separation-denying title of Moss's book *says,* "I's" are actually "We's."[5]

We come now to a pivotal point: in the belief that destiny has worked a saintly transfiguration upon him so that he might be able to manipulate these "energies," these post-Newtonian "quanta," these transformational vibrations or currents or wavelengths in a state of "unconditional love," Moss sets about *learning to radiate,* to change himself into a kind of "atomic reactor" (IW, 1) of healing forces moving among the sick and disturbed. "Transformation is *radiated,*" he writes (30, my emphasis), "not rationally taught, and rational processes must be wisely set aside to help receive the deeper impress." Shortly after his supernatural change, Moss "personally" has the "experience" of "transmuting" the "energy" within him for the benefit of others: "I shifted my awareness and simultaneously asked my consciousness to release this energy into unconditional love. *Miraculously,* I was suffused with a *radiant* warmth that seemed to *project* from the chest" (23, my emphasis). Working on this ability, Moss "finally" learns "to place [his] awareness at the heart" and begins "to learn how to *transmute energy consciously*" (26, my emphasis). Not only does Moss go on about this at some length, but he does so in terms that explicitly recall the work of Daniel Stern (1985) on *affective attunement in infancy* and early childhood. "As the consciousness of the healer ... begins to transform into a subtler realm," states Moss, the "I-am-separate-from-you approach is finally seen as illusory ... There is a far deeper blending and interpenetration of energetic forces. When these forces are *consciously attuned by the healer,* a new and finer energy is attained in the interaction" (86, my emphasis). Thus "procedures" can "go sour" if "the *attunement is lacking*" (87, my emphasis).

A person "whose consciousness has awakened can *effectively suggest a doctor-patient match,* or, even more important, teach individuals to *attune* to each other and to the deeper forces in such a way as to maximize the potential of the interaction" (87, my emphasis). In this way, it is the "consciousness of the healer" that "becomes vitally important" (87). Here are further examples which make it clear that Moss, at some level, is aware of the transference issues involved: "The release of goal and the *attunement* to the fineness of the energetic" is what the healer must "develop," he maintains (IW, 141, my emphasis). And then, "as one facet of this new form, the importance of the imbued teacher cannot be underestimated. One way to consider such a person is as a refined energetic ... To enter into relationship with such a presence" may result "in addiction and dependency of such magnitude that it can outrival the most powerful narcotic" (141). Moss calls this "the old guru-disciple process" (141). Here is a final instance, this time from the volume *How Shall I Live?* "All I was doing [in my healing work] with people was listening for wholeness—for that space where *their energy seemed most available*—and feeling when *the separation between us fell away* ... As I listened from this state of *meditative attunement* ... I realized that ... my being in the most receptive energy state possible facilitated an automatic high energy state in my visitors. This process ... led me to understand that at the level of the deeper *energy we really are one body* (HL, 14–15, my emphasis).[6] Once again, "I's" are "We's."

From the standpoint of psychoanalysis, what Moss is doing in all this is perfectly clear: he is fostering transference relationships; he is learning how to slip psychically into the inner worlds of people in a mesmerizing way and establish himself there as a partner in vibrational fusion, vibrational (or affective) attunement, dual-unity, merger, a "continuum" of regressive, symbiotic togetherness ("we really are one body"). Moss's belief in his miraculous, saintly powers, "cosmically confirmed" (IW, 8), along with his belief in the actual presence of a vibrating "stuff" that can be sent and received,[7] is merely the *rationalization, the screen* for his narcissistic indulgence in transference exchanges. Moss "heals" (to the extent that anything happens at all, of course) by *holding* the client in an intense psychological bond, by returning him/her unconsciously to the dual-unity situation in which the baby is *held* (and narcissistically gratified) by the all-powerful and unconditionally loving transformational object who possesses the "supernatural" capacity to turn discomfort into pleasure, or relief. As everyone knows, we see variations upon this ancient theme over and over again on TV where the rheumatic individual is brought into the presence of the numinous "healer" who extends his hand and *transduces* (Moss

likes this word) the power of God into a curative vibration which relieves the afflicted joint, thus "transforming" the subject. To put it another way, Moss learns how to adopt the omnipotent parental (and, in
particular, maternal) role in the transference relationship and in that
role to regress the suffering client into a state of soothing fusion
wherein the client experiences a measure of relief and emotional security, both of which recall at the unconscious level the first transformational union with the radiant maternal figure, the original dispenser of
"unconditional love." Can it come as a surprise to anyone that a good
many physically ill and/or emotionally dissatisfied people are seeking
change, alteration, transformation, that they are apt to respond posi-
tively to a "saintly" healer who goes about "radiating" a supernatural
"energy" which is supposed to take the illness and/or dissatisfaction
away and replace it with "unconditional love," the very kind of love
through which mothers attune affectively with their vulnerable babies?

Writing about patients with predominantly psychological problems in a manner that is easily extrapolated to those with psychosomatic complaints, Bollas (1987, 22) observes that "the search for the
transformational object" in the emotionally disturbed "is in fact an internal recognition of the need for ego repair and as such is a somewhat
manic search for health." Patients seek a "special ambience" with the
doctor, whose "interpretations are initially less important for their
content and more significant for what is experienced as a maternal
presence, an empathetic response." Indeed, declares Bollas (22), the
patient may actually "assert" his "illness" as a "plea for the arrival of
the regressive object relation." Essential to bear in mind here is that
Moss as saintly healer, as someone who has abandoned "traditional
medicine" to become a saintly healer, moves along a two-way psychological street. It is not only the patient who experiences fusion as the
dyad of attunement is created: Moss experiences fusion too. I would
suggest, in fact, that Moss fashions this entire arrangement not only to
indulge his grandiosity and his narcissism (probably his chief concerns)
but his own longing for symbiotic merger as well. Moss becomes part
of the "attunement" to the "fineness of the energetic," part of the
"interactional continuum," part of the perfect "doctor-patient match."
This explains, in some measure at least, why Moss's writings are endlessly preoccupied with, endlessly absorbed in, a denial of separation, a
denial of differentiation, and an insistence upon the connection of
everyone to everyone else: The I That Is We. Moss the spiritual healer
is out to gratify all the "levels" of his appetitive, human character,
from the narcissistic "level" to the symbiotic "level," and it is in the
process of doing that that he "heals" the seekers after transformation
who come unto him, or unto whom he comes.

That Moss's system of cure is based upon an unconscious return to early, primal affect and in particular the "unconditional love" that informs mother-infant attunement emerges strikingly from the logic of his writing, from the psychological formulations he fashions through the pivotal terms of his discussion. More specifically, as the individual undergoes an increase in vibrational energy he *simultaneously* undergoes an increase in his capacity to love: heightened energetic currents or frequencies *mean* heightened proficiency at *radiating* love. In turn, the heightening of the ability to love *means* transformation, *means* that one has undergone a transcendent alteration of "psyche and soma" (IW, 73). Thus *vibrational energy* is linked inextricably to the *transformational* moment, and we have, psychoanalytically, the "formula" for the restoration of affective attunement, for the restoration of the "unconditional love" that characterizes dual-unity, the mirroring symbiosis during which caregiver and baby discover themselves on the same affective *wavelength*, and also during which the empathetic parent continually *transforms* the infant's discomfort into pleasure, or relief. "The first step in a genuine movement toward awakening," writes Moss (IW, 24), "is the realization that all experience is ... the direct consequence of its underlying energy dynamic ... The second step lies in acknowledging that the ability to refine energy requires a commitment to and direct realization of unconditional love." The "embracing" of "unconditional love," in turn, "is the essential commitment in transformation" (28), and the formulaic circle is complete. Permit me to develop this with few more vivid citations from Moss's work. He declares: "The awakening into higher energies results in a major transformation ... Unconditional love is the energy that encompasses and supports this process" (49, 55). Again, "Unconditional love is a radiant current that intrinsically unifies the psyche and embraces within its transformative power the whole spectrum of human experience" (103). Once more, this time with explicit reference to healing: "All healing experiences, whether laying on of hands, penicillin injection or surgical procedure, are essentially energy modifying ... The nature and quality of this alteration is an expression of its relative intensity and vibrational frequency ... A new sense of reality (transformation) emerges as a refinement of energy ... is bestowed by the contemplation of unconditional love" (109, 111). Here is a memorable example from *The Black Butterfly*: "Fundamental transformation is a radical shift in the energetic structure; it is the new note that eventuates when the old system makes a quantum leap to a higher energy level ... Transformation produces a new energetic system of broader sensitivity that in turn radiates greater love" (BB, 149). Finally, from *How Shall I Live?*: "Transformation implies a refinement and extension of the radiant energy or aliveness that permeates one's being ... A presence radiates from this space that has physical, mental, and spiritual impact on those around us ... The transformative moment can also be described as a growth to a greater capacity to love" (HL, 46–47). Is it not remarkable how simple and straightforward Moss's system turns out to be? When we cut through all the New Age rigmarole, when we set aside the post-Newtonian quanta, the particles and waves, the butterfly on the nose, Handel's *Messiah*, the roof in India, the lives of the saints (Moss's self-proclaimed brothers), and the very Cross on Calvary itself, we come down to this: a disgruntled doctor who claims to possess a miraculous power to heal regresses his gullible, suffering clients to the time of symbiotic bonding, to the time of unconditional maternal love, and in the process not only makes them feel better ("transformation") but also gratifies his own needs for admiration, connection, and control. Here is New Age healing stripped down to its essentials, and rather reminiscent of that timeless children's tale, "The Emperor's New Clothes": duped by the tailor and believing he is sumptuously attired, the Emperor goes around in the buff until a small child, who has yet to be intimidated by royalty, cries out, "Mama, the Emperor has no clothes on!" The question arises, of course, what's wrong with New Age healing as it is exemplified in Moss's books and tapes and lectures? Why *shouldn't* people do this if they wish to? I reply, there is absolutely nothing wrong with it *as long as people see it for what it is*. If a person is feeling poorly and wants to curl up in bed and suck his thumb, who cares? If a person is feeling poorly and wants to be held and loved by others, so what? We are all just human beings. But when we regard such behaviour falsely, when we distort the facts of the matter by ascribing the "cure" to supernatural forces or mysterious quanta or saintly interventions, we cross the line into superstition and error. We blind ourselves and others to what is actually occurring. If I may use an old-fashioned expression in this deconstructive, postmodern age, we *strangle the truth*. Nothing, in my view at least, is more dangerous and more damaging to our heritage as human beings than that.

The Ultimate Mother

The philosophical or spiritual context in which Moss presents his system of healing discloses in a striking, unforgettable way, *the emotive direction from which he is coming as healer*, along with, of course, *the kind of transference relation* he offers the client who turns to him for assistance. More specifically, Moss develops a philosophical context that *justifies regression*, that justifies an emotional backslide toward early levels of psychosexual development where differentiation disappears and where absorption into the *corpus maternum* prevails. Moss writes, "If we let go and surrender our outer reason there must be something that we fall into, otherwise the release of our limiting egocentric reality would just result in chaos ... In making this jump one enters a dimension of formlessness governed by feeling states and intuitive knowing that do not respond to, or participate with, our traditional ways of learning. The ego structure through which we perform in our life is constantly distinguishing between ourself and so-called external reality ... But there comes a natural point in human development where this very process must be reversed [why?], where the boundary between self and experience must be allowed to relax in order for a new level of perception to enter [again, why?] ... It is a fundamental return to the beginner's mind, to the child state, to Beingness prior to conditional and memorized images about life ... This is what I believe is meant by the injunction, 'save as ye be as children, ye shall not enter the Kingdom of Heaven'" (IW, 31–33). But Moss does not want his prospective clients to enter his kingdom of transformational healing as mere *children*: "It is the *undifferentiated state of consciousness that belongs to the infant* who can perceive and appreciate the whole of experience simultaneously" (33, my emphasis) that he is after. And it is the "qualities of trust and surrender" which "must be regarded as essential for realizing the unconditional state," for "at this point trust is no longer a word. It is an energy field organizer. It is like a formless gelatin mould providing an integrity for the self at a critical time of instability where no dimension of rational consciousness can function. Trust and its sister, surrender, *are like a womb* in which all of consciousness can gestate ... In this *womb* rational faculties are not lost but they become blended with a formless, numinous quality of self" (66–67, my emphasis). Having moved the potential patient toward the "womb" of "trust and surrender," Moss proceeds to move him/her toward the Great Mother in whom that womb, and everything else in the world, resides.

Writing of his own "awakening," his own "rebirth," his own attainment of an "undifferentiated state," Moss asserts (IW, 91), "I knew somehow that the whole earth was my new mother ... With each wave of energy [the regressive reactivation of vibrational or affective attunement] I surrendered a little more, and finally there was no more resistance ... I simply entered another level of reality ... The sense was of *formless existence as a feminine principle—an ultimate mother*—that bequeathed life by the fact of existence itself. I felt in direct relationship, *inseparable from this great feminine consciousness*" (94, my emphasis). Just as the Witches draw the initiate toward their version of the *magna mater* during the course of the rebirthing ceremony, so Moss draws his potential followers toward his version of the Great Mother during the course of his theoretical introduction to healing. It is separation, differentiation, autonomy that must be broken down for the magical system to work: "At slow vibrations or lower energy states our separatist human individuality appears as reality to us; I-Thou duality dominates ... At the faster vibration or the higher energy levels of consciousness, our apparent individuality becomes more and more of an illusion [again, regression to vibrational merger]. The interpenetrating fields of energy unite all life in a continuum ... We exist as a nonpersonal, nonphysical interpenetrating continuum of tremendously high energy and high vibration" (165–67). The curious word *nonphysical* here captures the infant's total absorption in symbiosis, fusion, dualunity, out of which the awareness of *his own body* as separate and distinct from the object's only gradually emerges, as we saw in Mahler.

Moss simply will not let up on this score, driving home the *preverbal* nature of the ultimate reality in which we ostensibly exist, and to which we must *revert* if we are to be *healed*. Writing still again of "the awakening" during the course of which "the unity of all life became clear" to him, Moss declares (BB, 231, my emphasis), "I was suddenly aware of recapitulating my own birth ... It was preverbal, a state in which there were no words or concepts ... It was a state in which *I experienced existence as the Mother* ... I had come from the inside out—out of myself into Existence, the Mother." Is there a hint of the grandiose fantasy of self-creation here? "Know that, in the very act of perceiving, you Are," states Moss (231) in his best gospel style, and saying nothing. "You are safe in Mother Consciousness, just as surely as you were an infant in your mother's loving arms" (231). Assuming Moss is able through his writings and/or his presence to move his potential customers toward the "undifferentiated state," to soften them up in this particular manner, one cannot imagine Moss encountering great difficulty in moving them toward the next "state" in which his miraculous ministrations transform sickness (of whatever sort) into well-being. Indeed, Moss as healer, Moss *as he heals,* becomes simply *another aspect* of the maternal reality he has projected onto the entire universe. It is Moss's "loving arms" into which the patient "surrenders" himself. It is Moss's "mother consciousness" unto which the patient "entrusts" his welfare. To re-echo Christopher Bollas (1987, 22), the patient seeking transformation experiences through Moss the "regressive object relation" or "maternal presence" that Moss has been describing for us at the macrocosmic level with his "spiritual" presentation of the world as "the ultimate mother." As always, it is a two-way psychological street, comprising not only transference but counter-transference as well. Moss and the patient create, as the healing process goes forward, a version of the original dual-unit, with the miraculous par-ent-healer over here and the needy patient-child over there. *Both* recap-ture symbiosis; *both* re-experience fusion, the affective, vibrational *mirror* of primal attunement. Along with the patient's, Moss's regres-sive requirements are gratified, for, having *become* the "loving mother's" *equivalent*, Moss no longer needs the *actual* mother in the way that he once did. Having taken the mother's *place* (his role in the transference), Moss *has* the mother again in his own unconscious mind. In Moss's system of healing, *all* who seek shall find, including the saintly dispenser of "unconditional love."

As the spiritual healer gets down to the actual business of "trans-ferring healing energies" (HL, 127) to the patient, of enfolding him in what Moss (118) calls "the Energy Embrace"—a version of vibrational attunement—the healer "opens to the thought" that he has "nothing to *give* or *receive* except love" (124, my emphasis). He then "brings his hands together," as if "there was a small ball between them," and moves his hands toward the patient (124). However, "he *does not* actu-ally make physical contact" (124, my emphasis). Instead, he holds his hands "gently away" from the patient's "body surface" and "begins to *attune* to the sense of presence" (124, my emphasis). He "senses the energy connection in the subtle contact" (125). He "gives himself over to the perfect wholeness of the moment" (125). He "lets the connection and his sense of relationship to Life become the same thing" (125). Eventually, the healer "releases the connection" and "withdraws" to his own "physical boundaries" (125). Moss concludes (126): "The per-son with whom I was sharing ceased to exist as someone separate from me. *We became One* in that Presence, that palpable Aliveness ... Quite commonly, the Energetic Embrace itself produces a calmness or inner silence, and a new sense of rapport and fellowship. We may feel a fine *vibration* (what I call 'molecular aliveness') within the body; it may be generalized, or focused in specific areas like the head, chest, or abdo-men" (my emphasis). I doubt that the most skilful psychoanalytic cli-nician could elicit more effectively than this the behavioural essence of what happens between mother and infant as they join in affective attunement, as they create the dual-unit which comprises the core of early, symbiotic fusion.[8] The "I-Thou duality" Moss wants to over-come with his mother-centred "Existence," his "feminine principle" of the universe, is not some philosophical or spiritual duality. It is the duality that prevails when symbiosis ends and the separation of mother and infant begins. It is not the universe or existence that is "the ulti-mate mother" of human beings. The *actual* mother is the *ultimate* mother in the mind. All the other "mothers" that we may fashion up for our own emotional purposes are *projections of that one.*

The Group

What occurs when Moss heads up a "group energy sharing," as he expresses it (IW, 148), is simply a magnification or amplification of what occurs when patient and healer "share energy" on a one-to-one basis. Indeed, Moss is interested in groups *because* they magnify, or amplify, the potentialities for regressive merger. He writes (158), "By its very nature the dynamics of group energy held in a unified focus at the highest possible quality of consciousness creates a force field that transcends the issues of individual human concern." And again, "The heightened energy of the group provides a quality of resolution and healing that penetrates to a much greater depth than if it were attempted at a lower energy state in the more energetically balanced one-to-one modes of therapy." And finally, "The energy available in a dynamic of two is greater than that available to a solitary individual, but is far less than that of a larger group." I am not denying, of course, that other intrapsychic and interactional events transpire as Moss "orchestrates group energy" in an effort to "accelerate personal transformation" (159). We will look at a few of these other events momentarily. I am suggesting only that regressive merger is the principal thing and that the other occurrences are inextricably connected to the regressive slide. So "deep" is the "energy sharing" in what Moss terms his "conference work" (137) that many of his customers discover their lives "transformed virtually in an instant" (153). How does it go in Handel's *Messiah:* "changed in the twinkling of an eye"? Moss is "tempted" to call such transformations "miraculous" (152). Yet they do, he assures us, happen on a regular basis. "We are on the threshold of demystifying the power of love and of collective human energies in the configuration and evolution of man," he declares (153) under the spell of group transformation and in words that can only raise goose bumps on the flesh of New Age readers. It might be instructive here to remember something Ashbach and Schermer (1987, 6) have to say about the group in their definitive psychoanalytic study, namely that it (the group) "often takes on the qualities of the maternal object," and that "group fantasy and ritual are simultaneously ways in which the membership defends against primitive anxieties." We don't have to puzzle long at this point in our study of New Age thinking to figure out the "primitive anxiety" against which the members of Moss's group will be defending themselves: it is the anxiety engendered by the separation stage of development, the *bête noire* of New Age thinking as a whole. It might also be instructive to note that Moss himself maintains group processes place "great emphasis on the *feminine* nonrational and intuitive mode of being" (137, my emphasis), the "mode" Moss elsewhere (94) dubs the "great feminine consciousness" that is "existence itself." Is Moss's "energy group," by any chance, another version of "the ultimate mother"? Let's look more closely at the business.

In his role as group leader, Moss devotes himself to what he calls the "heightening" of "group energy." But it is not simply a general heightening that he is after; it is a heightening that leads to "the state of unconditional love" (IW, 118). Moss writes, "The heart of my own work is the volitional attempt at group heightening around the state of unconditional love. I believe unconditional love is essential for two reasons. First of all, for the purpose of *transformation*, contrast must be created with our ordinary levels of consciousness ... The state of unconditional love becomes the 'air' into which conditional consciousness leaps in order to behold a new dimension" (118, my emphasis). Now, when we recall Moss's "formula" for regressive merger, namely heightened vibration or energy *as* the "unconditional love" that returns the participant to affective attunement, to reunion with the *transformational* object who changes discomfort into pleasure or relief, we recognize not only the reason for Moss's great interest in collective power but the *kind* of experience participants in the group are urged unconsciously to embrace—that is, the experience of dual-unity, fusion, symbiosis—which brings us to the "second" reason for Moss's "focusing the group dynamic around the sense of unconditional love" (120). "Although the initial intimations of unconditional love can be shared as presence (and thus you can be guided toward it by a person who has realized this state)," he observes (120), "the realization in oneself is powerfully expedited and deepened by group energy." In other words, the individual can *use* the group *fully* to achieve his own, personal sense of fusion; he can *attach* himself to the group as he did to the *original object,* the original dispenser of "unconditional love" (transformation). The group is the transformational object "writ large." Thus we see how the group breaks down the very same "I-Thou duality" that is broken down in individual healing sessions. As Moss expresses it, "Group energy focused at the unconditional levels of Beingness can move the sense of Self into a direct realization that bridges our continuous tendency to split the part from the whole" (122). Still again, the "I" becomes part of the "We," the "We" as the group, the "We" as *collective* healer.

Here are a few sentences in which Moss describes critical facets of "the group process" (IW, 123): "I emphasize to the participants the concept of building an energy charge. The group dynamic is a powerful amplifier and refiner of energy and each individual tends to be able to hold this energy differently ... In general, the more receptive and open one becomes, *the more creative and unconditional one must become in the expression of energy* so that balance is sustained ... *This allows a gradual merging into the larger energetic* . . . People gain the freedom to hold more energy consciously" (my emphasis). With his customers "holding more energy consciously," with his customers *loaded* and *merging*, Moss directs them toward "the coin game"; that is, he instructs them to demonstrate their energetic capacity by locating through a kind of telepathic touch coins concealed in the pockets of other group members. Moss explains (124): "Such localization is possible because metal seems to create irregularities in the energy field that radiates from the body surface and this can be sensed by the hands." Everyone succeeds at this to one degree or another, he claims, for "once the required shift into a different perspective in consciousness is understood and practiced, such subtle perception is relatively simple to develop." Indeed, "some people find the coin with nearly 100 percent accuracy" (124). From a psychoanalytic perspective, we have here Moss's attempt to foster in his customers sensations of omnipotence and mastery, along with, of course, the narcissistic inflation that typically attends such sensations. The reason is obvious: as members come to feel empowered, they will come to believe in their ability to *transform* their fellows, to influence their fellows' attitudes and actions from what we may term the parental side of the symbiotic equation. If Moss's group is to function successfully, customers must be able to *shift* from the parental role to the infantile role and back again. Needless to say, some will be attracted to one role more than the other, but *all* will receive a regressive reward that reflects the tension surrounding the separation stage. The "parents" will no longer feel, temporarily at least, a longing for the transformational object, as they will have *become* that object themselves in the unconscious (just as Moss becomes that object in his one-to-one healings). The "infants," obviously, will plunge themselves into the re-establishment of transformational fusion. Accordingly, as soon as the coin game is completed, and "without prior verbal exchange with the person being examined, this same subtle ability [that is, the ability to find the coin] can be used to locate areas of trauma or to identify the presence of pain" (124). Group members begin to "direct energy from the hands or the eyes" (123) and with that energy to relieve the psychological and/or physical suffering of their fellows, who give themselves up in perfect trust to the emergent powers that now touch them. In some cases, the energy directed through "the hands or the eyes" (123) is employed to create the healing sensation of "love" (123). In other cases, customers "move into major life-changing realizations" (137); still others "are healed of serious illness" (137). The membership has entered what Moss entitles the "magical dimension" (125), where transformations and healings go forward at a brisk pace, and on a regular basis. "Emotions" are "transmuted"; "hearts" are "energized"; "telepathic" abilities are "activated" (124).

"Once a group comes into harmony," Moss asserts, "the energetic presence is palpable and wondrous ... What is subconscious at one level or vibrational of energy enters conscious authority at a higher level of energy" (126–27). Because he cannot see the regressive transference relations that dominate the group, Moss has this *backwards*. It is the *unconscious* wish for symbiotic merger, omnipotence, and narcissistic gratification that spins this plot. "Conscious authority" is the *illusion*. The "higher level of energy" indicates, as it always does in New Age thinking, the "lower," primal urge to *fuse* with the other, as either dispenser or receiver of "unconditional love." The members of Moss's group are *acting-out*.

Perhaps the most dramatic, and psychoanalytically revelational, kind of healing Moss pushes in his "conference work" is the group-on-one variety. Moss calls it "a sacred ritual" (IW, 148) and offers the following details: the members of the group, thirty-five or forty of them, sometimes a few more (122), gather around the afflicted client, who lies supine on a table. The intention of the members, under Moss's "orchestration," is to "share" with the client "an energy of unconditional love" (148). They begin by "focusing" their attention at the "centre" of their own "hearts." They then "consciously *attune* to the highest sense of inspiration and love" (148, my emphasis). Finally, they extend their arms and "allow" this love and inspiration "to flow" to the client "from the hands" and from their "whole sense of being" (148). According to Moss, this "sacred ritual" carries a "high level" of "healing potential" (150). "Relief" of "pain" is usually ... achieved in seconds to minutes," including the pain from "migraine, muscle tension or metastatic bone disease" (150). "Post-operative nausea" is relieved, a variety of "diseases" are "ameliorated," and "occasionally, unusually rapid bone healing" is "noted on X-ray" (150). Moss does not invite the reader to have a peek at the relevant "X-rays." In fact, because "most" of the "responses" to the "sacred ritual" are, in his own words, "subjective," Moss makes "no attempt ... to quantify the responses" or to "differentiate which treatment caused which result" (150). Yet he writes, in the face of this (and in a sentence that degenerates stylistically), "we physicians and therapists who were part of these groups had never seen, in our many cumulative years of traditional practice, experiences of such magnitude, or that conveyed such reverence for life" (150). Such remarks, in the context of Moss's "magical dimension" (125), speak for themselves. Moss and his fellow healers stand about and marvel at medical miracles that can *in no way* be verified or validated scientifically. "Physicians and therapists," Moss calls himself and his cohorts. That is not my way of understanding those professional titles.

As for the group healing, can anyone at this juncture possibly miss its psychoanalytic significance? The energy-transferring members become for the ailing client a huge, collective version of the transformational, vibrational object. They extend to him the kind of "frequencies," "wavelengths," "vibes," that mother extends to baby during the time of affective attunement, the time that *precedes* the dreaded separation phase of development. On his back, in difficulty, vulnerable, the customer gives himself over to the group's collective will, which "says" to him consciously, you will be changed, and *unconsciously*—where the dynamic affect resides—you are once again joined with the vibrational powerhouse who transformed your life on a daily basis throughout the symbiotic period and who has miraculously returned to you now to trigger another life-altering transformation. The unconscious wish for the transformational object, the wish that brought the customer to the ritual in the first place, has come true "in reality," for here is a *vibrational* group sending its "unconditional love" (transformation) to the passive receiver who wants more than anything else to experience an immediate (and positive) *change* in his condition. In the group-on-one healing process the membership comprises, to use Moss's helpful expression once more, "the ultimate mother." The "transferring" of "energy" from its "hands" to the client is actually the establishment of a *transference* relationship. That clients who undergo this often end up feeling better than they did before it started is hardly surprising: maternal love is a powerful potion, especially for those in discomfort.

Here is the *first* of several "key elements" Moss considers "necessary" for "creating a transformative experience with a group" (IW, 145): "A multidimensionally awakened individual who can initially provide the presence, wisdom and experience to move the interaction safely in new dimensions. Such individuals are capable of perceiving through one or more modes of subtle awareness; thus they are able to sense the energetic process that is moving within an individual or a group." These "awakened" souls, Moss continues, "can volitionally activate and refine their own energy level and are capable of activating specific energy centers. They are able to transfer energy through their presence and thereby induce an altered state of consciousness in those who are open to them. They usually can transfer energy through the voice and may be gifted at articulating dimensions that are beyond rational expression." Finally, "they are capable of maintaining several levels of awareness simultaneously and can sustain extended periods of deep concentration" (145). In all of this, of course, Moss is describing *himself*. He is the one who provides the "presence" to "move the interaction." *He* is the one with the "subtle awareness," the one who can "sense the energetic process moving within the group," the one who can "transfer energy with his voice," and thereby "induce altered states." *He* is the one who can, like a spiritual Houdini, "maintain several levels of awareness simultaneously" and "sustain extended periods of deep concentration." It is a *performance*, a *presentation*, and from the standpoint of psychoanalysis it has one and only one purpose.

Allow me to italicize the confessional lines which intimate that purpose rather clearly; Moss is describing the manner in which he "orchestrates" (IW, 159) the transformational moment: "The responsibility to carry and focus the energy of the conference process inevitably leads to *the presentation of only certain facets of my nature*. This results in a *particular kind of projection* that tends to *amplify the depth of my gifts* ... and this is necessary for some people in order to begin to realize *the same potential within themselves*. A sense of *the sacred and mysterious* is ... an important part of what allows some people to start on the *journey of transformation*" (143, my emphasis). When we recall once again what "transformation" *means* in Moss, namely "unconditional love," and when we recall as well Moss's earlier remark (118) that the "heart" of his "work" is the "volitional attempt at group heightening around the state of unconditional love," the nature of his *role* in the "group process" emerges unmistakably: Moss is there to *commence the regressive transference*, to encourage the membership *to attach itself to him* as it did to the transformational object during the early period. Indeed, the transformational object *reappears* to the membership in the guise of the "sacred and mysterious" group leader, the one with the energy-sending "presence" and the magical, charismatic "voice" (145). "To me, group energy is only a metaphor for the human family," writes Moss (BB, 52). Exactly! At the level of unconscious suggestion where the dynamics of "transformation" (fusion) reside, Moss's "presentation" (IW, 143) *transforms him* into the *head* of the "family," into a *parental* presence whom the members *internalize* (Moss calls this "the internalization of the guru principle" [140]) as they enter the "magical dimension" (125) and "journey" toward "life-altering realizations" (137). Moss is leading his flock toward the affective world that *precedes* the separation phase. It is *there* that the energetic "merging" (123) will transpire. Needless to say, Moss realizes intuitively, through his skill at manipulation, that once the regression gets going, once the unconscious takes over, all sorts of "miracles" can occur, for in the "magical dimension" (125) everything that happens is streaked with delusional mentation. The line between reality and wish-fulfilling alteration is blurred. Having been emotively *reactivated*, the omnipotent, transformational object is back again, and, as every unconscious mind knows, *that* object can do *anything*, literally *anything,* in the way of changing discomfort into pleasure, or relief. The "imbued teacher," declares Moss, "almost literally extends power out through the collective body" of the group (140). In other words, he *thrills* the membership into the infantile conviction that the all-powerful parent has returned unto them. "One way to consider such a person," Moss goes on (141), "is as a refined energetic or a larger context for Beingness." This "larger context" is simply the one that includes the unconscious dimension in general and the time of transformational symbiosis in particular.

Why does Moss do this—I mean, apart from the feelings of omnipotence and the narcissistic gratification that he must get from it? The answer is not difficult to discover. Moss fosters regression *to ensure his success, to please his customers* so that he can continue to attract them as a powerful and magical maker of transformations. In a nutshell, as "healings" go forward so does *success* go forward. At the time of composing *The I That Is We* (1981) Moss had successfully manipulated groups of people forty or fifty times (IW, 144). Currently, his Three Mountain Foundation is sending out brochures that encourage folks to sign up for transformation (it isn't cheap) and that offer Moss as the world-famous healer who will lead them into the promised land. After all, the man left "traditional medicine," with its traditional rewards, to take up the healing trade: it had *better* work.

As Moss's symbiotic healings go forward certain additional intrapsychic and interactional events transpire among the membership. I am not referring to the endless stroking and chit-chat which typically go on at New Age gatherings ("thank you for sharing with me this inspirational moment"), but to events that are considerably more compelling from a psychoanalytic angle. "Quite common in the transformational process," writes Moss (IW, 150), "are phenomena of altered perception." Participants are apt to find themselves "levitating" or "floating." They "see brilliant light and colors, symbols, columns or vortexes of energy, and auras." They also "hear unusual sounds" and "smell unusual fragrances." What does Moss make of these "experiences"? His "only response" is to "appreciate" their "reality." Indeed, writes Moss (150), "I have had them many times myself." Really? Has Moss really "levitated" many times? Does he go about "hearing unusual sounds" and seeing "vortexes of energy"? Is this the "wise, awakened individual" who can "move" the group "safely into new dimensions" (145)? But there are more "responses" to "transformation" to report, responses that, as Moss puts it (151), "encompass a broad range." They include "alteration in respiration, feelings of vibration or tingling, muscle trembling, large-scale muscular contractions, swallowing and intestial peristalsis, crying and emotional release, strongly perceived alterations in temperature, and more" (151). Thus, as we envision ourselves in attendance at one of Moss's "group energy sharings" we must also envision ourselves among customers who are weeping, sweating, trembling, panting, writhing about with stomach cramps, and struggling to swallow their saliva. What has Moss to say of *these* experiences? Well, it goes like this: "There is no point in going into this very deeply since we already know that energy is a bridge between psyche and soma" (151). Talk about diagnostic superficiality and denial walking down the spiritual highway hand in hand! Once again we must ask, *exactly* as we asked a moment earlier, is this the "wise and awakened individual" who can "move" the group "safely into new dimensions"? With the "data" Moss extends, we cannot, of course, make detailed and specific psychoanalytic interpretations of these vivid and rather disconcerting symptoms, for we know nothing of the clients who are weeping, trembling, and cramping-up. Yet we can say with assurance that *all* of these "responses" to Moss's carefully orchestrated effort to *regress* his followers to early stages of psychosexual development, to *break down* their sense of differentiation and autonomy, are precisely the kind of anxiety-laden, delusion-laden responses that characteristically accompany the fragmentation of the personality and the partial destruction of the ego. Certain similar reactions, needless to say, may also be witnessed in the psychoanalytic setting as the transference relation between doctor and patient develops. Analysands cry and tremble on a fairly regular basis, for example. The difference between *that* and what we witness in Moss's "conference work" may be rendered as follows: in the psychoanalytic setting (individual or group) a qualified psychiatric practitioner deals carefully and responsibly with the client(s) who has come to him/her under the burden of specific emotional or psychosomatic problems (traditionally known as neuroses), which will be addressed along well-developed and continually tested theoretical and clinical lines. In Moss's "group energy sharing," by contrast, a former physician and self-styled saint sends his miraculous vibrations of love out to several dozen seekers after transformation who wish to be healed and changed "virtually in an instant" (153). In his own words, Moss claims to possess the "gift" (143) of fostering the "transformation" of individuals "directly" through his "presence," and of triggering "life-altering realizations" with his "voice" (143, 145). I don't know of any licensed analysts (or therapists) who are putting forth similar claims to prospective clients. On the contrary, most practitioners are quick to point out their own limitations as "healers" and to stress that progress is slow, painful, elusive, and even uncertain. Surely it makes a good deal of sense for people to think carefully about where, and with whom, they choose to do their regressing. An inward return to the time of symbiotic fusion can be fraught with very serious psychological perils, particularly when it is "orchestrated" by an alluring guru and by the presence of fifty other people, each of whom is more or less under the spell of that "orchestration."

Like Benjamin Creme, Moss is eager to see what is happening in his groups happen all over the planet. As a matter of fact, he believes that this is currently going on, and that it comprises what we know popularly as the New Age. "I believe we are at the threshold of what I have referred to as the collectivization of mind," he writes (IW, 220). "The united personal consciousness is being transcended and a consciousness is being prepared that is capable of handling much higher energies, and directly experiencing its intrinsic connectedness with all humanity, so that it can function as a unit amidst a much greater wholeness." Moss continues, "There are now many experiments involving focused group energies springing up throughout the planet. In one ashram I visited in India the guru transfers energy to an individual in an overt ritual while hundreds of disciples simultaneously focus their awareness on him. The effect on the recipient of the energy can be quite dramatic. The laying on of hands by healing circles is another form of the same thing. Evangelical healers who catalyze an audience and then invite people for healing are also tapping the higher energy process" (132). Moss is fascinated by the way in which the media appear to be inducing similar reactive "processes" in the wider world: "Through the media, we are tuning into the same input at the same time. Millions of minds are receiving the same signal and responding to the same input simultaneously. It is as if we are unconsciously fostering *the same process that I attempt to catalyze in the groups*" (131, my emphasis). And then, "Are people as a result of this becoming more psychic? . . . Are we perhaps feeling and sensing each other more deeply and more of the time? I speculate that this is in part the basis for the so-called New Age" (132). Yet for Moss, as for Benjamin Creme, it is not electronics but the emotional dynamics of the interactive group that will ultimately nourish the New Age fully into existence, that will ultimately induce the "collectivization of mind" which will mark our "transformation" as a species of life. "As a physician," Moss declares (220), "I saw perhaps 10,000 patients individually. When I left that work and experienced the awakening of higher energies, I found myself in the exploration of group consciousness. Over the past five years I have done hundreds of group sessions that demonstrated the capacity to bring people temporarily into levels of telepathic and energetic rapport.[9] Very few people can withstand for long the energy of even twenty or thirty people brought into a unified focus; they must then enter a deep process of rebalancing and integrating that involves the whole of their lives. But already the experiment is entering into work with much larger groups. The energies are astronomical" (220–21). What is "required" for this "challenge" to be successfully met, says Moss, is "one basic realization—unconditional love" (221). Thus it is "unconditional love" and that alone which finally triggers the planetary millennium, which finally "catalyzes" the kind of "collectivization" which Moss regards as the highest potential of humankind. But *we know now* what "unconditional love" (or "higher energy") *means*—that is, from the psychoanalytic angle. *We know now* that "unconditional love" translates psychoanalytically into the regressive return of the vibrational, transformational object, the regressive return of dual-unity, of symbiotic fusion, of affective attunement and the mutual mirroring that characterizes the interaction of caregiver and infant during the early period. *We know now* that "unconditional love" comprises the denial of separation, the restoration of the before-separation-world, the garden, paradise, pre-lapsarian merger.

"To begin to generate a unified energy in my work" Moss writes (BB, 196) in a passage that strikingly recalls the planetary ambitions of Benjamin Creme, "I use two basic modes: the resonation circle and the Sacred Meditation. Both ultimately involve the same quality of attention, but the resonation circle is not as formally ritualized. Visually, the resonation circle appears as a group of people sitting or standing and lightly holding hands. Everyone is asked to give their inward attention to the deepest sense of Being they can intuit. The word *resonation* speaks to the process of summating and amplifying the energy of individuals into a more coherent or unified quality." The "effect," asserts Moss (197), is "profound," and "after a few days everyone has moved into a higher energy awareness ... The senses are intensified, and it becomes very easy to enter into deep rapport with other people." Thus do "we begin the remarkable exploration of the interface between individuality and collectivity"; thus do we begin to "transmute" the "egoic me" (197). What Moss *renders projectively*, then, through his "collectivization," through his worldwide "heightening" of the species into *one great resonating circle*, is a macrocosmic version of the original *vibrational* object affectively fused with the symbiotic neonate. Moss wants to see the world, *the whole world*, return to the dual-unity situation. He wants everything and everyone fused harmoniously together at the conscious *and unconscious* levels. He wants the all-out erasure of the differentiated, autonomous, "egoic" self, the source of his dreaded "I-Thou duality" (IW, 166). *That* is the principal way in which his wish-fulfilling work fits perfectly into the longings of the New Age as a whole. "Transformation" on the planetary scale means overwhelmingly the return of the transformational object of infancy. Indeed, the utopian urge, the utopian theme, is itself an expression of the wish to join once more with that object. What occurs between the individual caregiver and the individual baby during the transformational period, the period in which the "apparition-like presence of the mother" (Bollas 1987, 33), transforms the baby's reality over and over again, replacing discomfort with pleasure or relief on each occasion, is recalled projectively and unconsciously by the utopian schemer who would have all that restored on a global scale. The whole environment will re-experience the perfection it enjoyed when the transformational object was the whole environment.

The Blessings of Cancer: Moss among the Sick

The healer needs the sick one as much as the sick one needs the healer, for without the sick one where is the healer to find his fulfilment? Moss's groups gather people who are experiencing difficulties in their lives. They come to Moss with anxiety, with low self-esteem, with aches and pains, with problems at the workplace or at home, and they comprise, when taken together, a fertile soil in which Moss may plant himself as transference-inducer, miracle-worker, magical, mesmerizing guru. But the problems of Moss's groupies pale by comparison with the problems of those who cope with serious, life-threatening illness. These people are in *crisis*; they face *death*; they are harrowed by the prospect of their final and permanent *separation* from the world and everything in it, including their family and friends. Here, Moss may ply his trade as healer with outstanding chances for success, with outstanding chances for powerful response to his saintly, radiating presence. Here, among the disease-ridden ("and he shall go forth among the sick and the maimed"), Moss may discover the perfect audience for what he calls "the kind of projection that tends to amplify the depth of my gifts" (IW, 143).

Moss has a very lively sense of the opportunity with which disease presents him. "As I observe people with major disease," he writes (IW, 101, my emphasis), "it is clear that they *are being reduced at the personal level and coerced into entering a more expanded awareness* to whatever degree they are capable." In other words, the disease *breaks down* the ego, the "egoic me" (BB, 197), the dreaded "I-Thou duality" (IW, 166). It *softens people up for* regression, transference, fusion, for "expansion" into the symbiotic realm of mirroring and joining. "Consider the choices one confronts," Moss explains: "possible maiming surgery, potent radiation and chemical agents with debilitating side effects, realization that one's life may be ending, temporary or permanent change in work and lifestyle, and profound effects upon one's key relationships" (102). The "very roots of one's being are shaken," Moss concludes (102). Thus—and we come now to cruicial assertions by this New Age healer—"it is in moments of crisis, *health crisis in particular*, that the door of transformation may be opened to us" (HL, 53, my emphasis). Health crisis becomes an "opportunity" to "join in the larger impulse that is even now moving us collectively," an "opportunity" to "radiate out to all other lives" (xiii). Health crisis "is but one face of the transformational impulse" (xiii). It could hardly be expressed more explicitly than that.

We don't have to puzzle very long at this point in our chapter to understand what Moss's "transformational impulse" signifies: the "heightened energy" or "heightened vibration" that equals "unconditional love." Nor do we have to puzzle long to understand what *that* means psychoanalytically: regression to the symbiotic stage, regression to dual-unity, regression to the affective attunement that marks the interaction of infant and caregiver, the interaction that *precedes* the separation stage. As the sick one suffers and degenerates, as the sick one moves toward the surgery or the chemotherapy room, as the sick one stares death in the face, he/she may understandably experience a longing for the transformational object, for the soothing and reassuring maternal presence he knew and internalized during the first years of life. Not only does Moss intuitively grasp this as someone with an instinct for regressive emotions, he is *there* to encourage it, to spark it, to get it going and to *join in* as part of the *transference relation*. For this is Moss's province; this is where he wants to be, among those who look to him for wondrous "changes," for "miraculous realization," for "spiritual breakthroughs." When "we feel *weakened*," Moss writes in one place (HL, 53, my emphasis), "a deeper force can act through us," and we "jump to a new energy." He writes in another place (IW, 103), "People faced with the challenge of major disease can heighten toward an experience of love to a degree that they probably never touched before in their life. The awful friction of the disease process helps to create the transformation. One might almost speculate that the missing ingredient all along has been love: love in the deepest and most unconditional sense, love, not as an emotional connection, but as a radiant current that intrinsically unifies the psyche and embraces within its transformative power the whole spectrum of human experience." And then, "At this point they [that is, the sick] can be ... *guided* to ... the potent energies inherent in their situation" (103, my emphasis). Let's begin to concentrate intensively upon the way in which Moss characterizes this "guidance" in his work.

For the sick one to capture the "transformative potential" of "disease," says Moss (HL, 93), he must first of all learn to "let go." Indeed, our experience of illness "has little power to change us until the moment of let-go" (93). But what is it that one lets *go of*? It is, according to Moss, the "ego-dominated viewpoint" (90) or the "consecration to 'me'" (92). "At the moment when a shift occurs," and the sick one moves from the "me" to "the Whole," Moss declares (92), he, the sick one, "becomes unified." The "sense of 'me' and the sense of the greater Whole" blend together, and the "transformational moment," the "moment of deepest healing," is at hand (93). We know, then, what it is that one lets go of. Yet what is it that one lets *go into*? Moss answers (92): "At best," the context into which we release can be intuited but not known directly while we remain in the separate 'me' dynamic. Thus letting *go into the unknown* is the essence of transformative process" (my emphasis). In another place he writes as follows: "The way of radiant growth requires us to cease our usual efforts" and to "leap *into the unknown*," for "no conscious intent can permit transforming to a wholly new level of energy" (52, my emphasis). Now, what we must do at this juncture is call to mind again the *inception* of all this "letting go" in Moss, its tight connection to his "crisis," his "transformation," his self-styled beatification, his realization of "unconditional love." From this direction, I believe, will spring very rich psychoanalytic insight into Moss's system of guidance for the diseased.

During the course of his struggle toward "transformation," writes Moss (IW, 93), he reached a stage in which he "recognized" that it was time to "drop [his] old identity," to "become invisible," to "be with experience on its terms." This stage of the "process," Moss goes on, "was anguishing almost beyond [his] ability to stay with it" (94). "If I stay with this experience . . . I am just torturing myself . . . If I leave, it is because of fear" (94). "Finally," states Moss (94), "I *let go* of any struggle" (my emphasis). And then, "*letting go* was like choosing to sacrifice my sanity and my whole human history. I felt as if I were passing backward in time and simultaneously forward . . . With each wave of energy I surrendered a little more and finally there was no more resistance . . . I simply entered another level of reality" (94, my emphasis). What level, we may ask? Where is Moss's "letting go" taking him? Here is the answer: "While words cannot convey the experience, the sense was of formless existence as a feminine principle—an ultimate mother—that bequeathed *life* by the fact of existence itself. I felt in direct relationship, inseparable from this great feminine consciousness" (95). Again, in a passage that summarizes the entire "crisis" (91), "Recognizing a process of rebirth, I knew somehow that the whole of the Earth was my new mother, and through her I would discover a truer sense of being." Moss's truer sense of being, the result of his "transformation," is, of course, "unconditional love." The upshot? As I suggested a moment ago, *this is exactly what Moss is attempting to trigger in the diseased.* They are also to "let go" and *thereby to discover* the very same "formless existence," the very same "feminine principle," the very same "ultimate mother," the very same "transformation" toward "unconditional love," that Moss discovers when *he* "lets go." For let us bear in mind that when Moss "lets go" he does not know what he is letting *go into.* What it turns out to be, as we've just seen, is the mother. When he urges the diseased to "let go," he tells them they must do so "into the unknown." But *he knows* what "the unknown," or "formless existence," *means.* Indeed, he knows exactly what this "process" entails. Moss is inducing through the *crisis of disease—a variation* upon his own self-proclaimed "crisis"—a regression to the same "feminine principle," the same "ultimate mother," that *he* finds when *he* "lets go." Why does he wish to do this? For many reasons, needless to say, including narcissistic and omnipotent ones, but per- haps most of all because Moss fears and detests the "I-Thou duality," the "egoic me," the *differentiated, separate self.* The sick ones, soft- ened up by crisis, present him with a splendid opportunity to deny over and over again through regressive transference, regressive fusion, *breakdown*, precisely those fearsome and detestable items. To see the sick ones embrace the "ultimate mother" and to join them while they do so is pleasing to the healer's deepest unconscious proclivities. The sick ones are, finally, Moss's *converts.*

In support of all this, let us note, first, that the sick one cannot find the "ultimate mother" by himself. "Such a transformation," ob- serves Moss (HL, xiv), "is never accomplished alone, especially when it is centered around health crisis." The sick one must "enter" into a "deep rapport" (10) with the healer, whose business it is to foster an "attuned interaction." Moss writes in a crucial passage (IW, 86) that the "consciousness of the healer becomes vitally important" in "sensing the energetics of illness ... As long as the *illusion of a self that is sep- arate* continues within" the healer, his "approach" will be "mechanis- tic." However, "as the consciousness begins to transform into a subtler realm, this *I-am-separate-from-you approach is finally seen as illusory.* Now ... there is a far deeper blending and interpenetration of energetic forces," which, when "consciously *attuned* by the healer," can allow the sick one to "feel loved" (my emphasis). The healer's "powerful, en- ergetic presence" fills the sick one with "a sense of love" (88). But, as always, it is a two-way street: the healer's "level of consciousness ex- ists as the *radiant* quality of energy that interpenetrates every act and defines what is conceivable. This is also true of the patient. When the two are together it is the quality of consciousness that is their relation- ship, as well as the collective consciousness from which their beliefs

and techniques emerge, that ultimately defines the potential for healing within the interaction" (89, my emphasis). This "quality of consciousness," Moss tells us (90), is quite simply "love." Thus, as healer
and sick one cross into the "energetic continuum," they join in what
Moss calls (and we have seen this notion before) the "energy embrace"
(HL, 114). United upon the same "vibrational frequency," they
"breathe" together, "flow" together, "attune" together (124). The
healer's "connection" to the sick one and the healer's "sense of relationship to Life become the same thing" (125). To grasp the psychoanalytic
essence of this last remark, think once again upon Moss's observation
(IW, 94) that his transformational breakthrough, the culmination of his
"crisis," conveyed "the experience . . . of formless existence as a feminine principle . . . that bequeathed *life* by the fact of existence." Clearly,
Moss is regressing the sick one to the time of affective attunement,
symbiosis, fusion with the loving caregiver. He is fostering the kind of
"transformation" that recalls, or reactivates, the transformational
object of the early period, the magical "transmuter" of discomfort and
pain. He is moving the sick one emotively back into the mother's
"vibrational" arms, and *he is present transferentially as the mother*. "I
have been with individuals so powerfully eroded by the cancer process
at the level of external power and control," Moss declares (102), "that
profound *energy* and (formerly unexpressed) wisdom *radiated* from
them" (my emphasis). Let's call to mind here Moss's earlier claim
(26, 30) that he learned during the course of his own transformation
"how to transmute *energy* consciously . . . In fact, transformation is
radiated, not rationally taught" (my emphasis). The sick ones with
whom Moss "interacts" are beginning to "radiate" like him, to *look
like him*. So goes the *conversion*. So goes the "opportunity" of disease
to produce the kind of *loving disciples* by whom Moss wishes to feel
himself *surrounded*.

In this way, illness itself, disease itself, cancer itself comes to be
regarded by Moss *as a blessing*: "For those who allow themselves to be
transformed in the process, cancer, the modern day symbol of death,
has become the greatest blessing, the grace that transforms their lives"
(IW, 104). (For "allow themselves to be transformed" we may read
"allow themselves to be regressed.") And again, this time from *The
Black Butterfly* (134): "Cancer is a transforming force . . . a high-energy
disease . . . With cancer, it is as though a signal has been given to transcend the age-old limitations on growth." Do we not have here New
Age thinking's *ultimate distortion*, its ultimate refusal to look squarely
at the tragic face of life, at the realities of separation and death, each of
which is an emotive aspect of the other? "Where the fear of death is
concerned," writes Bernard Steinzor (1979, 118), "it is the uncertain

ties to the living world at all ages that shake us more than the awareness of biological mortality." If cancer is a "blessing," if disease is "growth," if degeneration and suffering are positive experiences, then why should we hold them at bay, combat them, defeat them? "Despite all protestation," declares Moss (IW, 104, my emphasis), "one gets the deep sense that many individuals need ... to be *catalyzed into a transformation process through disease* ... Who is to say that this ... is not a necessary and appropriate part of their growth?" Is there not a strong suggestion here of the self-confessed "crucifixion" Moss undergoes each time he heals? "For myself it feels like a crucifixion to come to another and offer energy for healing. I am drawn to the other in love yet feel a subtle violence to my deeper nature" (BB, 179). Is not Moss *projecting*, through his talk of "transformational" illness and "radiantly" dying patients, a view of *disease* which transforms *it* into the sick one's *cross*? I do not believe that anyone "needs to be catalyzed into a transformation process through disease." Nor do I believe that cancer is a "necessary and appropriate" part of one's "growth." Indeed, from a psychoanalytic standpoint, such ideas are loaded with sado-masochistic overtones; they attest to a "subtle" unconscious conflict in the "deeper nature" of their proposer. Moss, the saintly, maternal dispenser of "unconditional love," is not without his own ambivalent attraction to the "violence" of life and death. Less "transformation," less "crucifixion," and more honest confrontation with the distressing side of existence, I say.

Moss's discussion of disease and its role in the "transformational process" culminates in his notion of "the ultimate hospital," a kind of theoretical institution which Moss would like to see translated into reality. He writes, "The Ultimate Hospital *presumes that life is an inseparable whole* ... Imagine entering a hospital where, several times each day, the staff meditates and celebrates with all patients who are able to participate. They might sing, dance, hum, or *sit quietly together in Energetic Embrace.*" Moss continues: "Imagine the emergency room, surgical, and ward teams understanding how to tap their *collective energy* and thus create a *high energy milieu*. Because everyone would be continuously exposed to *higher energies*, each person would be challenged to master his or her own personal process." Finally, "In the Ultimate Hospital, every medical procedure will involve energetic preparation and *attunement* among the patients' families and staff ... The Ultimate Hospital is the expression of a way of life that honors the *mystery of transformation*" (HL, 140–42, my emphasis). There is no "mystery" here, however. Moss's key terms and expression—"life" as an "inseparable whole," the "Energetic Embrace," "higher energies," "attunement," "transformation"—in the context of his specific ideational emphases make crystal clear the persistence of his distinctive, habitual agenda: regression to the symbiotic stage, the restoration of affective (or vibrational) attunement, the denial of differentiation, separation, autonomy, and a generous dose of the "unconditional love" which *equals* "transformation"—that is, which *equals* the reactivation of the transformational object of infancy. Moss admits that "such a hospital might sound utopian," yet goes on to say that "in practice it would be a transformative cauldron" (HL, 140). The problem, of course, is that the word *transformative* as Moss employs it *is in fact* "utopian." Rather than creating the distinction for which Moss strives, it marks the unconscious return of the before-separation-world, the prelapsarian realm of paradisal merger and "unconditional love" which eventually and inevitably gives way to the "fall" of the separation phase. There is nothing original or new, *ultimately*, in Moss's notion of the ultimate hospital. Indeed, the ultimate hospital is but *another projective version* of the "ultimate mother" (IW, 94) who resides emotionally and conceptually behind Moss's productions as a whole, and behind New Age thinking as a whole, to boot.

"Conscious transformation and unconditional love" are not for "cowards," writes Moss (IW, 107). "One is no longer in the realm of simple answers ... One is in the cauldron through which the heart is opened." Finding one's spiritual path to this "cauldron" requires, Moss informs us (104, my emphasis), "that *one release the fear of death*." If cancer as a "blessing" is the ultimate *distortion* of New Age thinking, then surely this last notion is the ultimate *superficiality* of that thinking. Release the fear of death? Just "release" it? Can Moss be dreaming? One simply releases with a "conscious" effort the deepest, most pervasive and tenacious fear of humankind, the fear that inspired the pyramids, the fear that hoisted the huge cathedrals of Europe, the mosques of Arabia, the temples of Asia, the fear that haunts millions, nay billions, of ordinary individuals like you and me on and off throughout the course of their lives? Release the fear of death? Release the *muse* of art, music, literature, science, and religion? Why does not Moss simply ask us to step out of our psychic skins? That would be just as easy. The whole "transformational process" that Moss is pushing, among both the sick and the well, is *predicated* by the fear of death, which, in the unconscious, connotes separation. As usual, Moss has things *backwards*.

Not everyone, as it turns out, yields to Moss's saintly influence when it comes to death and dying. "I am reminded in particular," Moss writes (IW, 102), "of a well-known psychiatrist with whom I shared the last weeks of his life. He was deeply respected and loved for his openness and loving nature. In the last year of his life he rapidly succumbed to a brain tumor ... In my involvement with him it was soon clear he was involved in a deep transformational process for which nothing need be done. I observed that, *although the energy I came to share was never taken in by him*, with each visit his wife became more and more at peace and able to release him" (my emphasis). Here, apparently, we have an individual who experiences no desire or need for Moss's "unconditional love," for Moss's "radiating" presence, for Moss's "spiritual embrace." The healer comes to "share energy," to "project his gifts," to fashion one of his "presentations," and he gets nowhere. Moss assumes this man's unwillingness to "take in" what he has to offer is rooted in some other kind of "transformational process" the man is undergoing, but we don't know. Well, *I* am reminded here of *another* "well-known psychiatrist," one who refused to turn away from death's reality, one who refused to indulge in illusions and saccharine comforts, one who steered clear of the purveyors of "transformation" and "unconditional love" and all the rest of it. I wonder if Moss would consider *him* a "coward" for not rendering himself up to a "higher energy" at the end? I see Freud's old, bespectacled face in my mind.

The Dangers of Sainthood

A good many of us may remember the débâcle at Jonestown, and most of us witnessed on television some portion of the disastrous events at Waco. We've seen the dead bodies, the conflagrations, the grieving survivors. We know the dangers that lurk in guruism, in powerful transference relationships, and of course in delusions of grandeur as they take shape in both individuals and groups. Moss and the vast majority of his fellow New Age healers, given as they are to mushy, regressive love-ins and to the relatively harmless trumpery of "transformative processes" and "Energetic Embraces," will probably never present us with scenarios similar to those mentioned in my opening sentence. At the same time, to go about, as does Moss, in the belief that one has experienced a miraculous "change" from which stem a variety of supernatural powers and capacities, to go about with the conviction that one has become of a sudden a radiant, energy-emitting first cousin of the Buddha, Jesus, and the saints, may well lead to occurrences which make the psychoanalytic investigator sufficiently uncomfortable to ask the question, what is going on here? With what, and with whom, are we dealing? What follows are three occurrences which made me, the psychoanalytic investigator, uncomfortable in the extreme.

* * *

Shortly after his "transformation," shortly after having entered into "another state of being" (IW, 37), Moss finds himself at home and in the presence of a one-year-old boy who frequently visits the Moss family as a "guest." Flushed with his newly acquired supernatural powers, Moss has "the idea" that he "could communicate" with the child "through energy fields" (38). He writes, "We were on the bed together and the child was watching me. I shifted my internal focus and began to project a current of energy toward him. Immediately he began to cry. It was not at all what I expected. I tried to comfort him but I felt inept and clumsy, and he just cried all the harder" (38). A moment later, noticing that the frightened youngster has "brought his hand in front of his face," and feeling helpless to stem the crying, Moss brings his own hand in front of his own face. The ploy works. The child recognizes the familiar game of peek-a-boo and starts to interact with Moss in a playful, happy fashion: "We began to crawl around ... He found the coiled spring door-stop that makes a thwanging sound if you flick it ... He thwanged a few times, giggled, and moved on ... And so we shared an hour together" (39). Now, this is the way Moss *interprets* the episode as a whole: "I understand through this child that *what he perceived, he was*. The moment I joined this reality I let the labeling process of my conscious-ness fall away and just began to experience. I followed his example" (39). But Moss has "understood" *nothing* here, nothing at all. Indeed, by shifting the burden of the exchange *from himself to the child* he misses all the important psychological and interpersonal significances.

When Moss decides to "shift his internal focus" and "project a current of energy" toward the child, he begins to gaze at him, to stare at him, to lock on to him with a kind of grinding, catatonic intensity. In a word, he behaves *unnaturally*. The child begins instantly to cry because the child knows at once through his own unclouded percep-tion that he is in the presence of a weirdo. Moss is scaring the baby out of his wits, and he is too full of himself, too bloated with his own gran-diosity and omnipotence, to appreciate it. When Moss drops the gran-diosity, drops the omnipotence, drops the assumption of supernatural powers and gets down to an ordinary game of peek-a-boo, the child recovers. Among adults, needless to say, Moss is able to get away with this sort of "presentation," this sort of manipulation and "projection," this sort of egoistic, self-indulgent nonsense, for adults, by the time they have reached that state, are sufficiently confused, cowed, and gull-ible to be taken in. Over the years they have been loaded up with hokum and diminished in their perceptual capacities by physical and mental stress in general and by separation anxiety in particular. Had Moss not been blinded by his own narcissism, he might have *learned* something from all this. He might have seen the child in Wordswor-thian terms as the "best philosopher," and through the child have come to a truthful realization of the oddness of his own conduct, the disturbed quality of his omnipotent posture, the kooky aspect of his "internal shifting" and "focusing" and "projecting." But then, as I have suggested, Moss interacts with the baby shortly after his self-canonization. He is on the verge of world-shaking events. This is no time for Moss to be pulling back from the miraculousness of his own "transformation." The man is on the loose.

* * *

Working to "open" one Theodora to the "transformative power" of "energy sharing," Moss allows himself to interact with a beautiful cancer patient[10] in a manner that discloses further the clear and present dangers which lurk in the adoption of sainthood. "I tried to understand and resolve," he writes (BB, 121), "the subtle push-pull that I felt in myself when I interacted with her. I knew that I was attracted and simultaneously intimidated by her beauty and talent. I knew that I longed for her as an energetic counterpart, as I have for many others who energetically represent continuations of my own body and being." Moss goes on, "There was a recognition of depth and of possibility that drew me into personal involvement. Thus I was in direct conflict with a deeper wisdom that knew I could not serve her fully in this way. Theodora was like a magnificent meal that I couldn't quite let myself taste … Clearly, I was being seduced and, in retrospect, it is easy to see that I wanted to be" (120–21). What emerges here immediately, of course, are the sexual implications of the *tone* and the *language*: push-pull, attraction, seduced, magnificent meal, taste. Moss is perfectly aware, "in retrospect" at least, of his "personal" interest in this talented and beautiful female. He is also perfectly aware of the problematical (or unprofessional) aspect of that "personal" interest: "I could not serve her fully in this way."

Moss resumes the narrative by remarking, "I also knew that when such a state is triggered in me [that is, "personal involvement"], it is not only my process; I am resonating in the energetic dynamic of the other. I wondered what it was about Theodora that both invited and obscured, opening with promise and closing at the same time" (BB, 121). This "resonance" comprises in significant measure the *transference relationship*, of course. Moss experiences not only his cathexis of the lady; he experiences also her interest in him, and I *don't* mean simply her sexual interest. Of Theodora's motivation we do not know a great deal because Moss writes mostly about himself. However, he does observe shortly after having penned the passage at which we've just glanced that Theodora "turned to [him] desperately for help" as a "doctor and therapist" (122). The point is, we cannot divorce the *sexual* component from the *transference* component without distorting what occurs. As is invariably the case in these "personal" therapeutic situations, the *dependency*, the *need*, the regressive "desperation" of the patient get mixed into the "attraction" to the doctor. The sensual cravings of maturity *harbour* the earlier, infantile longings for closeness, succour, "transformation." We must also keep in mind as we go that *Moss* is the professional, the guide, the "therapist." Responsibility for the nature of the interaction is ultimately *his*, no matter how much Theodora makes him "resonate" with her "energy," as he puts it.

Although Theodora "could not allow the vast energetic depth" that Moss "senses" in her "to merge with her personal self," on one particular day, "all of a sudden," she "opens" (BB, 121). Moss is evidently describing something that happened during a specific "therapeutic" hour: "As the energy of the conference built to a finer and finer note, it began to dissolve her self-control. At first she was agitated and invoked all kinds of mental questioning to tie up her energy. But finally there was nothing she could do and she lost control. The sense of separation gave way and, for a little while, I could *taste* the promise that had always been there. But while Theodora became more energetically available, her subjective experience was that of great terror" (121, my emphasis). This is a bit confusing to me. Just what is it that Moss is describing? What is it that he is "tasting"? Is it the "magnificent meal" to which he referred earlier? Has Theodora "lost control" of her *body*? Or is Moss shifting the discussion *away* from the sexual, "personal" sphere (about which he feels *guilty*) to the purely "energetic" one? "Ignoring an inner discomfort," Moss writes a moment later (122), "I joined with her energetically to intensify and refine the quality of her space, and perhaps to help her break through ... I had her breathe deeply. In a few moments she reached a state of release." And then, "with my help Theodora reached a state of peace ... but rather than transcending the dynamic to a higher level, she had dissipated or discharged the energy. She was in the calm that follows an orgasm" (123). Again, I find this confusing. How has Moss "joined" with Theodora, *exactly*? What does it *mean*, in this context of "personal interest" and guilt, to unite with her "energetically"? Any why does Moss use the word *orgasm*? Is he referring to an *actual* orgasm, or is he making an analogy? I've looked through his writings and I can't find any other usages of this term. Are we in the realm of "spirit" and "energy" at this juncture, or are we in the realm of sexual interaction? Or, better, are we in the realm of *both* as both are *confused* in Moss's practice? "I understand why people believe in demons," states Moss; "feeling the energy pouring through her [that is, Theodora], and seeing her fear, one might think that something diabolical was occurring" (123). Yes, one might very well think so, and one might also think that the "diabolism" has as much to do with the doctor as it does with the patient.

Moss begins to interpret the narrative: "Theodora could not release the egocentric perspective. This was not a conscious choice; it is just how the process occurs at times ... Theodora's energies were heightened and she came to the boundary of her egoic structure ... But she never entered the transcendent sense of integration ... She could not trust" (BB, 123). Theodora could not "release the egocentric perspective"? Theodora could not pass beyond her "egoic structure"? *Her* "egocentric perspective"? *Her* "egoic structure"? Has not Moss's "perspective" on this vulnerable, beautiful patient been colossally "egocentric"—even by his own guilt-filled admission? Surely it is *Moss's* "egoic structure" that has determined the stressful, "personal" nature of these "conferences." Theodora might well have "transcended" her "ego" had not Moss been regarding her all along as a "magnificent meal" ready for "tasting." Moss declares that Theodora "could not trust" (123). *Trust?* He has been mind-f——ing the woman for some considerable time, and he has the temerity to declare that *she can't trust him?* If this is all somewhat confusing and problematical to the writer (and perhaps to the reader), imagine how confusing and problematical it must have been to poor Theodora.

We come now to the pivotal passage—that is, to the passage in which Moss sums up the interaction in its entirety: "There are ways I might have helped Theodora out of my experience. Becoming emotionally involved was the last thing she needed. This shackled my capacity to act as a transformational door. In retrospect, I understand my deep love of her more clearly. I see that, *while this love had its roots in a completely impersonal space*, it became confused with a more personal involvement. This is an easy confusion and many of us make it ... Being a teacher is at times a very lonely work" (BB, 127, my emphasis). Just as Moss missed entirely the psychological and interpersonal significance of his interaction with the little boy he frightened, so he misses entirely the psychological and interpersonal significance of his "therapeutic" encounter with Theodora. His "love" for the woman did *not* have its "roots" in a "completely impersonal space" only to become "confused" with a "personal involvement." On the contrary, Moss's "love" had its "roots" in the "space" of the *transference relationship*, in the powerful emotional interaction that invariably springs up between individuals when one of them assumes the parental, healing role and the other assumes the role of the ailing, needy child. It is hard to see how Moss can overlook this when he writes (121) of having "longed" for Theodora as an "energetic counterpart" and proceeds to confess that he *similarly* longs "for many others" who "represent continuations of [his] own body and being." Surely such "longing" is anything but "perfectly impersonal." Surely it is "rooted" in one's deep, *feeling perception of the other*. Or is Moss claiming in this passage by implication that his "unconditional love," the love that equals "heightened energy," which in turn *equals* "transformation," is "impersonal"? Of course he isn't. That would go against everything he has been preaching since his *own* impassioned "transformation." In most cases, the "energy" Moss shares with his clients may be described as *de-sexualized libido*. It moves the patient regressively toward the transformational object of the early period, and the symbiotic fusion that marks life's initial stages. But it is nonetheless *libido*. It is loaded with the emotional weight of humankind's original and most compelling cathexis, the love of the baby for the parent, and of the parent for the baby. With Theodora, this de-sexualized libido simply *gets sexualized*. The transference relationship of doctor and patient becomes streaked with physical attraction. Because Moss apparently attempts to keep Theodora in the sphere of "energy exchange," because he never examines the sexuality openly and honestly, because he insists upon being one thing (dispassionate healer, guru) while he is in fact another (appetitive, "personally involved" male), he makes the woman *hysterical*: she pants, she trembles, she "loses control," she "releases," and all of this in a fog of sublimation and frustration, a fog of *interpersonal ambiguity*.[11] In a word, Moss torments his patient by trying to transform sexual attraction into regressive merger, disguised at the conscious level as "energy sharing." This brings us to a crucial observation.

Moss has no genuine, professional awareness of what he is doing here, because he has no genuine, professional awareness of the deep, personal, emotionally charged nature of the transference relationship. In his own mind, he goes about as saintly healer transferring divine (or non-egotic) "energy" to people who then "heighten" toward the "transformation" which equals pure, "unconditional love." Moss does not see the "process" as it is "rooted" in the early period, in the mirroring union of caregiver and neonate. He does not see the *regression*, the *cathexis*, the "personal" *dependency*, and thus he cannot deal professionally with situations like the one on which we have been concentrating. Moss titillates Theodora as he regresses her; he arouses her as combination parent, saint, doctor, healer, lover. And he ultimately *confuses* her because his "energy sharing" drips with a prurient interest. In the end, instead of grasping the whole business and facing it squarely Moss retreats into a self-indulgent, narcissistic cocoon. He is the "lonely teacher" (BB, 127) burdened with his commitment to humanity.

Moss is dangerous. He is dangerous because he cannot or will not see the psychological significance of what he is doing with, and to, people. He is dangerous because he is acting-out his delusions of grandeur as saintly healer in the belief that he is primarily the dispenser of pure, spiritual love. As Dr. Johnson said during the course of the eighteenth century, "Beware of philosophers; they discourse like angels but they live like men." To repeat the words with which I closed the previous section on the traumatized one-year-old boy, Dr. Moss is on the loose.

* * *

Parting with a depressive, debilitated client whom he had seen some weeks earlier for the treatment of hepatitis, and learning that "she felt there were two evil spirits in her," Moss notices "an oppressive ... darkness and heaviness pervading the room" (BB, 91). "Immediately," Moss writes, "a powerful voice within me silently commanded, 'Be gone!'" The result? "At precisely that moment, a wave of heat passed through us and she [the client] burst into tears. Some weeks later she wrote to thank me and ... said that from the moment of her spontaneous tears her hepatitis ceased, and she was feeling wonderful ... She asked me if I had any idea of the power of the forces I was dealing with. Instantly I was thrown into terror" (91–92). Dr. Moss in "terror"? Dr. Moss endangered by powerful, diabolic forces? Well, what happened? "Quite spontaneously," declares Moss, "I began to sing with all my soul of the fear that was holding me and of my need for help. I was oblivious to the fact that I was on the front lawn of my house in a rather sedate suburban neighborhood. I sank to the ground like a character in a Wagnerian opera. (None of this was consciously directed or premeditated.) Suddenly I could hear my voice reverberating in the trees as if I were far above myself. At the same time, the energy moving through me was a fine hum and I fell into utter peace and stillness" (92). Thus concludes the wondrous, chilling event.

At this mature stage of our study of Moss and New Age healing we do not have to subject such material to a lengthy analysis. It speaks for itself. On the one hand, we have a sickly, superstitious patient going about in the delusional belief that "evil spirits" inhabit her body. On the other hand, we have a doctor-exorcist given to omnipotence of thought and grandiosity casting out these devils (the "oppressive darkness," the "wave of heat"), then falling victim to diabolical terrors. What Moss discloses for us here is the medievalism that underlies and informs his behaviour as "therapist" and "teacher." We are returned by this material to the hoary literature of the Christian saints, the literature in which champions of the spirit do battle with the supernatural forces of wickedness. Who knows what truth there is in Moss's account. His parenthetical remark "(none of this was consciously directed or premeditated," appears *very* fishy to me. Yet he *writes* the account. The physician turned spiritual sage actually *writes* it, asks us to believe it, perhaps believes it himself. Surely that's enough for us to grasp unequivocally the psychological and intellectual level upon which Moss's "energetic" practice goes forward. Shall we leave Moss thus, prone upon his suburban lawn, beneath the trees, exhausted by his struggle with "evil spirits"? I think so. It is a fitting final picture of this representative New Age healer.

New Age Healers Everywhere

The kind of pitch Moss offers us as healer may be discovered in dozens upon dozens of New Age advertisements and writings—I mean, down to the very fine print about mysterious particles, atomic reactors, powerful vibrations, heightened frequencies, and transformational energies. Here is a recent, juicy example from a monthly publication called *Shared Vision* (1994, 9). The guru in this instance is one Brian Grattan: "Experience the Mahatma Energy. A once-in-a-lifetime opportunity for those called to be in attendance. Those present at this rare and powerful event, through highly energized group mediations, will experience an unequalled vibrational Group Vehicle of the highest vibrational frequency. The Mahatma Energy, through Brian Grattan, acts as an Atomic-Accelerator, discharging lower frequency patterns. This allows the dense physical-atomic body to become transformed into Pure Light—the actualization of Physical and Spiritual Ascension. You will be introduced to your Cosmic Heart, and the subatomic particle called Microtron, which will bond with you and electrify your 4-body system. The time has come. The Cosmic Heart awaits." This full-page ad is complemented by a picture of Grattan himself. With his chin resting firmly upon his fist, he looks straight out at the potential customer (Grattan doesn't come cheap) with wide, penetrating eyes, and with a faint smile upon his lips. I trust the courteous reader, who has patiently indulged my investigations, will be able at this point to examine such a pitch with *his own eyes* wide, wide open, and with a faint smile upon *his* lips.

Notes

1. This advertisement appears at the back of Moss's volume, *How Shall I Live?* (See the reference section for full bibiographical information.)

2. *The I That Is We:* Further references to this volume will take the form IW. Further references to *The Black Butterfly* will take the form BB, and further references to

How Shall I Live? will take the form HL. For complete bibliographical information see the reference section below.

3. See note 2.

4. For an excellent discussion of recent scientific attempts to explain consciousness see John Horgan's "Can Science Explain Consciousness" in *Scientific American* (July 1994, 88–94). Horgan makes it crystal clear that consciousness is as much a mystery to us today as it was to our forebears. Moss's unsupported claim that "modern physics" is drawing close to understanding consciousness is simply nonsense.

5. Moss's attempt to dress his ideas up scientifically reaches its nadir in *How Shall I Live?* (46 ff.), where he strives to give *mathematical* expression to his "system." Low energy and low perceptual states are designated A and their opposites A prime. Apparently Moss believes his readers cannot keep track of this simple dichotomy.

6. See note 2.

7. In psychoanalysis, "vibrations" are always *affective* or *psychological*. There is no attempt to give them concrete physicality, let alone to try moving them about in a way that might be called therapeutic or healing.

8. Moss sometimes uses the word *fusion* in his work and says that it is characterized by a "heightening of energy" as when "two people fall in love" (*The I That Is We*, 211).

9. In another place Moss states that only about forty of these conferences achieved remarkable success (*The I That Is We*, 144).

10. Moss indicates that the patient with whom he interacts in the narrative to follow suffered not only from cancer but from an emotionally disturbed adolescence and early adulthood. In my view, this makes his treatment of her all the more remarkable for its utter irresponsibility.

11. In the unconscious, the sexual culmination of regressive merger usually feels incestuous. Theodora's hysteria may be linked to the undoing of a powerful repression.

References

ASHBACH, C., and V. SCHERMER. 1987. *Object Relations, the Self, and the Group*. London: Routledge and Kegan Paul.

BOLLAS, C. 1987. *The Shadow of the Object: Psychoanalysis of the Unthought Known*. London: Free Association Books.

CUNNINGHAM, S. 1988. *The Truth about Witchcraft Today*. St. Paul, Minn.: Llewellyn.

HORGAN, J. 1994. "Can Science Explain Consciousness?" *Scientific American*, July, pp. 88–94.

MOSS, R. 1981. *The I That Is We*. Berkeley, Ca.: Celestial Arts.

———. 1985. *How Shall I Live?* Berkeley, Ca.: Celestial Arts.

———. 1986. *The Black Butterfly*. Berkeley, Ca.: Celestial Arts.

SHARED VISION MAGAZINE, October 1994, p. 9 (Grattan advertisement).

STEINZOR, B. 1979. "Death and the Construction of Reality." *Omega: Journal of Death and Dying*, 9: 97–124.

STERN, D. 1985. *The Interpersonal World of the Infant*. New York: Basic.

CHAPTER V

A LITTLE GALLERY
OF NEW AGE THINKERS:
INTERVIEWS AND EXPERIENCES

W<small>HAT</small> follows is meant to be read only in the light of the context. I cannot control the reader, but I will say emphatically that unless he has digested the discussion to this point, he will miss a great deal. I present my interviews and experiences directly and offer no analytic comments or interpretations. I want the material to speak for itself. As we have seen, an individual's involvement in New Age thinking may engage all the levels of his psychosexual development. It can be heavily imbued with the wishes of infancy, with the longing for fusion, omnipotence, and narcissistic inflation; it can display a rebelliousness and a search for identity, characteristics we commonly associate with adolescence; and it can evince a genuine concern with the well-being of others, with social and environmental issues—the quest for justice, equality, physical and emotional health. Typically, all of these levels are operative in the New Agers, but some are considerably more operative than others in individual cases, as I believe my materials will show. The coven meeting, too, will challenge the reader's ability to explore what I may presume to call "the data" in a fluid, multilevelled way. Finally, I have worked in all cases to conceal the subjects' identities without altering the substance of my notes and tapes. While I have perforce done some editing, I have also attempted to leave things pretty much as they were presented to me, even at the risk of some repetition and disorganization. For psychoanalysis, of course, disorganization and repetition sometimes disclose unconscious intention, and I did not want to sacrifice that potential to a flawless narrative flow. Here, then, is a cross-section of New Age thinking, from the proverbial horse's mouth.

Pauline (Crystal Healing)

Pauline invited me into her lovely seaside home near Vancouver on a sunny afternoon during the spring of 1995. A tiny woman of forty-eight years with striking green eyes and short, blonde bangs, Pauline was attired in a mid-calf blue dress, hose, and low-heeled white pumps. She seated me on a leather sofa in her spacious den, poured me a cup of herbal tea, and allowed me to stroke her sleepy tortoiseshell cat.

MDF: Tell me a little bit about your background. I'm particularly interested in religious and spiritual influences.

Pauline: My parents were not very religious, or spiritual. We went to church on Sunday and observed the usual holidays, but that's about all. There were certainly no heavy religious or spiritual influences. My father was a pipe-fitter for many years and also worked for the post office. Mother was home most of the time doing what moms usually do when raising a couple of kids. I have a younger brother, James.

MDF: A typical, normal home life, then?

Pauline: On the contrary! My family, like all families, was completely dysfunctional, only you couldn't see it. All sorts of awful things were going on, in the privacy of the home, as they say. My parents claimed to love us, James and me, but we felt unloved, uncherished, out in the cold emotionally. I've talked with my brother about this at great length. We were both abused physically and verbally, with strapping and shouting. I suffered additional abuse.

MDF: Additional abuse?

Pauline: I'd rather not talk about it or name names, but it was sexual in nature and it went on for several years.

MDF: I'm sorry to hear that.

Pauline: Well, it led to several years of psychotherapy during my thirties. I was married by then, with one daughter, and as the years went by the inner pressure continued to build. I had to have some relief.

MDF: Did the therapy help?

Pauline: Let's say it was the beginning of a recovery which took place over many years. While I was struggling to get better emotionally I was also preparing myself to be a teacher and counsellor by taking college courses. By the time I was in my late thirties, about ten years ago, I was qualified to teach and to counsel in the primary grades.

MDF: When did you become interested in healing?

Pauline: During my years as a counsellor in Victoria [the capital of British Columbia, about forty-five kilometres southwest of Vancouver] I became gradually aware of my gift. I mean, I began to *see* it. Parents came to my home before and after school hours to discuss their own issues, their past hurts, their anxieties, their problems at work, their mental and physical blockages. I became not simply the school counsellor but the district therapist, you might say. I realized my true calling was not in the educational system but in the healing arts. It was during this period, around 1985, that crystals first came to my attention. This was an important time for me, full of synchronicity. No sooner would I read a book on crystals than someone would come over and *show* me a number of beautiful stones. It was as if some higher power was marking out my path.

MDF: What made you believe specifically that crystals had the power to heal?

Pauline: I knew it intuitively. I just knew it. It all comes from knowing. This isn't something that can be proved in the usual sense. One goes to another dimension, another level of being, where intuition makes things very, very clear. Then too, my channelling was well underway by this time, and it helped me to see the crystal's potential. The knowledge didn't come simply from *me*, but from the guides I was channelling. It is a whole sensory experience, a whole movement, on several levels at once.

MDF: Can you describe the beginning stages for me?

Pauline: They covered several months, and they included many wonderful occurrences. I recall suffering from a particularly severe headache. I put a large piece of quartz on my lap and meditated over it for a few minutes (my head hurt too much to start channelling). During the course of the meditation I felt a shift. A moment later my headache was gone, gone for good. That was a key experience for me. My head felt clear and serene. I was filled with a kind of joyousness. Crystal healing was no longer an issue for me, if it ever was one. I knew the quartz had the energy to heal and I wanted to go further with it. Friends began to bring me stones, and I began to study intensely. I was on my own at this time [divorced], and I wanted to understand fully the power of crystal, the vibration of crystal, and to assist others with my gift. That's when I purchased the stone on your left.

MDF: [I look to the left and see a thick, six-sided tan quartz piece about one metre high and shaved to a sharp point at the apex; it sits, or perhaps stands, in a wicker basket.] Did you want to tell me about this stone?

Pauline: When I saw it in the crystal store I knew I had to have it. I mean, not right away, but when I left. Walking away from it to my car, I began to mourn, to grieve. I felt terrible, like I was leaving a dear friend behind. It was a feeling of loss. It wasn't the beauty of the stone, although it *was* very beautiful; it was the sense of *relationship*. We were related. So I went back and bought it. It has become instrumental in my healing work.

MDF: How is that?

Pauline: It turns out to be a record-keeper. It is a stone that is programmed with specific information about the people who come to me for treatment. The information is contained in the tiny triangles which are scattered in great numbers throughout the stone [we go to the quartz; Pauline shows me many small triangular flecks just beneath the surface]. When I elicit the information with my fingers, the triangles are altered. I mean, they're still visible but they're different; they're depleted of their energy which I have taken out of them to use in healing.

MDF: Will you ever use them up, I mean all of them?

Pauline: Perhaps; but, as you can see, there are thousands and thousands, all over. The stone also contains keys.

MDF: Keys?

Pauline: Indentations or rough spots which can be explored through touch or sight. These also contain information that is useful in healing. You see, this is a special stone, one with an Atlantean history, and as it turns out, one that is intimately bound up with my own history. That is why I felt so much for it in the shop.

MDF: Could you tell me more about this?

Pauline: During one of my former lives, in the kingdom of Atlantis, I programmed this stone myself. I come to it now to get information about both myself and those I assist.

MDF: I see. And what is this information?

Pauline: It is simply the remembering of spiritual matters, where we went wrong spiritually, and what will help us to experience oneness, or integration. This information comes strictly from the other side. You have to cross the valley, so to speak, to discover it.

MDF: Can you describe a healing session for me, very briefly of course?

Pauline: With my client lying on the table, eyes closed and meditating, I journey to Atlantis, to the life I knew there long ago. As my past life regression goes forward, I am guided toward certain triangles on the stone [to MDF's left, as previously described]. Drawing power and information into my hands, I move toward the client to locate and to clear those chakras where energy has become blocked or diseased. These are the places that want healing; they may hold past emotional traumas (from former lives or from the present incarnation), and they may hold sick tissues and cells. Generally they hold both, as body and mind go together. As the healing images flow through my mind, usually beautiful scenes of ancient Atlantis, I release the energy and restore the chakras to a healthy, cleansed condition. But I have other methods, too, which do not involve past life regression. Sometimes a client simply needs a specific stone placed on a certain part of the body. When my hands detect extreme cold or heat I apply the appropriate crystal to clear the chakra. Then there is music.

MDF: Music?

Pauline: Yes. I sometimes strike chords on the piano. These often bring to the client's mind specific family members with whom the client has experienced disturbed relations. As the client focuses his/her attention upon this family figure, I clear the chakras of negative energy. I have crystal in my hand, or pocket, as I do this. I'm a stickler for work, and my clients know it. When they come here it's work, work, work, and that means clear, clear, clear—clear the chakras, clear out the blockages, free the life energy. My gift is for healing, and for metaphysics, and I want to share my gift, even if it means wearing my clients out!

MDF: Do you strive in some instances for physical healing— I mean, healing specific physical ailments?

Pauline: Yes. I do. A client recently came to me with severe bursitis in her shoulder area. I managed to clear it with a beautiful piece of bluish quartz. I had no idea I would be using that to clear but the guide I channelled that afternoon led me directly to it. When my client left, the bursitis was gone, and it hasn't returned, at least to my knowledge. I'm currently writing all this up, by the way. I'm not a very good writer but I do want to bring out a book on crystal healing in the near future. I feel I have enough knowledge and experience, now, to move ahead with this, to begin to share it with others who live far away from me. Perhaps I'll send you a copy of the book when it's finished.

MDF: I'd be delighted. By the way, do you know of a book by Bowman titled *Crystal Awareness*?

Pauline: I certainly do. It is an excellent discussion of the field. I've read it twice. In fact, I have a copy of the book upstairs, in my study.

MDF: Bowman claims the power of crystal to heal is related to the Earth's mineral kingdom and ultimately to the universe itself as a divine source of healing and spiritual energy. How do you feel about this?

Pauline: It is the very basis of what I do. We all come from the same place, don't we? I mean, we all come from the power that made the world, the stars, the oceans, everything. Crystals have long been recognized as a very rich source of this power, this energy. Think of it. A piece of crystal can make a wrist-watch go for years, or a computer. The ability of the crystal to heal, or to locate the source of spiritual suffering and psychological wounding, is not *simply* tied to this energy. The crystal has to be *used* by someone who understands the world of the spirit and the meaning of health. Just going around with crystal earrings or pendants isn't going to make everyone better. [Laughs] But the *source* of the healing power is the universe itself. And because the universe itself has a divine origin, the crystal is also touched with divinity. *We* are the makers of the whole situation in all its complexity; the crystal is our instrument.

MDF: Bowman says sleeping with a piece of quartz under one's pillow, or taking a piece into the bath, is a good idea. Is it, in your view?

Pauline: Well, yes, but I don't think anything very specific will be accomplished by that. The presence of crystal energy can aid sleep and relaxation in a very general way, but to address specific blockages, or spiritual problems, or energetic depletions, a person needs to engage a well-trained expert, or at least to study intensely and at great length himself. There are no quick fixes, and I don't believe in gimmicks, if that's what you're asking. As I said before, I am a stickler for work and for study. You get out of something exactly what you put into it. I am certain only that the crystal is the *basis* of a great and blessed science, a science of the universe and of the soul. Wait here.

[Pauline leaves the room for a moment, and then re-enters. She hands me a small, shiny, triangular stone of a yellowish tint.]

Pauline: Take this. I want you to have it. In my opinion, this is the best way to find out about crystals. Let's call it a beginning.

MDF: That's very kind of you.

Catherine (Shamanic Healing)

Catherine met me cordially at the door of her North Vancouver town house. The morning was wet, and I stepped gingerly inside. We walked down the hall past her two young sons, aged nine and eleven (home from school with colds), and into her study in the centre of which sat a hefty massage table covered with a patchwork quilt. Catherine was a tall, big-boned woman of forty, with large, prominent facial features and long grey-blonde hair hanging loosely over her shoulders. We sat facing each other in well-used, cloth-covered armchairs.

MDF: Tell me a little bit about your background.

Catherine: I was born and raised in England, coming to Canada— Edmonton, actually—at the age of fifteen. Dad was a successful graphic artist and Mom a very popular high-school teacher and vice-principal. We were not a religious family (I have two older sisters) but both Mom and Dad emphasized serving the community, doing good turns for others, being generous of oneself. I had trouble fitting into the system, however, and my years in Alberta were spent hanging around with hippie types and not doing very well in school. I did lots of marijuana, booze, and petty thievery. My parents were concerned, and even reported me to the police on one occasion. Eventually, though, I settled down, took a teaching credential (following in Mom's footsteps), and even found myself a husband. [Laughs]

MDF: When did your interest in shamanism begin?

Catherine: Well, it's a long story. When I was in my late twenties, my son, Craig, was diagnosed with leukemia. He was only three. I took him to the cancer clinic in Edmonton where he began to undergo chemotherapy. It was awful. He suffered terribly, and I knew in my heart he was going to die. There was nothing I could do. A few days after his treatment began I had a mystical experience. I suddenly realized that I could save Craig if I could find an *inner space* in which to hold and nurse him psychically. I had to get him away from the clinic and I had to *contain* him in a certain, spiritual way. At this time his skin was transparent and his white cell count was in the neighbourhood of 67,000. Two days after my mystical experience a friend brought Olga Worral to my attention. Olga was an elderly spiritual healer based in Philadelphia. I telephoned Olga, spoke to her for a few moments, and then told her my son's name. She asked me to put my hands on him for five minutes while concentrating on the sound of her voice, and to do this every day for one week. As the days passed, Craig began to improve— I mean, dramatically. His skin looked more and more healthy and normal, his strength returned, and, most of all, his white cell count began to drop into an acceptable range. When the doctors at the clinic got word of these developments their anger was incredible. How could I betray them, and my son? How could I turn away from modern medicine? How could I resort to quackery, psychic healing, and so on. Yet Craig recovered, and I'm convinced his recovery was made possible by the healing capacities of Olga Worral and by my own intuitive understanding of the situation. When I called Olga to thank her for the miracle of Craig's recovery, I learned she was dead. All of this taken together constituted my introduction to shamanism, for shamanism takes us down to the level of direct, intuitive experience. It gives us access to the power and energy inherent in the human organism. We don't fool around here. This is where we *live*. This is where the forces of life and death express themselves.

MDF: What happened after Craig's recovery?

Catherine: What happened? I went into crisis! I was thirty years old and unable to live the life to which I had become accustomed. Everything began to crumble around me. I resigned my teaching job—I just couldn't do it any more. I asked Peter (my husband) to leave—which he did. And I decided to have a new kind of existence, a new way of being which would take me away from the artificiality, the *death*, I saw going on all around me in the world. My love for my son had revolutionized my life. I needed to go inward. I needed to go in the direction I experienced with Olga Worral. Six months later I was on the Hawaiian island of Maui studying Huna with Joseph.

MDF: Tell me about Huna.

Catherine: Huna means "secret" and is used in connection with the shamanism of Hawaii. Kahuna means "keeper of the secret" and is the title to which the apprentice shaman aspires. It is not something one masters quickly. My studies continued on and off for a period of nearly six years. I would spend a few months with Joseph, return to Canada to work and support my children, return to Maui, and so on. After several years Joseph came to regard me as a qualified practitioner.

MDF: Of what did your training consist?

Catherine: It was an entire way of life. We lived communally, about eight of us (it varied), in a donated house well off the beaten, tourist path. We worked together in the fields, we participated in group discussions, we cooked, we cleaned, we assisted others in nearby communities, and we danced. Mostly, we danced.

MDF: Danced?

Catherine: A person's character and temperament are disclosed in the way he *moves*. Think of a hula dancer in the midst of a traditional, ritualistic performance, and then think of a Nazi storm trooper goose-stepping down the boulevard. The motions of one's body—one's arms, chest, shoulders, torso, legs—are a key to the shape and the quality of one's inner energy. People's energy, in a word, is caught in their bodies, and it is only when the person's body *shifts* that the energy *shifts*. Spiritual change, spiritual development, is connected to such shifting, for until the body is fluid and free in its energetic motions, the spirit, the soul, cannot be free to develop its higher potentialities. Think of the way the Hawaiian dancer moves his hips and ass. Can you do that? Have you developed that kind of freedom, fluidity, relaxation? When Joseph watches me dance, when he looks at my hips and my ass, he can see exactly where I am in terms of my spiritual development. He can see into my character, into my psychology, into my essence and soul. He can *see me*. And he can direct me, encourage me, discipline me, train me, guide me past the old conditioning which has rooted itself in my body, in my shoulders and hips, in my ass and genitals. For three full years I struggled with this dance; for three full years I was thrown back on what my body had *become* during the course of my experience. Then came the breakthrough.

MDF: Tell me about that.

Catherine: I was sweeping some glass up in the yard at the front of the house. Joseph walked by and watched me for a while. He then said, "Little iddy bits, little iddy bits." In other words, as I later understood, I was dealing with fragments, with scattered pieces, with details, and not with the whole picture. I was hurt, devastated, wounded to the core. Joseph was telling me I had power but was not allowing it to come through. Later that afternoon I was splitting logs on a stump. Joseph was standing nearby. I hated him. As I struck a log vertically to split it from top to bottom, I went all the way through and split the stump as well. "Huna!" cried Joseph as he saw. "Huna!" My power was beginning to crest. That evening as two of my fellows were massaging me I became a four-year-old girl again. I returned in my emotion and fantasy to my family home, to Mom and Dad, and I *saw* the truth of my childhood, and indeed of my whole existence since that time. My parents didn't love me; they only pretended to love me. To *get* their love I had to be exactly as they wished me to be, not as I was. My whole life was spent conforming to the will of my parents rather than developing my own personality and character. I was a lie. I was a false mask. I was the keeper of a brittle, artificial "Huna," not the "Huna" of the way. I didn't exist. That night as we practised around the fire I *danced*—I mean, I really *danced*—for the first time. My body was my own, my hips were my own, my ass was my own, my legs and arms and genitals were my own. I danced; I moved with my energy, my *power*; I *flowed*. Joseph watched me closely with a smile on his face, and when the dancing had concluded he came over to me and touched me on the forehead with his right index finger. It was midnight, and for some reason my sons couldn't sleep. They were up and watching me too. They were happy. It was the night of my transformation, the night of my change. I was becoming me, finally, after thirty years of being a plaster statue. I could breathe; I could move; I could live. I continued to study with Joseph for three more years, perfecting my techniques of alignment and massage, and eventually became "Kahuna."

MDF: Can you tell me what you do for people, in this room?

Catherine: Do you see that open fan on the wall? It means openness, relaxation, *expansion*. I ask my clients to ponder that fan. Do you see that mirror on the wall? It means reflection, self-image, appearance. I ask my clients to ponder that mirror. When people come to me they are 95,000 miles away from the truth. They are conditioned, constrained, distorted, unaligned; they are loaded with emotional baggage, emotional stress, emotional disloyalty. They are living *other* people's lives, usually the parents', not their own. I know this. I know it through my considerable psychic powers which take me straight into the psyche of the individual who comes here, and straight into that individual's chakras where the energy sits bound and festering, like a terrible lump of death. What I do for people is this: I bring them to high health, or try to do so, for sometimes it is very difficult. I try to align their bodies with their essence. I try to make a *space* for them, as I did for Craig, in which we can together get rid of the ill health, the trauma, the accumulated disease of their lives. This is, of course, terrifying to most people. They want to be free and clean, yet they don't want to go through the work and the effort. We are all this way. That is why the shaman's way is a way of compassion and care, a way of understanding. My son took me to Hawaii and to myself. For six years I journeyed toward wholeness with Joseph. For six years I worked to get past the time of my childhood.

MDF: How did your work with Joseph come to an end?

Catherine: I realized one morning that Joesph was my father. I mean, I realized that I had all along linked the two men in my deeper mind. When the course came to a close a few days later I knew it was the end of my involvement. I had put something together, and out of it came my own identity. I didn't need my father any more, and I didn't need Joseph, either. There were no more psychological secrets, psychological mysteries. My life had somehow become my own.

MDF: Can you describe a shamanic treatment for me, very briefly of course? We were on to that a few moments ago, and we somehow drifted by it. What exactly do you do?

Catherine: I *look*. I *see*. I feel the client, the *inner* client, with my whole intuitive presence. This isn't something that can be easily described. You have to *experience* it, *do* it, have it *happen in you*, and in the other person. By looking, by seeing, I locate the person's energy blockages, the chakras that need attention, the kundalini energy that lies there waiting to enliven the energetic centres. When I have located the disturbances through my vision, I ask the client to lie down upon the table you see there. Then I run my elbow up and down the frame, searching the muscles, the organs, the bones, and in this way I pick up further concepts, further clues. I pick up the clustered memories of past events which are stopping the kundalini, preventing the chakras from functioning properly, keeping the body down, trapped, distorted, essentially lifeless at the core. When my diagnostic picture is complete I induce *trance*, and massage and pull the negative forces out of the afflicted parts. Sometimes I do this while talking softly to the client, releasing him with hand and word. As the healing work goes forward, I go deeper and deeper in *sight* and deeper and deeper in physical manipulation of the body. I find other organs, other centres that require cleansing and freeing.

MDF: Do you always experience success?

Catherine: All sessions are fruitful but some far more than others. Certain clients have to return ten or twenty times. In some instances, only a final parable will work. I tell a Hawaiian tale of the fish and the sea, the wind and the boat, the storm and the calm. Then the client sees. This can be very dramatic and often involves weeping, writhing, and vomiting.

MDF: May I ask your fee?

Catherine: One hundred dollars an hour. However, if you would like to experience a treatment as part of our interview, I would be happy to exclude the fee.

MDF: Would you do that for me?

Catherine: By all means; just remain in your chair.

The Treatment (Huna)

Catherine pulls her chair more directly in front of mine and squares herself around to me. I sit up straight, place my hands upon my knees, and look across into her pale blue eyes. We sit like this for a few moments, in perfect silence. I feel vaguely nervous, uncomfortable, anxious, yet curious too. After perhaps five or six minutes, Catherine begins to screw up her face; her brows knit together, her eyes narrow and glaze, her mouth twists unnaturally, her teeth protrude. The effect is quite remarkable, a kind of terrible Chinese mask or something. As the facial distortion deepens I feel increasingly apprehensive. Catherine's eyes are entirely glazed over and actually rolling; she appears to be in a full-fledged transport; and yet her body remains passive, almost motionless in the chair.

Catherine begins to belch. I mean, she begins to bring up full, sonorous pockets of air from some deep place in her abdomen, or her chest. The belches come in great numbers, one after the other in quick succession, rich and loud and seemingly without end. Startled, and more apprehensive than ever (this is a *big* woman), I manage to remain still, to keep my hands upon my knees and to hold my composure, although I do notice an increase in the rate of my breathing. As her belching reaches an incredible intensity, Catherine rises. She is perhaps one metre away from me. She takes a step toward me, leans over me, still belching through her distorted face, and places her hands on the top of my head. She then lets her hands slide down over my cheeks, and come to rest on either side of my neck, just at the inner portion of my shoulders. The belching has subsided. We remain like this for about two minutes. I still feel slightly apprehensive, and notice the pressure of the woman's hands on my neck and shoulders. Looking up at Catherine's face, I see her flaring nostrils, and a quantity of flaxen hair upon her upper lip.

Finally Catherine speaks: "You have tremendous intensity, of mind and of body," she says. "This is remarkable in one who possesses such a loving and compassionate nature. Yet you can have this intensity of body and mind without creating the energy blockages I detect in your neck and your shoulders. You believe for some reason that your intensity of intellect *depends* upon your intensity of muscular comportment. This is not so. Relax. Relax your neck and your shoulders. Relax your face. Relax your back and your spine. Let the kundalini rise, let the kundalini flow; let the life energy run through you like the river's water. How old are you? [I tell Catherine my age.] I see. You are a fine, loving person. You are a fine, loving man. You will find the release and relaxation your face and neck are seeking. You will find them." Catherine smiles down at me. I cannot refrain from bringing up all the belching; I want to know if it means something, from the shamanic perspective. When I do so, Catherine stares at me hard and says, "I belch." She then presses me gently on the chest with the knuckles of her right hand. Two minutes later I am walking through the rain to my car.

Carol (Pranic Healing)

Carol and I shook hands in the foyer of Capers, a trendy health-food cafeteria on the west side of Vancouver. The afternoon was sunny, and we decided on a window table overlooking congested Fourth Avenue. Carol was a middle-aged brunette of average height and weight, with small, even features and inclining toward pretty, in my view. Dressed in a soft green sweater and combed-cotton slacks, she sported a pair of rather thick-lensed, gold-rimmed glasses attached to a tan leather neck chain. We ordered specialty coffees and exchanged the usual pleasantries.

MDF: Tell me a little bit about your background.

Carol: I was raised by my father, my mother having died of cancer when I was six. We lived in a small town [Nelson] in the interior of British Columbia, surrounded by mountains and filled for one half of the year with skiers and for the other half with hikers and campers. Dad worked for the railroad, in a supervisory capacity, and was something of the village atheist, as the expression goes. He was constantly arguing against the authority of the Bible, looked upon Christianity as an abomination, read popular scientific books and magazines, and considered a belief in God to be a weakness of the mind and character. A union man, who didn't say no to a whisky and who loved a good time, he was nevertheless a very good parent—responsible, tender, full of care. We're still in close touch; and since my divorce several years ago, he's become particularly close to my two sons as a sort of substitute father. We spend lots of time with Dad during the summer months (he's retired now). He stays with us in Richmond, where I own a town house, and we visit him frequently in Nelson, too. I think it was Dad's scientific interests that guided me toward the medical field.

MDF: You studied medicine?

Carol: Well, I thought about it all through high school and college but failed to get accepted when I tried for admission to med school. When I knew I wasn't going to make it, I went into a funk for a year and just travelled around aimlessly, visiting friends and wondering what to do. When I got bored with that I decided to settle upon nursing, which went right along without a hitch.

MDF: What sort of nursing do you do?

Carol: I'm a psychiatric nurse and have been for about fifteen years. I worked at Riverview [a mental facility in Vancouver] until the government closed it down, and now I am at Vancouver General, the psychiatric division. The work is very intense and very draining but I love it and wouldn't dream of walking away from it until I have to.

MDF: When did you become interested in New Age thinking?

Carol: My interest in metaphysics began in 1984 when I came across Shirley MacLaine's *Out on a Limb*. I then picked up various writings by Edgar Cayce, the works of Rudolf Steiner, Krishnamurti, and Carlos Castaneda. I began to visit New Age bookstores on a regular basis. Something was drawing me in a metaphysical direction and I wanted to combine that interest with my nursing skills. I knew my dad would not approve, so I actually concealed several of my "far out" books when he came to visit. I just didn't want to set off his argumentative nature. I wasn't afraid he'd stop loving me, or anything. [Laughs]

MDF: When did your interest specifically in healing commence?

Carol: I began talking with my massage therapist about the potentialities of spiritual healing during the summer of 1985. I enrolled a few months later in Wild Rose [an unaccredited "college" of

New Age studies located in Vancouver] and took several classes in energy work. I studied the chakras, kundalini, crystals, channelling, the Native American healing tradition, and Chinese herbal remedies. Eventually, and quite on my own, I discovered Pranic healing, which is what I currently use in my healing practice. I find that I get quick and very satisfactory results with it. I channel, and then go directly to Pranic work, and, believe me, it is very effective.

MDF: I see. Can you tell me more about channelling and Pranic healing?

Carol: Channelling, in this context, at least, means simply opening oneself up through one's crown chakra to the healing energies of the universe, which one pulls in or channels in and then applies to the client who has come for Pranic treatment. Prana is energy or life energy, or the energy that informs all things in the world. Disease works, thrives, succeeds, only in the absence of Prana, and Prana is capable of driving out disease, no matter what it is, where it is, how it began, or how long it's been there. Do you want to see Prana? Well, just look around you: the people walking, the plants and trees swaying, the dogs barking, the cars running—everything that moves, breathes, operates, works, lives is Prana. We can't see it often because it's everywhere. But when you learn about it and learn how to use it, you have the key to well-being. The individual who is losing Prana is like a fish that is flapping in the bottom of a boat: alive in shallow water, yet dying in the air.

MDF: How do you go about channelling Prana through the crown chakra?

Carol: I invoke. Invocation is the basis of Pranic healing. We can do nothing on our own, nothing unaided, nothing as *egos* wrapped up in our own illusions and schemes. If we want Prana to stream in through the crown chakra we must invoke the aid of the Masters, the Beings who exist on the spiritual plane and govern the events in which we participate "down here."

MDF: Could you tell me more about this? How exactly do you invoke the Masters? Who are they?

Carol: The Masters are the Guides, the angelic presences who govern the great forces of the cosmos, gravity, planetary motions, the big bang, the quantum universe. To invoke them is simply to ask in all sincerity that they may work through you, not for your benefit but for the benefit of your client. When I invoke the Masters, I say, "Angels, Masters, Rulers of the World, give me energy, Prana, with which I may relieve the suffering of this person, your son or daughter, and your suffering servant. Send the power through my crown chakra and on to my arms and my hands that I may transfer it to this precious client."

MDF: Do you say *that*, those very words, the ones you're saying now?

Carol: Well, perhaps not those very words, but something quite like them. Yet there is nothing special, nothing unusual about this, in case you're thinking there is. *You* could invoke the Masters; *you* could invoke the Guides; anyone could. You just have to *do* it. You just have to *be* in the channelling state, the spiritual state, a sort of meditation or trance in which the sincerity of your intention, or the *love* behind your intention, can find its way up to the Masters. This isn't like asking for a new car, or a new suit, or a Christmas present. [Laughs] You have to find your way to an altered state of consciousness; then you invoke.

MDF: What does the client do as you go about invoking the Masters?

Carol: I always ask my client to join me in the invocation. When practitioner and client invoke *together* the benefits can be enormously enhanced. Prana flows more easily, more beautifully, I might say, when the invocation is doubled. Usually I sit across from my client and we invoke together until I can feel the Prana entering my crown chakra. It's at *that* point that the treatment commences.

MDF: Of what does the treatment consist?

Carol: I begin by scanning the chakras with my fingers and with my spiritual vision. I have unusually developed psychic powers and can often *see* inside the client with whom I am working. As I scan I generally come upon congestions, or depletions, in the energy fields. I mean, some chakras are under-activated, and some are over-activated. Some chakras are shrunken or caved in. When it is a matter of depletion or shrinking I use my channelled Prana to *fill* the starving energy centre, to fill the gap, to fill the emptiness, which ultimately means the weakness or even the sickness of the person, for although no disease is *there*, absence of health is presence of illness—mere emptiness can be construed as disease. On the other hand, when sickness is present, when the chakra is swollen with malignancy, with sick, contaminated energy, I use the power of Prana to *sweep* the chakra clean, to clear it, to sweep out the contamination, get rid of it. As it happens, mostly I find myself *sweeping*. The chakras I deal with, these days, at least, are not so much empty as loaded with illness and waste.

MDF: Where does the illness go when you have swept it away?

Carol: That's a very important point. The negative or diseased energy that I sweep away with Pranic healing must ultimately be stored or contained just as nuclear waste must be stored or contained. For this purpose I use salt water, usually in a pail or bucket. The salt water binds the diseased energy, holds it, traps it safely until it is neutralized and made harmless. I'm not exactly sure how Pranic healers came to learn of the power of the salt water to do this, but it is a tried and true aspect of the healing and never fails.

MDF: Forgive me, but I am not exactly sure *what* it is that goes into the pail, or how it gets there.

Carol: Diseased energy, diseased power, goes into the pail—negative quanta, negative microparticles—and they are *swept* there by the motions of my hand. This is not visible to the eye, in the usual sense, but it is visible to the spiritual sight.

MDF: This must mean the purchasing of many, many buckets and pails.

Carol: Not at all. Unlike nuclear wastes, the wastes that one sweeps from the chakras are relatively short-lived, about three days. After that the salt water may be safely dumped and the container used again. During the three-day span, however, the energy in the bucket is deadly. I have about ten containers at home, and that seems quite sufficient.

MDF: Do you always practise at home, when it comes to Pranic healing?

Carol: Not always. Sometimes at work I will sweep the auras of my fellow nurses, when they come to me with their problems. This isn't as complex a procedure as clearing or sweeping the chakras, and it is often quite effective and worthwhile.

MDF: Could you tell me more about this?

Carol: Well, you've probably seen examples of Kirlian photography— I mean, the photography that captures the energy field that surrounds our bodies. We usually call this energy field the aura, and if you look closely at the Kirlian photography you can see that it [the aura] consists of energy quills, or energy hairs. Emotional problems and physical ailments dis-align the auric quills—that is, the hairs or spikes cluster and bunch, or extend in opposite directions. To sweep the aura is to comb the auric hair, to re-align the energetic field in a harmonious way. This is done through Pranic massage during the course of which the practitioner's hands remain slightly above the body of the client, catching and rearranging the auric quills. When the aura is re-aligned, when the energy strands are swept into a harmonious pattern, the whole self is re-centred, re-integrated, calmed, and restored. When I first offered to do this for my friends at the hospital, they laughed and kidded me, like I was some sort of kook, but there's no more laughing now. I can't keep up with them. They're all over me!

MDF: With what sort of problem do you deal?

Carol: Oh, you know, separation, divorce, break-ups, debts, colds, flu, whatever makes us miserable. [Laughs]

MDF: Can Pranic healing actually get rid of the flu?

Carol: No question about it. Recently, for example, my teenaged son came down with a dreadful case of Asian flu: congested chest and throat, coughing, horrible blowing and sneezing—the works. After invoking the Masters and applying Pranic energy to the chest and throat, the symptoms subsided. He was back in school the next day.

MDF: How do you explain this? It seems almost miraculous to me.

Carol: I think you must mean "explain" in some sort of scientific sense, and for this I refer you to the quantum world. It's clear from modern physics that everything is energy, everything is force and power and field. Prana is simply a *manifestation* of this energy, and a *manipulation* of this energy along spiritual lines. The Masters, remember, love us, care about us, look after us. *They* are the miracle workers. If we invoke their powers with love, those powers will come through to assist us. Nothing can withstand the Pranic force. Flu? Flu is a tiny matter. Prana can heal the most advanced cancers and heart ailments, as well as severe physical injury and trauma, from stab wounds to severed limbs. If it were fully accepted by the medical community, and intensely applied to patients, we'd live on a healthy as opposed to a diseased planet.

MDF: Do you believe a bond exists between the Pranic healer and the client, and if so, what sort of a bond is it?

Carol: Yes. I believe a bond exists, and it is without question a bond of love. I learned this powerfully through my teacher, to whom I went for training after my graduation from Wild Rose. Her name was (and is!) Nina Fuentes. She is a former nun from Manila, and was originally trained at the Institute for Inner Studies (in the Philippine Islands). I didn't go to her simply for training, however; I went to her for *healing*. I went to resolve many issues in my life, issues that were still a source of trouble to me. As we worked together, we touched on many, many aspects of my psychological development, my childhood, the loss of my mother, the personality of my father, my disappointment over medical school, my marriage, my role as wife and mother. I went into everything with Nina, everything, and as I talked, as I *confessed*, she touched me and she healed me. She cleansed the wounds; she swept the contamination from my chakras; she emptied me of the diseased and malignant energy that had clustered in my centres of power. She could *see* it. She could see right into me, reach right into me, and she got the negative stuff and removed it. I've never known anyone who could channel and employ Prana like this woman. She taught me more than I can ever tell you. Believe me, I'm speaking from painful experience. No psychotherapy ever worked like this. No therapist, no *shrink*, ever did for me what Nina did. I came to life again under her loving hands and eyes. I returned to the world in her care. It was a bond of spiritual love, and it is exactly this kind of bonding that I strive to establish with those who come to work with me. You know, my childhood was not quite as benign as I indicated earlier. I mean, it was mostly good and loving but there was some emotional abuse, nothing physical, mind you, but emotional. Nina got right to that. She became my Pranic rebirther by clearing all that away. *I'm* in control now. *I'm* in charge of my life. It isn't an intellectual thing; it isn't the will, or the mind. It's allowing the Masters, the Guides, to express their Pranic intentions through me, as the vessel, the instrument.

MDF: Is the field of Pranic healing doing well?

Carol: I don't know about well, at least yet. But it is spreading in Canada and I believe in the States. The bookshelves increasingly hold texts on the subject. Let me write down one or two especially good titles for you.

MDF: You're very kind.

Carol: This book [she writes down a title] is especially helpful. It tells you how to *sweep yourself*. That's right. You can heal yourself with your own participation in the power of Prana.

MDF: I'll have a look at this text very soon.

Boris (Channelling)

It was during the lunch hour that I walked across the lobby of the Hotel Georgia in downtown Vancouver to shake hands with Boris, a channeller whose advertisements appeared in the monthly New Age publication *Shared Vision*. A stocky, blond fellow in his late twenties, with large grey eyes set wide apart in his broad, clean-shaven face, Boris sported a long braid beneath his San Francisco Giants baseball cap. A tan leather jacket, black polo shirt, jeans, and white canvas sneakers completed his casual attire. We found a cosy, comfortable corner in the hotel lobby and smiled at each other in happy anticipation of the interview that was about to occur.

MDF: Tell me a little bit about your background, particularly as it relates to your spiritual activities.

Boris: I came to Toronto with my large Rumanian family at the age of two. I'm very proud of my Rumanian heritage and have visited Bucharest on four different occasions, staying with relatives and friends. My father was a naturopath and physician with outstanding credentials from the Rumanian medical college in Bucharest. Actually, my entire family is involved in healing endeavours—aunts, uncles, brothers, sisters, and grandparents. You may know that Transylvania is a very special part of the world, filled with powerful mystics, seers, channellers, and healers. I believe our family was for generations part of a great spiritual and healing tradition. We brought this with us to Canada when we came over in the sixties. My spiritual and psychic capacities surfaced very early on, at the age of four. My grandmother saw them right away and encouraged me greatly. She was a famous Rumanian channeller and astrologer, and I believe the most powerful and talented of all the members of our family, including my father. He also saw my gifts early on, and he used me freely in his own healing endeavours.

MDF: Used you?

Boris: Father asked me to sit with patients, and frequently to touch patients. He knew that special, divine energies were radiating from my body and my spirit, and he wanted his patients to benefit from these powers. A good portion of my evenings and weekends as a child was spent in Father's office, or treatment room, at home. I sat next to his patients in a special red leather chair with a red leather footstool, I remember; and when Father found an afflicted organ in a patient, or a bad cold, or indigestion, or an emotional problem, he asked me to concentrate, to visualize, and to reach out. By the time I was seven or eight years old patients came to Father and to me on a regular basis. He called me the little Buddha, a title my grandmother made up for me actually when I was two, and I would often hear him calling me away from the TV, or from my games, with that name. "Little Buddha," he would say, "come to the treatment room." On the way there, I would sometimes pass my grandmother, who was sitting in the den. She would look at me with luminous eyes, and smile. She knew I possessed her gifts, and I believe she saw me as an extension of herself. When Grandmother died last year I felt devastated for three months. Only when I located her spirit in a distant constellation and established firm astral contact with her did my sense of loss and mourning begin to diminish. We now have daily, channelled contact, and much of my present success as a healer and a channeller is linked directly to her loving example.

MDF: Can you tell me more about your channelling and spiritual activities in childhood?

Boris: In my early teens I began to channel in earnest, and also to practise therapeutic massage. My first channelled beings were exclusively connected to UFOs; they were a colony of space travellers, from a very remote corner of the universe, and they would offer me information on the relationship of earthly illness to gravitational forces. They saw from their spacecraft the extent to which the clients who came to me for treatment were struggling with gravitational misalignment. Their [the clients'] bodies were strained, distorted, pulled apart unnaturally. My job was to align these bodies, to massage them into harmony, *pull* them into concord, and *that* meant into alignment with the gravitational forces of the Earth. My space travellers transmitted invaluable information to me from the spacecraft. As they were just outside the Earth's gravitational field and *weightless*, and as they knew the gravitational nature of many parts of the universe, they were uniquely able to see precisely what my clients needed. For seven years I practised gravitational massage and re-alignment in Toronto. It was only when my channelling experiences began to change radically that I knew I had to move on to other areas. Is it not interesting that weightlessness should accompany space travel? Surely there is a spiritual dimension to that fact. As we move out to the universe we leave our gravitational bodies behind, so to speak. We move toward the weightlessness of *spiritual* being.

MDF: Yes. Can you tell me how your channelling experiences began to change? You were about twenty years old, I believe.

Boris: That's right. I was just entering the decade I am about to leave. [Laughs] Well, I began to channel the entities I have come to rely on in my present healing endeavours. I am referring to two important angels mentioned in the Bible, Michael and Gabriel, and I am referring also to the Masters of the outer galaxies—these are spiritual beings who were present when the universe was created. They are able to provide me with extraordinarily potent *energies*, the very powers we associate with the divine bang, the birth of the cosmos (I will come to another channelled presence, Lavou, later). Curiously, however, these ancient, galactic Masters have no names but only numbers. I am currently in close association with 777 and 999. They are huge and somewhat terrifying entities, but, unlike some other spiritual forms available to the channeller, they are completely benign. I can channel them alone, I mean by myself. When there is a threat of diabolical forces entering into my energy field, as there sometimes is, I have another person present in the room. I also began in my twenties to channel certain medicine men, or shamans, from the plains of ancient Siberia, and Huna shamans from the ancient kingdom of Hawaii. My early twenties, as you can imagine, were very fruitful and busy years for me. I studied hard, read voraciously, healed with groups and individuals on a regular basis, and strove to establish the foundation of my present practice and my future institute.

MDF: Your future institute?

Boris: My deepest quest in life is to reconcile science and metaphysics. I believe the world is sadly split into two camps with the scientists over here and the spiritualists over there. This need not be so. The theories of science, particularly physics and chemistry, are merely intellectual abstractions or intellectual versions of spiritual occurrences and events. To channel is to *see* this, as the spiritual origins of matter are *directly* communicated to the channeller by the forces (we could say the Masters) that brought matter into existence in the first place. If my channelling endeavours continue successfully, if the future brings me the financial rewards I am currently experiencing, I will be able to open the institute in about five years. It will be called the Leonardo da Vinci Centre for Scientific and Metaphysical Studies. Leonardo, as you may know, was one of the first reconcilers of the scientific and spiritual worlds.

MDF: Can you tell me of specific experiences—I mean, in relation to your channelling and healing?

Boris: When I came to Vancouver five years ago I was having trouble with my eyes. My vision was blurred, and often I could not see at all in bright light—on a bright summer day for example. I was afraid I would go blind. I healed my eyes. I mean, healed them completely, by concentrating on channelled messages from a Siberian shaman named Nootka. When I meditated and induced my channelling trance I noticed Nootka right away. I was receiving several messages in turn, but Nootka's message was clearly the most important. He told me the problem with my eyesight was directly linked to a traumatic experience I underwent in childhood. One night in Toronto I awoke in the midst of a terrible thunderstorm. I went into my parents' bedroom for comfort, and as I entered I was almost blinded by several incredibly bright flashes of lightning. The thunder was so loud and the lightning so bright that I closed my eyes in terror and decided to keep them closed. I didn't want to see anything. Subconsciously, my sight was affected over the years by this occurrence. When Nootka brought all this to my attention, when he narrated the events of that night to me through the channelling process, my vision cleared up, I mean totally. I was so excited after Nootka came through that I said to myself, you can become an airline pilot now! Ha! It was only a joke. I am a channelling healer and that is all I wish to be—for the present, anyway. Another important experience occurred at a workshop I attended here in Vancouver three years ago. I was in the presence of a great channeller from England, Daniel King. In the midst of his lecture on the spiritual realm he looked straight at me and asked "Can you read my aura?" I could, of course, and I replied to that effect. "Then hold up your open hand," said King. I did so—my right hand, actually—and suddenly it was burning with laser heat right in the centre of my palm. King smiled and said he knew I was particularly sensitive to energy. This was not a healing experience, needless to say, but it further established in my mind the quality of my special powers and gifts. I had been doing group channelling sessions at the time of King's workshop; when King's visit to Vancouver concluded I decided never to do group work again. I would deal only with individuals, only on a one-to-one basis. I would concentrate and specialize, hone my skills to perfection, and not try to deal loosely with the problems of ten people at once. This was a turning point for me and immediately preceded my meeting with Lavou.

MDF: Yes, Lavou. Who, or what, is Lavou?

Boris: Three years ago on Salt Spring Island [a small residential island near Victoria] I was channelling for a client who had just been through a painful divorce. He wanted some guidance for the future, and some relief for a severe depression. In the midst of my channelling trance, Lavou just popped in; it isn't easy to describe him but I will say that he is an androgynous intergalactic being surrounded by white light, and intent upon assisting me in all my healing efforts. In fact, since the appearance of Lavou on Salt Spring my channelling sessions involve Lavou primarily. He channelled wonderful advice through me for my divorced client who has since remarried and started a successful business. His depression is gone. The only problem I have sometimes with Lavou is his thick Irish accent. He speaks with what is popularly known as a brogue, and I have to listen very carefully.

MDF: What kind of problem do you deal with, typically? How do you assist people, exactly, with your channelling skills?

Boris: I assist them in several ways. First, I help them avoid what I call *messes.* I help them avoid things they shouldn't get into, areas they should steer clear of. This would include personal involvements, work-related issues, and substance abuse. Secondly, I help individuals find constructive and positive ways to live, to develop their talents and to direct their energies. I also help people get rid of physical and emotional ailments, to clean their chakras of negative energy, to clear them [people] of blockages and thus restore them to health. All of this comes directly with Lavou's assistance.

MDF: Can you describe a channelling session for me?

Boris: Sure. In my apartment [*always* at home], I sit across from my client and establish *the intent.* That is, I establish what it is the client wants or needs, what it is that has brought the client to me, how I may help the client resolve the problem. When the intent has been established I close my eyes and meditate. This leads to a deep trance state, achieved in about five minutes, which leads in turn to the invocation. I call upon Lavou to assist me here, to advise me here, to direct me here; I ask with love and humility for his guidance. After perhaps three minutes, if all goes well and if no diabolical spirits try to interfere, the message of Lavou comes through my crown chakra and into my throat and vocal chords. The message is usually quite specific and lasts for about ten minutes. My voice always goes up in pitch or becomes considerably higher when really important material is coming through. When and if I have trouble receiving messages from Lavou or from other beings, I sometimes shiver or shake to stir up energy, friction, which can make the reception better by loading my aura with raw electricity. In most instances, however, I am able to sit quite still and channel information.

MDF: Can you tell me of a recent client, a recent session?

Boris: Well, last week a woman came to me with severe marital problems (it was a lesbian union). She just didn't know what to do. I established intent, focused, invoked, and found myself channelling both Lavou and another companion of his whom I had not encountered before. They spoke in turns and they emphasized above all this woman's great *impatience*. She would not allow anything in her life to *develop*. She had to have her answers, her solutions, *right away*. The session made it very clear to her that unless she developed patience nothing in her life would go right. It took about forty minutes to get all this across to her, but she left very relieved and very eager to return to her everyday activities.

MDF: Impatient to get back to things, eh?

Boris: [Laughs] Yes! That's good! Impatient to get back to things!

MDF: Have you ever recorded your channelling sessions, and if so, may I listen to a recording?

Boris: I made two attempts, both of them unsuccessful. It can't be done. That's all.

MDF: What happened?

Boris: The first time I attempted to record Lavou on tape, nothing was there. I had a solid, quality machine plugged into the wall, and a brand-new tape. When I re-wound and attempted to play it, there was nothing there, just hissing. The second time I tried, the guts of the recorder melted together. I opened the back and looked inside and there was just this mushy plastic stuff. I took it to London Drugs, completely stumped, and the guy said, "What did you do, put this thing in the microwave?" I haven't tried to record Lavou or anyone else since then and I won't be trying in the future. The spirits of the universe, apparently, do not take well to prying technology.

MDF: What do you feel is the channeller's main function in regard to matters of healing?

Boris: Ill health is primarily the *blocking of energy*, something that can result from physical injury, emotional trauma, or the trag- ical events of former lives. The beings whom I channel, and most importantly Lavou, are able to give me a precise energy *map* of the client who has come to me for assistance, for heal- ing. The channeled entities can *see* with powers of which we are only dimly aware. They can see the body, the spirit, the soul of the client, for they are enormously powerful entities existing on a spiritual level far beyond our earthly understanding. That this *sight* can be channeled through me, can be communicated through me, can only be regarded as the gift of a loving god- head. The channeler is ultimately the vehicle for creating energy *maps*, and the maps are ultimately the vehicles for locating the chakras that need either clearing or re-charging. When the channel to the spiritual realm is open, all things are possible. May I give you a few of my cards? Perhaps you'd be good enough to pass them along. [Boris gives me his card. It reads as follows: Boris Lupu, Psyhic (sic) Consulations (sic), Channelling, Cranial, Sacrial (sic).]

I put the card in my wallet and, after shaking hands with Boris, I exit the hotel into the grinding traffic of Vancouver's main thorough- fare.

Natalie (Witchcraft)

I met Natalie around one in the afternoon at a small Spanish restaurant in Richmond, a Vancouver suburb. She was a tall, slender woman of thirty-two, with dark hair and eyes, a glowing olive complexion, and graceful, athletic movements. Attired in a grey running suit and white sneakers, she spoke of her quest for a master's degree in counselling psychology and of her interest in therapeutic massage. After chatting amicably for a few moments, we commenced the interview.

MDF: Tell me a little bit about your background—your family, religious beliefs, and so on.

Natalie: I was born in Winnipeg. My family was heavily into Christianity (United Church of Canada) and I was obliged to attend services from an early age. I never really took to it. I mean, I was never drawn into the religious ideas and feelings of the Church. It just wasn't me. I was confirmed at fourteen but I can remember that by the time I was fifteen I found the whole thing ridiculous, and quit. I guess I resented having to attend Sunday school and services all those years, so it felt really good to chuck it.

MDF: Were your parents upset?

Natalie: Yes; I can remember the quarrels we had about my not going to church any more, but I should clarify that my dad died when I was eight and that by the time of my confirmation I was living with my mom and my stepdad, who also claimed to be a believer.

MDF: How did you get on with your stepdad?

Natalie: Not very well. I think I resented his intrusion and I felt he was rather wish-washy compared to Dad, who was more decisive, more involved in the family, although Mom was always the real centre of things. I can remember trying to get much closer to Mom and to my brother after Dad died and I guess I saw my stepdad as interfering with that.

MDF: What do you mean, "Mom was really the centre"?

Natalie: She was just always at the hub of things, like the central post office where you have to go to pick up the really important stuff. I was always close to her and always relied on her. A few years ago when I went into therapy I realized I may have been too close to Mom, sort of emeshed in her. She told me how to live, how to be; and yet at the same time I always had the feeling I was the centre *for her*, like she lived through *me* and *my brother* during the time I thought I was living through her. When I had therapy Mom used to come to some of my sessions because my therapist said we had a lot of separation work to do. It came out that Mom was a rather anxious person, not very happy in her marriage and not very happy in her sex life.

MDF: Do you see your mom very often now?

Natalie: She's dead. She died four years ago.

MDF: What about your stepdad and brother?

Natalie: My brother is in therapy, and we're having our problems, but I seem to be getting on better with my stepdad, although I don't see him much. We went to dinner together a few weeks ago and we both got a little drunk on wine. He asked me, with his hand on my arm, if we ever did anything naughty together when I was young. I said I didn't think so. Then he told me I was very beautiful and that he would "f—-" me at the drop of a hat. We were both drunk by then, but that wasn't unusual. There was a fair bit of drinking, mostly secretive, in my family, in spite of the Christian beliefs. Mom too. For the past year, in fact, I have been going to AA meetings in an effort to get past this thing. When I say AA I mean AA for gays and lesbians. I'm now a lesbian.

MDF: Would you be willing to tell me about that?

Natalie: I had lots of boyfriends as a teenager but nothing seemed to go well. In my early twenties I lived with different men but again it wasn't very successful. I was always unhappy and somehow dissatisfied. Then I met Karen. She was teaching at a college I attended and we began to spend a lot of time together, eventually including weekends. We have an equal, open relationship; it has its ups and downs, but we've been together for nearly three years now and I have the feeling it will go on for a while.

MDF: Tell me something about your involvement in Witchcraft. How did it begin?

Natalie: I confess my involvement in organized Witchcraft has been waning of late. It's a long story, but my interest has always been in New Age thinking, women's issues, the environment, politics. Witchcraft sort of entered into these more than I entered into Witchcraft. I've been a feminist for several years. But I've always had spiritual or even mystical inclinations, too. My family background has some Celtic in it so naturally I have always been interested in healing, something Witches do. Anyway, a few years ago I went to the Witches' camp in the Gulf Islands [near Vancouver] during August. Starhawk [Miriam Simos] was there and many other accomplished Wiccans. The camp was great. After a while I felt completely at home with these people. They seemed able to harmonize everything; I mean, spiritual, political, feminist, ecological. It all came together, including *play*, in one total expression of feeling. By the end of two weeks I'd decided to become a Witch. I don't mean that I wanted to gaze into crystal balls or say abracadabra with a pointed hat on. For me, the main things are feminism, the environment, and peace. But I felt connection there; I felt I belonged. These were my kind of people, and I wanted to be with them. I returned to Vancouver, was initiated, and joined a coven. As time went on, however, some problems developed.

MDF: How is that?

Natalie: I have a strong need for conflict resolution, and I find that the coven and the Witches can be superficial in that respect. They deny things and project things. They use the Craft and the group to act-out their own shit. I began to get ambivalent about the coven almost from the very beginning. Maybe that was because I am a strong feminist and environmentalist, with a political orientation. I mean, I never had any big conversion experience as such, even when I was initiated. That doesn't mean I don't have a strong spiritual nature, though. I've had mystical moments all my life and feel as capable as any Witch in this respect. When Mom died I underwent several very powerful altered states, real mystical experiences in which I felt joined to her; and I got this, too, after break-ups with men, the feeling we were still together, although eventually I was able to let go of them. I can still find Mom when I really need her. I meditate, to relax and centre, and also to find those I need, Mom mainly. I also feel very connected to the Earth. I've always felt this way. It's a warm, glowing feeling all through me, like I really have a connection.

MDF: Could you amplify this?

Natalie: For me, the Earth is a living body, a living entity, an organism; Witches call it Goddess, and I regard myself as an eco-feminist here. I believe that the Earth is alive, that it is the mother of all life, that it must be saved from the polluters, and that men should see the female as central, and stop treating women badly, just using them. I actually hug trees, hug them as part of the Earth's body, and I get warm feelings with my arms around them. When Mom died I went to the beach and felt this tie to nature. I knew I wasn't alone. I was linked to the world—more than to people, who aren't like nature to me. I often don't feel I'm really part of the community. People just do too much denying and projecting. They dump on you and try to control you. I feel more a part of nature, more at home in nature than with other people. I left the coven because of the games and the denial. People are all clammed up. They don't say what they mean; they don't even *know* what they mean. The coven was a lot of aggressive games and conflict, when what I wanted was mediation.

MDF: What were the circumstances surrounding your departure from the coven?

Natalie: Gloria, the High Priestess, wanted everyone's power. That's really all she was after. At first I deferred to her and shut up. I let her know through my expressions and bodily posture that she could have power from me. I suppressed myself and gave her the power. That's all power is, actually. It is regard, the projection of energy into another person through regard. She loved it, from everyone. She was like an actress, all dressed up in exotic clothes and jewellery, playing the part of Priestess in a theatrical way, more like a movie star than the leader of a religious group. And she wanted hierarchy. She wanted a court, with favourites and servants. Eventually I couldn't stand it and so I began to take my power back. My expressions and body language said I was taking it back, and she noticed right away. A few weeks later there was an explosion. I told her she was a phoney, an insincere manipulator. She hated me, although she pretended not to, like I was a poor crazy person. I had to leave the group, of course, and I don't want to rejoin it or any other group right now. When I see her she smiles and pretends to be friendly but it's all BS. I don't trust her, or the other coven members. They saw it all, and they see her for what she is, too; but they don't say anything. They just go on with the show, the projective games, the master-slave thing. They're silent. They won't take sides.

MDF: But you still practise, do you not?

Natalie: Yes; I practise on my own. Gloria wrote me a twenty-page letter accusing me of disloyalty and all sorts of things; it was another psychological game, but very aggressive. I didn't answer. I'm going more and more into psychology now, getting away from the projection and the denial—what I call the BS. And I also feel more and more drawn to the nature groups, the Greens, Greenpeace, Friends of the Earth, organizations like that. As I see it, the spiritual, psychological, and environmental all go together, as part of the same effort to improve our situation on the Earth. I'm planning a trip into the bush, a retreat; that seems more meaningful to me now than a coven meeting.

MDF: Tell me more about your solitary practice as a Witch. What do you do, typically, and how often?

Natalie: It varies, but I usually practise about once a week, in my living room. I begin by making a circle, tracing it on the floor with a stick or knife. Sometimes as I trace the circle I hum or sing. Then I do the directions. I ask the spirit of the north to be here, then the spirit of the west and south and east. I ask them to bring me healing energy, to take away my tension. When that's done I take water with salt in it (I think of it as spiritual sea water) and rub it on my face and body to cleanse and purify. After relaxing for a few moments, or perhaps grounding (which means feeling my connection to the Earth), I invoke the Goddess from the centre of my circle. I ask Her to come into my sacred space, to be with me in my circle.

MDF: How do you know when She comes?

Natalie: I feel a shift in energy. I feel powerful, centred, peaceful, grounded. I feel complete in the circle with the Goddess, like there's a ribbon around me, a place for me to be and feel good in.

MDF: Anything else?

Natalie: I feel I get the power to take risks when I am in the circle. I feel I can do things I would not ordinarily be able to do, at work or in university. I mean, assert myself in situations with other people, which I now do. The good feelings in the circle also lead me to meditate. I sit quietly for a few minutes and think about the things I want to accomplish. I sometimes chant, or sing, or image the people and situations that please me. This is usually the last thing I do, or almost the last thing.

MDF: What do you mean?

Natalie: I always thank the Goddess for coming to me. I know She leaves at the end, but I *hope* She stays. I ask Her to stay with me even though the rituals are over. And I thank the directions for their gifts, just as I thank the Goddess. All that remains, of course, is to banish the circle, but for me saying goodbye to the directions *is* banishing the circle. This doesn't mean I feel suddenly disconnected, however. The feeling of connection can go on for hours. I once felt the Goddess's presence for an entire weekend.

MDF: I understand that Wiccan gatherings can be very colour-
            ful and very moving. Don't you ever want to practise with
            others? Is this all you need?

Natalie: Occasionally I mull over the idea of going to a festival, or sab-
            bat, or group meeting, but I haven't been doing that. Right
            now it feels good to be on my own. I feel more like working
            with a few women on the environment, or on some political
            issue. My therapy seems to be heading me in that direction.
            I'll just have to see what happens down the road.

Richard (Witchcraft)

I met Richard at his rented home in Kitsilano, a quiet neighbourhood
of tree-lined streets and older frame houses in the Victorian style about
two miles south of downtown Vancouver. It was 1:30 in the afternoon
and Richard, casually dressed in jeans and a black t-shirt, was babysit-
ting his twin daughters who were in the midst of their afternoon nap.
Thirty-eight years old, of medium height and build, with brown eyes
behind gold wire glasses, and rather long, straight brown hair, Richard
was currently spending his days writing a Wiccan newsletter and
attempting to organize a coven of which he was to be the leader. His
common-law wife was working as a registered nurse and, according to
Richard, resisting his attempts to involve her in the Craft. This seemed
to annoy him. After chatting over herbal tea for fifteen minutes or so,
we began the interview.

MDF: Tell me a little bit about your background, your family, reli-
            gious persuasion—that sort of thing.

Richard: I was born in Hamilton [Ontario] in 1952. My mother
            belonged to the Anglican Church and was fairly devout. She
            attended services regularly, involved herself in Church activ-
            ities, and enrolled me in Sunday school, which I attended for
            several years, until I was twelve. My father was of no partic-
            ular religious persuasion. He stayed clear of all that, but I
            believe he and my mother were involved in a serious conflict
            over the role of religion in the family. And over other things
            as well. They had a very stormy marriage, with lots of quar-
            relling and weekly threats of separation or divorce. Much of
            this obviously stemmed from my father's drinking. He was a
            full-fledged alcoholic, constantly drunk, constantly storming
            around like an animal, scaring the hell out of us day-in and
            day out. When I was eleven he left, for good.

MDF: How did you feel about this?

Richard: Do you mean was I upset? Not at all! I wanted him to leave. He was a self-blinded man, closed off, defensive, violent, and unable to give or receive affection. I haven't seen him or heard from him since, and I have no desire for contact. I'm not saying it was easier after he left, only that it was less scary. I don't know how my mom managed to raise us all during those years. I was the eldest of six children, two brothers and three sisters, and it seemed we got by mostly on part-time jobs, severe restraint, and some governmental assistance. I'm very grateful to my mother for hanging in there. I tried to help out as much as I could along the way.

MDF: Were you and your mother close?

Richard: Extremely. We had, and we still have, a very special bond. We're mother and son, and also best friends. She is as good as they come, and I missed her a great deal when I first went off to university.

MDF: Which university did you choose?

Richard: I was on scholarship at McMaster, actually. It was 1971. I'm exceptionally bright, much brighter, in fact, than my transcripts might indicate. I performed adequately in the public schools, enough to get my scholarship and enough to get chosen for several appearances on TV quiz shows; but I never threw myself into my studies completely and could have done even better had I really tried.

MDF: What did you study? What degree did you take?

Richard: I entered the independent studies program with an eye on Canadian lit, but I left in 1975 without taking my degree. I was only a few credits shy, but somehow I had no incentive to finish. I spent the next few years working at odd jobs, reading, and exploring various political groups and ideas. This was in Toronto.

MDF: How did you happen to find your way to the Craft?

Richard: It had everything to do with the death of my closest friend, in 1978. I was a Marxist and an atheist at the time, very radical politically, very disillusioned with the establishment, very materialistic in my outlook, a kind of cynical communist. But when Dale was killed everything began to change. I was totally devastated, totally crushed by his death, and yet found

I had no way, no *inner* way, to deal with it. I kept coming up against my materialist philosophy. I couldn't cry, couldn't mourn, couldn't even honour his memory. I felt sealed off within myself, like a prisoner. At the Catholic service an old friend of ours put his arms around me and whispered in my ear that Dale was with Jesus. What shit, I thought. Is that what people say to console themselves? Am I supposed to say that? Going home on the train I began to write poetry to the Goddess, to the power of life, to the great wheel of the year, the cycle of the seasons. I had heard about the Goddess on and off for years and had read about matriarchy and the seasonal myths of the Greeks and Romans during high school and university, but I had never thought about it much and now for some reason it came pouring out of me. I began to realize that everything derived from the same creative female force and went back to it in the end. Death no longer seemed horrifying, empty, arbitrary, but part of a timeless pattern. I began to feel awkward and guilty about being an atheist. It suddenly seemed wrong, and blind, like a bitter stubbornness rather than a philosophical position. I wanted a spiritual life; I wanted spiritual fulfilment. I wanted to complete a part of myself that was there, alive, awake, and starving. And I felt the power of the Goddess, of the Earth, of the female. I knew it in a way I had never known it before. I think women are strong, even though they don't have cocks. Male gods, Jesus and the others, don't make sense to me. Women are at the foundation of things, the very creation of the world, and they aren't cut off from their bodies and their feelings as men are. When I read *The Spiral Dance* in '79 I found not only many great ideas to add to my own thinking; I also found many of the ideas I had had on the train expressed beautifully. *This* made sense. This was a view that I could totally identify with. There is no doubt in my mind that *The Spiral Dance* is one of the best and most important books ever written. My spiritual crisis was resolved as I turned the pages, and by the end I was converted, in my own mind, to the Craft.

MDF: Could you be more specific about what it was in *The Spiral Dance* that really grabbed you?

Richard: The theology was true. The view of *everything* was true. The female is the dominant force and gender; the male is adjunctive to the female, and subordinate. The book had it right. Also, the model of maleness that the book presented was one I could identify with. It wasn't an aggressive or destructive model; it didn't appear that way to *me*, and it didn't appear that way to women either, as I have discussed the subject with them. This book taught me that I didn't have to go around raping women to be a man, and I also didn't have to be castrated to be a feminist. I am a fully heterosexual male. I am manly, strong, and confident. You can see what I am just by talking to me, and I don't have to hurt others or be macho-patriarchal to prove anything.

MDF: Were there other themes in *The Spiral Dance* that intrigued you?

Richard: I was very taken with the ecological emphasis, and that, along with world peace, is still a huge part of my thinking. When I realized that Dale's death meant ultimately that he had reunited with the Goddess or the maternal power (to which we're all joined whether or not we know it), I also realized the Earth had to be protected, kept whole and clean as an expression of the living Goddess. It seemed awful to think the very ground we get buried in could be poisoned with chemicals. This aspect of the book was very important to me. The more I read, and the more I discussed my ideas with Sarah [Richard's girlfriend at this time], the more I was convinced by the Craft's conception of things. Finally, I underwent my first possession, or trance, my first true mystical encounter.

MDF: Could you tell me about that? When did it occur? What was it like?

Richard: It was about one year after reading *The Spiral Dance*. Sarah was withdrawing from me at the time. We were beginning to disagree on a number of things and I felt I was on my way to developing my own ideas, my own philosophy, apart from everyone else. I wanted my own connection with the Goddess, with the divine. Sarah did too, and perhaps she sensed what I was going through, but I remember being alone that night and wanting to feel my own power, my own strength, by myself, with no one around and no one else's ideas in my head. I cast a circle, called in the directions, and chanted and danced for a while. I then began to feel another being taking over my body. I felt something moving my arms and legs. Something was expressing itself through my limbs. A few moments later it moved into my belly, so sharply and so forcefully that I grunted. My dancing began to stem from my belly, my centre, the area directly behind my navel. This continued for perhaps ten minutes, until Bran appeared.

MDF: Bran?

Richard: The ancient Celtic fertility god. I had become acquainted with him through the literature but had never paid any particular attention. Yet here he was, directly present in my consciousness, a part of my mind. I knew instantly that my role on earth was to assist Him, to serve His cause. I am here to aid Bran, was my thought. The God is speaking through *me* to others. Not only did my atheism disappear once and for all, but my priesthood began. I bore Bran's message, and it was within *my* circle, cast by me, that my mission got underway. I wanted to go further with Witchcraft after this, to bring my experience to other Witches, and share my vocation with them, too. I began to attend Wiccan festivals, to participate in a coven in Toronto, and to deepen my spiritual life through reading and study. That's the big change. I now have a spiritual existence where before I had only my Marxist doctrines.

MDF: Why Bran? What do you think? You've read of a good many Goddesses and Gods.

Richard: I believe it is connected to my reading of Robert Bly. His poetry makes it very clear that we all have a wild man within, a kind of pre-civilized, untamed masculine power—very sexual, very masterful—and that most of us never manage to live fully in and through this aspect of our nature. It gets socialized out of us, pushed down. As I danced and chanted in my circle I began to feel its presence; it came surging up in me, my masculine capacity and strength. I was in the process of breaking up with Sarah at the time. It was clear that we were not going to make it, although the disengagement was slow for both of us. And suddenly Bran comes in and says to me, here is your manhood; here is your power; here is your mission. I was linked to the archetype and became the kind of Witch whose spiritual and philosophical roots reach back to that particular figure.

MDF: Were you initiated into the Craft immediately after Bran's visit?

Richard: No; not immediately after. When Sarah and I broke up I decided to spend some time on a communal farm in southern Ontario; it was there that I met Pam and started the relationship that is currently going on. I needed a retreat to nature, a close communion with the Earth, the plants and animals. However, I eventually began to feel the need to return to the social world and the pressing issues of the day. I travelled to Buffalo with Pam, made contact with the Wiccan community, and in 1983 formally became a Witch. It was one of the biggest moments in my life, one of the big four, as I think of it. First there was Dale's death, then *The Spiral Dance*, then the appearance of Bran, and finally my initiation. My goals began to solidify. I knew I was a priest; I knew that I wanted communion with the divine, and I knew I wanted to work with and serve others, bring them to the world of Wicca. It's the fastest-growing religion in the world because neither men nor women are satisfied with traditional faiths, traditional roles, traditional culture. All that stuff is in the process of destroying the Earth, destroying Gaia [an ancient Greek earth mother], destroying the Goddess.

MDF: Do you regard the Earth as a sentient, living organism?

Richard: Of course. How can anyone miss it? The Goddess exists *as* Earth, and the Earth exists *as* Goddess. We are part of Her, an expression of Her consciousness and being. The very atmosphere of the planet sustains us, nourishes us; it is part of a unified, coherent, living system. Everything works together at the physical and spiritual levels. We don't have to think of Her, strictly speaking, as *consciousness. We* are her thinking process; we are part of her total body. Our liver doesn't have to think; we think for it, take care of it, nourish it. Our liver isn't conscious in a definite way, but neither is it without consciousness as part of us. The world is a system, and the Goddess is interfused throughout the system as its foundation and organizing principle.

MDF: In my reading of Wiccan texts, including of course *The Spiral Dance*, I've noticed that Witches are concerned with the use of power, particularly personal power. Could you tell me something about that?

Richard: Power is a *force*, a manifestation of the primal universe. It is out there, all around us. What has to be borne in mind is that we get power to give power, and then we get it *back* again from that to which we gave it, as Gardner [Gerald B. Gardner, a prominent modern Witch] points out. If I project power into the circle it doesn't matter where it comes from. The circle becomes a portable temple because I project my power into it; but then I get power back from the circle as I invoke the

Goddess and develop a particular ritual. It is give and take, a two-sided relation, a source and a receiver.

MDF: But do you have a particular strategy for getting power?

Richard: I *ask* for it. I ask the Goddess to bring it to me, from her domain or being; or if I feel it dwelling inside already, I just summon it up. It's a matter of changing awareness, or clicking in to it, or being open to it. There's no need to define it in that sense. It works, so why worry about it?

MDF: I gather that magical practice is an integral part of Witchcraft today. How, in your view, does magic work?

Richard: It has everything to do with power, with what I just told you. If I have a magical purpose to accomplish I link my awareness to the power source and then send the power out to do the job. In my trances I may collaborate with specific outside forces of a divine nature but I can't go into that. I don't mean to say I don't have my own inner sources of power, either. I have enormous energy, great power of my own, as everyone does, and it is through this, finally, that collaboration proceeds. I think of it in my own mind as producing the great vitality, the source of all magical accomplishments worldwide. I don't use wands; I don't use crystals. I rely upon the circle and my own powers of communion.

MDF: What about magical practice in the coven?

Richard: It works very much the say way. We cast the circle, we call in the directions, we light the candles, join hands, ask the Goddess and the Gods to be with us, and then we experience the influx of energy. We may chant, or dance, or meditate as we raise our cone [of power]. It is all very basic, very elemental, very raw, in Bly's sense. We are naked and we are in a place that is halfway between the world of the Goddess and the world of mortals. It is a place that is not a *place*, a time that is not a time. It is the centre of the universe, a special kind of relativity, the circle that is all circles, and one. When we've sent our power to its goal, whatever that happens to be, then we celebrate with hugs and kisses. There is no hesitation or embarrassment. Wiccan men and women interact on a different plane. We are equal, spiritual, devoted in our eclectic pantheon. I like the mixed group, the men and the women together. Male groups don't work for me. I want both sexes present, both sexes participating, as they do in the natural order.

MDF: You mentioned directing power to its goal. What sort of goal
            did you mean?

Richard: We heal when we learn of someone who requires it. We stop
            logging where it shouldn't be going on. We stop the develop-
            ers from turning farm land into shopping malls; we stop
            employers from excluding women from executive positions.
            We visualize the situation, we visualize the desired outcome,
            and we send the power to accomplish it. We may visualize a
            valley saved from the polluters and destroyers; or a cancer
            patient cured of a malignancy; or a difficult birth proceeding
            smoothly; or a politician changing his reactionary stand on
            an important social or environmental issue; all of this. For us,
            the divine is not static. It is our activity. The Wiccan crusade
            is a union of spiritual and political ends.

MDF: Will the coven you are organizing be meeting in the near
            future?

Richard: Pam and I have only been here [in Vancouver] a few months,
            and the organization of the coven is turning out to be a very
            slow process. I've asked Pam to be one of the participants but
            at this time she doesn't seem to be willing. She's continuing
            her study of Witchcraft, however, and I feel she'll eventually
            be initiated, and our children too. I have a Pan-like influence
            on people; my power eventually gets to them. That's why I
            am referred to in so many Wiccan articles and books. People
            remember me.

MDF: Have you written books and articles yourself? May I read
            them? I am most eager.

Richard: I will write the books when the time comes. Right now my
            business is to organize the coven and to get involved in the
            Wiccan activity on the West Coast. It's a new life.

At a Coven Meeting

We gathered in the living room of a Victorian-style home situated on
Vancouver's east side at half past seven in the evening. The room was
large, with a highly polished hardwood floor from which two or three
oriental rugs had been removed and piled in one corner. On the mantel
above the unlit fireplace were several antique statuettes of female deities and several large, luminescent pieces of crystal. The walls of the
room were tastefully covered with a mauve paper highlighted by a

sinuous floral pattern. A sofa and several high-backed chairs in the Victorian style had been circularly placed at the living room's periphery, and at the centre of the floor stood four large candles and holders arranged rectangularly, a bowl of clear water, a saucer of salt, and a large blue canvas bag tied at the top and resembling a hiking pack. In the adjoining dining room a good-sized oak table had been laid with plates of fruit, vegetables, and cheese, and with two large pitchers of what turned out to be apple juice. There were no lights on in the living room, which was illuminated by the chandelier in the dining area. All nine members of the coven (seven women, two men) had been informed in advance of my participation. As people arrived, they sat or stood about chatting and smiling. By ten minutes to eight attendance was complete and the meeting began.

The Grounding

At the suggestion of the Priestess, a tall, fair, middle-aged woman attired in a floor-length white gown, we formed a circle in the living room, standing with hands joined. After a silence of perhaps two minutes, the exercise in grounding commenced as follows: we were told, first, to extend our arms upwards toward the sky and to visualize the clouds, the moon, the stars, and the galaxies, all of which were "manifestations of the goddess."[1] We were then told to imagine an opening in the tops of our heads into which we were to pull "the power of the cosmos." After four or five minutes of what the Priestess called "reaching for the sky," we were asked to sit, again in a circle but with hands disjoined, and to visualize our "roots," which emerged from our abdominal or genital areas, extending themselves into the ground. More specifically, we were asked to visualize these "roots" discovering their way into the Earth's "crystals, or caves, or mud, or into the bones of the dead." All of this was suggested by the Priestess in a firm yet soothing tone: "ground and centre." As we focused, as we pushed our roots into the planet, the Priestess asked us to join hands and continue with the grounding. We were, in her words, "reaching together to the centre of the Earth" for "power," for "fresh energy." We were also "dumping" our egotic preoccupations and petty problems into the world's "hot centre," where they would evaporate, thus leaving our "souls" in a "cleansed" condition. As the group's effort proceeded, one member began to rock back and forth and chant. The others seemed to be deeply absorbed in thought or in meditative states. This continued for perhaps ten minutes, at which point the Priestess slowly rose, and the members of the circle rose with her. Smiles were exchanged at this juncture, and lots of eye contact was initiated. People stretched their necks and shoulders, moved their hips, breathed deeply, and shared a brief remark or giggle. Shortly thereafter, the Priestess requested us to sit again and suggested that Peter begin to call in the directions.

The Directions, the Circle, and the Ablutions

Employing a copy of *The Spiral Dance*,[2] which had somehow appeared, Peter, a young red-bearded man in floppy blue cotton pants and a kind of loose-fitting Mexican shirt, read aloud:

> Hail, Guardians of the Watchtowers of the South, Powers of Fire, We invoke you and call you, Red lion of the noon heat, Flaming One! ... Be here now! (p. 56)

As Peter recited, the Priestess rose and, with a pearl-handled knife that sported a blade of perhaps eight inches, made a semicircular motion in the air. At the conclusion of his recitation, Peter lit one of the candles at the centre of the floor and handed *The Spiral Dance* to another coven member (female), who had been designated by the Priestess a few seconds earlier. The new reciter intoned as follows:

> Hail, Guardians of the Watchtowers of the West, Powers of Water, We invoke you and call you, Serpent of the watery abyss, Rainmaker, Grey-robed twilight, Evening star! ... Be here now!"

Once again this was orchestrated with the Priestess's circular motions, and concluded with the lighting of a candle. After the final two directions were "called in" in a similar manner, the Priestess stepped outside the circle of seated bodies and, with her knife pointed downward, walked once around the group to her original position, announcing,

> The circle is cast. We are between the worlds, beyond the bounds of time, where night and day, joy and sorrow, meet as one.

She then entered the circle's centre and placed her knife on the floor next to the blue canvas bag. She took up the salt, poured it into the water, returned to her place with the bowl, sat down, and uttered a few sentences the gist of which was a request for purification through the Goddess. After touching the salted water to her hands, arms, and forehead she passed the bowl to the members of the coven, each of whom repeated her ministrations and the last of whom returned the bowl to the centre, next to the knife, bag, and candles.

The Goddess Comes

After members had been sitting quietly in the circle for two or three minutes, Sarah, a heavy-set, blonde, bespectacled woman of perhaps thirty-five dressed in jeans and a black sweater, suggested that we "call in the Goddess." I was startled a few seconds later to hear the coven members begin to chant, call, and sing most energetically on an individual basis. I am not certain who commenced the din (it was not the Priestess), but it continued for at least five minutes. I recorded the names of various deities, including Isis, Diana, Hathor, Maat, Istar, Eros, and Nabu, as well as the names of several of the coveners. Apparently some were calling to the Goddess by calling to each other, or to themselves. Toward the conclusion of this remarkable outburst, members began to pause and look at one another, squeeze each other's hands, grin, laugh, and embrace with remarks such as "She's here!" and "She's come!" and with questions such as, "Can you feel Her presence?" and "Is She with you too?" When the man seated next to me (Charles) asked me whether I could sense the Goddess's presence, I smiled at him warmly, then looked away.

As the commotion gradually died down, the group began to focus its attention on the Priestess, who announced the evening's work. In a serious, low voice she told us that one of the coven members, Stephanie, had been recently and unexpectedly diagnosed as diabetic. Obliged to inject herself three times a day with insulin and to live with an uncertain future, Stephanie was presently in a severe depression. Members listened intently to the Priestess and then turned to Stephanie with expressions of commiseration and concern. A tiny woman barely five feet and ninety pounds, with short black hair, a pronounced aquiline nose, and pearl horn-rim glasses, Stephanie smiled softly at her fellow coveners and seemed on the verge of tears. When the soothing and commiseration declined, Peter undertook what I quickly discovered to be a healing chant. He asked the Goddess to touch Stephanie with Her healing powers. As Peter chanted, the members of the coven rocked, swayed, and chanted softly with him until another chant began, this time from Sarah. Hers, I found out, was a "water chant," also designed to pacify and heal the "patient." Again the group swayed and rocked and chanted softly to themselves.

As it turns out, however, all this chanting had a crucial, additional purpose, namely to "raise power" for the central rite, which got underway when the Priestess rose, went over to Stephanie, assisted her to her feet, and began to undress her. Stephanie was wearing a long black cotton dress that was loosely fitted and that was simply lifted over her head after she had removed her flat canvas walking shoes. She did not have a brassiere on, and after her dress was laid neatly to one side she removed her underwear. Naked, she was led to the circle's centre, which had been quickly cleared of objects. The Priestess then lowered Stephanie gently to the floor where she lay flat on her back, her legs fully extended and her arms straight down at her sides. After staring at Stephanie intensely for a moment or two and then nodding with satisfaction, the Priestess took up the blue canvas bag, removed its tie, and reached inside.

Her hand returned with a smooth, flat, circular stone about the size of a tea saucer. She handed this stone to Peter and then reached in for another, which she handed to me. A few minutes later the bag was empty and each member of the circle had in his possession three stones. Leaning down to Stephanie, the Priestess placed two stones on her upper chest and another between her breasts. Following suit, coven members, including the writer, placed stones on different parts of Stephanie's anatomy until she was virtually covered with them; they rested on her legs, her arms, her belly, her pubis, her forehead, as she lay flat and still. There was no talking during all of this, and no flinching on Stephanie's part when a stone tumbled off her calf and had to be replaced.

Then, for perhaps ten full minutes, in complete silence, the group focused its "power" on Stephanie's stone-covered body. The aim, of course, was to heal her through an enormous concentration of energy and with the aid of the stones, laden as they were with the natural force of the Goddess. The ritual as a whole, I was subsequently told, was designed also to call up the "patient's" own "healing powers." The group, in other words, was helping Stephanie to help herself. Thus, at the centre of the magic circle and naked as a new-born babe beneath her blanket of maternal stones, Stephanie basked in the glow of the group's collective *wish* that she get better.

A faint stirring in the room marked the close of the focusing and wishing. The Priestess rose, went to the dining area, and returned with a cotton blanket. She knelt by Stephanie, removed the stones (which coven members quickly put back into the bag), and covered her up. At this point, everyone converged on Stephanie with smiles and soft, soothing words. They stroked her hair, arms, and shoulders, whispering congratulations. After smiling back and occasionally touching the faces of fellow Witches, Stephanie began to speak from a benign, peaceful, inward place: "Thank you," she said over and over again, "My god, I feel so wonderful!" "I love you!" "This is unbelievable!" A few moments later she got up, dressed, and rejoined the circle that had newly re-established itself with members holding hands and with the Priestess in her commanding position.

For five minutes or so everyone chatted, laughed, smiled, relaxed, and remarked on what had just occurred. "It was great!" "I felt so much!" "She's going to get better!" "Did you feel the *power*?" "The

Goddess was here!" When the group's attention finally shifted back to the Priestess, she asked, after a few moments of complete silence, "Shall we say goodbye to the Goddess?" There was a quick, general assent followed by individual farewells on the part of coven members who began to chant, sway, and sing. I recorded: "Kali, thank you for being here." "Stay if you will, go if you must." "I will keep you, I will keep you, I will keep you" (this from Peter). A few moments later, the same people who had called in the directions bid them adieu with, for example, "Farewell, power of the North who brought to us the strength of the healing Earth," and "Farewell, power of the West who bathed us with the waters of spiritual rebirth." This time, however, *The Spiral Dance* did not appear to direct the verbalizations of the ritual. Finally, when the last direction had been addressed and the last candle snuffed, the Priestess rose and pronounced, "The circle is open but unbroken. Blessed be." A feeling of solemnity and success was clearly in the air at this point, as if nothing could compare with the wonderful healing of Stephanie that had just occurred. With the Priestess's final blessing, the smiling and chatting coven members arose and moved to the dining area to partake of the food and drink. As people munched and milled around between the two rooms Sarah said loudly, "May you never hunger or thirst!" Those closest to her nodded and smiled affirmatively; others paid no attention. The socializing continued for perhaps thirty minutes amidst talk of the next meeting, the distribution of notices and newsletters, and frequent salutations to Stephanie, who seemed very much restored. As departing coven members made their way to the front door, the Priestess was on hand to exchange a final word or two with them. To me she said soberly although not unpleasantly, "Let us know if you wish to join our circle again."

Notes

1. Quotation marks indicate direct quotations from my tapes or from my notes. In many instances I do not cite explicitly the individual source of the verbalization, either because the context makes the source clear or because the significance of the passage does not require an explicit designation.

2. Miriam Simos's [Starhawk's] *The Spiral Dance* is among the most influential texts of modern Witchcraft. I make extensive use of it in chapter 3, and I refer the reader to the bibliographical information at the end of chapter 3.

CHAPTER VI

THE GREAT HOLOGRAMAMA: CONCLUDING REMARKS ON NEW AGE THINKING

Nᴇᴡ Aɢᴇ thinking's projective goal of restoring to the centre of the individual's psychic life the before-separation-world of infancy and early childhood extends itself beyond the quotidian, beyond the concerns and problems of everyday existence, to the universe itself, to the entire, surrounding, gigantic, cosmic spectacle. We live at a time when the nature of the universe has come to be a matter of widespread speculation, a time when popular science in general and popular physics, biology (evolution), and cosmology in particular have discovered a place in the rumination and discourse of very large numbers of people, including of course the professional and semi-professional middle and upper classes. What sort of a world, what sort of a universe, do we live in? And perhaps more important for New Age thinkers, do the views of the world and the universe which emerge from the work of the experts, the physicists, evolutionists, cosmologists, and scientific philosophers, support in some significant measure the spiritual-religious-mystical perspective that is close to our hearts? New Age thinking has no intention of confining its projections to the sphere of daily living, to the issues of the person in the ordinary social world. On the contrary, New Age thinking wants to tell us what *everything* means, what *everything* discloses about the quality and purpose of our lives. For after all, if the universe itself announces at the macrocosmic level the same spiritual truths or principles that we have discerned down here, at the level of our mundane activities and behaviours, then *how can we be wrong?* Ultimately, what New Agers have to say about the cosmos will assist them in the fulfilment of their individual, worldly agendas.

Dr. Pribram and Dr. Bohm

Here is the way the essentials of the matter are set forth in what *USA Today* calls "the handbook of the New Age," namely Marilyn Ferguson's *The Aquarian Conspiracy.*[1] In a section devoted to the "hologram" and to the "holographic world" which it reveals, Ferguson (1980, 177) informs us that "some scientific discoveries are premature." They are "repressed or ignored until they can be connected to existing data," and she has in mind Mendel's disclosure of the gene, Polanyi's espial of absorption in physics, and Avery's identification of DNA in biology. "Recently," Ferguson goes on (177), "a Stanford neuroscientist, Karl Pribram, proposed an all-encompassing paradigm that marries brain research to theoretical physics [read the theories of David Bohm]; it accounts for normal perception and simultaneously takes the 'paranormal' and transcendental experiences out of the supernatural by demonstrating that they are part of nature. The paradoxical sayings of mystics make sense in the radical reorientation of this 'holographic theory.'" Well then, we may ask, what exactly is a "hologram"? Declaring that it is "one of the truly remarkable inventions of modern physics," Ferguson (179) chooses to give us an operational definition which gets at the "principle" of the thing. As the process of engendering the hologram commences, "light falls onto a photographic plate from two sources: from an object and from a reference beam, the light deflected by a mirror from the object onto the plate. The apparently meaningful swirls on the plate do not resemble the original object, but the image can be reconstituted by a coherent light like a laser beam. The result is a 3-D likeness projected into space, at a distance from the plate" (179). Ferguson then italicizes what is apparently the most compelling aspect of all this: *"If the hologram is broken, any piece of it will reconstruct the entire image* ... The whole code exists at every point in the medium ... The brain may decode its stored memory traces the way a projected hologram decodes or deblurs its original image." Accordingly, "stored mind is not a thing. It is abstract relationships." Ferguson is careful to point out (177) that Pribram's initial interest in the hologram was in no way tied to a spiritual or religious agenda. The man was simply doing science.

In 1971, Ferguson's presentation continues, "a distressing and ultimate question began troubling Pribram. If the brain indeed knows by putting together holograms ... *who* in the brain is interpreting the holograms? ... Who does the actual knowing?" (1980, 180). Lecturing at a symposium one night in Minnesota, "Pribram mused that the answer might lie in the realm of gestalt psychology, a theory that maintains that what we perceive 'out there' is the same as—*isomorphic* with—brain processes." He blurted out suddenly to the audience, "'Maybe the *world* is a hologram!'" (180). Maybe "its concreteness is an illusion" (180). Shortly after this, Pribram spent some time with his son, a physicist, discussing the question and searching for answers. This is where Bohm comes in.

Pribram's son, notes Ferguson (1980, 180), "mentioned that David Bohm, a protégé of Einstein, had been thinking along similar lines. A few days later, Pribram read copies of Bohm's key papers urging a new order in physics. Pribram was electrified. *Bohm was describing a holographic universe.*" Having given us the gist of Pribram's holographic theory, Ferguson proceeds to give us the gist of Bohm's "new order." We might keep in mind as we read the next few sentences that Bohm's ideas have thus far been greeted with scepticism by the vast majority of his colleagues, none of whom doubt Bohm's intelligence but nearly all of whom doubt gravely his underlying theoretical assumptions (see Talbot 1991, 53).

What appears to be "a stable, tangible, visible, audible world," said Bohm, "is an illusion. It is dynamic and kaleidoscopic—not really 'there.' What we normally see is the explicate, or unfolded, order of things, rather like watching a movie. But there is an underlying order that is father to this second-generation reality. He called the other order implicate, or enfolded. The enfolded order harbors our reality, much as ... DNA ... harbors potential life." Thus "all apparent substance and movement are illusory," Ferguson (1980, 181) observes, following Bohm. "They emerge from another, more primary order of the universe ... the *holomovement*." The "true nature of nature" is in "another order of reality, another dimension where there are no *things*." The "blur" on the holographic sheet "is the basic reality," and "transcendental experiences," or "mystical states," may "allow us occasional direct access to that realm" (181). Ferguson sums up: "Our brains mathematically construct 'hard' reality by interpreting frequencies from a dimension transcending time and space. The brain is a hologram, interpreting a holographic universe ... Individual brains are bits of the greater hologram" (1980, 182). While there are many items here that merit psychoanalytic attention, and while there are many items still to come before the hologramama of New Age thinking emerges in its entirety, I will pause and concentrate upon two central notions which issue from this portion of Ferguson's handbook. I have in mind, first, the idea that every part reflects the whole ("the whole code exists at every point in the medium"), and second, the idea that "reality" is the dynamic, energetic, *vibrational* substrate which underlies the realm of "things."

The Illusion of Separateness

That every part reflects or somehow contains the whole—the whole code, the whole vast, underlying, energetic "holomovement"—might be characterized simply as the *idea of universal interconnection*. New Age thinking, always on the lookout for materials that challenge the psychic reality of separation and happy to employ the old enemy, science, in the service of its regressive wishes, fastens onto this idea like a bulldog and won't let go. Here is an array of citations from influential New Age texts. It will not take the reader very long to get the hang of things.

Substituting the word "holoverse" for "universe" in his volume *Space, Time, and Medicine*, Larry Dossey (1982, 116) declares that "*we cannot separate* our own existence from that of the world outside. We are *intimately associated* not only with the earth we inhabit, but with the farthest reaches of the cosmos" (my emphasis). Dossey proceeds to outline on page after page the "healing" potentialities of this "holographic" realization. The "holoverse" becomes *an object* that brings the divided, sick, alienated "self" together (118, 124, 129, 139).

In his book *The Holographic Universe*, which is devoted largely to the work of Pribram and Bohm, Michael Talbot (1991, 48, my emphasis) asserts that "everything in the universe is part of a continuum. Despite the *apparent separateness* of things at the explicate level, everything is a seamless extension of everything else, and ultimately even *the implicate and explicate orders blend into each other*" (the restoration of symbiotic fusion with the object). "Take a moment to consider this," Talbot (48) instructs us. "Look at your hand. Now look at the light streaming from the lamp beside you. And at the dog resting at your feet. You are not merely made of the same things. *You are the same thing*. One thing. Unbroken. One enormous something that has extended its uncountable arms and appendages into all the apparent objects, atoms, restless oceans, and twinkling stars in the cosmos" (the internalized object once again *is* the environment; here, the hologramama is even given "arms" and "appendages"). There is an "undivided wholeness" among "all things," insists Talbot (48); the "parts" of the "universe" are "*no more separate* from one another than different patterns in an ornate carpet" (my emphasis). Talbot (55) goes on, "We can view ourselves as physical bodies moving through space. Or we can view ourselves as a blur of interference patterns enfolded throughout the cosmic hologram. Bohm believes this second point of view might be the more correct, for to think of ourselves as a holographic mind-brain looking at a holographic universe is an abstraction, *an attempt to separate two things that ultimately cannot be separated* ... We are not looking at the hologram. We are part of the hologram" (my emphasis). Thus "we are beings without borders" (the abrogation of ego boundaries in the restoration of symbiotic fusion), and it is "the mystics" who are "able to peer beyond ordinary explicate reality and glimpse its deeper, more holographic qualities" (60, 63). "All boundaries are illusory," Talbot (70) informs us; "the lack of distinction between part and whole and the interconnectedness of all things" are "qualities one would expect to find in a holographic universe." Note this series of short quotations from a single page (285) of Talbot's book: "In a holographic universe ... *separateness ceases to exist*; we are all thoughts in the mind of God; we cannot ask if the part is creating the whole or the whole is creating the part because the part is the whole." Finally, Talbot's accent falls on the Garden, the prelapsarian realm, the before-separation-world toward which, of course, all of this "interconnection" has been pointing from the start: "There is a Hindu myth that human consciousness began as a ripple that decided to leave the ocean of consciousness as such, timeless, spaceless, infinite and eternal. Awakening to itself, it forgot it was part of this infinite ocean, and felt *alone and separated* ... Adam and Eve's expulsion from the Garden of Eden may be a version of this myth, an ancient memory of how human consciousness ... left its *home in the implicate* and forgot that it was part of the cosmic wholeness of all things" (300, my emphasis). Thus the implicate order, the energetic essence of the hologram, is our original *home*, our original *Garden*, our original *Paradise*. Surely even the most conservative reader cannot fail to spy the Great Mother, or the Great Hologramama, lurking just behind such images, at that very point where the realm of the unconscious begins to stretch away.

Hyped by Bantam Books as "the Bible" of those interested in "mind-altering physics," and by the journal *Parabola* as "a new education for a New Age,"[2] Gary Zukav's *Dancing Wu Li Masters* informs us, "There really may be no such thing as *separate parts* in our world ... The idea that events are *autonomous* happenings is an *illusion*. This would be the case for any *separate parts that have interacted with each other at any time in the past*" (denial of the separation phase) (Zukav 1979, 296, my emphasis). Zukav goes on, "What happens here is intimately and immediately connected to what happens elsewhere in the universe, which, in turn, is intimately connected to what happens elsewhere in the universe, and so on, simply because the *separate parts of the universe are not separate parts*. 'Parts,' wrote David Bohm, 'are seen to be in immediate connection ... One is led to a new notion of unbroken wholeness'" (297, my emphasis). (Zukav tells us in his Acknowledgements that Bohm read the manuscript on its way to publication.) Here is Zukav pushing the central theme with the concept of an "organic" or *living* hologramama explicitly in his mind: "All of the things in our universe (*including us*) that appear to exist independently are actually parts of one all-encompassing *organic* pattern ... *No parts of that pattern are ever really separate from it or from each other*" (48, my emphasis). Zukav asks in one place (255), drawing a parallel between science and spirituality, "What does physics have in common with enlightenment?" He replies: "Physics and enlightenment apparently belong to two realms which are *forever separate*. One of them (physics) belongs to the external world of physical phenomena and the other of them (enlightenment) belongs to the internal world of perceptions. A close examination, however, reveals that physics and enlightenment are not so incongruous as we might think." And then, "the physical world, as it appears to the unenlightened, consists of many *separate parts*. These *separate parts*, however, are *not really separate*. According to mystics from around the world, each moment of enlightenment ... reveals that everything—*all the separate parts of the universe*—are manifestations of the same whole. There is only one reality, and it is whole and unified. It is one" (255–56, my emphasis). Zukav titles one of the chapters in which he makes such assertions "I Clutch My Ideas." Setting aside the esoteric Eastern meaning of these words and looking at them from the psychoanalytic angle, one might suggest that Zukav's "biblical" negation of "separate parts" in the "universe" is an "idea" onto which the New Age has been "clutching" enthusiastically for the past two decades.

The "universe" may be regarded as a "giant hologram," writes John Casti (1989, 464), joining the parade with *Paradigms Lost*. He goes on, "Beneath the world of surface phenomena there is an undivided, seamless whole," namely "the domain of quantum objects" (464). Every quantum object "carries a trace of every other object with which it has ever interacted" (464). Thus Casti links up with Marilyn Ferguson (1980, 177), and with countless other New Agers, in regarding the "hologram" as the new "paradigm" through which we may gain an accurate understanding of the cosmos.

Here are a few sentences from *The Web of the Univers*, the work of a University of Wisconsin physicist named John Hitchcock who holds a Ph.D. in the phenomenology of science and religion from the Graduate Theological Union and the University of California at Berkeley: "It seems to be more and more clearly the case that there is a unified real-ity behind the diversity of the *living cosmos* ... The new paradigm of-fered by the 'new physics' *forbids the separation* of the human from the nature of reality" (Hitchcock 1991, 1–2, my emphasis). Again, "There is a widest possible structure which *binds all of us in this cosmos* ... Not to be bound to a relatively minor culture, one which, for example, represents only part of a planet, is the prerequisite to perceiving the *overall binding of finite creatures by the oneness, or unity, or physical consistency of our cosmos*" (69, my emphasis). And again, "The whole question of integrity, as my integrity, must *begin with the ego* ... and *extend outward*. Its logical extension is an actual *cosmic unity*, in which I can be aware of the Totality" (223, my emphasis). Hitchcock is particularly concerned throughout his volume with the manner in which the opposites of quantum theory (particle/wave, etc.) lead one to an understanding of the interconnectedness of all things. We'll hear more from Hitchcock later.

Here is Fritjof Capra (also a physicist) writing in *The Tao of Phys-ics*, another New Age "bible" that attempts to wed science to Eastern spiritualities: "The Western way of thinking ... mirrors our view of the world 'outside' which is seen as a multitude of *separate objects* and events. This natural environment is treated as if it consisted of *sepa-rate* parts ... In the Eastern view ... the cosmos is seen as one *insepa-rable* reality ... The basic elements of the Eastern world view are also those of the world view emerging from modern physics" (Capra 1983, 24–27, my emphasis). Capra continues, "In modern physics, the uni-verse is ... experienced as a dynamic, *inseparable* whole which *always includes the observer* in an essential way. In this experience, the tradi-tional concepts of space and time, of *isolated objects*, and of cause and effect lose their meaning" (81, my emphasis). "Everything is dynami-cally connected with everything else," maintains Capra (88), and "as long as our view of the world is fragmented, as long as we are under the spell of *maya* and think that we are *separated from our environment and can act independently*, we are bound by *karma*" (my emphasis). For the truth is, according to Capra (88, my emphasis), "*there is no sep-arate individual self.*" Both "modern physics" and the "Eastern world view" have found "the unity and interrelation of all things and events" to be the essence of our universe (99). The "universe" is "an *insepara-ble* whole" (291, my emphasis).

Allow me to proffer a few brief quotations from the influential New Age volume *States of Grace*, by the feminist Witch Charlene Spretnak (1991), presented by HarperCollins as a "guide" to the "con-nectedness" of the world. "At subtle levels of perception," Spretnak claims, "we are ever changing and ever aware of our connectedness with other humans, the rest of nature on Earth, and the whole of the universe" (20). Indeed, Spretnak goes on, "Hundreds of discoveries in contemporary science have ... indicated a world based on inherent interconnectedness" (21). Well, what "discoveries" does Spretnak have in mind? They are these: "Everything is composed of a subatomic flux of wavelets and particles, chaos and pattern. Boundaries are fluid. Possibilities are endless. *Unrelated separateness is an illusion.* Interconnectedness is reality. Process is all" (21, my emphasis). And then, with Einstein's relativity and Pribram's hologram in the immediate background: "Any point in the universe can be regarded as the fixed point, the center. *You are the center of the universe*" (the re-establishment of mother-infant mirroring) (33). Thus you must "find a way that reveals to you the joy of *our profound unity,* the subtle interrelatedness of you and every being, every manifestation of the unfolding universe" (78); for *"our seeming separation* from the rest of the natural world is a matter of perception, a view that does not hold up at subtle levels of awareness. Atoms exhibit responsiveness to other atoms ... Subtle mind is aware that nature is aware" (the internalized object *lives* projectively) (86, my emphasis). "We are all related," Spretnak (100) concludes; the *"apparent multiplicity and separateness* of phenomena yield ultimate unity" (my emphasis). At the "center of human life are experiences of deep communion with the cosmos," the *"vast organism in which we are embedded without separation"* (103, my emphasis). Surely that final sentence sums up very well this particular aspect of what we have chosen to characterize as the Great Hologramama.

The reader may think I've been cleverly selective during the course of the last few paragraphs. Just the opposite is true. In all of this I have chosen but a few representative illustrations from a veritable plenitude of possibilities. Were the reader to spend a couple of afternoons in a well-stocked New Age bookstore he would discover not dozens but hundreds of citations identical to those which I've included here: everything is connected to everything else; everything that ever *was* is connected to everything else; everything that ever *will be* is connected to everything else; *there is no separation; there is no separation; there is no separation;* we are *held,* we are *contained,* we are *embedded in* the vast organism-universe-cosmos-hologram. In psychoanalysis we call this *an obsession:* it is one that New Age physics *shares* with New Age thinking as a whole. The New Age may be regarded as an unforgettable attestation to the traumatic power of separation in human life.

Physicist John Hitchcock is not the only New Age author to employ the metaphor of "the web" when attempting to communicate his conception of the "living cosmos" (Hitchcock 1991, 1). The metaphor appears everywhere in the New Age literature arising from the so-called new physics. "More and more," writes Talbot (1991, 43), "the picture of reality Bohm was developing was not one in which subatomic particles were *separate* from one another and moving through the void of space, but one in which all things were part of *an unbroken web* and embedded in a space that was as real and rich with process as the matter that moved through it" (my emphasis). The "physical world according to quantum mechanics," says Zukav's *Dancing Wu Li Masters* (1979, 72, my emphasis), "is not a structure built out of independently existing unanalyzable entities, but rather a *web of relationships* between elements whose meanings arise wholly from their relationship to the whole." In Fritjof Capra's view, "The whole universe appears as a dynamic *web of inseparable* energy patterns" (1983, 80, my emphasis); "quantum theory has shown that particles are *not isolated* grains of matter but are probability patterns, interconnections in an *inseparable cosmic web*" (203, my emphasis). Each person on the Earth has a part to play in the drama of the universe, maintains Charlene Spretnak (1991, 134); one must "articulate as deeply and fully" as one can one's "ontological potential" as a "weaver of the *cosmic web*" (my emphasis). Spretnak (158, my emphasis) continues in another place: "We are constitutionally connected with the manifestations of being that surround us ... *Everything that appears in the cosmos emerges into this web.*" At its "primary level," asserts Marilyn Ferguson (1980, 171), "the universe seems to be paradoxically whole and *undifferentiated*, a seamlessness that somehow generates the intricate tapestry of our experience" (my emphasis). And then, "the ultimate reality is an underlying *web of connection*" (184, my emphasis). Finally from John Hitchcock himself, and in keeping, of course, with the title of his book: when we "look at" the manner in which molecular atoms "fit" together and "resonate" with the "local field" they engender, "we see the simplest form of the *web of the universe*" (1991, 38, my emphasis). I believe it is the traumatic power of separation in human life that sparks not only the New Age's projective, obsessive insistence upon universal interconnection generally but its widespread projective employment of the metaphor of the *cosmic web* particularly: the web *holds* us, *attaches* us, *links* us, and above all *catches* us (it is "unbroken, seamless, rich, real"); that is to say, it prevents us from *falling* into the abyss of separation and non-attachment, the primal *angst* of human existence as it takes shape during and after the differentiation phase of development (Mahler 1975) when the forces of culture (the symbolic realm) rush in to fill the gap left by the disruption of symbiotic fusion, the mirroring merger of caregiver and infant. The "cosmic web" is the metaphor that most compactly renders the *emotional purpose* to which New Agers would put their creation of a holographic universe and of a Great Hologramama, which is its unconscious, projective expression.

The blur on the photographic plate becomes the web of the implicate order, the dynamic, seamless whole that contains us and sustains us at the deep, emotive level where the dread of separation (including death) manifests its very considerable *energies*.

Universal Vibrations

According to our New Age experts in the ultimate nature of the universe, the organic, webby, holographic cosmos in which we are all embedded is an essentially *vibrational*, resonating entity. The days are long gone when we might look upon the cosmos as "an agglomerate of Newtonian objects," writes Stanislav Grof (1991, 186) in his volume *The Holotropic Mind*: "We now have a universe that is an infinitely complex system of vibratory phenomena." In Judith Blackstone's (1991, 67) view, the "basic affinity" among "human beings" extends toward "everything" in the universe. We are able to "resonate" with plants, animals, and even "mineral life," because "all forms are created by the same laws, out of the same spectrum of vibration." Zukav (1979, 155) maintains in his *Dancing Wu Li Masters* that the "world of matter is a relative world, and an illusory one: illusory not in the sense that it does not exist, but illusory in the sense that we do not see it as it really is." He goes on, "The way it really is cannot be communicated verbally, but in the attempt to talk around it eastern literature speaks repeatedly of dancing energy and transient, impermanent forms. This is strikingly similar to the picture of physical reality emerging from high-energy particle physics." Capra (1983, 194) is of the same persuasion: "Modern physics ... pictures matter not at all as passive and inert, but as being in a continuous dancing and vibrating motion ... The universe has to be grasped dynamically as it moves, vibrates, and dances." And again, "The quantum field is seen as the fundamental physical entity; a continuous medium which is present everywhere in space. Particles are mere local condensations of the field; concentrations of energy which come and go, thereby losing their individual character and dissolving into the underlying field" (210). This cosmic holding environment, moreover, is not vibrational only in and unto itself; it operates upon a frequency we can *share*. Indeed, say our New Age cosmologists, when we manage to gain an accurate, stable view of things we may harmonize with, *merge* with, the holographic super-entity at the energetic, vibrational level of our own being. Writes Talbot (1991) in *The Holographic Universe*: "The objective world does not exist, at least in the way we are accustomed to believing. What is out there is a vast ocean of waves and frequencies" into which we are "enfolded" (54–55). Once we "drop" the "disguise" of the "body" we become "a vibrational pattern comprised of many interacting, resonating frequencies ... We are a frequency phenomenon," and "our consciousness is contained not in the brain, but in a plasmic holographic energy field that both permeates and surrounds the physical body" (235–36). Were we able to "see" with more than our "eyes," claims Talbot, it is precisely *this* that we would discover (236). "Consciousness is ultimately a pattern of vibrations, or frequencies," a kind of "radiation" (239). We can "contact" or "enter" Pribram's "frequency domain" and *stay* there as we develop our ability to transcend ordinary awareness: "Our consciousness—the thinking, perceiving part of us—can detach from the physical body and exist just about anywhere it wants to" (234). Declares Hitchcock (1991) in *The Web of the Universe*: "Resonance occurs when something matches," and "frequency matching is resonance." An "excellent model" of this, says Hitchcock, is "the process of falling in love"; the "field of consciousness is narrowed, the power of symbol is enhanced, and the sense of patterning is heightened: 'this is perfect; this is meant to be'" (40–41). Hitchcock continues: "When the fundamental patterns of the universe are actualized or fulfilled, things fit, and the flow of energy is felt with beauty and luminosity," for "each particle in the universe is co-extensive with the universe. So the outer fringes of all the waveforms of the atoms overlap each other. Thus the shaping field subtly shapes the larger forms, especially the living forms, in the cosmos ... The cosmos as a whole shapes us; and thus, in a reciprocal sense, our actions shape the cosmos" (41–42). The universe and the human creature can "resonate" together as "lovers." What is required to accomplish this is an energetic "restructuring" of our "souls" (47). But perhaps the passage that pulls together perfectly the emphases on interconnection and vibration is the following one from Spretnak's *States of Grace* (1991, 52): "When the apparent boundaries of the body dissolve" in moments of "clear observation," the "vibratory nature of one's form and the surrounding world are experienced as one minutely pulsating ocean of flux." The projective quality of the New Age cosmos is beginning to emerge in earnest.

Not only does the Great Hologramama contain us and sustain us, it *vibrates* within us, *resonates* within us, *as* it contains and sustains; furthermore, if we perceive things rightly and work on ourselves spiritually, we can *blend* our vibrations, *merge* our frequencies, *with it*. In a word, as microcosms or little ones we can *mirror* the quantum realities of our macrocosmic environment—the colossal, webby, organic, living cosmos that surrounds us. The unconscious wish in all of this could hardly be plainer: to erase separation and restore not simply symbiotic fusion but the *affective (or vibrational) attunement* (Stern) that characterizes the mirroring stage. The vibrations of the "quantum world" fascinate and compel the New Age because they can be projectively converted into the vibrations of the early period. The parallel is simply too obvious for a regressive unconscious to ignore: the universe is fundamentally vibrational and the early period is fundamentally vibrational, fundamentally a matter of mother (the environment) sharing her affective frequencies with baby. We "come from" Bohm and Pribram's "frequency domain," the so-called "implicate order," and we also "come from" the world of the internalized object; we ponder the primal vibrations of the cosmos, and we recall in the deep unconscious the blissful vibrations of affective attunement, the realm of dual-unity and mirroring: presto-changeo, the world of the internalized object *becomes the universe*, and we are "enfolded" in our vast, vibrating, cosmic "home." Hologramama is like the *crystal* which binds us vibrationally to the earth's mineral kingdom, or the *power animal* which links us energetically to the eternal, shamanic reality, or the *guardian angel* whose channelled frequencies take us to the spiritual kingdom, or the *Wiccan circle* in which we discover the immortal power of the Goddess, or the *Energetic Embrace* of New Age healing where patient and healer become one in the exchange of miraculous vibes. Accordingly, Hologramama is not merely a version of affective attunement, it is a version of *evoked companionship* as well. To *read* the New Age literature about the cosmos is to evoke the maternal companion of life's first years. The vast, surrounding cosmos "out there" feels just like the vibrational object "in here." We are comforted and reassured; we are humming inwardly. No wonder books on New Age physics make money for publishers and distributors. They offer the purchaser a pleasant, wish-fulfilling fix each time he sits down to read. And no wonder, too, that New Age cosmologists allude to the universe in terms that explicitly recall *the parent*. We are "descended from the fireball," from the big bang, writes Spretnak (1991, 17); the "ongoing process of cosmological unfolding" has "birthed" us (134), has given us "our cosmological lineage" (20). Thus "everything in our life experience is kin to us, the result of a cosmic birth during which the gravitational power of the event held the newborn particles in a miraculously deft embrace" (79). We can regard the "Big Bang as our birthday party," declares Sylvia Fraser (1992, 344) in her *Book of Strange*; "We humans are womb-mates to the brightest quasars on the fringes of the known world" (344). John Talbot (1991, 52) goes still further by way of constructing our cosmic family tree: "Despite its apparent materiality and enormous size, the universe does not exist in and of itself, but is the *stepchild* of something far vaster and more ineffable" (my emphasis). How does it go in the Bible: Adam begat Seth, Seth begat Enosh, Enosh begat Kenan ...? What this finally gives us, of course, is the Great Hologramama as the *parental body* and New Age cosmological projection as the unconscious attempt to re-find and re-attach to that body. As Spretnak (1991, 52) puts it, referring to the cosmic energy: "We are it. It is us. No illusions of separation, so no alienation." Collapsing the subject/object dichotomy can be done for philosophical or for emotional reasons; I believe we can safely say that we have an instance of the latter here. "No separation, no alienation": it could be the motto on a New Age scutcheon.

Cosmological Evolution

At various points in the context of this book we touched upon the role of *evolution* in New Age thinking; more specifically, we noted how New Agers employ the term loosely to describe "change" or "transformation" to a "higher" spiritual level. Now we will see the idea of evolution attached to the "implicate order," to the originating fireball, to the webby, birthing, cosmic matrix itself, the Hologramama. Further, we will see the way in which *we* are "implicated" in the evolving nature of the cosmos, for, as always in New Age thinking, what the cosmos is doing "out there" is reflected directly in what *we* are doing "down here." That is, I grant you, a very strange idea, yet it is axiomatic to the propositions of the writers with whom we are dealing.

Behind the New Age belief in an evolving universe stand three historical items: the investigations and publications of nineteenth- and early twentieth-century biologists (Darwin, Wallace, T. H. Huxley), the acceptance of evolution in some shape or form by very large numbers of people, and most important for New Age thinking, the inspirational writings of Pierre Teilhard de Chardin, a Catholic theologian-paleontologist who strove to wed scientific evolution to mystical Christianity during the 1930s and 1940s. "The world is a-building," wrote Teilhard (1961, 92), who looked out at the material cosmos and saw a process of "ascent" toward what he called the "Omega Point," a perceptual summit at which *the spirit inherent in matter* (or "spirit-matter") would finally and fully achieve its God-given destiny through man. "No mechanism of *evolution* could gain a hold on an entirely passive *cosmic material*," declares Teilhard in his *Hymn of the Universe* (1961, 104, my emphasis), a notion that he refines and amplifies in *The Phenomenon of Man* (1965, 258), where cosmological evolution becomes explicitly the attainment of "supreme consciousness" among humans.

That the macrocosm is not simply infused with spirit but somehow *becoming* or *evolving into* spirit is the notion on which New Age thinking eagerly pounces. Employing Teilhard's word *complexification* to describe mankind's gradual, evolutional ascent toward the noetic sphere, Copthorne Macdonald (1993, 12) declares in *Toward Wisdom*:

"Without a grasp of *evolutionary processes* we have little sense of our deep *kinship with the universe.*" In addition, Macdonald goes on, "we fail to sense the role that we humans are now playing as active agents of evolution." Thus our *familial relationship* with the cosmos, our "kinship," is considerably enhanced by our appreciation of its *evolving nature.* Moreover, it is not simply the universe that is evolving; *we,* as *part* of it, as *linked* to it, as *related* to it, are *also* evolving as its "active agents." As we "follow the tracks" of our "spiritual evolution," writes Talbot (1991, 301), we "penetrate deeper into the implicate" order of things. Indeed, we witness the "unfolding" of the "original source of our being" (300). To be "heading toward Omega," Talbot asserts, echoing Teilhard explicitly, means mounting an "evolutionary thrust toward higher consciousness" (299). In New Age thinking, then, it is not simply "the world" but Bohm's "implicate" order—the vibrational heart of the Hologramama—that is, in Teilhard's expression, "a-building." According to Marilyn Ferguson (1980), "evolution" is the "paradigm" that most accurately describes not only the purpose of New Age thought and practice but the impetus of the world and the universe around us (157). Referring again and again to the work of Teilhard (25, 43, 68, 130, 184, 225, 243, 289, 393), Ferguson declares that the "whole" of which we form a "part" is an essentially "evolving" super-entity, a "flickering web of events" integrally tied to ever-changing patterns of atomic and molecular behaviour (169, 171). If "society is to evolve," observes Ferguson (187), "we must match our lives to our new knowledge," and she has in mind specifically the "knowledge" we gain from Pribram, Bohm, and Teilhard. Turning directly to Teilhard's notion of "spirit-matter," Hitchcock (1991, 25) maintains that this is "the stuff out of which everything in the cosmos is formed." In order to see "the sweep of evolution as a whole, and as the unfolding of a divine potential," Hitchcock continues, "we must perceive the presence of spirit in the simplest of atomic forms. As an example, one of the spiritual potentials of humanity is freedom. We can see elements of freedom in the nature of atoms [!], and for this reason Teilhard called atoms 'elementary freedoms' ... *Evolution of spirit-matter has produced us,* with our distinct though rudimentary freedom" (25, my emphasis). In this way, it is "erroneous" to view the "human" as somehow "given"; rather, the "human" has "evolved from the primal hydrogen of the cosmos" (22). It is the "evolving stuff of the universe" (209) that accounts for our presence and our consciousness.

Now, the evolving cosmos of New Age physics is connected inextricably to the *central theme,* the central *bent,* of New Age thinking as a whole: I am referring to the theme of, to the questing after, *transformation.* An evolving universe *means* to New Age thinking a

universe that encourages, indeed catalyzes and makes virtually irresistible, the transformational urges of its denizens. Evolution, and in
particular the evolution of the cosmos, is of no interest to New Age
thinking in and of itself, *scientifically*, any more than quantum theory
is. The evolution of the cosmos interests New Agers because, like the
vibration of the cosmos, it offers them fertile psychological soil in
which their regressive wishes may take root; it interests them because
it facilitates the fashioning of projective associations which magically
restore the past. " 'Son of man,'" cries Teilhard as he is quoted in Hitchcock's *Web of the Universe* (1991, 101), "'bathe yourself in the ocean of
matter, for it is that ocean which will raise you up to God.'" In other
words, the vast, evolving Hologramama, the ocean of molecules and
atoms, is the "ocean" of *transformation*, the ocean that will *change*
one fundamentally, heighten one's being "up" to the very godhead, the
supreme source and origin of everything. Hitchcock (1991, 42, 27) calls
the "physics" associated with this miraculous capacity the "physics of
transformation," or "transformative restructuring," and claims that its
pursuit is our highest spiritual destiny in a universe given to "transformative growth." Writes Ferguson (1980) in her *Aquarian Conspiracy:*
"Molecules and stars, brainwaves and concepts, individuals and societies—all have the potential for transformation ... All wholes transcend
their parts by virtue of internal coherence, co-operation, openness to
input ... Evolution is a continuous breaking and forming to make new,
richer wholes ... Particles make sudden transitions, quantum leaps, behaving at times like units, yet mysteriously wavelike on other occasions. One current theory sees the universe as a scattering matrix in
which there are no particles but only relationships between events"
(169–71). And then, "Experiments show that if paired particles (which
are identical twins in their polarity) fly apart and the polarity of one is
changed by an experimenter, the other *changes instantaneously*. They
remain mysteriously connected" (171, my emphasis). Ferguson groups
these transformational wonders of the universe under the heading "the
science of transformation" (162). "There is now incontrovertible evidence," she writes, with Teilhard's "dazzling" *Phenomenon of Man*
explicitly in her mind, "that we have entered upon the greatest period
of change the world has ever known" (50–51). Just as evolution has
"enveloped" the universe, Ferguson concludes (50), so it will "envelop"
our planet, for "nothing in the universe" can "resist" the "ardor" of
"transformed persons working together." Evolution is the "condition"
to which "all theories must bow." The "world view" of "particle physics," writes Zukav (1979, 194) in *The Dancing Wu Li Masters*, "is that
of a world without 'stuff,' where what is equals what happens, and
where an unending, tumultuous dance of creation, annihilation and
transformation runs unabated." What we "have been calling matter,"

Zukav goes on, "is being constantly created, annihilated, and created again." All-embracing and continuous "transformation" is the "chaos" that resides beneath the apparent "order" (194). Fritjof Capra (1983) could not agree more: the "ultimate essence" of the "universe" cannot "be separated from its multiple manifestations. It is central to its very nature to manifest itself in myriad forms which come into being and disintegrate, *transforming* themselves into one another without end" (189, my emphasis). Once "mass" is seen "to be a form of energy," it is "no longer required to be indestructible, but can be *transformed* into other forms of energy" (201, my emphasis). Thus Einstein's famous equation gives us a cosmos with *transformation* at its core.

We do not have to struggle here to discern the *psychoanalytic meaning*: just as a *vibrational* cosmos attracts the unconscious attention of New Agers yearning for the restoration of affective attunement, so does a *transformative cosmos* attract the unconscious attention of New Agers seeking to restore the transformational object to their lives. The transformative cosmos of New Age physics unconsciously projects the before-separation-world in two of its most compelling psychological aspects: the transformational ministrations of the caregiver, and the primal gratification and security that such ministrations induce in the neonate. In this way, the Great Hologramama does not merely hold us in its webby vibrations; it does not merely protect us from the abyss of separation and non-attachment; it does not merely offer us the solace of evoked companionship and vibrational mirroring; the Great Hologramama also returns us affectively to the oceanic environment of infancy in which the mother's transformational behaviours continually *change* the infant's discomfort into pleasure, or relief. Simply to *read* of a transformative cosmos, simply to *contemplate* a macrocosm in which evolution is continually going forward and taking us with it, is to get a significant *hit* in the part of the self that longs to reconnect to the object. Transformation is occurring all around us, claim the New Age cosmologists; it is everywhere; the very *universe* is transformative; we can't evade evolution and change. *All of this says to the unconscious of the reader or contemplator:* "Relax; the transformational object of infancy is still at hand; you are not entirely disconnected from the early period; indeed, you are about to re-experience the delicious kind of change that you knew on a regular basis in the foundational past; the universe has the power to metamorphose you, to alter you, to grant you your wishes; the transformational object is *there*, just behind that brilliant quasar, or perhaps that shimmering galaxy." This is the unconscious message that inheres in the New Age version of the cosmos. This is what the pages, and the sages, are suggesting. This is the *hook* in the New Age *use* of modern science.

The Soul

To understand the New Age universe as a detailed, full-fledged projection of the object helps us to fathom the New Age preoccupation with the soul, for the soul in New Age thinking, quite simply and straightforwardly, is also a wish-fulfilling projection of the object. Indeed, we might think of "soul" as the *microcosmic version* of the vibrational, immaterial *macrocosm* which has emerged from New Age physics. In one or two instances, remarkably enough, this microcosmic soul has even been accorded *holographic* qualities. The "soul" of the individual, writes Itzhak Bentov (1988, 95) in *A Cosmic Book*, may be thought of as "consciousness" or "mind," an expression of "the universal mind" which is the cosmos itself, the "great hologram called Creation." Within a "quantum model of consciousness," declares Danah Zohar (1990, 87) in *The Quantum Self*, perceptions are "molecular wave patterns" or "vibrations," the "mathematics" of which are those of a "hologram" and thus of the surrounding universe. If we adhere to Descartes's "interesting" view that perceptions are "excitations of the underlying soul," then we may regard the soul and the hologram as *reflective expressions* of each other.

Let us note carefully here that Gary Zukav, who gives us *The Dancing Wu Li Masters: An Overview of the New Physics* (1979) subsequently gives us *The Seat of The Soul* (1990), a New Age classic on the universal spirit. "How remarkable," writes Huston Smith on the cover of Zukav's later book, "to find that one of our finest interpreters of frontier science is equally conversant with the human spirit. This augurs well for our times." But there is nothing "remarkable" here at all. On the contrary, the business is entirely expectable and logical when we remember that "frontier science" in the hands of a New Age writer like Zukav is science dragged off to a wedding with Eastern mysticism—in other words, science as *soul food*. As to whether or not this "augurs well" for our times (augury? divination from omens?), the reader can decide for himself.

"The soul *is*," declares Zukav (1990, 37), as he commences his maternal projections. "It has no beginning and no end but flows toward wholeness. The personality emerges as a natural force from the soul ... Each personality is unique because the configuration of energy of the soul that formed it is unique" (the ego emerges from the interaction with the object, particularly the vibrational or energetic interaction). "The personality does not operate independently from the soul," Zukav (37) continues in a statement which observes simply that the object is internalized. "To the extent that a person is in touch with spiritual depths, the personality is soothed because the energy of consciousness is focused on its energy core" (it feels good to feel the good object inside). "The personality sometimes appears as a force running rampant in the world," says Zukav (37); "it is the result of the personality being unable to find its reference point, or connection, to its *mothership*, which is the soul" (my emphasis) (the soul as a projection of the mother, *explicitly*). "The conflicts of a human's life are directly proportional to the distance at which an energy of personality exists separately from the soul" (life's troubles boil down to separation from the object). Finally, "When a personality is in full balance, you cannot see where it ends and the soul begins" (37). We have in this a collapse of the subject/object dichotomy toward *fusion*, the vibrational realm of affective attunement, the undifferentiated state. It is *the baby* who does not know where he/she ends and the environment (the mother) begins; it is the baby who does not "operate independently," who is "focused" on his "energy core," who must constantly "connect" to his "mothership." The entire passage at which we have been looking comprises a huge, revelational *slip* in the classic Freudian sense.

Observe how the projections continue in *The Seat of the Soul* (Zukav 1990, 91), this time with the emphasis on the soul and the surrounding cosmos: "The soul is not physical, yet it is the *force field* of your being ... Therefore, it is not possible to understand your soul or your *higher self* or your intuition without coming to terms with the existence of non-physical reality" (my emphasis). "What is non-physical reality?" Zukav then asks. "Non-physical reality is your *home*" (92, my emphasis). It is "the universe in terms of light, frequencies, and energies of different frequencies." This is *not* "metaphorical," Zukav insists (96); "it is a natural and powerful way to think of the universe." Here is the *dynamic cosmos*, the atomic *field* of modern physics, the vibrating, energetic Hologramama all over again in mirrored, macrocosmic opposition to the "non-physical" soul that is the source and the essence of our "being." What appear to be *distinct, differentiated entities*, namely the part and the whole, are in actual fact *united* in a "higher" synthesis (remember, in New Age thinking "higher" always implies symbiotic regression).

Continually in New Age thinking and frequently in New Age physics we discover a consuming interest in the union of opposites. This is a very big topic because it speaks unconsciously for merger, fusion. Writes physicist Fritjof Capra (1983, 114): "The Taoists saw all changes in nature as manifestations of the dynamic interplay between the polar opposites *yin* and *yang*, and thus they came to believe that any pair of opposites constitutes a polar relationship where each of the two poles is dynamically linked to the other." Capra goes on to maintain that "modern scientific theory," and in particular "quantum theory," has "confirmed" these "profound insights" (114). The waves of the ocean appear to be separate and opposite, declares Marilyn Ferguson (1980, 381), some of them crashing to the shore, some of them pulling back out. However, such separation and opposition is an "illusion," for there is only "one ocean." Similarly, the separate and opposite items in the universe are ultimately joined to the "great Self," to the "Thou art That." (380). It is precisely "this wholeness," Ferguson concludes (381), that "unites opposites." One side of a circle is called *yin* and the other side is called *yang*, states Zukav (1979, 158) in *The Dancing Wu Li Masters*: "Where there is yin there is yang. Where there is high, there also is low. Where there is day, there also is night, where there is death, there also is birth." All of this, Zukav claims, is just "another way of saying that the physical universe is a whole which seeks balance within itself." The "opposites" of the "universe" certainly do exist, maintains Hitchcock (1991); yet they emanate from the dynamic "Center" (113), which extends the potential for integrated union. Ultimately, these "opposites," including "the opposites in physics," may be regarded as "the web of the physical cosmos" (130). The point is, the "soul" in New Age thinking is a projective, self-indulgent celebration of an *already completed fusion* of "opposites," namely the neonate and the internalized caregiver who is the *origin* of the subject/object dichotomy. Finding the "soul" is simply *focusing upon the object in the self* and *being there with it*, in the self. Hence Zukav asserts in *the Seat of the Soul* (1990, 87): "Communication between the personality and its soul is an in-house intuitive process ... Your personality and your higher self are of your soul." Again, "The personality is never separate from its soul, and the soul and its personalities are continually assisted and guided with impersonal compassion and wisdom" (89). The "personality" seeks to "align itself with its soul" (that is, to recover affective attunement), to "become the physical embodiment of its higher self" (that is, to feel itself fused with the object) (90). For Zukav, then, "nonphysical reality," which is Bohm's "implicate order," our "home," and our "soul," also signifies *the original Eden*, the pre-lapsarian realm in which we all experienced perfect communion: "The distance between you and your understanding of the creation of matter from energy is equal to the distance that exists between the awareness of your personality and the energy of your soul ... Are you not metaphorically within a Garden of Eden? ... Will you create Paradise [that is, live in fusion with the object] or be Cast Out" (that is, persist in psychic separation)? Note how closely Zukav ties his paradisal musings to the themes of evolution and transformation, for as always in New Age thinking it is the transformational object that lurks unconsciously behind the spiritual agenda: "Eventually you will come to authentic empowerment ... You will evolve beyond the human experience, beyond the learning

environment of space, time, and matter. You cannot not evolve. Everything in the universe evolves. It is only a question of which way you
will choose to learn as you evolve" (159). And then, "When you return
home, when you leave your personality and body behind, you will
leave behind your inadequacies, your fears angers and jealousies ... You
will perceive with loving eyes ... [and] choose to allow your soul to
move through you ... This is the work of evolution ... the work that
you were born to do" (159–60, my emphasis). Finally: "We are destined
to evolve beyond the nature of duality," to "journey home" to our
"non-physical plane," to discover "the perfection of all that is" (181).
In other words, we are magically fated to recapture the fullness of symbiotic merger. Thus "frontier science" in Zukav and in New Age thinking as a whole actually leads, through the "soul," to the dual-unity, the
mirroring, the attunement of life's early, internalized stages during the
course of which the immortal object reigned. How cunningly New Age
thinking uses both the scientific world and the religious world to
achieve projectively its unconscious aims.

I mean, the idea of a vibrational universe is currently gaining acceptance among physical scientists; the idea, in fact, may soon be attaining lofty, paradigmatic status. In a recent issue of *The Sciences*,
Haisch, Rueda, and Puthoff (1994) offer us "a first glimpse of a postmodern physics in which mass, inertia and gravity arise from underlying electromagnetic processes" (26). "Indeed," these physicists go on,
"if that view is correct, there is no such thing as mass—only electric
charge and energy, which together create the illusion of mass. The
physical universe is made up of massless electric charges immersed in
a vast, energetic, all-pervasive electromagnetic field" (26). Yet Haisch,
Rueda, and Puthoff do not proceed to discover a spiritual significance
in this. They do not project psychological objects, or make theological
claims; they do not bring up "soul," or "Thou art That," or the divine
"web of the cosmos." There is simply the all-pervasive electromagnetic field; that's it; that's the *factual possibility*, which they *present*.
New Agers, by contrast, extrapolate such "data" toward the supernatural realm; they spy analogies at the conscious level because the unconscious *wish* creates in them a *keen eye* for projective potentialities,
for "spiritual" meanings that gratify the *regressive aim*. As we have
seen, this aim is generally *symbiotic* in nature; it seeks to end the *gap*
of separation, of differentiation, and it frequently harbours the omnipotence and narcissistic inflation that may accompany symbiosis. The
New Age, one may observe with impunity, will not take No for an answer here. It knows perfectly well that the theories of David Bohm
have been rejected by the vast majority of Bohm's peers. "Most physicists are sceptical of Bohm's ideas," writes Michael Talbot (1991, 53) in

The Holographic Universe. And it probably knows perfectly well by now that Zukav and Capra are not taken seriously by experts in the field. Declares prize-winning physicist Leon Lederman (1993, 190–91) in *The God Particle*: "Fritjof Capra and Gary Zukav in *The Tao of Physics* and *The Dancing Wu Li Masters* ... jump from solid, proven concepts in science to concepts that are outside of physics and to which the logical bridge is extremely shaky or non-existent." In fact, Lederman continues (191), Zukav's central theses are "way off the mark," and Capra, who "starts with reasonable descriptions of quantum physics," proceeds to "construct elaborate extensions, totally bereft of the understanding of how carefully experiment and theory are woven together and how much blood, sweat, and tears go into each painful advance." The "cosmic hypothesis" of New Age physics is very like the Gaia hypothesis of New Age Witchcraft: discredited by the scientific community and given credence only by the scientifically innocent.[3] New Age physics is mostly *wishful thinking*, and I use that expression with its full psychoanalytic connotation in mind.

The maternal significance of the soul in New Age thought does not emerge only from the writings of Zukav and his fellow cosmologists, of course. Here are some revealing projections from another New Age classic on the subject, *Facing the World with Soul*, by another New Age guru of the spirit, Robert Sardello (1992, 18–19). Following the Greek tradition of referring to the soul as Sophia, Sardello declares, "She was present at the origin of the world"; she is the "archetypal figure of all sectors of existence"; we could "travel the world seeking her manifestations and she would never be exhausted, such is the extent of her depth" (18–19). She is "Isis, the rainbow, beauty, form, creation, everything in the world" (25). As Paracelsus held in ancient times, Sardello goes on, Sophia is both "the great mystery" and "the mother of all" (19). As for "intellectual thought and abstraction," it is the "source of the world's malaise" (28). Accordingly, to find Sophia, to find the soul, is the best method of *ending* that "malaise." When we immerse ourselves in the "magic of soul" we see the "connection of everything to everything else," and in this vision we are "transformed" (75). Just as in Zukav, then, the soul in Sardello gets associated with the maternal object in *several* key ways: the soul is origin, environment, form, mystery, and, last but not least, transformation.

It is perhaps the maternal meaning of the soul in the unconscious that explains the pathetic quality of Thomas Moore's answer to the direct, blunt question, what *is* the soul? Moore, a former Catholic monk and the author of the immensely popular New Age volume *The Care of the Soul*, is asked this question by interviewer Michael Bertrand (1993, 4) for the review *Branches of Light*. Moore replies: "The soul is a dimension, a level of experience. There's a level of spirit or mind and a level of body or material world. Now what holds these together and makes them valuable and makes sense is the soul in the middle." The interviewer, wisely, drops this line of questioning. Surely Moore's inadequate, almost laughable answer to the inquiry, the sort of thing we'd expect from a college freshman—"in the middle" indeed!—may well be rooted in the soul's tight, unconscious connection to the object, the maternal internalization of life's first years. Moore can't see this, of course, because, like most New Agers, he refuses to look. He wants the pleasure and security of regressive merger, not analysis, not the "malaise" of the intellect. The "soul" is a hugely popular subject in New Age literature because people enjoy re-immersing themselves in the oceanic, vibrational caregiver of the early period. Like the Great Holo-gramama, the shamanic animal, the channelled guide, the crystal, the healer, and the Goddess, the soul becomes for New Agers but another in a series of *evoked psychic companions* with whom one may savour on the inside the old mirroring, the old attunement, the old dual-unity of before-separation existence. Reading about the soul, thinking about the soul, is simply cuddling up to the good object within, sensing the hum of the loving caretaker, one internalized deeply in one's infantile past. To be separate, to be differentiated, to be on one's own, is not an easy thing for many, many individuals, and it certainly is not an easy thing for those attracted to New Age ideas and practices. While the cult of the soul offers New Agers some protection from the storm, the price they pay for that protection, as always in New Age thinking, is extremely high: one's reason betrayed; one's emotional maturity forestalled; one's potential for honest, courageous confrontation with the realities of life unactualized. It is a sorry business.

Postmodernism, Psychoanalysis, and New Age Thinking

Toward the inception of this book I raised the issue of postmodernism's causal relationship to New Age thinking. To what extent has the postmodern world engendered New Age practices and beliefs? "In the face of poverty, crime, disease, pollution, bureaucracy, taxes, deficit spending, technology, terrorism, and whatever else composes the crisis of post-modernity," writes Wendy Kaminer (1992, 158), using the term *post-modernity* in a rather loose, all-encompassing sense, "people are likely to seek refuge in the dawn of a New Age." We may insert in Kaminer's hospitable "whatever else composes the crisis of post-modernity" such items as postmodernism's insistence that "the truth" is always loaded with some person's or group's will-to-power, its accusation that postmodern democracies are designed chiefly to further the goals of powerful interest groups and to suppress the ambitions of those who cling to the ladder's lower rungs, and its refusal to accord rationality a major role in human affairs: for postmodernism as a philosophical outlook, passion spins the human plot; the reasonable, enlightened self is mostly self-flattering illusion, and that includes not only the enlightened self of the individual psychoanalyst but the reasonable institution of psychoanalysis as a whole.

Doubtless this perspective has a measure of validity. We require desperately today a cultural environment that *holds* the individual with compassion, that *facilitates* his growth toward autonomy and self-expression, that *counteracts* the stress, stagnation, isolation, and frustration which are central to our current experience. As Thomas Ferraro (1994, 29) expresses the matter, we must work toward an environment that encourages people of both sexes and all ages to relinquish their "omnipotent, counterdependent attitude toward the social," to put aside their "entrapping aloneness and defensive, autistic addictions." This implies a "loss of control and power," states Ferraro (29), but it also implies a "gain in connection and intimacy." As for *psychoanalysis*, it must stop treating the social milieu in North America, Europe, and elsewhere as a kind of *neutral given*; indeed, it must *include* the problem of the social milieu *directly* in its therapeutic strategies. "The actual adult social environment in America," observes David H. Jacobs (1992, 544), "is far too well known and far too oppressive and deficient for the majority of adults, for psychoanalytic formulations to regard it as a benign, theoretical convenience." Jacobs continues: "Psychoanalytic thought on the topic of adulthood in general faces a clear choice. It can essentially ignore prevailing social conditions, and thereby remain a strictly clinical literature, or it can assimilate the empirical findings of the social sciences, which would require a new emphasis on defence against external stress" (545). Either "advanced social disintegration" finds a place in psychoanalytic thinking or psychoanalysis loses considerable efficacy as an ameliorative instrument. The defensive beliefs and behaviours of people—and that includes of course the beliefs and behaviours of people involved in New Age thinking—are bound up inextricably with the cold, hard, social realities in which people discover themselves.

At the same time, and in spite of all this, it would be a basic, dreadful error to regard New Age thinking as a spinoff of what Kaminer terms *post-modernity*. The aims, the wishes, and the underlying anxieties that comprise what we have chosen to call New Age thinking have been with us as a species for a long, long time—one might say forever. While the current social milieu gives these aims and anxieties a certain distinctive accent and perhaps a certain distinctive urgency it no more creates them, it no more breeds them, than chocolate cream pie breeds the compulsive eater. New Age thinking defensively addresses wishes and fears that are timeless, ubiquitous, ever-present and ever-pressing; they are an integral aspect of human experience because they are rooted in basic facets of human bodily and emotional life: separation, limitation, loss, and mortality (which in the unconscious is a form of separation). Writing beautifully in a section titled "The Awareness of Separation, Loss, and Death," Howard Stein (1985, 301) observes: "Initially, the mother's body, the social topography of kin and neighbors, the animate and inanimate physical environment, are not experienced as distinct objects in the world with a life and needs of their own; they *are* the world. They are one's earliest psychogeography. One experiences them as though they were an intrinsic, even if distal, part of the self; just as limbs are extensions of intentionality, these yet indistinct objects are extensions of boundary and need." Stein goes on (302), "Sometimes insidiously, sometimes abruptly hastened by walking and talking, one dimly begins to perceive that the world is distinct from the self. Long before one is cast out of preoedipal Eden by the demands of the Oedipal father for exclusive possession of mother's sexuality, one suffers the blessing and curse of self-awareness. One becomes self-exiled. The world is forever after beyond the self: equated with the tragic hammerblows of separation, loss, and death." And then (302), "Over the course of human history universally, one enterprise that has occupied much time and energy has been the denial, reversal, and undoing of this catastrophic realization." Through religion, through ritual, through a wide and endless variety of beliefs and behaviours, people employ culture to change reality into fantasy: the dead are not really dead; there is no final separation; we can have what we wish; our apparent limitations can be "transcended." Yet, as Stein (302) points out, "even the alleged unity, cohesiveness, and continuity of culture are themselves a cherished illusion—or perhaps ... delusion, for it is a false belief toward which one acts as though it must be true. Mutable reality intrudes upon immutable wish for merger with one's culture. Boundaries can be violated, and as a result once again one is thrust upon renewed awareness of one's distinctness. Losses of symbols of self and group are heir to losses of early loved ones by separation and death: they reignite separation anxiety and give the lie to cherished illusions of immortality." Now, this is where *cult* comes in, including all the cultic aspects of New Age thought, from Witchcraft, to channelling, to shamanism, to crystal, to soul, to Hologramama, for it is *cult* that is designed to rejuvenate failed culture, to restore the symbiotic fantasy that culture has somehow let slide, to lessen the sting of separation, to create a transitional space (Winnicott) in which the anxious, wounded, deprived individual may take delicious refuge. In this way, we may regard culture in all its holding capacities, including cult, as a kind of "continuous therapy" for the "panhuman drama" of "separation and loss" (Stein 1985, 303). *Growing-up* psychologically and emotionally, then, implies *growing-out* of the yearning for and the indulgence in such "therapy," such *magic* of symbol and ritual. As Stein (304) expresses it, "Cultural symbolism and ritualization only forever postpone the solution; indeed, they incapacitate men by serving as cozening bromides that narcotize them away from reality." Odd and scary as it may sound to many, facing separation and loss as separation and loss is the only honest, mature way to cope with separation and loss.

Maxine Sheets-Johnstone (1990, 240, 242) points out in her volume *The Roots of Thinking* that "*in* is the first locative state and act to be linguistically understood ... with priority over *on* and *under* ... In the literature on linguistic development in children the primary acquisition of *in* is explained in terms of learning the rule that 'if (*x* is a container, put *y* inside it.' The rule is identified as a 'non-linguistic strategy.' Where the strategy comes from is a question never asked and thus nowhere investigated. Yet surely the 'strategy' or 'rule' is motivated: by knowledge gained from bodily experience, not just in the sense of *doing*, but in the sense of *being a body*. The cognitive rule from this perspective is in fact a rational extension from corporeal experience. Putting one thing inside another is how an infant has lived his active life from the beginning." Thus "insides are, or can appear to be, magical, not in the sense of sorcery ... but in the sense of being something beyond one's immediate ken and powers of understanding. It is just this character of insides that Leonardo da Vinci evoked when he anticipated the possibility of 'something *wonderful*' inside 'the great cavern' before him. It is just this character that both casts further light on paleolithic fascination with caves and suggests why paleolithic hominids would have been motivated to paint on their walls. What would otherwise be part of the typical everyday world with its familiar flora and fauna is transformed simply by being *inside*. The form and power of things inside is precisely *extra*ordinary—whatever is there appears magical, awesome, dumbfounding. To engrave or paint on the inside surfaces of a cave is precisely to enter actively into the potential magic of insides." Because being *in*—in life, in arms, in family, in relationship, in culture—has always been *in*, in favour, and because being *out*—alone, separated, rejected, alienated, divorced, dead—has always been *out*, out of favour, New Age thinking with its wholesale absorption in merger and symbiosis, appeals to very large numbers of people who are acutely aware of the *outs* that surround them in a postmodern society which seems to be breaking down, and in a scientific universe which no longer puts humans at the centre. Still, when Hitchcock

(1991) in *The Web of the Cosmos* insists that "modern physics," in spite of its awareness of "illusoriness at different levels of physical being," permits us to believe that "*something is there*" (55), and when he declares, further, that we need not "fall off the precipice" of "modern, rationalistic" doubt (75), he discloses "inside" needs that derive from the very ground of human existence, from the timeless awareness of separation and loss, and not simply from the strains of "post-modernity." So it is with Spretnak's (1991, 25) assertion that "we are not apart from the dynamic cosmos," an assertion which translates psychoanalytically into the basic bodily and emotional desire to be *in*, in relation, in family, in culture, *in the universe as a projective extension of one's inner life*, one's existence on the inside, including of course the caregiving objects one *internalized* during the course of one's psychosexual development. Something is there! We are not apart! This is the old, magical cry, the old, magical wish, of humankind, and it springs *directly* from the most tenacious and powerful of humankind's many anxieties, *separation*.

Regression in the Service of Regression and Transformation in the Service of Magic

Much of what psychoanalysis has to tell us about the course of our development as humans applies dramatically to the subject of our inquiry, New Age thinking. Psychoanalysis tells us, for example, that the "mental construction of reality" always involves "the interpenetration" of the person's "internal world" and "the environment" (Seinfeld 1990, 25). Everyone projectively shapes, and is shaped by, the reality in which he discovers himself. Thus we may regard New Age thinking, wholly, globally, as a particular instance of *interpenetration*, with New Agers projecting into the world their individual and group agendas. Psychoanalysis also tells us that our developmental existence consists fundamentally of "two antagonistic needs" (Solan 1991, 339); one, "for a complete reunion with the external object so as to eliminate the sense of the not-I," and the other "for being separate so as to safeguard one's own self." As we grow, as we mature, we are "challenged" to maintain "a subtle balance of merging-separation"; indeed, "all vital human communication represents both the separateness of the two individuals and their joining" (Solan, 340). To successfully negotiate this "challenge" is to erect the very scaffolding of our characters as reliable, responsible people interacting in the world. We might think of this "subtle balance" of "merging-separation" as a "dialectical model of attachment and separateness in the development of self-identity"

(Blass and Blatt 1992, 190). The "attachment line considers the quality of the individual's relationships—the capacity to form stable relationships and the ability to integrate these into a sense of self in relation to another person. The separateness line considers the development of the individual as a self-contained and independent unit. Individuation, differentiation, and autonomy are developmental achievements that lead to a stable sense of self as separate with a clear sense of goals and values. The relationship between these two developmental lines is intimate and complex, with the individual's overall self-identity emerging as a product of an ongoing dialectic between the self as separate and the self as experienced in its attachment to objects" (Blass and Blatt, 190). In all of this, we probably never completely outgrow our deep and largely unconscious wish for the "unitary state; it remains lurking in the background and provides a continuing matrix for later experience" (Berger 1993, 7). Accordingly, most people suffer to one degree or another from what Fred Pine (1992, 251) calls "developmental pathology and conflict"—that is, from an imperfect negotiation of the attachment-separation line, the urge to go *toward* the object regressively through substitutes and *away* from the object progressively through the gaining of a stable, fully differentiated self. About the best we can expect here—and it is actually a great deal—may be characterized as a person's gradual acceptance of his world as *there*, alterable perhaps, modifiable perhaps, but there. "In the course of development," writes Meissner (1992, 177), "the child's illusion of magical omnipotence and control over the transitional object gradually gives way to increasing degrees of disillusionment and optimal frustration, leading gradually toward accommodation to reality." When the struggle to negotiate the attachment-separation line becomes too much for us, when our urge to merge is frustrated, or our striving for autonomy goes unfulfilled, we may choose a wide variety of psycho-physical paths, from suicide, to substance abuse, to religion, to cult, to psychoanalysis. If we choose psychoanalysis, if that becomes our avenue of "transformation," the "guiding assumption," according to Carlo Strenger (1991, 205), is perfectly clear: "Increased self-understanding constitutes the main factor which enables and propels therapeutic progress and change. Once the patient becomes fully aware of the aspects of his mental life previously inaccessible to him, psychoanalysis assumes he can take more responsibility over himself and change. Psychoanalysis is *the* paradigm of a nondirective psychotherapy; the patient's insight is supposed to make it possible for him to use *his own resources* to abandon self-defeating strategies, infantile wishes, needs for omnipotent reparation, and whatever else he has come to know about himself in the course of his analysis ... This perspective on man as potentially mature and autonomous was voiced explicitly in several places, most strongly in Freud's passionate plea *The Future of an Illusion* (1927). There Freud defends the possibility of man to rid himself of illusions dictated by the regressive tendencies of wishful thinking. He is not overly optimistic about the ease with which this possibility can be realized, but he is intransigent in his insistence on man's duty to strive for maturity." While we may never entirely lose our psychological appetite for "illusion" and "cultural space" in Winnicott's sense of those terms, we can choose goals and beliefs which are more mature than misleading, more realistic than fantastic, more productive of genuine selfhood than defensive persona.

How does New Age thinking fit into this picture? Surely by now the reader knows perfectly well my view of the matter. I haven't been pussyfooting around for the last five chapters. I've been writing psychoanalytic critique. I've been making my position plain and explicit. All I plan to do here, in the brief psychoanalytic context that I've just set out and that comprises a capsule version of chapter 2, is state my position for a final time. New Age thinking, through crystals, through shamanism, through channelling, through Witchcraft, through psychic healing, and through the creation of the Hologramama, discloses unmistakably from the psychoanalytic angle an absorption in *magical omnipotence,* a devotion to the *merger* side of the separation-merger dialectic, an attempt to regain the narcissistic inflation, the attunement, and the mirroring that characterize life's early stages. New Age thinking would *restore the past* in an idealized form. Waging war on reality, it employs a variety of magical practices *to make the factual world go away,* and it then *replaces* that world with one which better suits its unconscious, regressive agenda. New Agers do not want the *responsibility* of their existence; they want to *share* that responsibility, as the small child does, with an omnipotent, projective entity discovered in the crystal, in the shamanic power-animal, in the guardian angel (or guide), in the Goddess, in the numinous healer, and in the evolving, transformational universe, their original *parent.* We do not have here the abandonment of infantile wishes; we have infantile wishes *gone wild;* we have infantile wishes *on the loose.* And that is, of course, why sophisticated philosophical logic is lacking entirely in New Age literature, why *anything goes* in the way of validating New Age epistemology: each person's subjective experience is both true and final—in other words, not to be questioned; if something "works" for an individual, don't bother to subject it to analysis; reality is a private affair, and that is that. To let rigorous reasoning in here would destroy the magical agenda, disclose the tautologous subjectivity, the wish-fulfilment passing as valid perception. Where there is *regression* in New Age thinking, then, it is *not* regression in the service of the ego, or the self; it is *not* regression as psychoanalysis, including the psychoanalysis of Jung, conceives of regression: the return to an earlier stage of psychosexual development for the purpose of seeing it, analyzing it, abreacting it, and finally *letting it go* so that one may be better able to perceive and to negotiate the hard realities, including separation and loss, in the midst of which one discovers himself. One does not in New Age thinking enter the crystal array, or slide down the shamanic tunnel, or contact the guardian angel, or sit in transmission meditation, or cast the Wiccan circle, or receive the Energetic Embrace to attain self-understanding and autonomy; on the contrary, one turns to these activities and states regressively *to find the object again*, the evoked companion again, affective attunement again, omnipotence, fusion, and primary narcissism again; one regresses to *erase* the reality of separation and loss, to discover *another reality* in which symbiosis and unlimited power become one's magical estate. This is not "mature" in the sense Carlo Strenger suggests when he refers to Freud's *Future of an Illusion*; it is, rather, *misleading*, a wholesale distortion of the facts and a wholesale infantilizing of the person who opts to indulge. New Age thinking is ultimately a *symptom* of what we might term *unfinished developmental business*.

The foregoing paragraph helps us to understand the persistent utopian strain in New Age thought, the strain that wishes to see the planet Earth become the garden of love and that believes such a "transformation" is about to occur. "Universal love is possible," writes Spretnak (1991, 177); the "particle world" discloses the reality of universal "harmony and perfection," declares Capra (1983, 257); we are all about to experience "the homecoming" to the Age of Aquarius "so long envisioned," states Ferguson (1980, 416). According to a Vancouver newspaper, "The countdown is on. Yesterday we were 2000 days from the year 2000. And if the Visioneers get their way, peace and love will suffuse the planet long before then. The Visioneers International Network [based on Desmond Berghofer's New Age novel, *The Visioneers*] has declared July 10 Day 2000. By January 1, 2000, the Visioneers say in group literature they 'intend to see innumerable relationships among people in every corner of the planet massively transformed in the direction of positive love and co-operation'" (*The Province*, July 11, 1994, A2). One could easily discover, of course, a thousand other such utopian gleams in and around New Age thinking. The point is, we have here a striking instance of what Ely Garfinkle (1994, 19) calls in his psychoanalytic paper *Quid Pro Quo: The Positive Talion* "the incomplete mourning of love freely given and freely received in the infant's interaction with the parent." Unable to relinquish such love in the unconscious, the New Ager would have it back again in the form of planetary transformation. As the parent's love was once the whole environment, so now the whole environment will become the parent's love. In a very real way, New Age thinking as a whole is an instance of such "incomplete mourning." Stung by the loss of the before-separation-world, it yearns for its retrieval and works through magical beliefs and behaviours to get it back. How tenaciously we cling to the past; how ceaselessly we mourn the disappearance of the Eden we knew in the caregiver's arms. However, from the psychoanalytic standpoint and with our eye unwaveringly on the splendid condition of autonomy, maturity, genuine selfhood, we realize that the only item to be mourned here is the regressive, gullible New Ager himself, the one who has missed, at least for the present, his chance to grow up and inherit his birthright of adulthood.

"Imagine America without self-help books," writes Wendy Kaminer (1992, 165), "imagine everyone grappling with their problems and forging their identities, using their own intuitions and powers of analysis and maybe some help from their friends. Imagine that. I can't. I have no cure for America's self-help habit and no advice to offer on how to find one ... I have no expectations that the 'problem' of self-help will ever be solved. Instead, I expect more self-help books, not less." What is the explanation for this cultural phenomenon? How are we to understand it? Observes Kaminer (164), "Merely buying a self-help book is an act of dependence, a refusal to confront the complexities of a solitary creative act and to endure the loneliness and failures that are the price of its surprises." I would agree. And I would offer an additional explanation rooted in both the context of this volume as a whole and in the easily demonstrable assumption that many of these self-help books are of the explicitly New Age variety: such books hold out to the reader the promise of a virtually instantaneous "transformation," the promise of a virtually instantaneous "change" that will either turn one's entire life around in some remarkable way or at least fix immediately some troubling issue that is detracting from the sweetness of one's presence on the planet. As we have seen, the idea of transformation is ubiquitous in New Age literature. According to the *covers* of many New Age books, in fact, all one has to do in order to undergo a transformational experience is simply *read* the text one has happened to pick up in the bookshop. "Just the act of reading this book will create an immediate and spontaneous transformation" in one's life, declares the back cover of Cunningham's (1992) Wiccan text *The Magic in Food*. "Within these pages you will learn exactly how to effect change in yourself," trumpets the jacket of Kaplan-Williams's (1987) *Changing Your Life: A New Psychology for Turning Your Life Around*. "Perhaps the most important book yet written on the process of inner transformation," heralds the cover of Kornfield's (1993) *A Path With Heart*; "reading this book will remind you of the promises inherent in the life of the spirit." Proclaims the cover of Curtis's (1993) *Helping Heaven Happen*: "If you want to change your life you have to change your thoughts. The author of *Your Thoughts Can Change Your Life* [a previous work] teaches us how to use our minds to change our lives for the better." Moss's (1991) *The I That Is We* is "for those who are struggling with their own transformative process," asserts its cover. "No one reading this book will be left unchanged." Jacquelyn Small's (1994) *Embodying Spirit* "carries us to the very threshold of transformation—and then leads us through." I won't go on. Anyone who has spent an hour or two looking over New Age texts knows exactly what I am illustrating here. The point is, New Age books of the self-help variety are addictively pursued by readers not for "dependence" in some wide-open, general sense, as Kaminer suggests; they are addictively pursued because *they hold out the promise of reunion with the transformational object of infancy and early childhood*. That is the "dependency" they work on. They say to the reader's unconscious, both as he browses and handles the volume and as he sits down with it at home, the transformational object of the early period is just around the corner; you are on the verge of regaining the apparition-like caretaker whose loving ministrations continually transformed your discomfort into pleasure, or relief; you are about to discover your Eden of transformation once again. In this way, New Age volumes of the self-help variety *hook* the dependent reader by dangling the transformational object in front of him, by allowing him to recoup in a mild, diffuse way the transformational miracle that enveloped him early on each time the ministering object changed the quality of his experience from negative or neutral to positive or blissful.

The "transformation" that is pushed by New Age texts and publishers, then, the "transformation" that attracts New Age readers as honey attracts flies, is *not* the kind of transformation that psychoanalysis has potentially in store when it offers the possibility of change to the client, and that includes of course the kind of transformation we discover in Jung. Change in psychoanalysis, including Jung, comes gradually, cumulatively, painstakingly, often agonizingly, and usually modestly as the patient courageously works through the problems of his present life, problems which are rooted in the struggles of his past. Indeed, change in psychoanalysis, including Jung, means largely the *recognition* and the *acceptance* of one's psychological imperfections; it means moving more relaxedly and more confidently in the emotional or affective reality that one's interpersonal past has created, and therefore it means also mastering and/or avoiding the interpersonal and intrapsychic pitfalls into which one habitually tumbled before one's courageous analysis began. Such change, such transformation, has *nothing to do* with what we might characterize as transformation New Age-style; it has *nothing to do* with reading self-help books that promise the psychological or "spiritual" quick fix; it has *nothing to do* with the book jackets adorning like magical objects the shelves of the New Age bookstores.

The question arises, if genuine psychological change cannot be garnered in the facile manner suggested in the New Age literature, will not the market for such stuff and nonsense shrink through disillusionment on the reader's part? The answer is, of course not; for the promise of "transformation" is immortal, it never dies; the unconscious memory of the transformational object never fades; the unconscious wish for miraculous "change" never ceases its clamouring, be it mild or intense. If *this* book didn't do the job, why surely the next one will, and in the process, let us remember, the reader receives the deep, unconscious pleasure of *feeling* the transformational object stirring within him again. Indeed, as I've been suggesting, the reader turns to the book in the first place *both* because he believes, in his conscious gullibility, that it will "transform" him and *also* because he believes, in his wishful unconscious, that it will bring him closer to the transformational object than he would otherwise be. He picks the book up *both* for the information it putatively contains and for the transformational *hit* he receives *as he reads*. The latter reward is always a sure thing. Just as the New Ager enjoys reading of "soul" or "guardian angel" because it allows him to cuddle up with the good object again, just as he enjoys reading of "power animal" or "Goddess" because it allows him to sense the presence of the omnipotent object once more, so he enjoys reading of "change" because it affords him the psychological luxury of returning to the transformational side of his infancy and early childhood.

Two Final Points

Let us say for the sake of argument that the universe *is* some sort of giant hologram; let us say that every particle, or wave, *is* related in some vibratory fashion to every other particle or wave; let us say that all things *are* "interconnected," that everything *is* "woven" together at the dynamic level of the cosmic "web." The question arises immediately from the psychoanalytic standpoint, *so what?* Are these assumptive physical factors supposed to cancel out, or diminish, or modify, even for one moment, the emotional, psychic realities of our developmental lives? Do New Agers actually believe that appreciation of such "cosmic" properties, such "dancing wu li" physical features, will alter, even for one moment, the tenor of our unconscious minds as those minds have been shaped in and through the internalizations of the past? Such assumptive, speculative factors, even if we believe them wholeheartedly, are but straws in the psychic wind of our actual, character-producing experience. Gary Zukav (1979, 250–51) writes: "The idea that objects exist apart from events is part of the epistemological net with which we snare our particular form of experience ... It profoundly influences how we see ourselves. It is the root of our inescapable sense of separateness from others and environment." Not only is this wrong, it is incredibly naïve; it appears to come from an individual who has no idea of what it means to be a person in the world. The sense of our separateness from others and environment comes from *the real separation* we confronted and coped with during the early period, and after. The sense of our separateness comes from *the real separation* we all had to go through as we moved toward differentiation and autonomy, both of which are *grounded* in separation. The unconscious does not hear the theories of Zukav and Capra, of Pribram and Bohm; the unconscious is not influenced or swayed by sophisticated theoretical ideas about the universe. The unconscious is clamouring for its needs to be met, as those needs are forged in the developmental, and often dysfunctional, past. One can talk about the tao of physics or the holographic universe until one is blue in the face and it will not have any effect on the urgency of one's unconscious requirements. Physics will never satisfy psychology. The way to deal with one's sense of separateness is, first of all, to acknowledge its permanent nature, its primary, integral role in catalyzing the formation of autonomous selfhood—in a word, its inevitability as part of the human picture. Once this has been done, an individual can begin to face up to his particular conflicts over and around the theme of separation; he can begin to analyze honestly and unflinchingly his own separation "hang-ups"—his denials, projections, aggressions, mergers, withdrawals, including of course his tendency to indulge in magical practices and beliefs, the kind we associate, now, with New Age thinking. When this has been accomplished, when one's hungers and defences have been thoroughly examined, one may begin to interact with "others and environment" in a manner that satisfies the natural human appetite for togetherness without sacrificing the autonomy, the maturity, one has gained through one's laudable commitment to growth.

Everywhere in New Age thinking we come upon the theme of "evolution," largely as it has been inspired by and inherited from the writings of Teilhard de Chardin. Humankind is heading toward Omega;

we are evolving in the direction of "higher consciousness," spirituality, understanding, love; we cannot escape this universal, evolutionary process; it comprises an integral aspect of the "cosmic web" in which we find ourselves embedded. If I may be permitted to use the word *evolution* in the loose, informal way in which it is used in such utterances, and if I may be permitted to remind the reader that *higher* in New Age thinking always means *lower*—that is to say, always implies the regressive impulse toward primary merger, or symbiosis—I would suggest the following: the evolutional development humankind desperately requires at this stage of its history is the evolution *beyond* the infantile omnipotence, the narcissistic inflation, the backward-looking fusion—in short, the magical thinking that characterizes the New Age as a whole. This would be an evolution toward direct, honest, unmediated contact with the world as it is and not as we would wish it to be; evolution toward the use of symbols primarily for communicational, informational, and aesthetic purposes; evolution toward acknowledging both our limitations as finite, mortal creatures and the ultimate mysteriousness, the ultimate inexplicableness of the universe that surrounds us; evolution toward spying illusion in *all illusion*, even the kind psychoanalysis, through Winnicott, considers beneficial for the purposes of day-to-day living.[4] For after all, once we *see and know* the emotional purpose illusion serves, we can no longer come to it disingenuously, as believers. The game is up. We either go forward to face the unknown stripped of illusion and armed only with our clear perception, or we go backwards into the realm of magical behaviour and belief. Throughout its pages, this book has been inviting the reader to go forward.

Notes

1. The comment from *USA Today* is reprinted on the cover of Ferguson's book.

2. See the Bantam paperback edition of Zukav's book for both comments. *Parabola*, a magazine in its nineteenth year of publication, originates in New York City. It features articles on myth, shamanism, Buddhism, soul, spirituality, Jung, and so forth. It calls itself a "magazine of myth and tradition."

3. See note 3 in notes to chapter 3.

4. I discuss this aspect of Winnicott's thought in the section of chapter 2 titled *The Tie to the Culture*.

References

BENTOV, I. 1988. *A Cosmic Book*. Rochester, Vt.: Destiny Books.

BERGER, L. 1993. "Psychoanalytic Neonate Models and Noncartesian Frameworks." Southwest Research Institute, San Antonio, Texas.

BERTRAND, M. 1993. "Soul Food." *Branches of Light*, 2: 4–8 [Interview with Thomas Moore].

BLACKSTONE, J. 1991. *The Subtle Self*. Berkeley, Ca.: North Atlantic Books.

BLASS, R., and S. BLATT. 1992. "Attachment and Separateness." *The Psychoanalytic Study of the Child*, 47: 189–203.

CAPRA, F. 1983. *The Tao of Physics*. Boston: Shambhala.

CASTI, J. 1989. *Paradigms Lost*. New York: Avon.

CUNNINGHAM, S. 1992. *Magic in Food*. St. Paul, Minn.: Llewellyn.

CURTIS, D. 1993. *Helping Heaven Happen*. New York: Weiser.

DOSSEY, L. 1982. *Space, Time, and Medicine*. Boston: Shambhala.

FERGUSON, M. 1980. *The Aquarian Conspiracy*. Los Angeles: Tarcher.

FERRARO, T. 1994. "Psychoanalytic Knowledge and Cultural Development." Presented to the American Psychological Association, Washington, D.C., April, pp. 1–27.

FRASER, S. 1992. *The Book of Strange*. New York: Doubleday.

GARFINKLE, E. 1994. "Quid Pro Quo: The Positive Talion." Presented to the Vancouver Psychoanalytic Association, March, pp. 2–26.

GROF, S. 1991. *The Holotropic Mind*. New York: HarperCollins.

HAISCH, B., A. RUEDA, and H. PUTHOFF. 1994. "Beyond E=MC^2: A First Glimpse of a Universe without Mass." *The Sciences*, Nov.–Dec., pp. 26–32.

HITCHCOCK, J. 1991. *The Web of the Universe*. Mahwah, N.J.: Paulist Press.

JACOBS, D. 1992. "A Critical Review of Psychoanalytic Adult Developmental Psychology." *Psychoanalysis and Contemporary Thought*, 15: 523–47.

KAMINER, W. 1992. *I'm Dysfunctional, You're Dysfunctional*. New York: Vintage.

KAPLAN-WILLIAMS, S. 1987. *Changing Your Life: A New Psychology for Turning Your Life Around*. Berkeley, Ca.: Journey Press.

KORNFIELD, J. 1993. *A Path with Heart*. New York: Bantam.

LEDERMAN, L. 1993. *The God Particle*. Boston: Houghton Mifflin.

MAHLER, M., F. PINE, and A. BERGMAN. *The Psychological Birth of the Human Infant*. New York: Basic.

MACDONALD, C. 1993. *Toward Wisdom*. Willowdale, Ont.: Hounslow Press.

MEISSNER, W. 1992. "Religious Thinking as Transitional Conceptualization." *Psychoanalytic Review*, 79: 175–96.

MOSS, R. 1981. *The I That Is We*. Berkeley, Ca.: Celestial Arts.

PINE, F. 1992. "From Technique to a Theory of Psychic Change." *International Journal of Psycho-Analysis*, 73: 251–54.

THE PROVINCE. 1994. Monday, July 11, A2 [Article on the Visioneers].

SARDELLO, R. 1992. *Facing the World with Soul*. New York: HarperCollins.

SEINFELD, J. 1990. *The Bad Object*. Northvale, N.J.: Aronson.

SHEETS-JOHNSTONE, M. 1990. *The Roots of Thinking*. Philadelphia: Temple University Press.

SMALL, J. 1994. *Embodying Spirit*. Center City, Minn.: Hazelden.

SOLAN, R. 1991. "Jointness as Integration of Merging and Separateness." *Psychoanalytic Study of the Child*, 46: 337–52.

SPRETNAK, C. 1991. *States of Grace: Recovery of Meaning in the Postmodern Age*. New York: HarperCollins.

STEIN, H. 1985. "Culture Change, Symbolic Object Loss, and Restitutional Process." *Psychoanalysis and Contemporary Thought*, 8: 301–32.

STRENGER, C. 1991. *Between Hermeneutics and Science: An Essay on the Epistemology of Psychoanalysis*. Madison, Ct.: International Universities Press.

TALBOT, M. 1991. *The Holographic Universe*. New York: HarperCollins.

TEILHARD DE CHARDIN, P. 1961. *The Hymn of the Universe*. New York: Harper and Row.

———. 1965. *The Phenomenon of Man*. New York: Harper and Row.

ZUKAV, G. 1979. *The Dancing Wu Li Masters*. New York: Bantam.

———. 1990. *The Seat of the Soul*. New York: Simon and Schuster.

ZOHAR, D. 1990. *The Quantum Self*. New York: Quill.

INDEX

The paper used in this publication meets the minimum requirements
of American National Standard for Information Sciences –
Permanence of Paper for Printed Library Materials, ANSI Z39.48-1992.

Printed by
Ateliers Graphiques Marc Veilleux Inc.
Cap-Saint-Ignace, Québec
in January 1996